W9-BZK-959

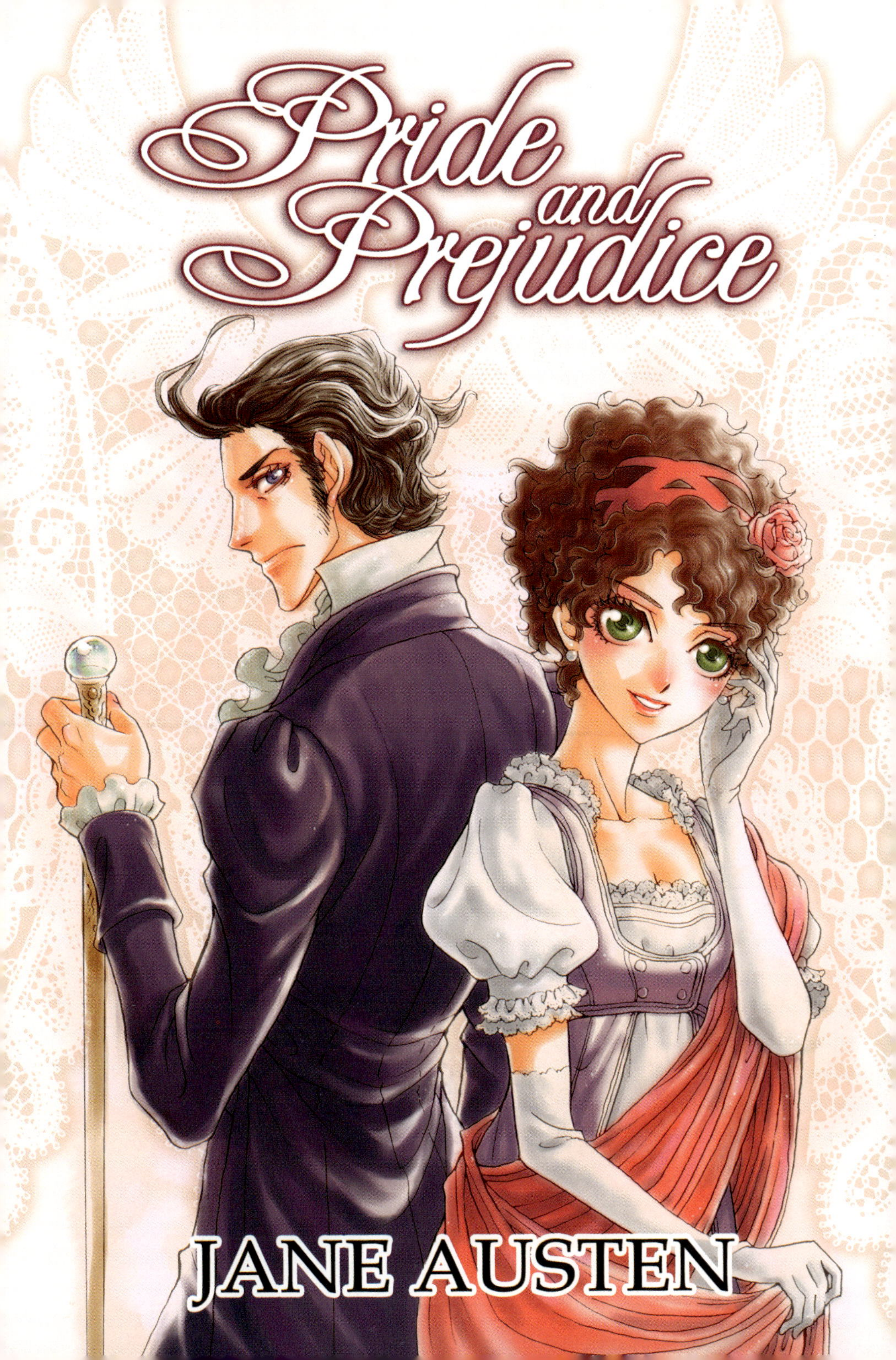
Pride and Prejudice
JANE AUSTEN

HOW TO READ MANGA!

Hello there, and welcome to **Manga Classics**! "Manga" is a style of comic book originating in **Japan**.

A manga book is read from **right-to-left**, which is **backwards** from the normal books you know. This means that you will find the first page where you expect to find the last page! It also means that each page begins in the top right corner.

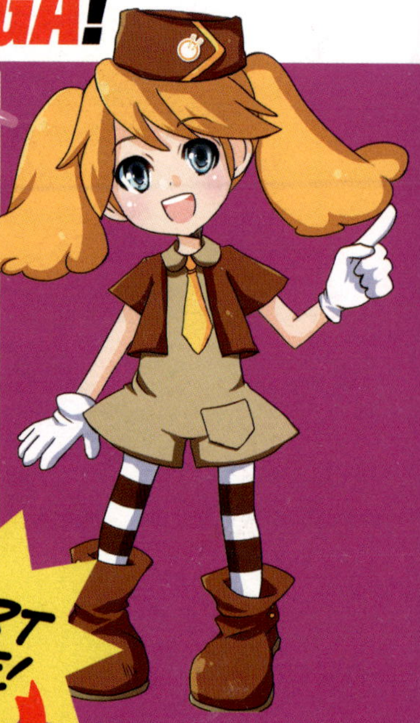

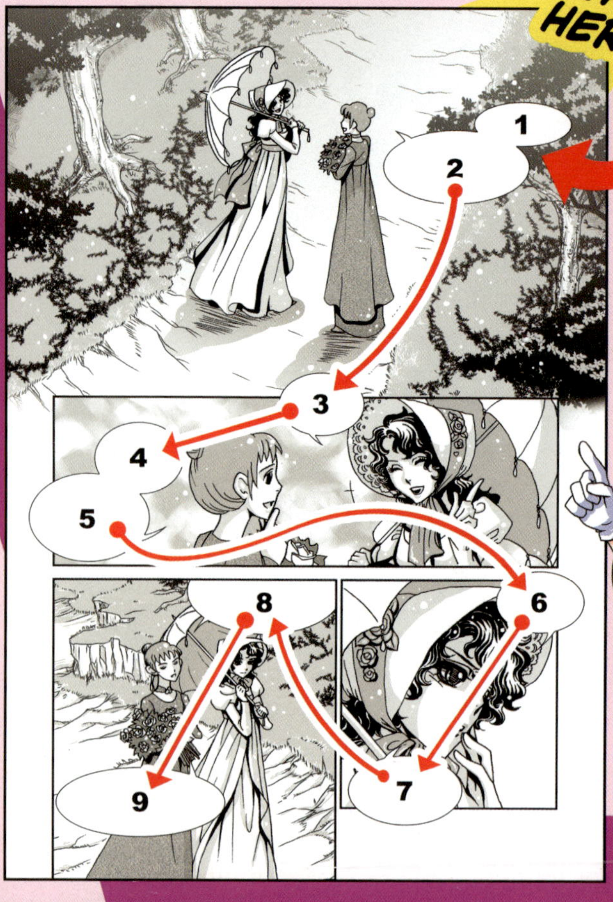
START HERE!
1
2
3
4
5
6
7
8
9

If you have never read a manga book before, here is a helpful guide to get you started!

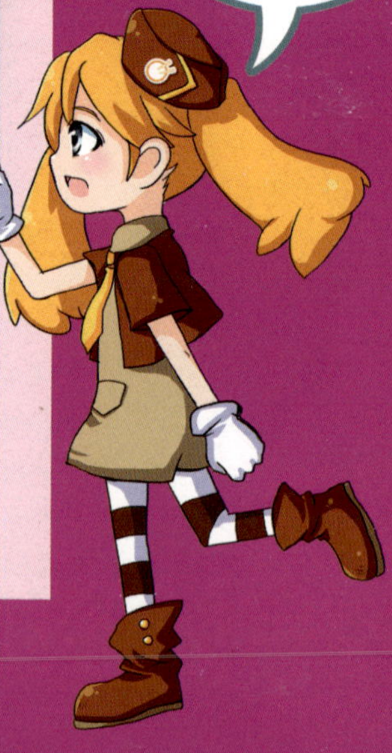

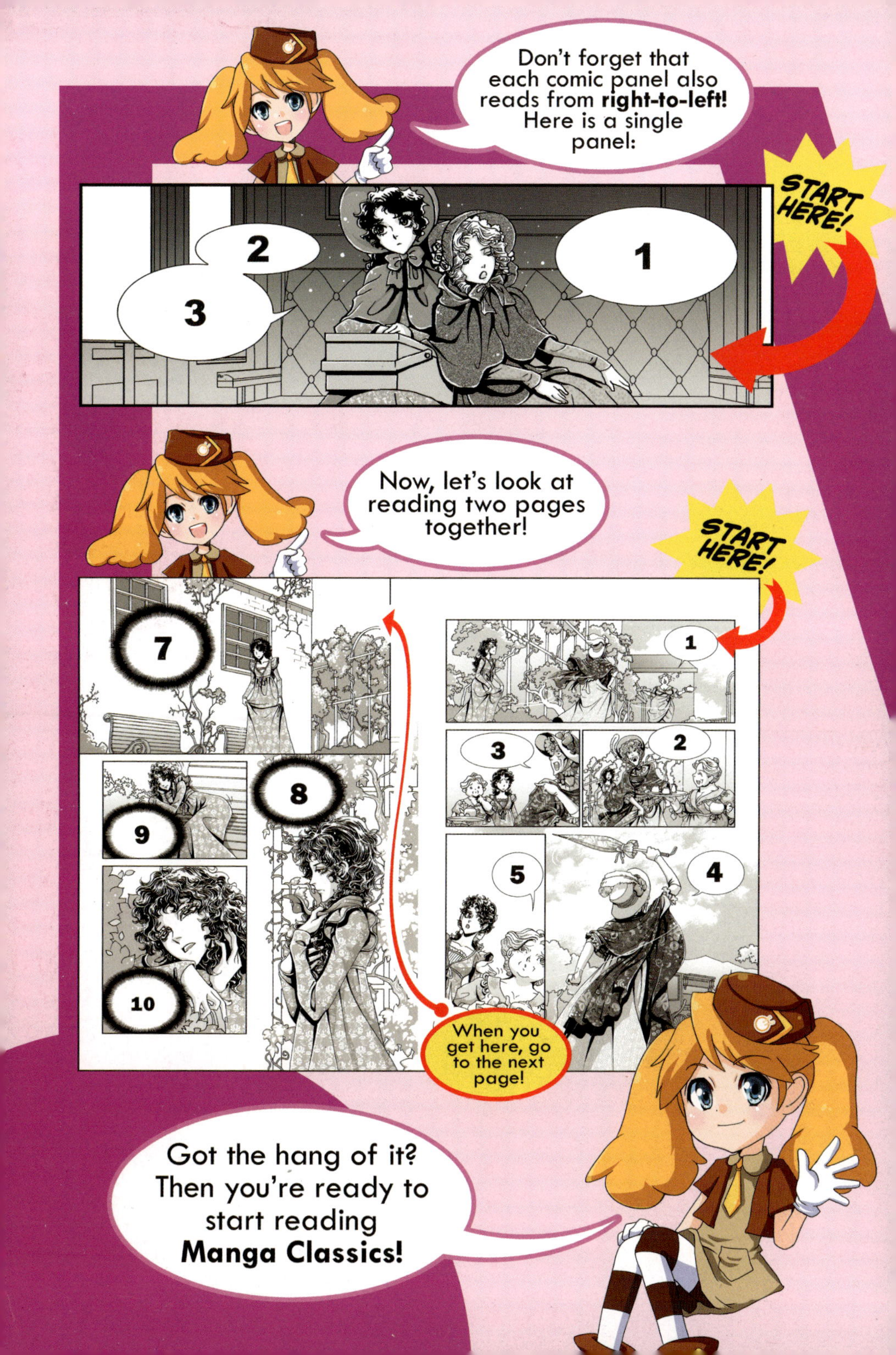
Don't forget that each comic panel also reads from **right-to-left!** Here is a single panel:
START HERE!
1
2
3
Now, let's look at reading two pages together!
START HERE!
1
2
3
4
5
When you get here, go to the next page!
7
8
9
10
Got the hang of it? Then you're ready to start reading **Manga Classics!**

CONTENTS:

Chapter 1

It is a truth universally acknowledged
that a single man with a good
fortune must be in want of a wife.
Whether he knows it or not...

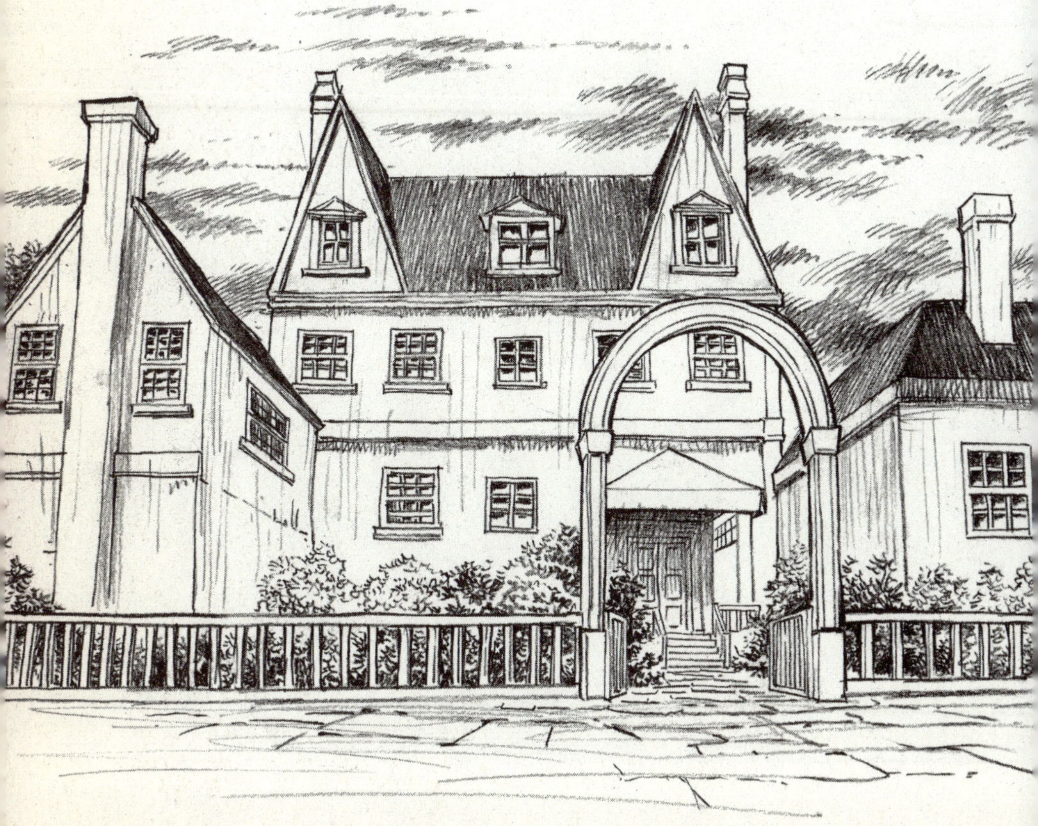

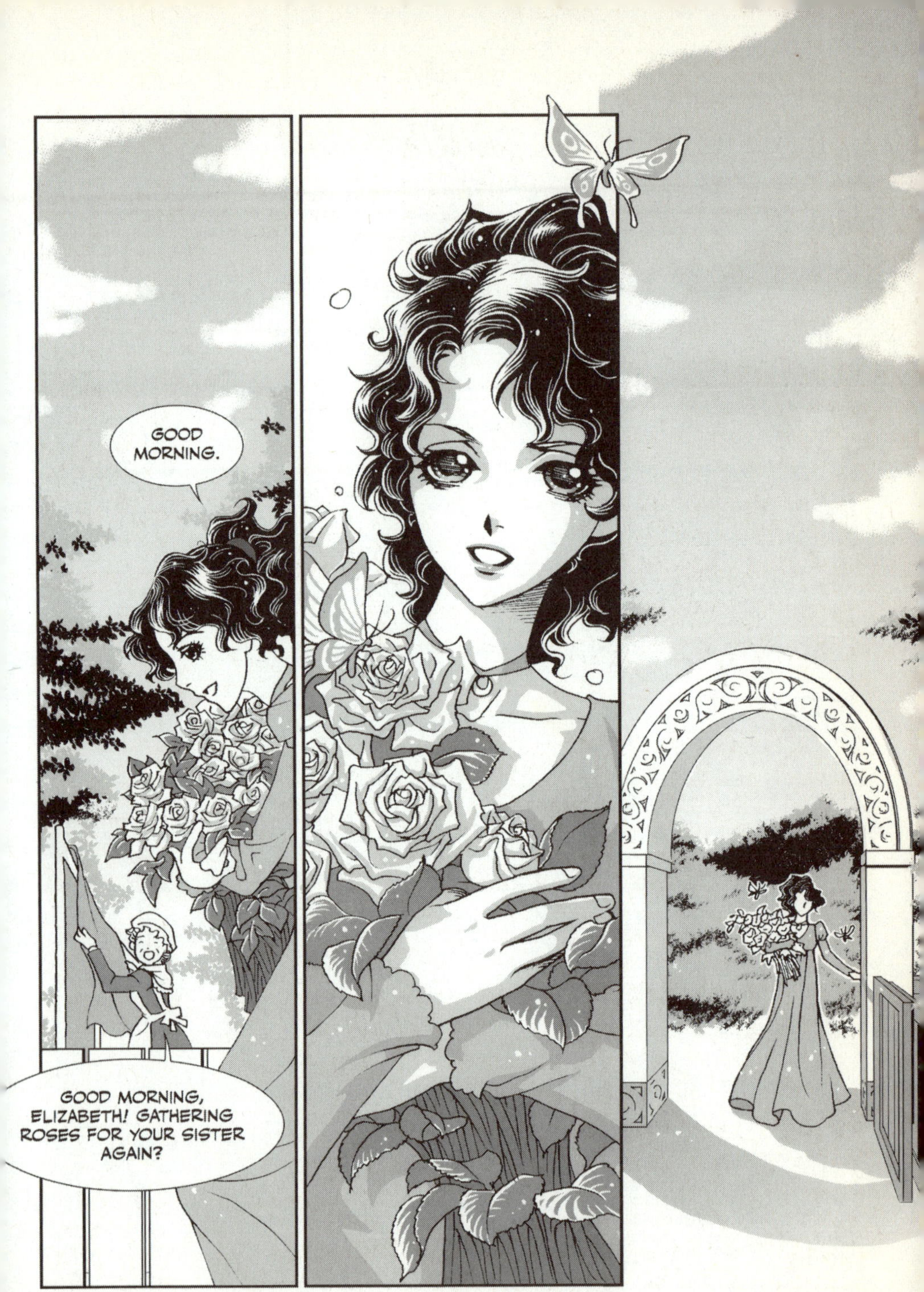
GOOD MORNING.
GOOD MORNING, ELIZABETH! GATHERING ROSES FOR YOUR SISTER AGAIN?

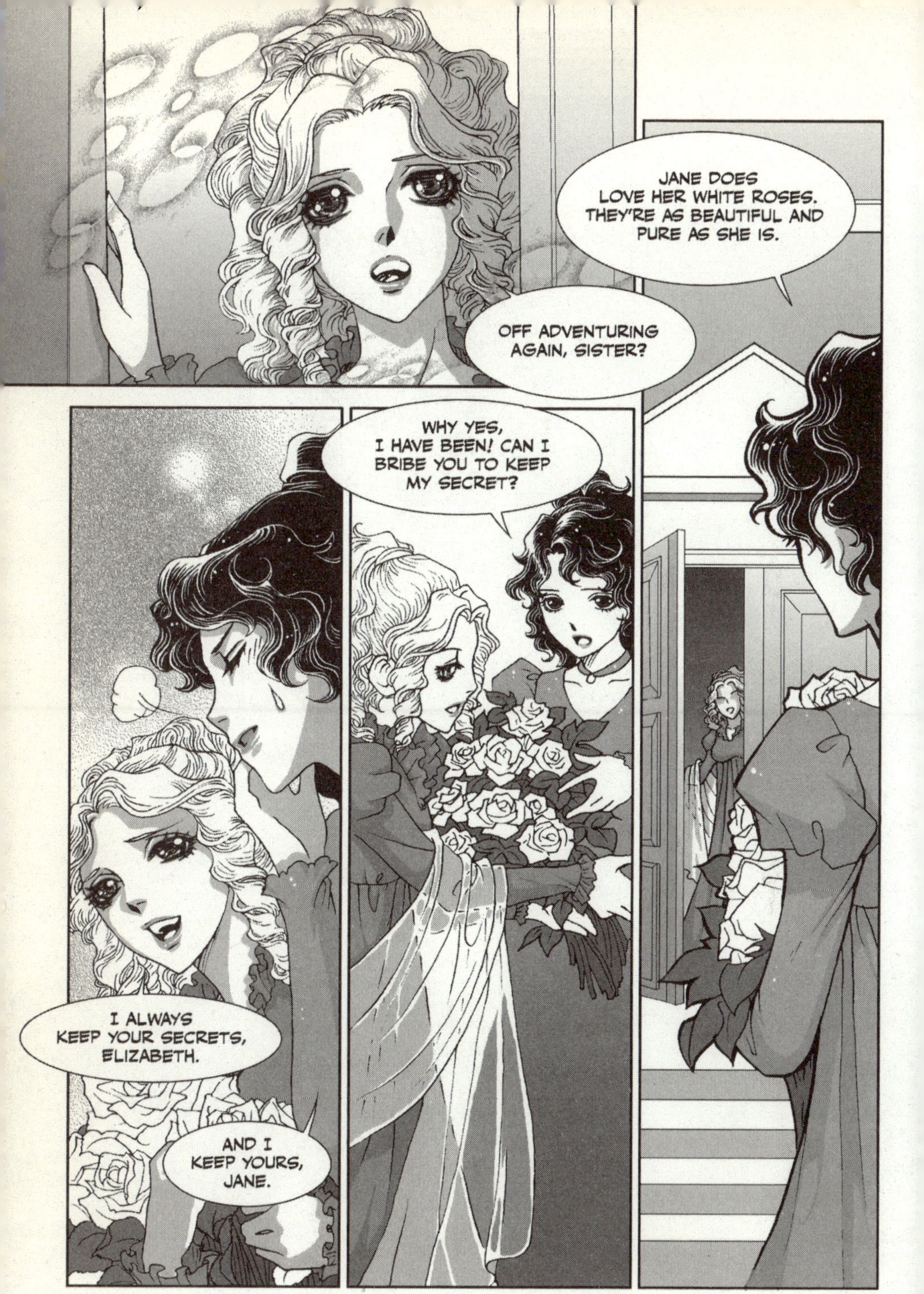
JANE DOES LOVE HER WHITE ROSES. THEY'RE AS BEAUTIFUL AND PURE AS SHE IS.
OFF ADVENTURING AGAIN, SISTER?
WHY YES, I HAVE BEEN! CAN I BRIBE YOU TO KEEP MY SECRET?
I ALWAYS KEEP YOUR SECRETS, ELIZABETH.
AND I KEEP YOURS, JANE.

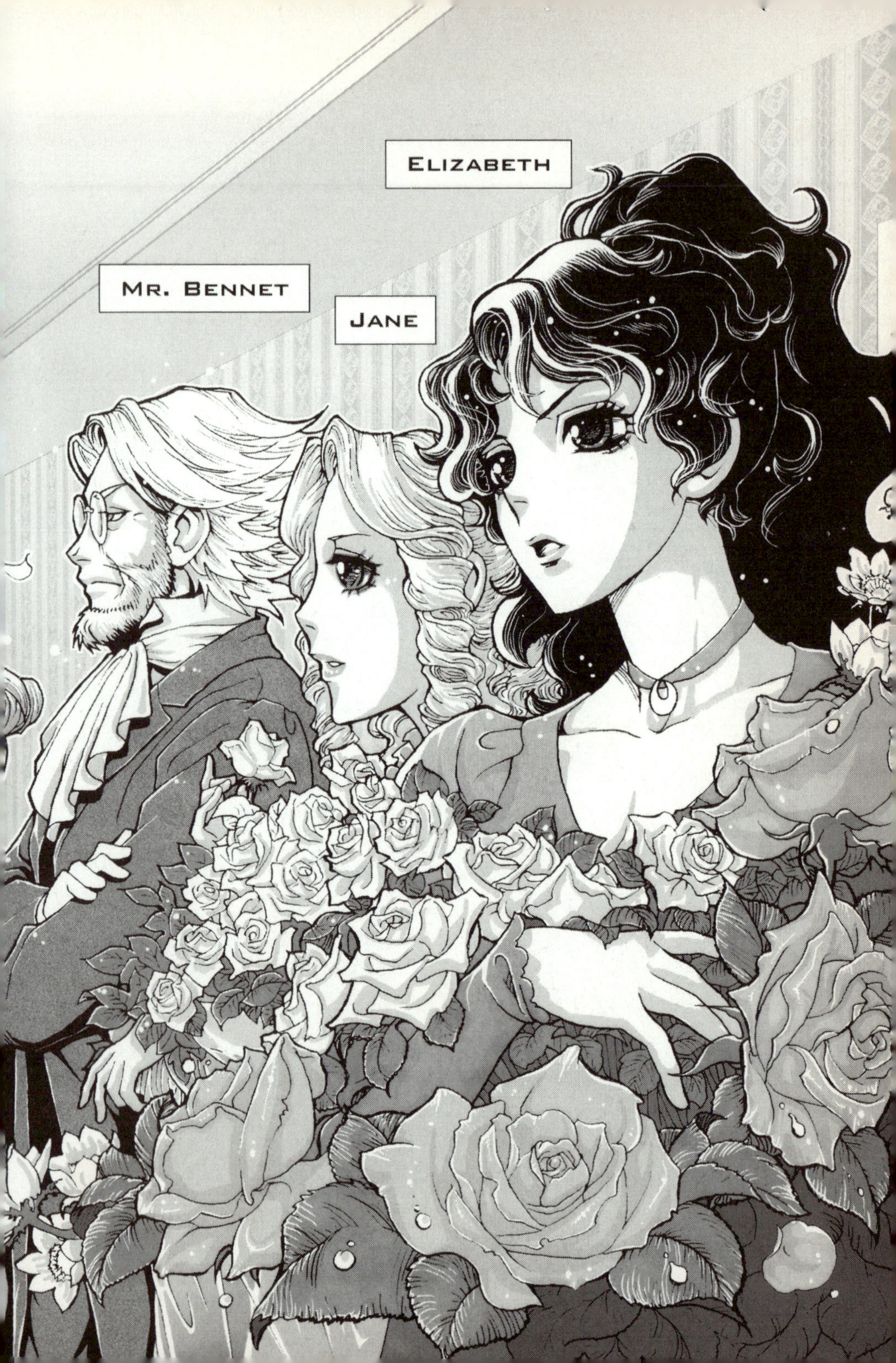

Elizabeth
Jane
Mr. Bennet

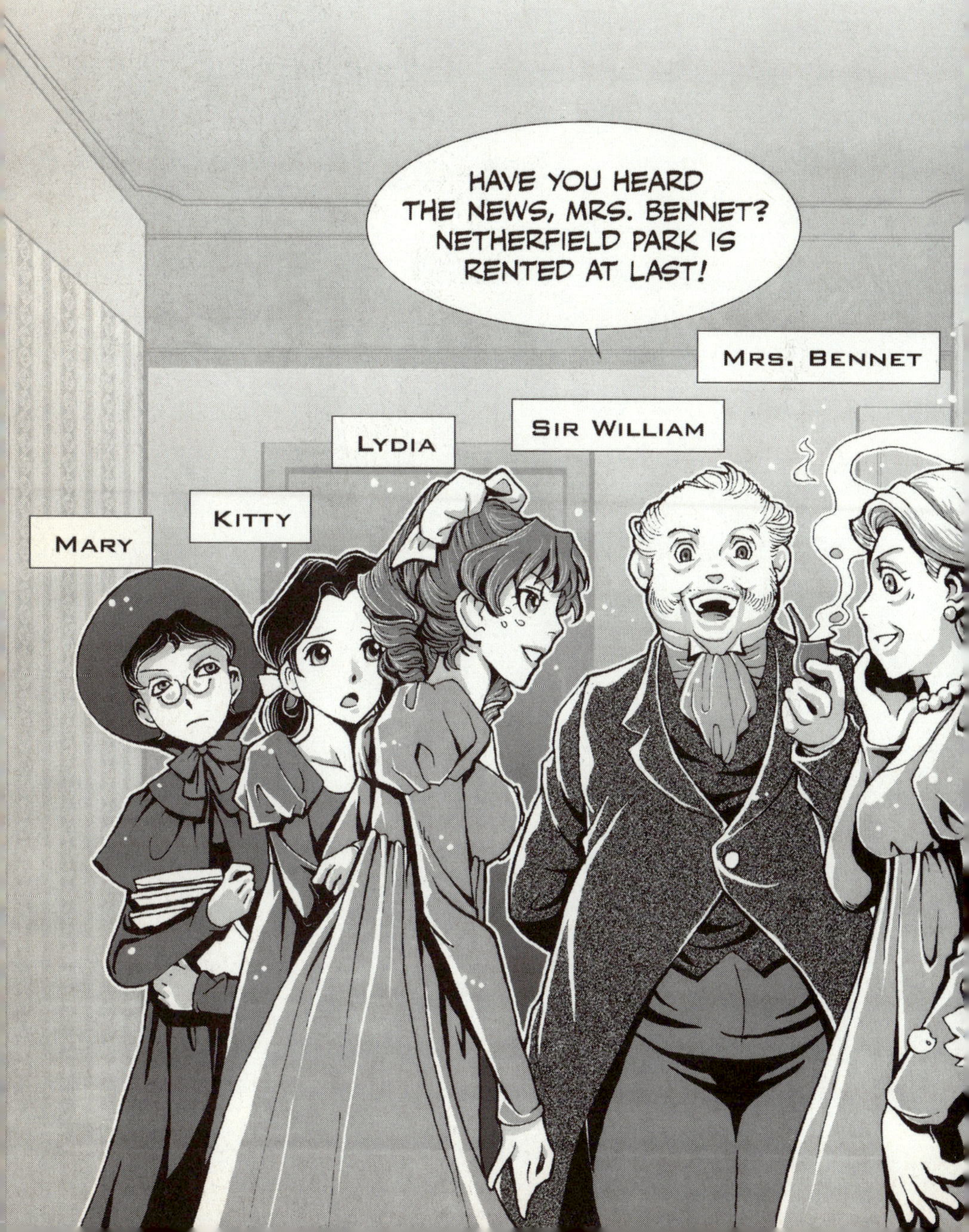

HAVE YOU HEARD THE NEWS, MRS. BENNET? NETHERFIELD PARK IS RENTED AT LAST!
MRS. BENNET
SIR WILLIAM
LYDIA
KITTY
MARY

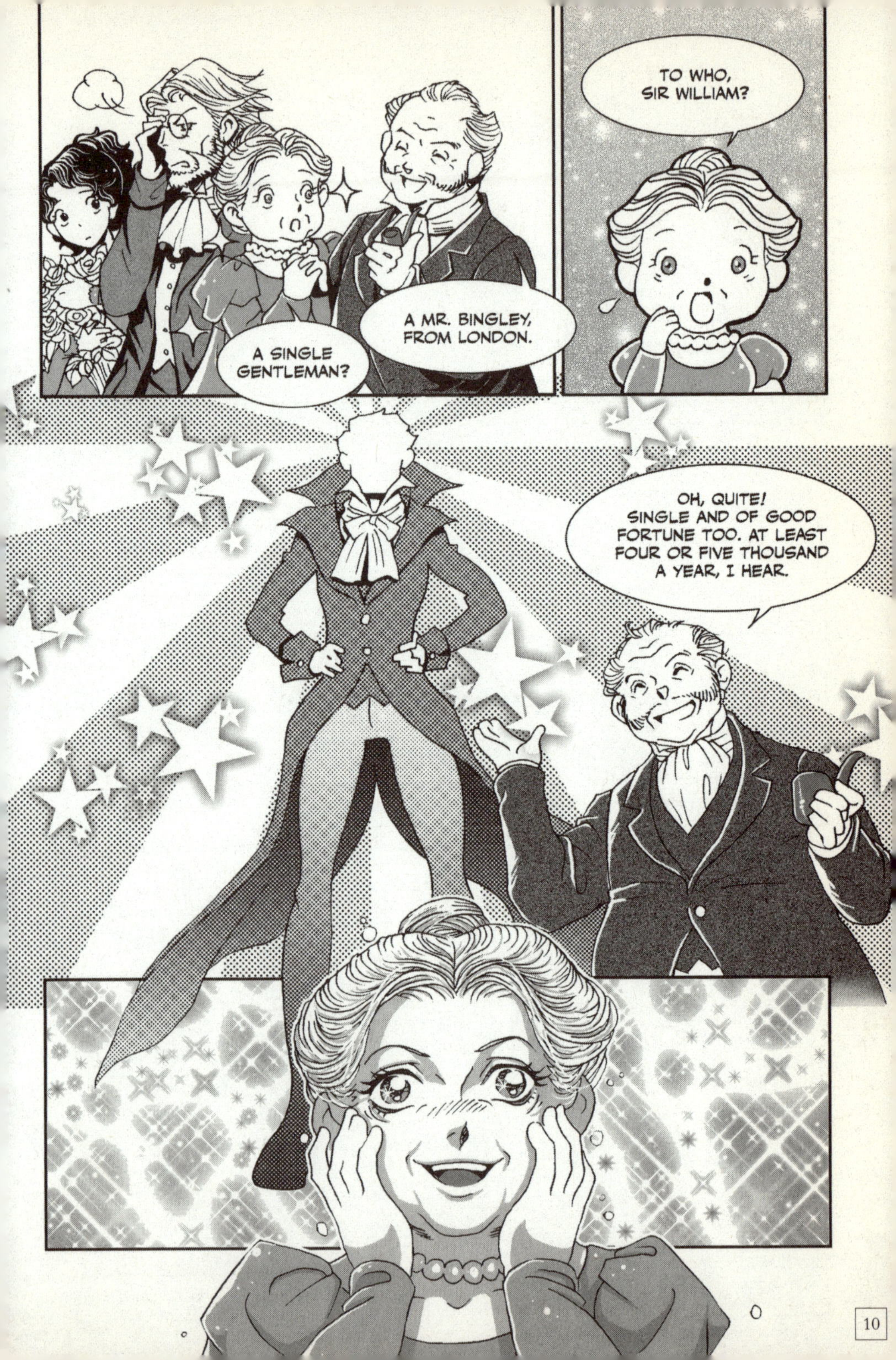
TO WHO, SIR WILLIAM?
A MR. BINGLEY, FROM LONDON.
A SINGLE GENTLEMAN?
OH, QUITE! SINGLE AND OF GOOD FORTUNE TOO. AT LEAST FOUR OR FIVE THOUSAND A YEAR, I HEAR.

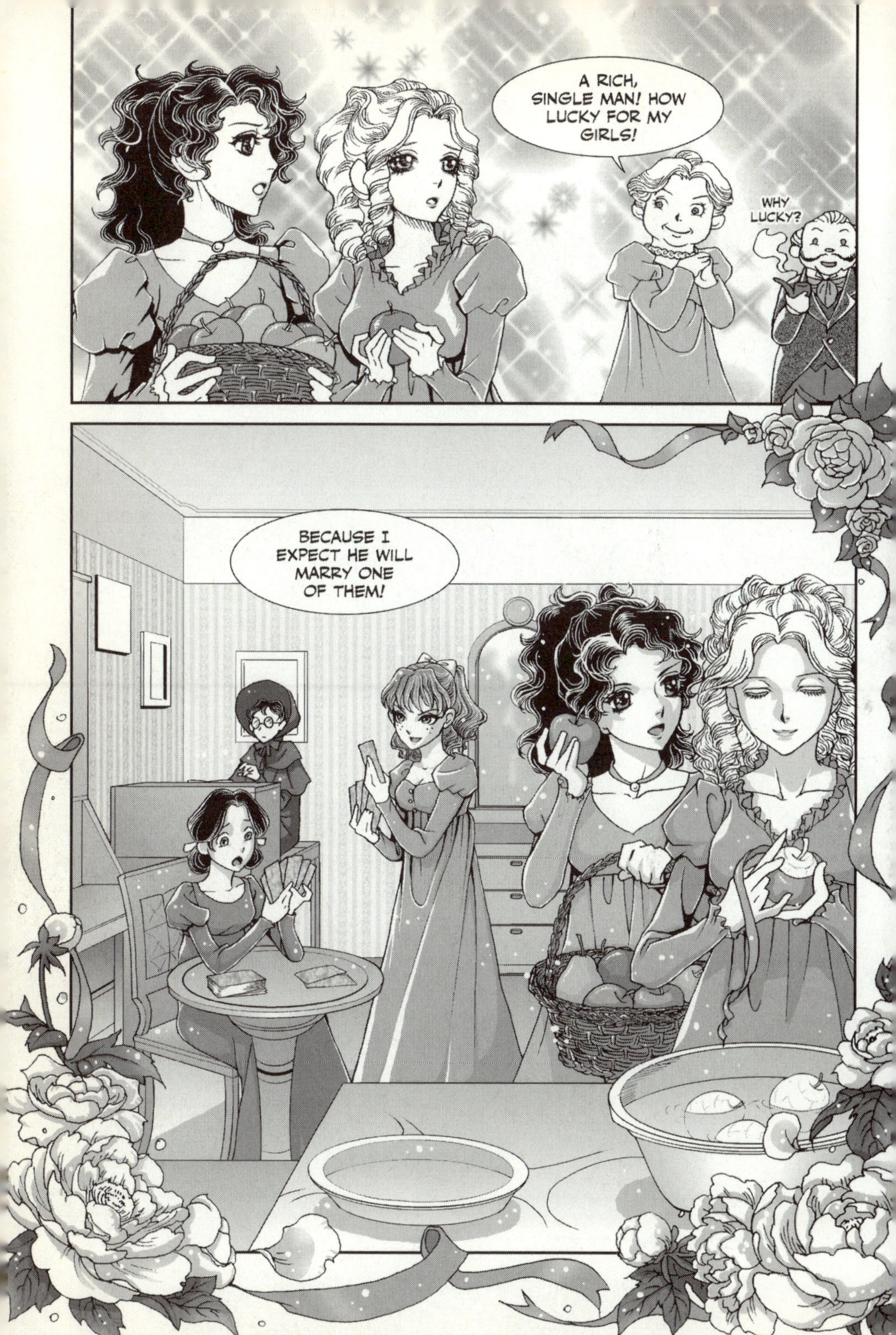
A RICH, SINGLE MAN! HOW LUCKY FOR MY GIRLS!
WHY LUCKY?
BECAUSE I EXPECT HE WILL MARRY ONE OF THEM!

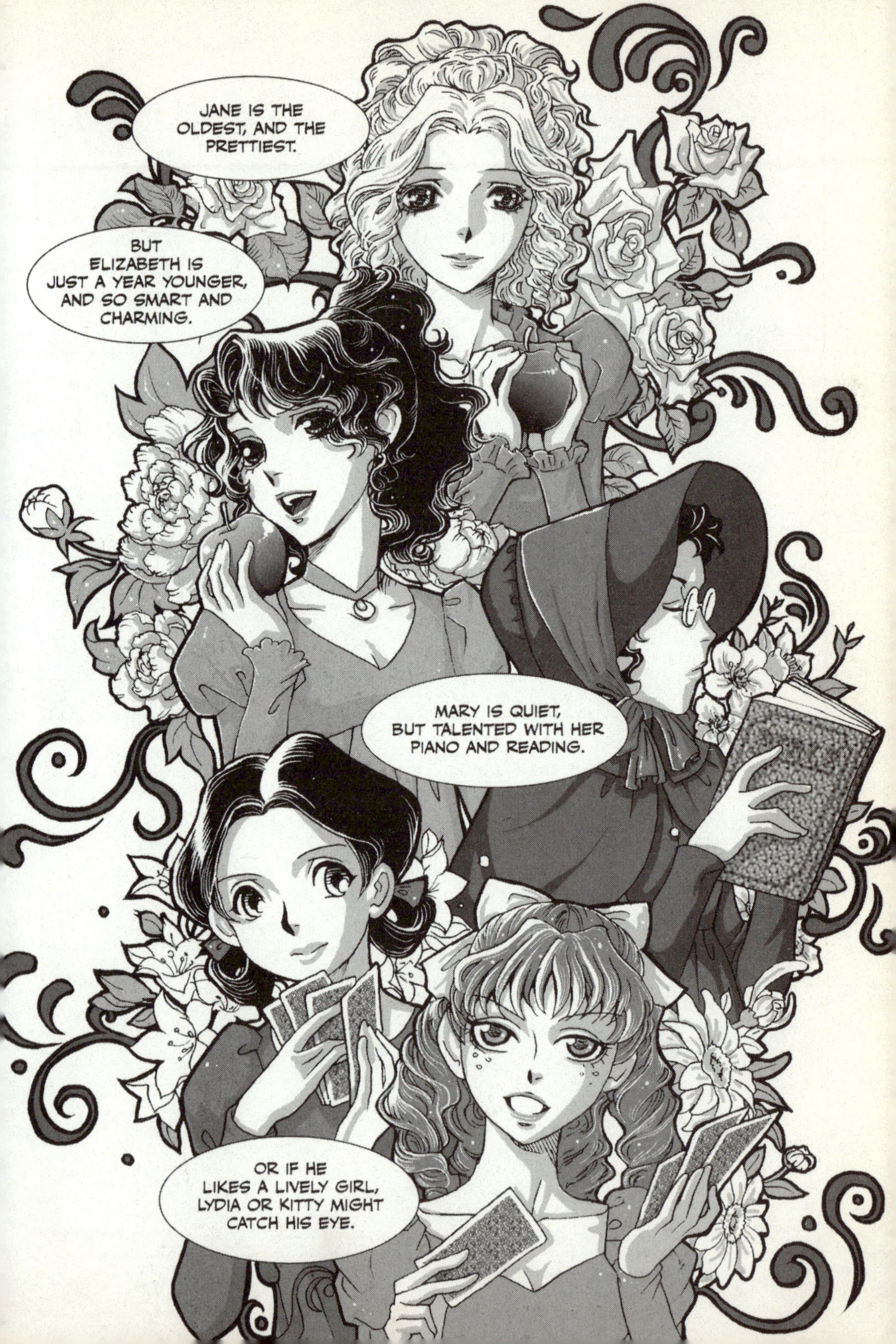
JANE IS THE OLDEST, AND THE PRETTIEST.
BUT ELIZABETH IS JUST A YEAR YOUNGER, AND SO SMART AND CHARMING.
MARY IS QUIET, BUT TALENTED WITH HER PIANO AND READING.
OR IF HE LIKES A LIVELY GIRL, LYDIA OR KITTY MIGHT CATCH HIS EYE.

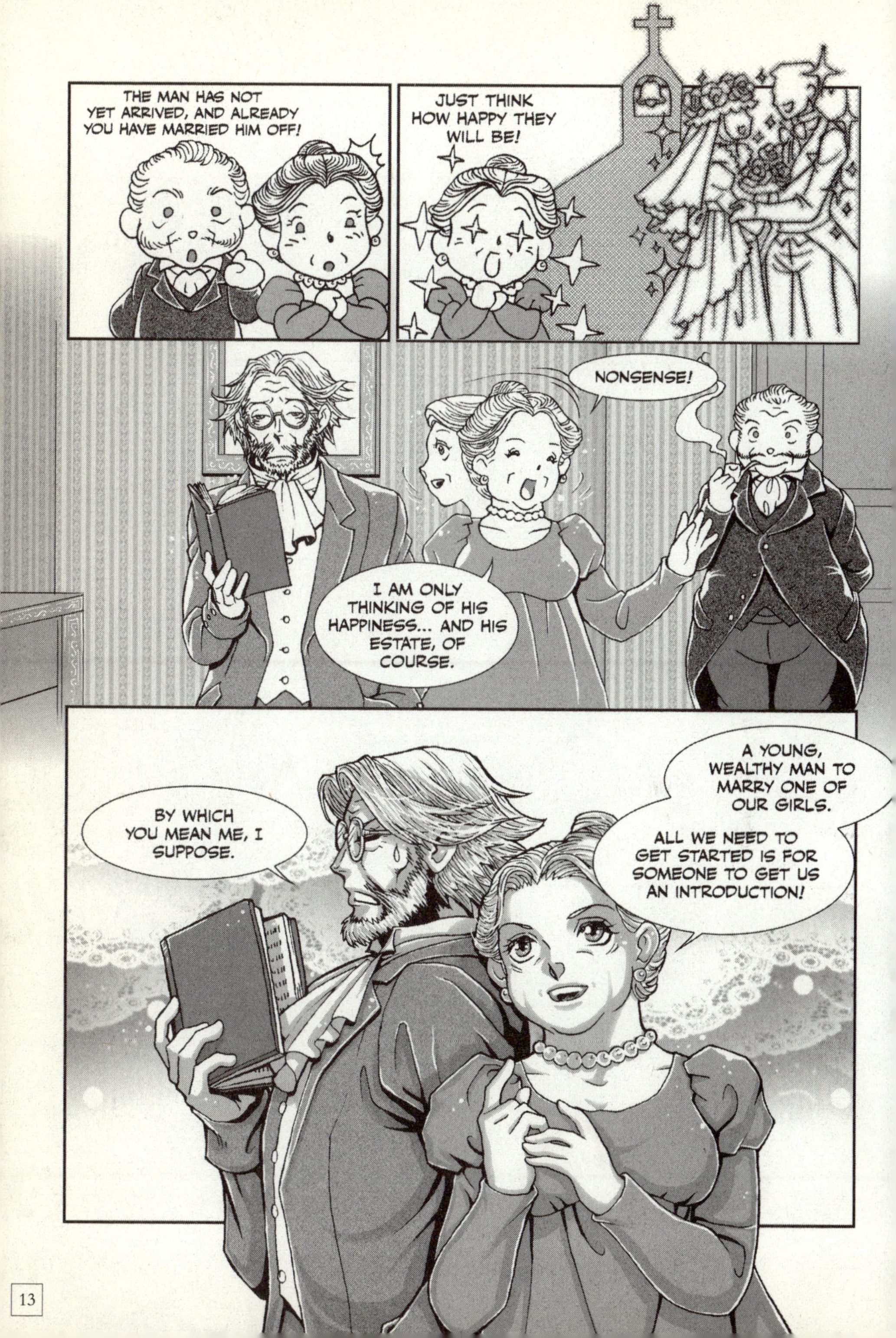
JUST THINK HOW HAPPY THEY WILL BE!
THE MAN HAS NOT YET ARRIVED, AND ALREADY YOU HAVE MARRIED HIM OFF!
NONSENSE!
I AM ONLY THINKING OF HIS HAPPINESS... AND HIS ESTATE, OF COURSE.
A YOUNG, WEALTHY MAN TO MARRY ONE OF OUR GIRLS.
ALL WE NEED TO GET STARTED IS FOR SOMEONE TO GET US AN INTRODUCTION!
BY WHICH YOU MEAN ME, I SUPPOSE.

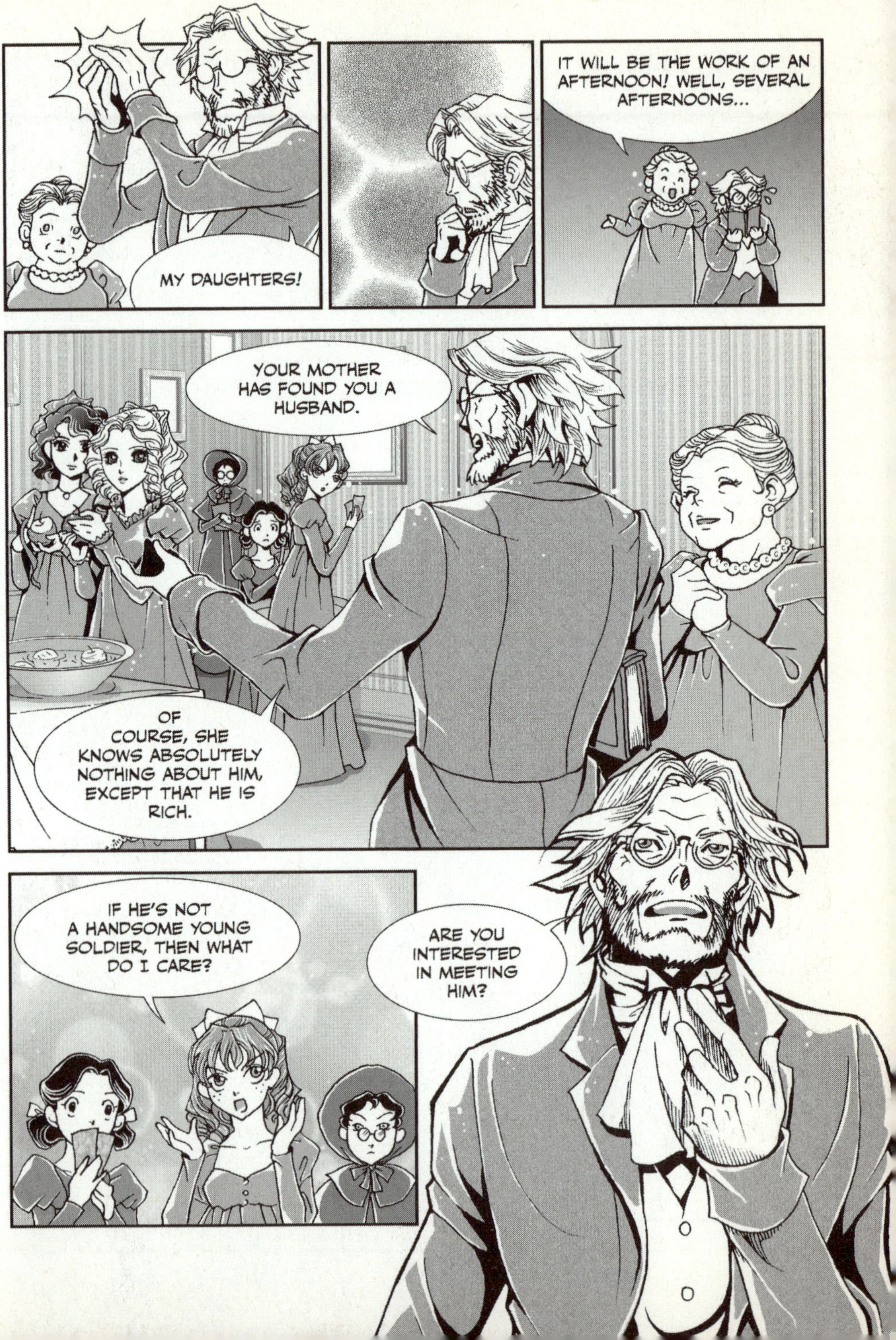
IT WILL BE THE WORK OF AN AFTERNOON! WELL, SEVERAL AFTERNOONS...
MY DAUGHTERS!
YOUR MOTHER HAS FOUND YOU A HUSBAND.
OF COURSE, SHE KNOWS ABSOLUTELY NOTHING ABOUT HIM, EXCEPT THAT HE IS RICH.
ARE YOU INTERESTED IN MEETING HIM?
IF HE'S NOT A HANDSOME YOUNG SOLDIER, THEN WHAT DO I CARE?

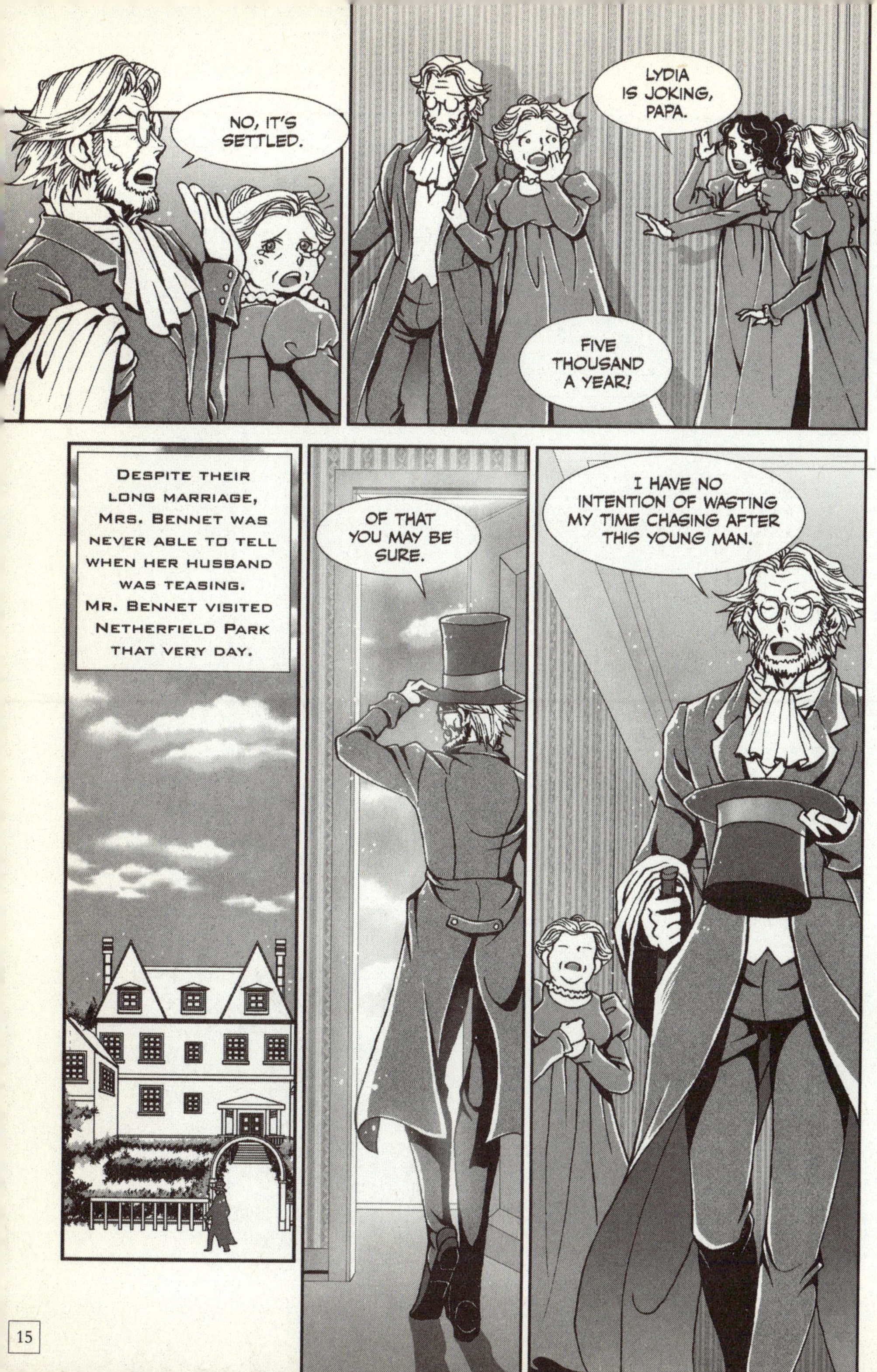
LYDIA IS JOKING, PAPA.
FIVE THOUSAND A YEAR!
NO, IT'S SETTLED.
I HAVE NO INTENTION OF WASTING MY TIME CHASING AFTER THIS YOUNG MAN.
OF THAT YOU MAY BE SURE.
DESPITE THEIR LONG MARRIAGE, MRS. BENNET WAS NEVER ABLE TO TELL WHEN HER HUSBAND WAS TEASING. MR. BENNET VISITED NETHERFIELD PARK THAT VERY DAY.

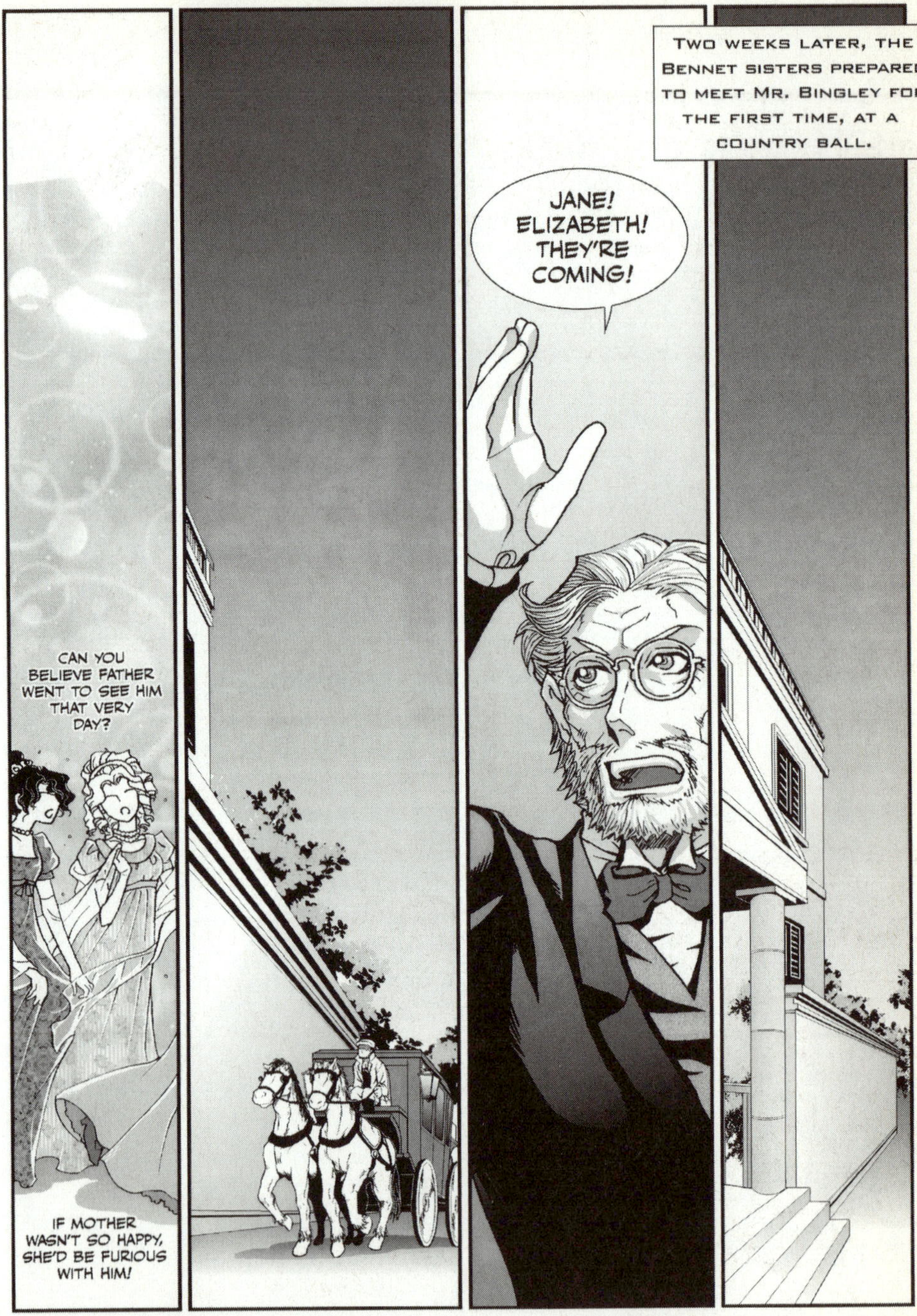
Two weeks later, the Bennet sisters prepared to meet Mr. Bingley for the first time, at a country ball.
JANE! ELIZABETH! THEY'RE COMING!
CAN YOU BELIEVE FATHER WENT TO SEE HIM THAT VERY DAY?
IF MOTHER WASN'T SO HAPPY, SHE'D BE FURIOUS WITH HIM!

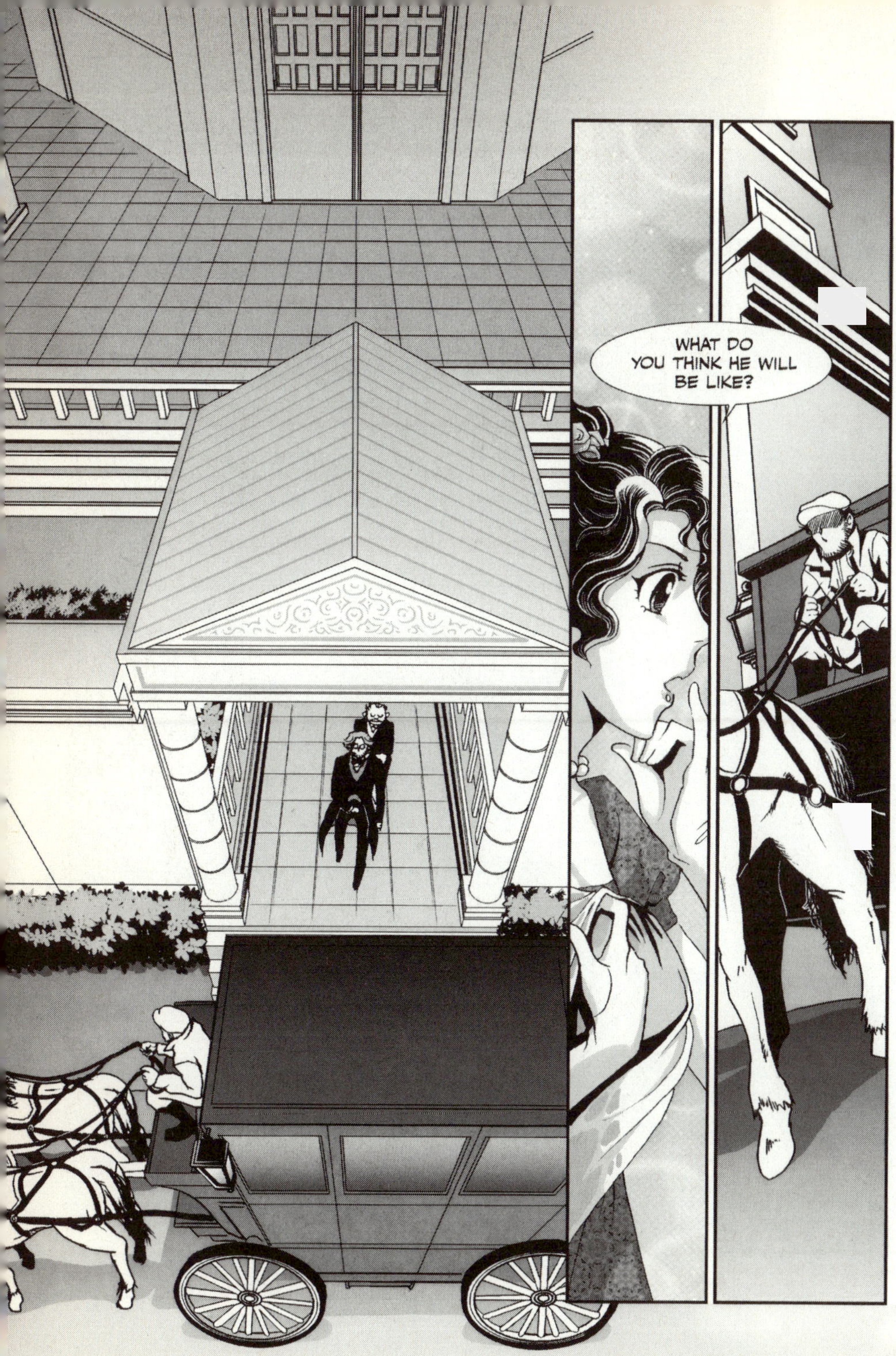
WHAT DO
YOU THINK HE WILL
BE LIKE?

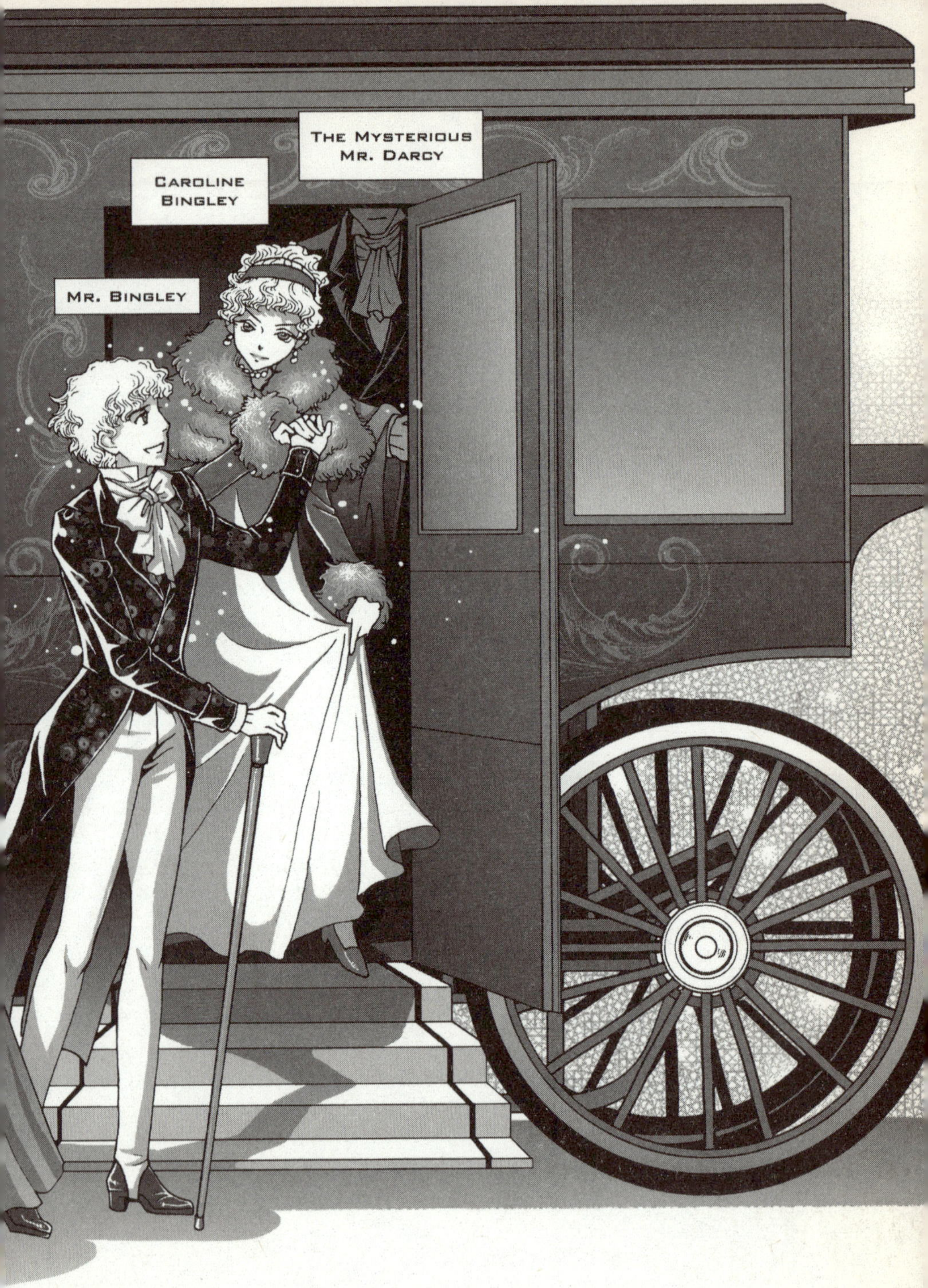
THE MYSTERIOUS MR. DARCY
CAROLINE BINGLEY
MR. BINGLEY

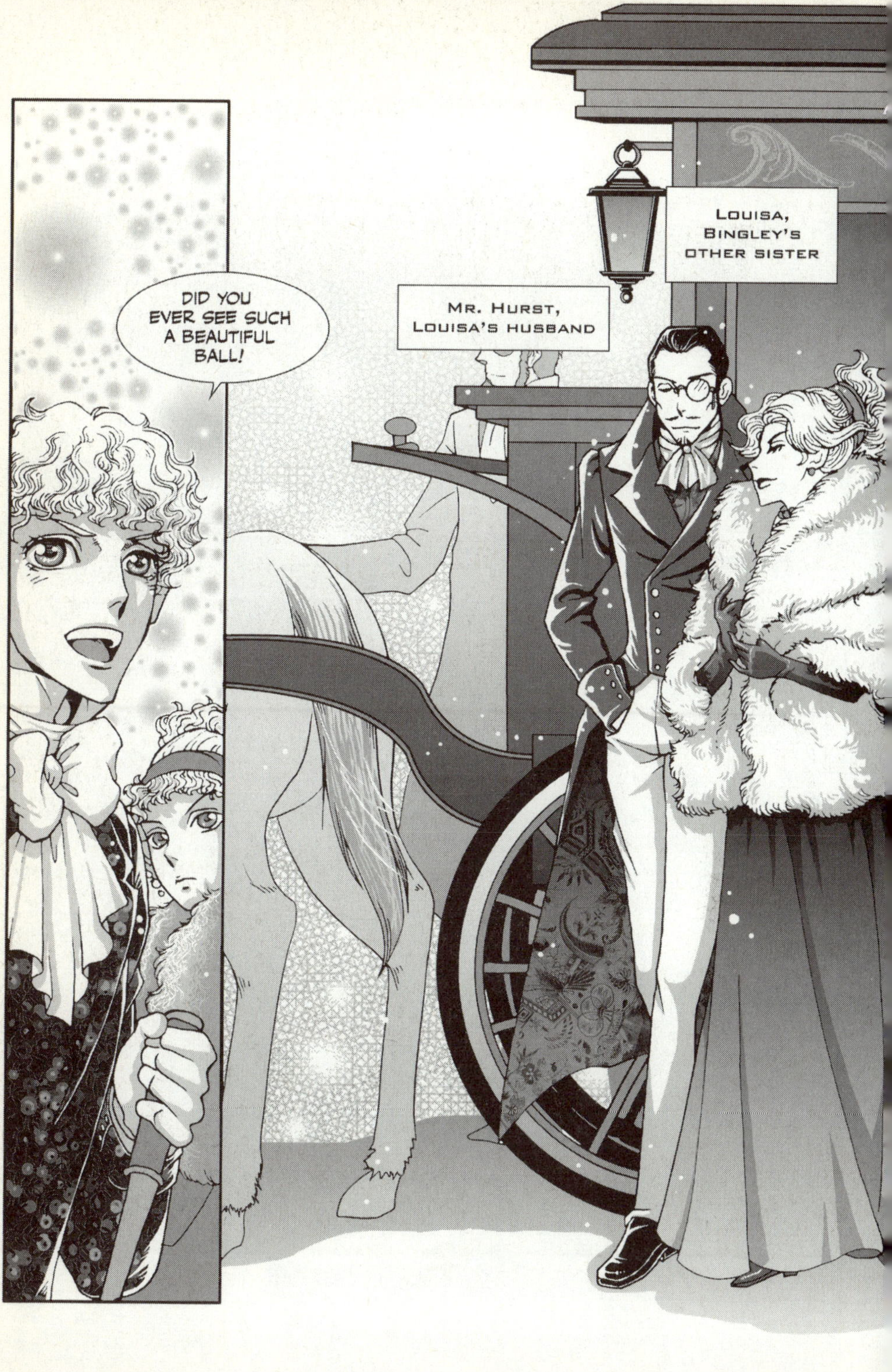
Louisa, Bingley's other sister
Mr. Hurst, Louisa's husband
Did you ever see such a beautiful ball!

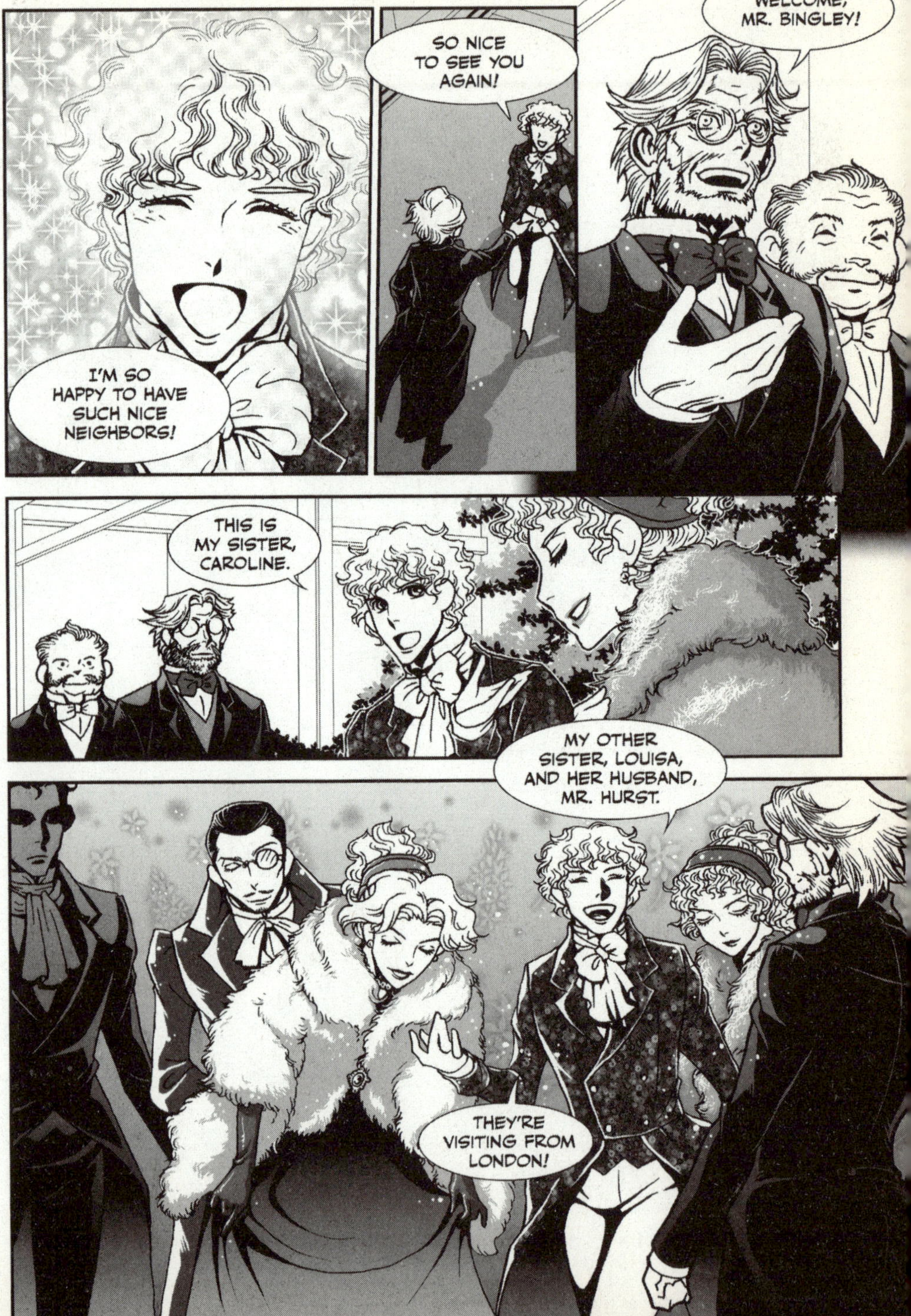
WELCOME, MR. BINGLEY!
SO NICE TO SEE YOU AGAIN!
I'M SO HAPPY TO HAVE SUCH NICE NEIGHBORS!
THIS IS MY SISTER, CAROLINE.
MY OTHER SISTER, LOUISA, AND HER HUSBAND, MR. HURST.
THEY'RE VISITING FROM LONDON!

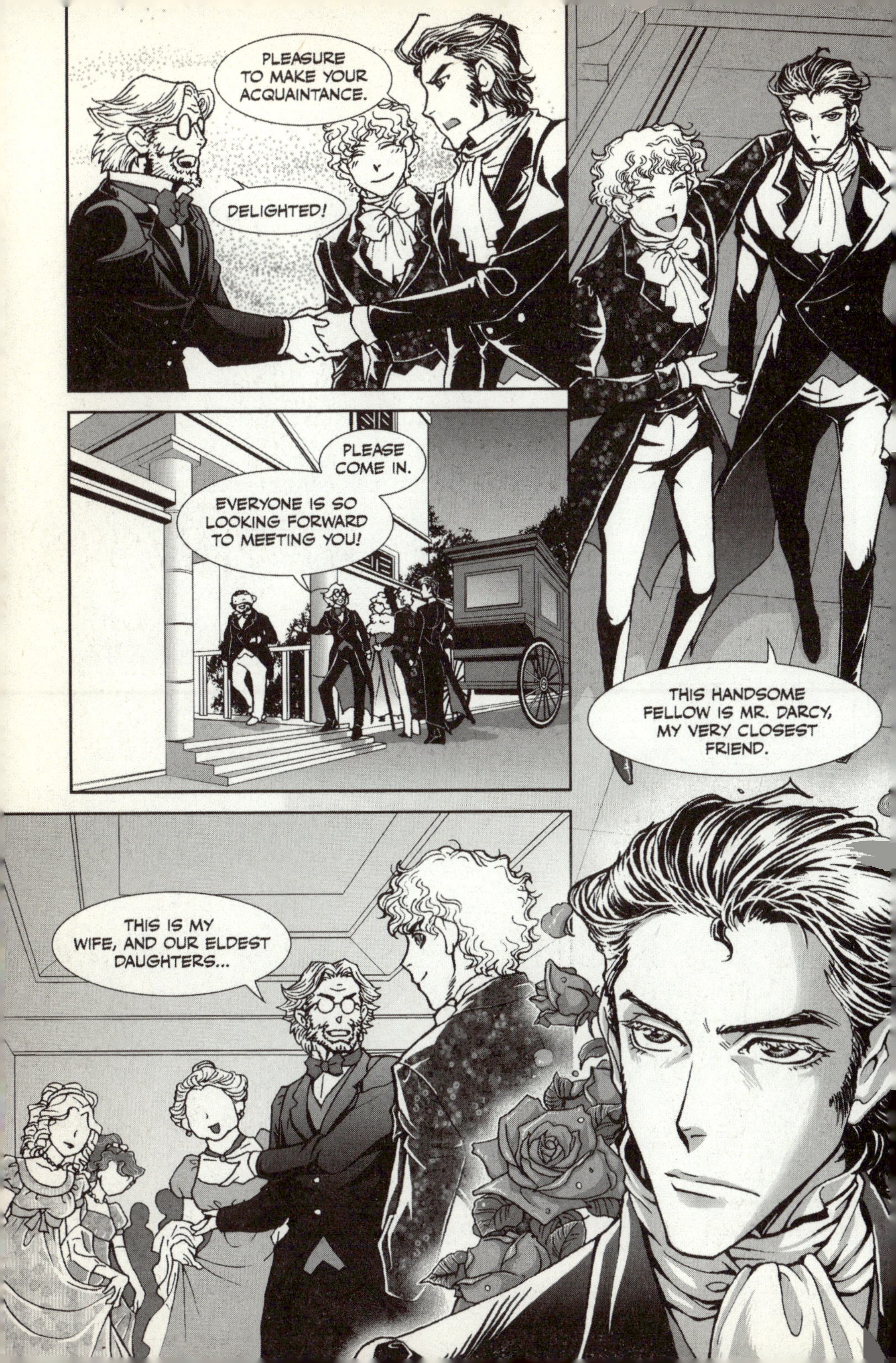
THIS HANDSOME FELLOW IS MR. DARCY, MY VERY CLOSEST FRIEND.
PLEASURE TO MAKE YOUR ACQUAINTANCE.
DELIGHTED!
PLEASE COME IN.
EVERYONE IS SO LOOKING FORWARD TO MEETING YOU!
THIS IS MY WIFE, AND OUR ELDEST DAUGHTERS...

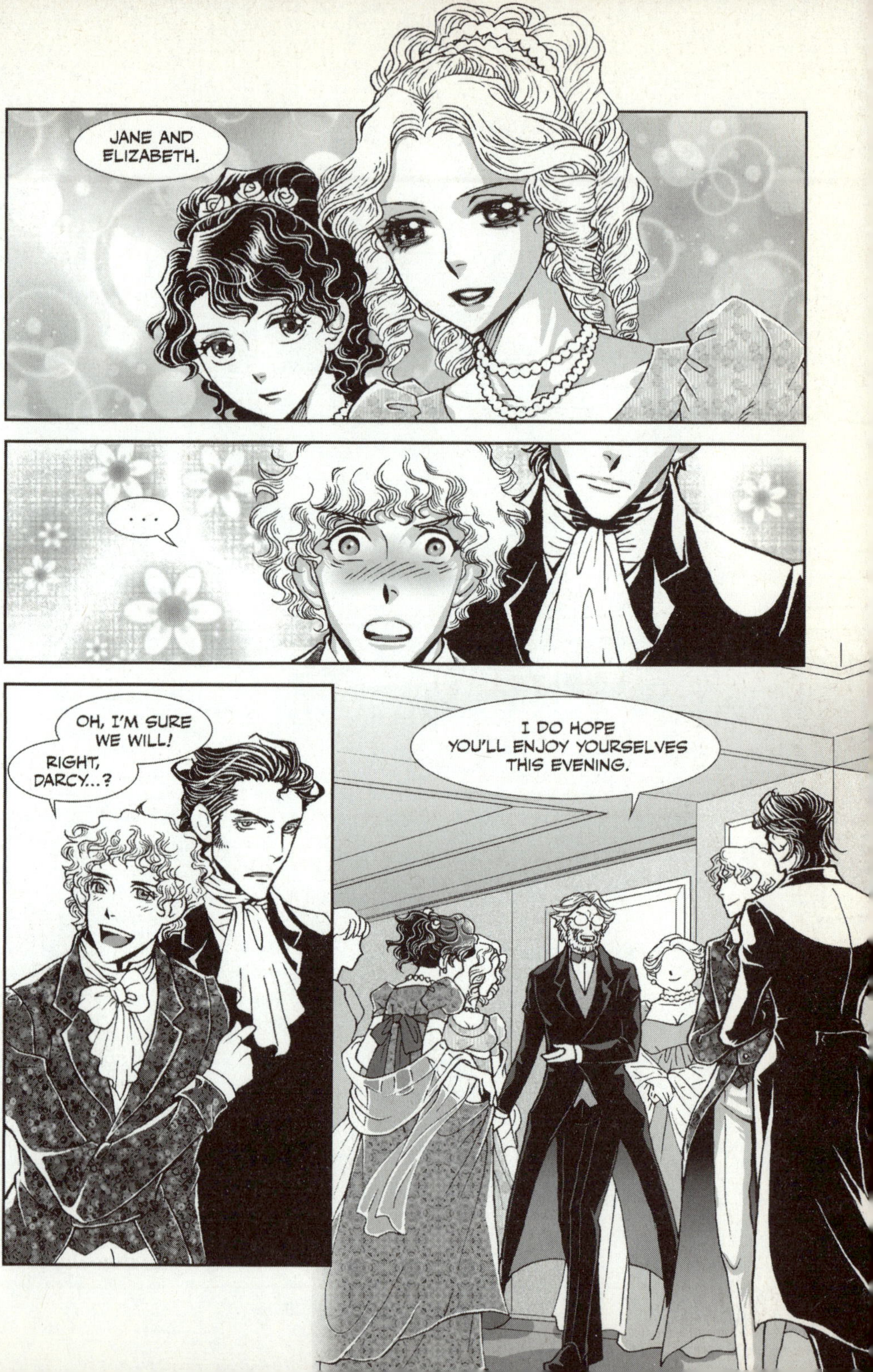
JANE AND ELIZABETH.
...
I DO HOPE YOU'LL ENJOY YOURSELVES THIS EVENING.
OH, I'M SURE WE WILL!
RIGHT, DARCY...?

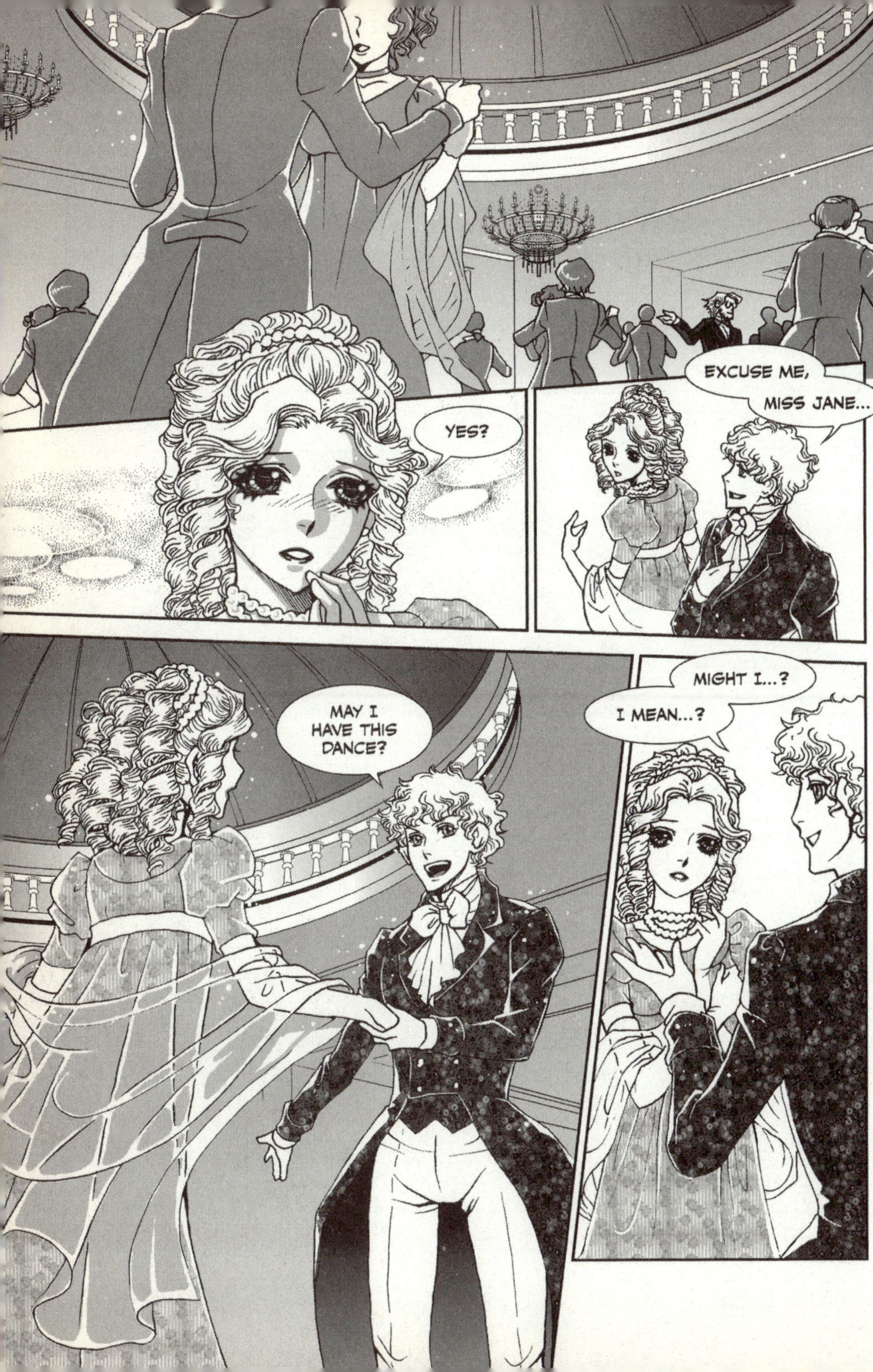
EXCUSE ME, MISS JANE...
YES?
MIGHT I...?
I MEAN...?
MAY I HAVE THIS DANCE?

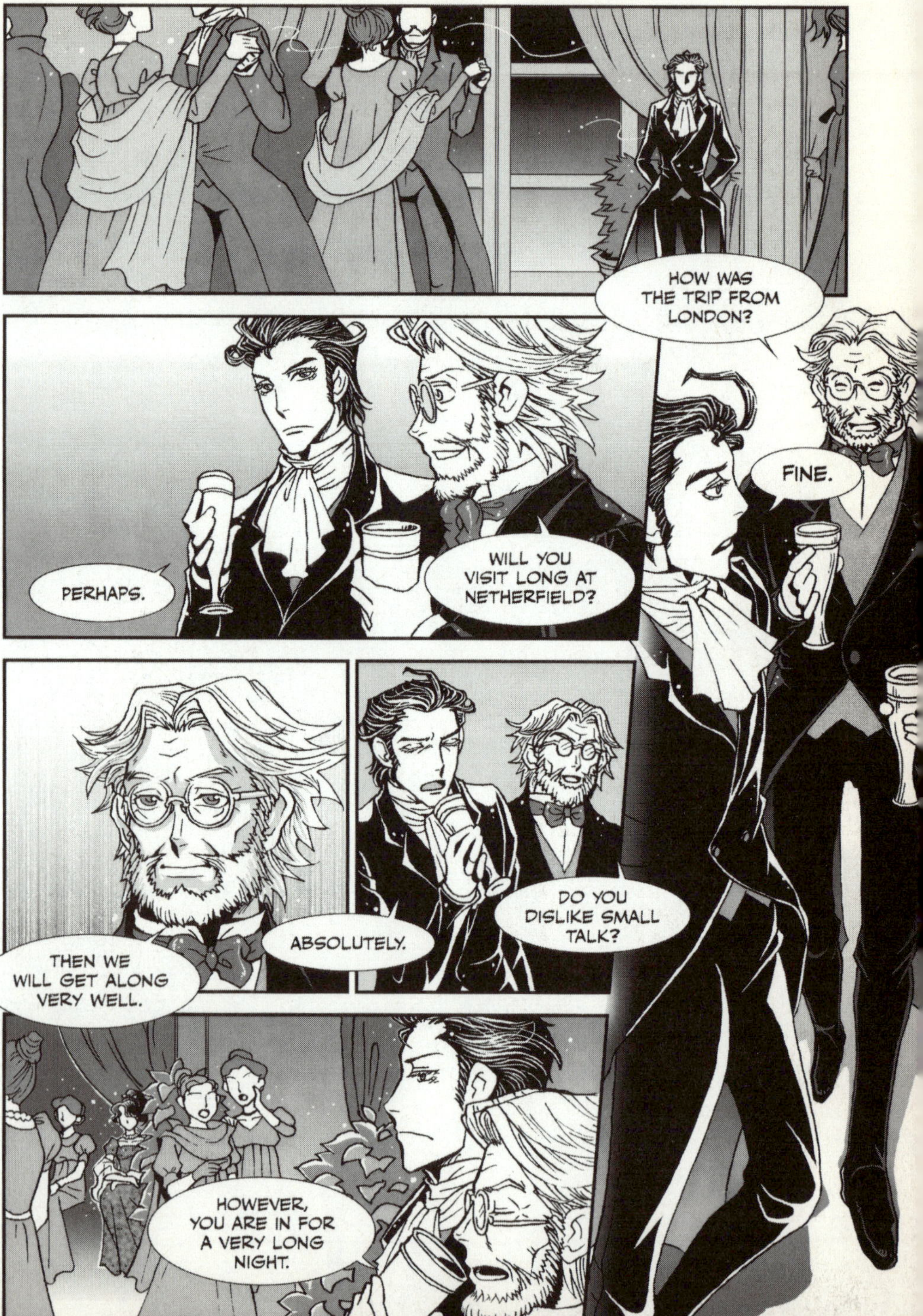
HOW WAS THE TRIP FROM LONDON?
FINE.
WILL YOU VISIT LONG AT NETHERFIELD?
PERHAPS.
DO YOU DISLIKE SMALL TALK?
ABSOLUTELY.
THEN WE WILL GET ALONG VERY WELL.
HOWEVER, YOU ARE IN FOR A VERY LONG NIGHT.

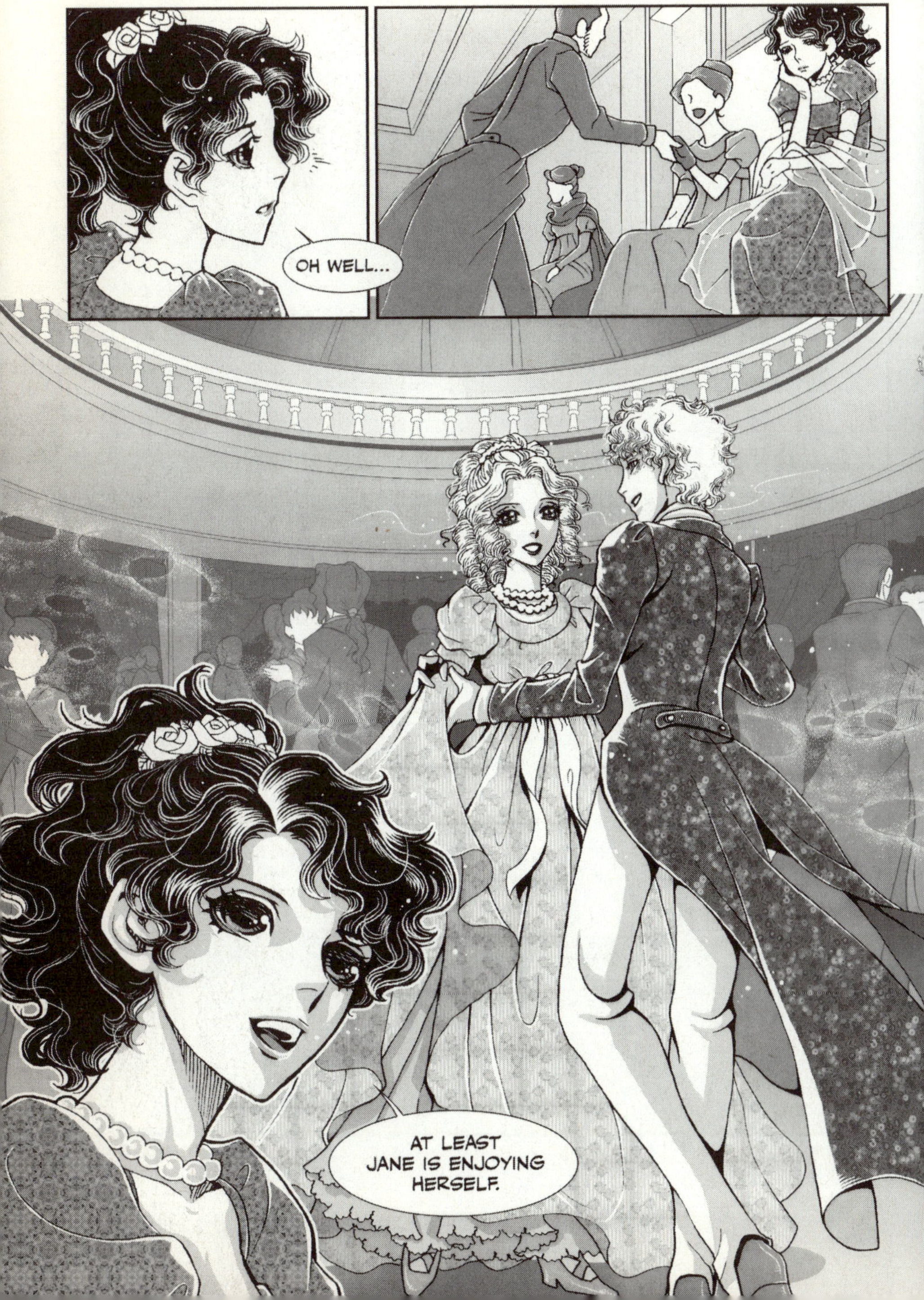
OH WELL...
AT LEAST JANE IS ENJOYING HERSELF.

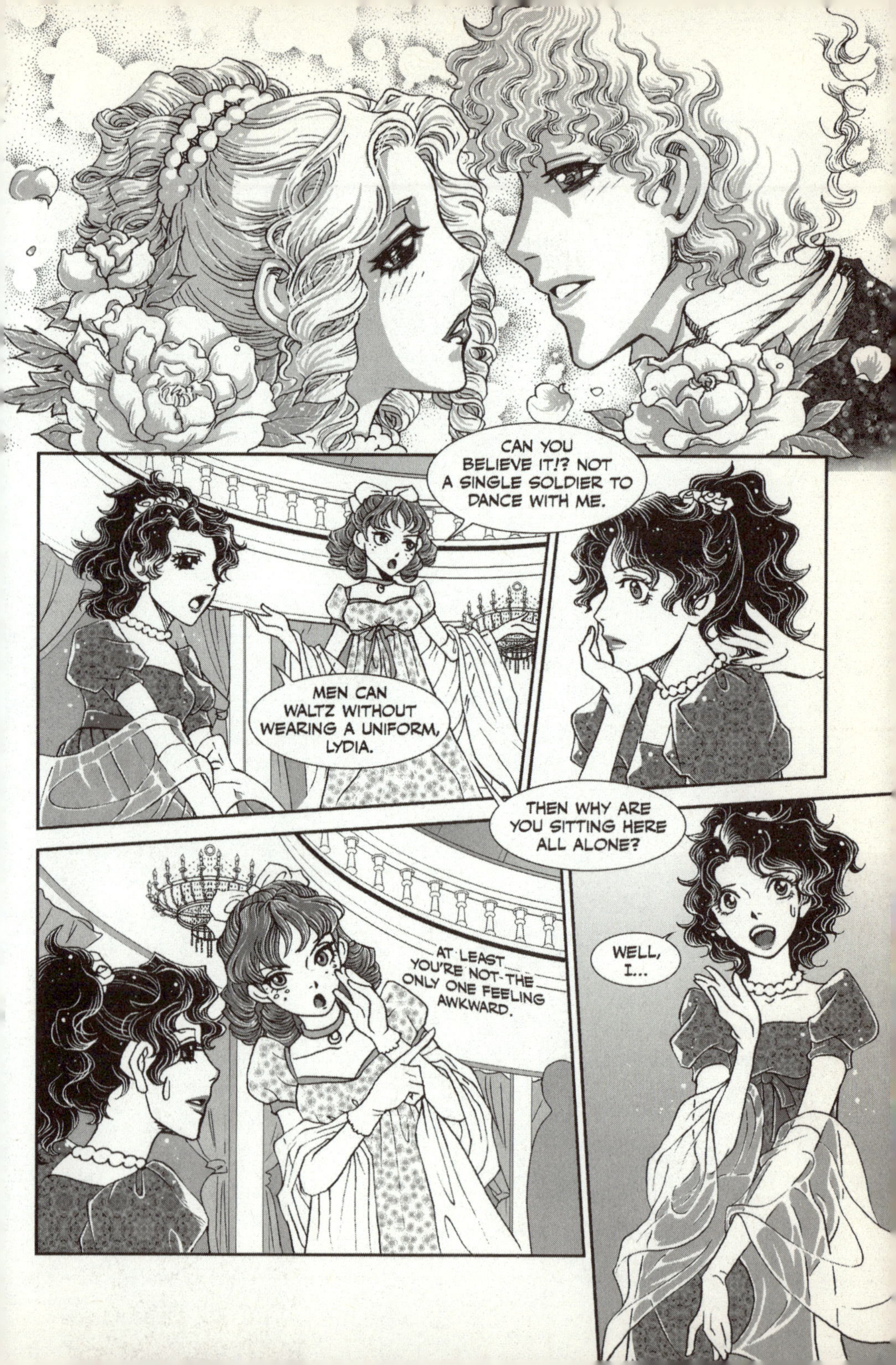
CAN YOU BELIEVE IT!? NOT A SINGLE SOLDIER TO DANCE WITH ME.
MEN CAN WALTZ WITHOUT WEARING A UNIFORM, LYDIA.
THEN WHY ARE YOU SITTING HERE ALL ALONE?
WELL, I...
AT LEAST YOU'RE NOT THE ONLY ONE FEELING AWKWARD.

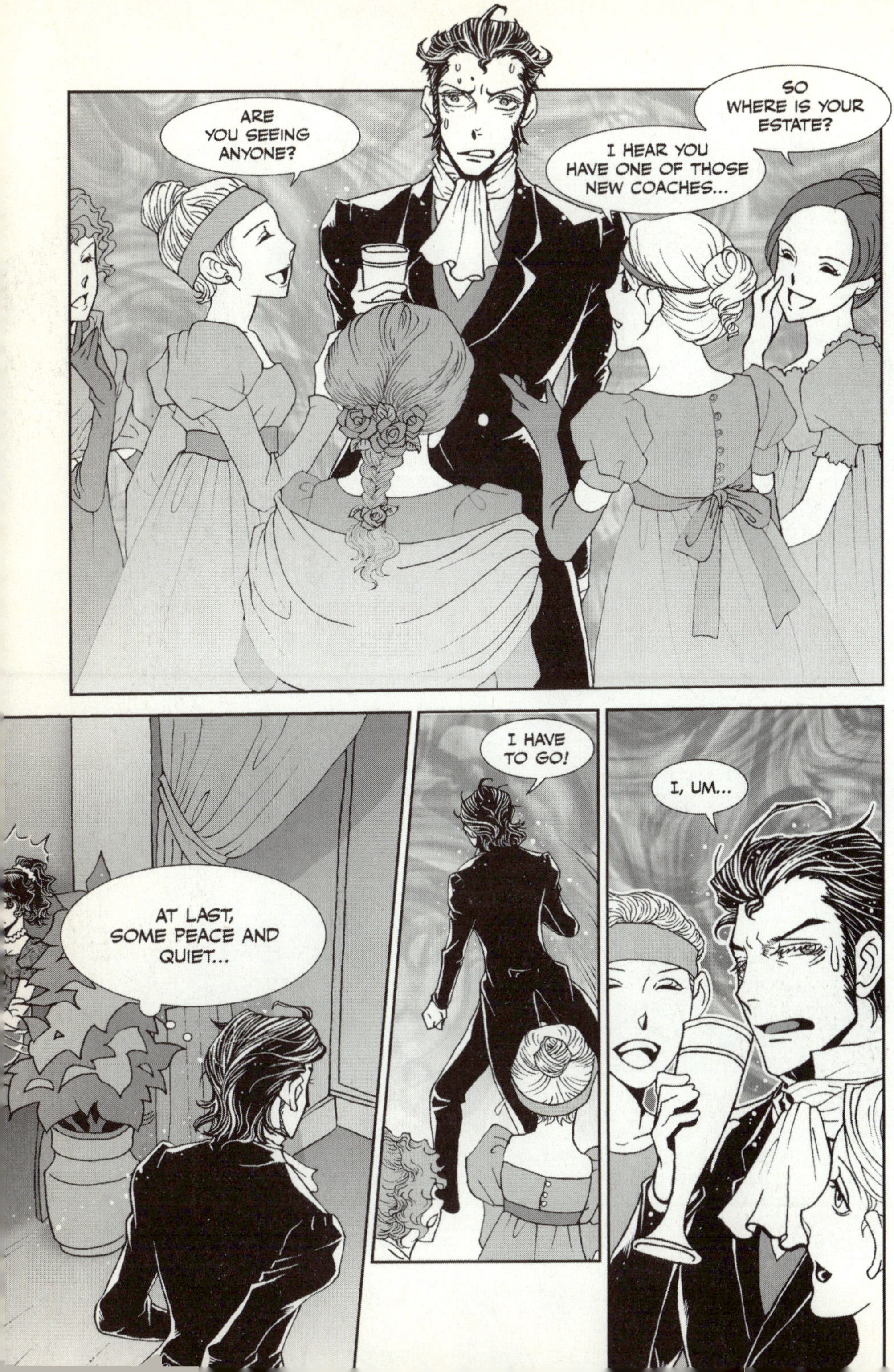
SO WHERE IS YOUR ESTATE?
I HEAR YOU HAVE ONE OF THOSE NEW COACHES...
ARE YOU SEEING ANYONE?
I, UM...
I HAVE TO GO!
AT LAST, SOME PEACE AND QUIET...

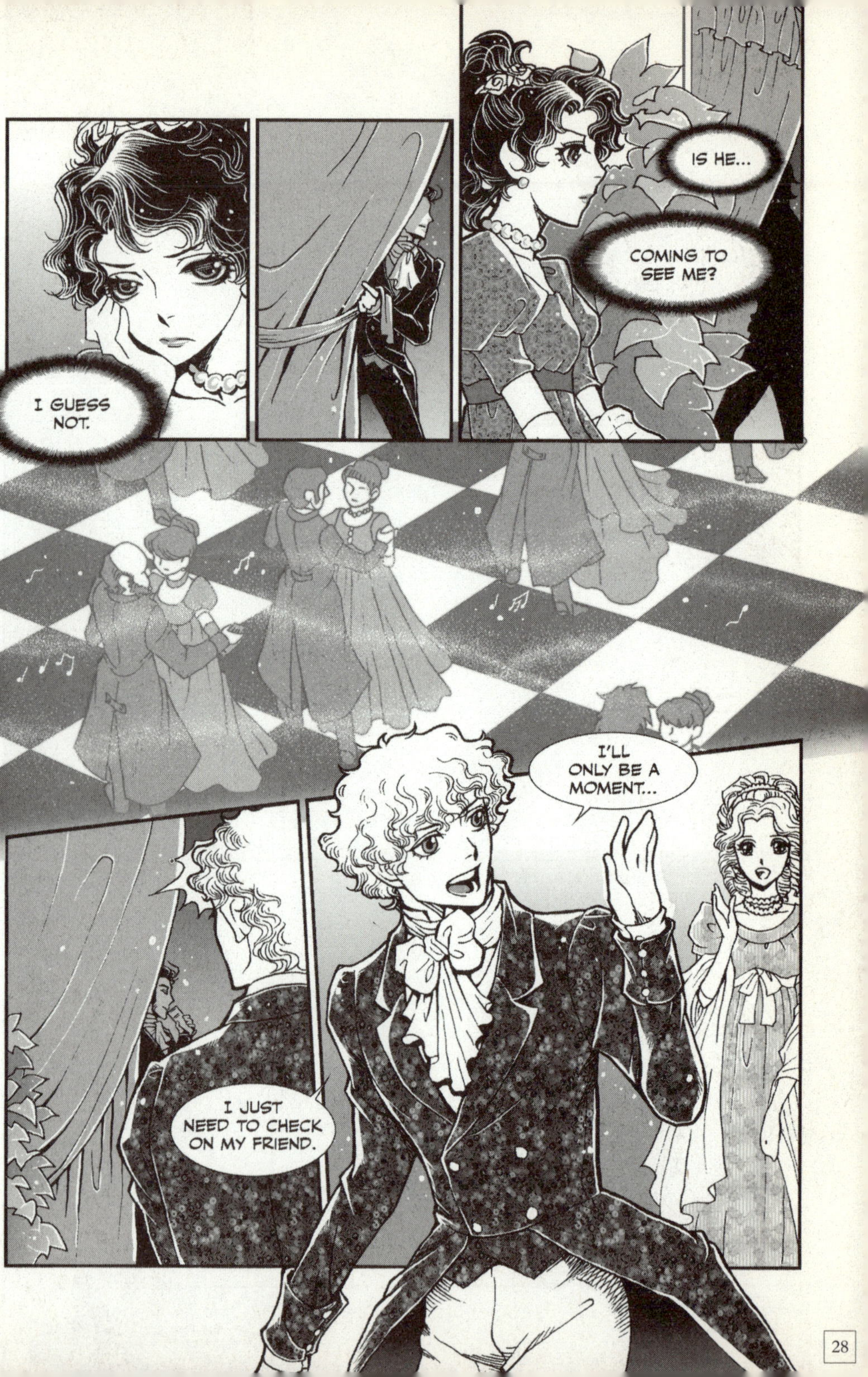
IS HE...
COMING TO SEE ME?
I GUESS NOT.
I'LL ONLY BE A MOMENT...
I JUST NEED TO CHECK ON MY FRIEND.

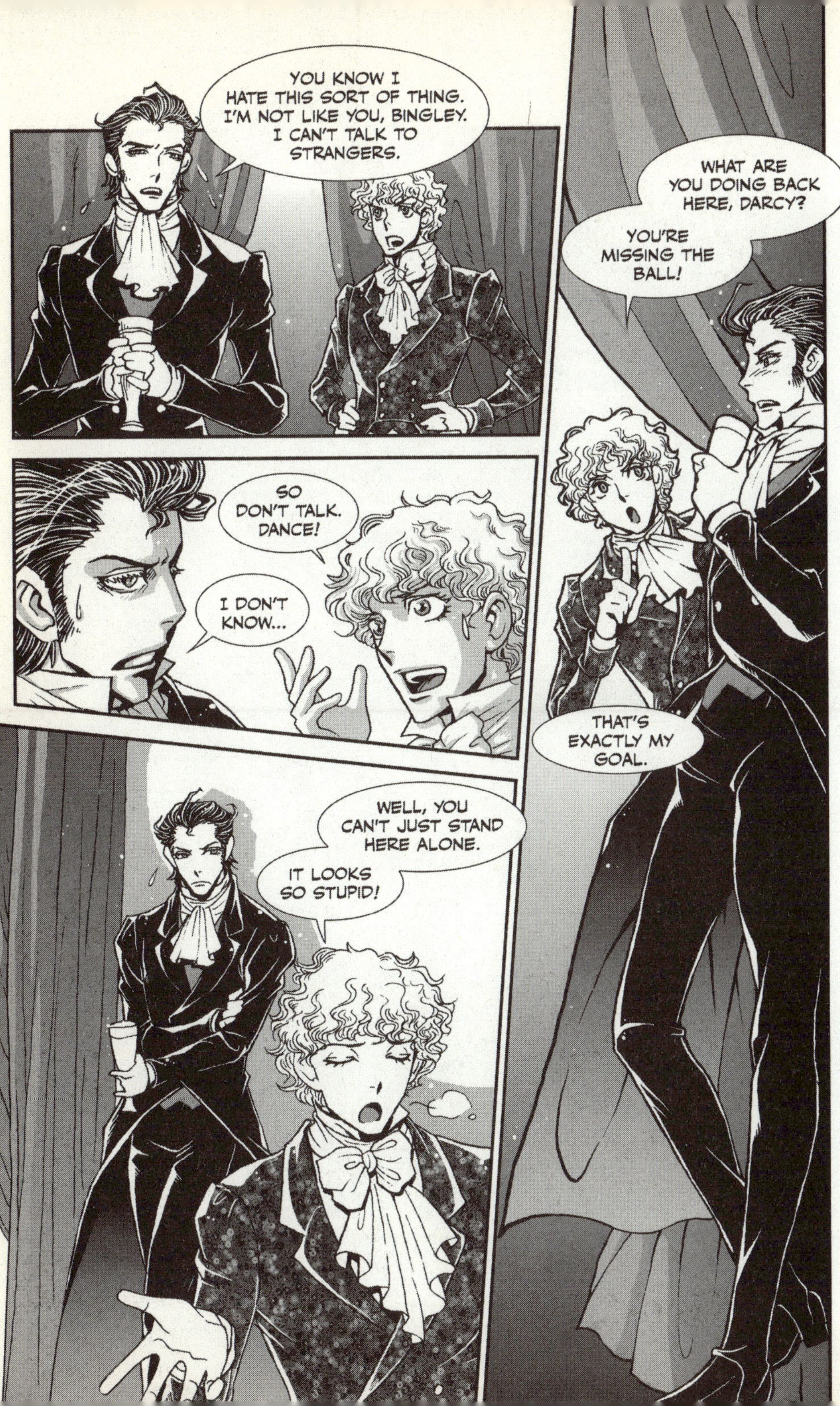
WHAT ARE YOU DOING BACK HERE, DARCY?
YOU'RE MISSING THE BALL!
THAT'S EXACTLY MY GOAL.
YOU KNOW I HATE THIS SORT OF THING. I'M NOT LIKE YOU, BINGLEY. I CAN'T TALK TO STRANGERS.
SO DON'T TALK. DANCE!
I DON'T KNOW...
WELL, YOU CAN'T JUST STAND HERE ALONE.
IT LOOKS SO STUPID!

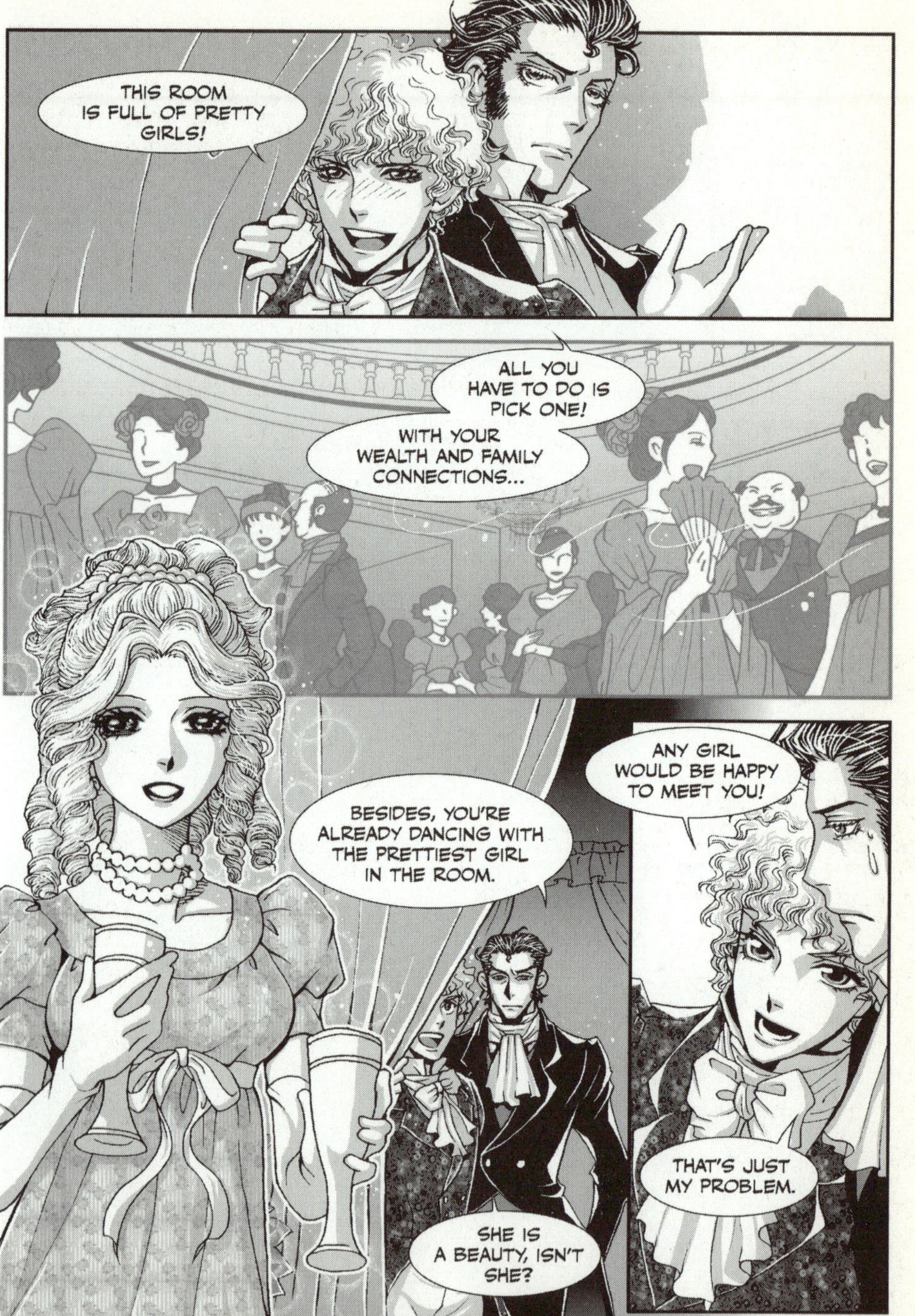
THIS ROOM IS FULL OF PRETTY GIRLS!
ALL YOU HAVE TO DO IS PICK ONE!
WITH YOUR WEALTH AND FAMILY CONNECTIONS...
ANY GIRL WOULD BE HAPPY TO MEET YOU!
THAT'S JUST MY PROBLEM.
BESIDES, YOU'RE ALREADY DANCING WITH THE PRETTIEST GIRL IN THE ROOM.
SHE IS A BEAUTY, ISN'T SHE?

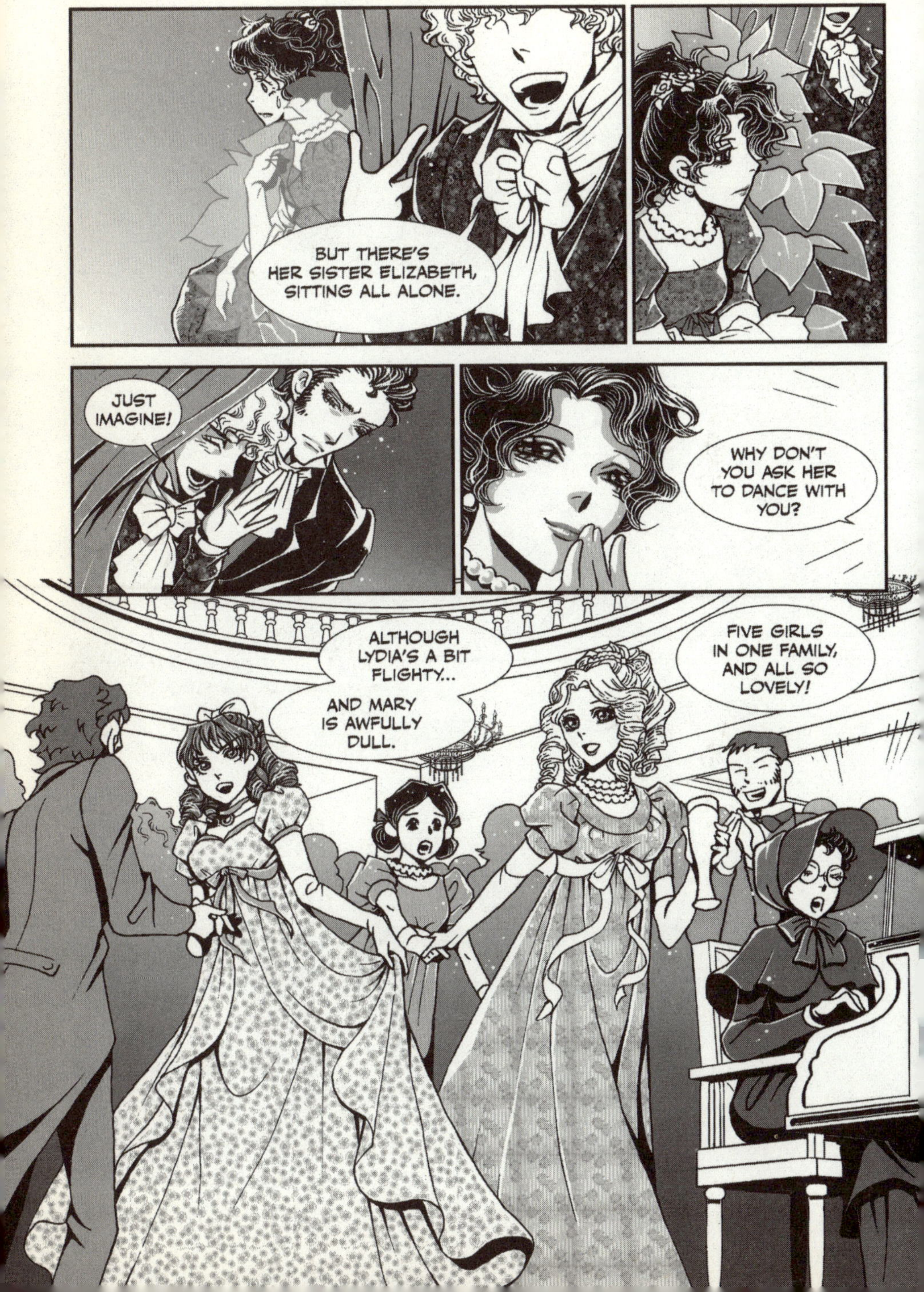
BUT THERE'S HER SISTER ELIZABETH, SITTING ALL ALONE.
WHY DON'T YOU ASK HER TO DANCE WITH YOU?
JUST IMAGINE!
FIVE GIRLS IN ONE FAMILY, AND ALL SO LOVELY!
ALTHOUGH LYDIA'S A BIT FLIGHTY...
AND MARY IS AWFULLY DULL.

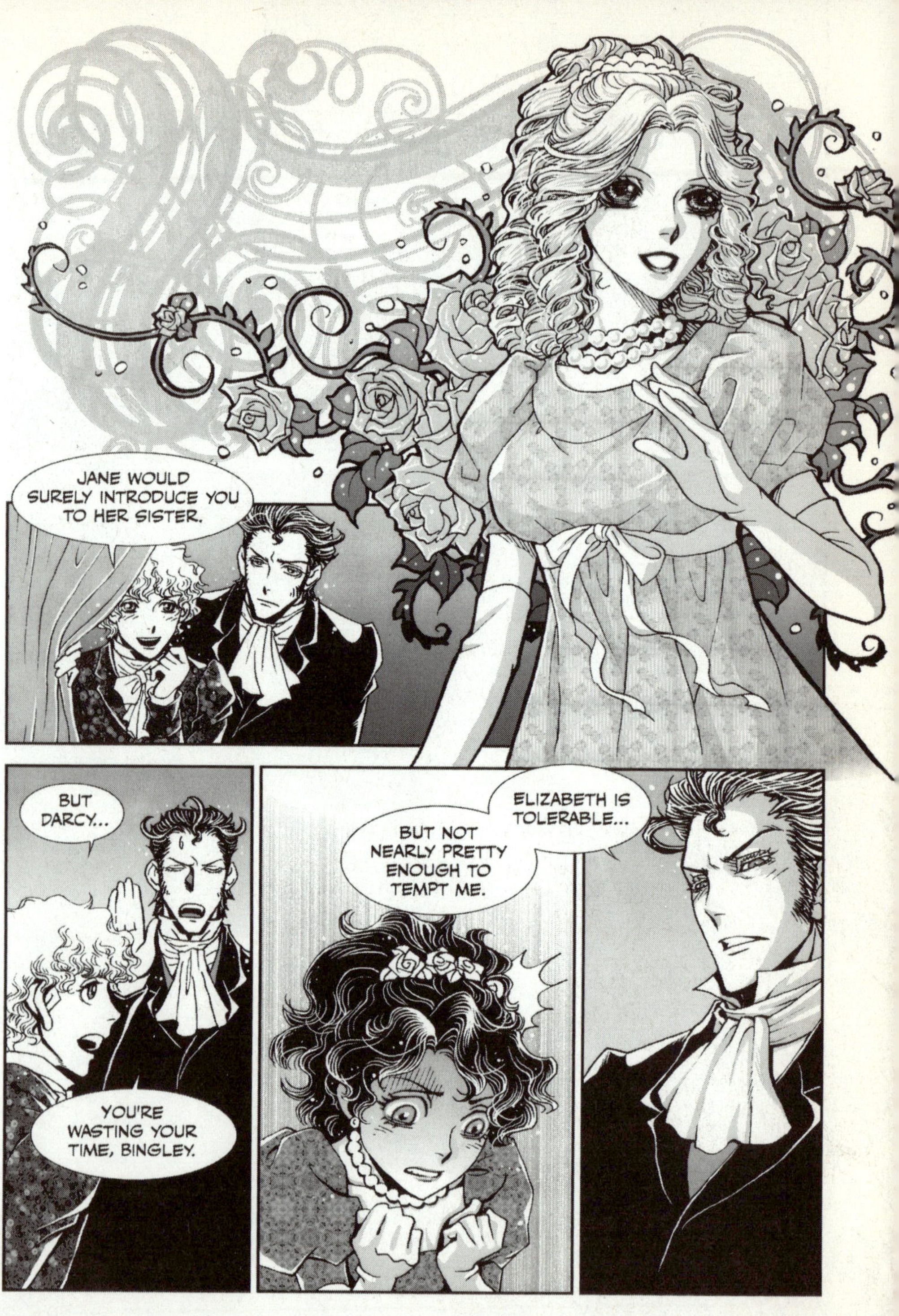
JANE WOULD SURELY INTRODUCE YOU TO HER SISTER.
ELIZABETH IS TOLERABLE...
BUT NOT NEARLY PRETTY ENOUGH TO TEMPT ME.
BUT DARCY...
YOU'RE WASTING YOUR TIME, BINGLEY.

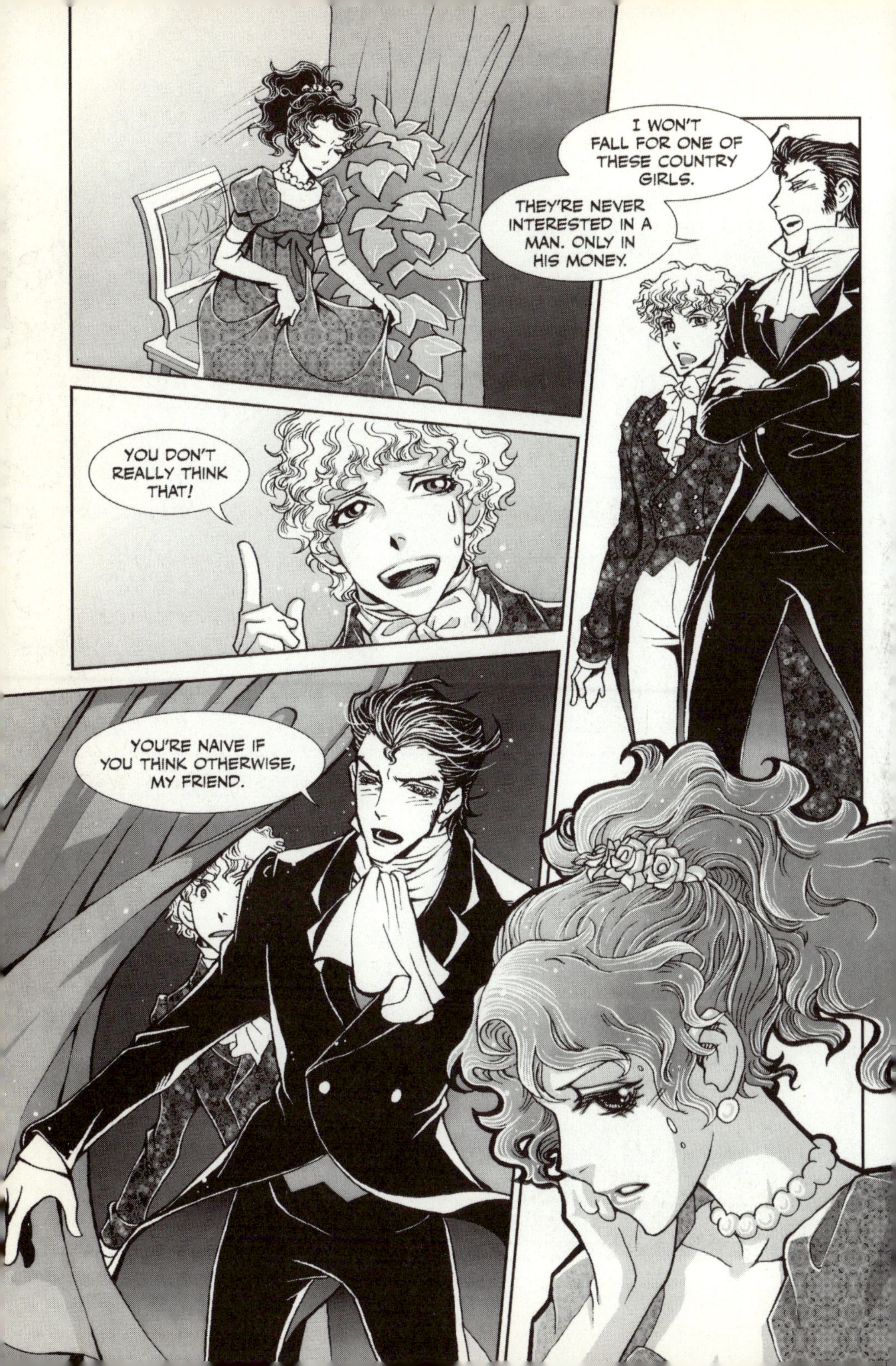
I WON'T FALL FOR ONE OF THESE COUNTRY GIRLS.
THEY'RE NEVER INTERESTED IN A MAN. ONLY IN HIS MONEY.
YOU DON'T REALLY THINK THAT!
YOU'RE NAIVE IF YOU THINK OTHERWISE, MY FRIEND.

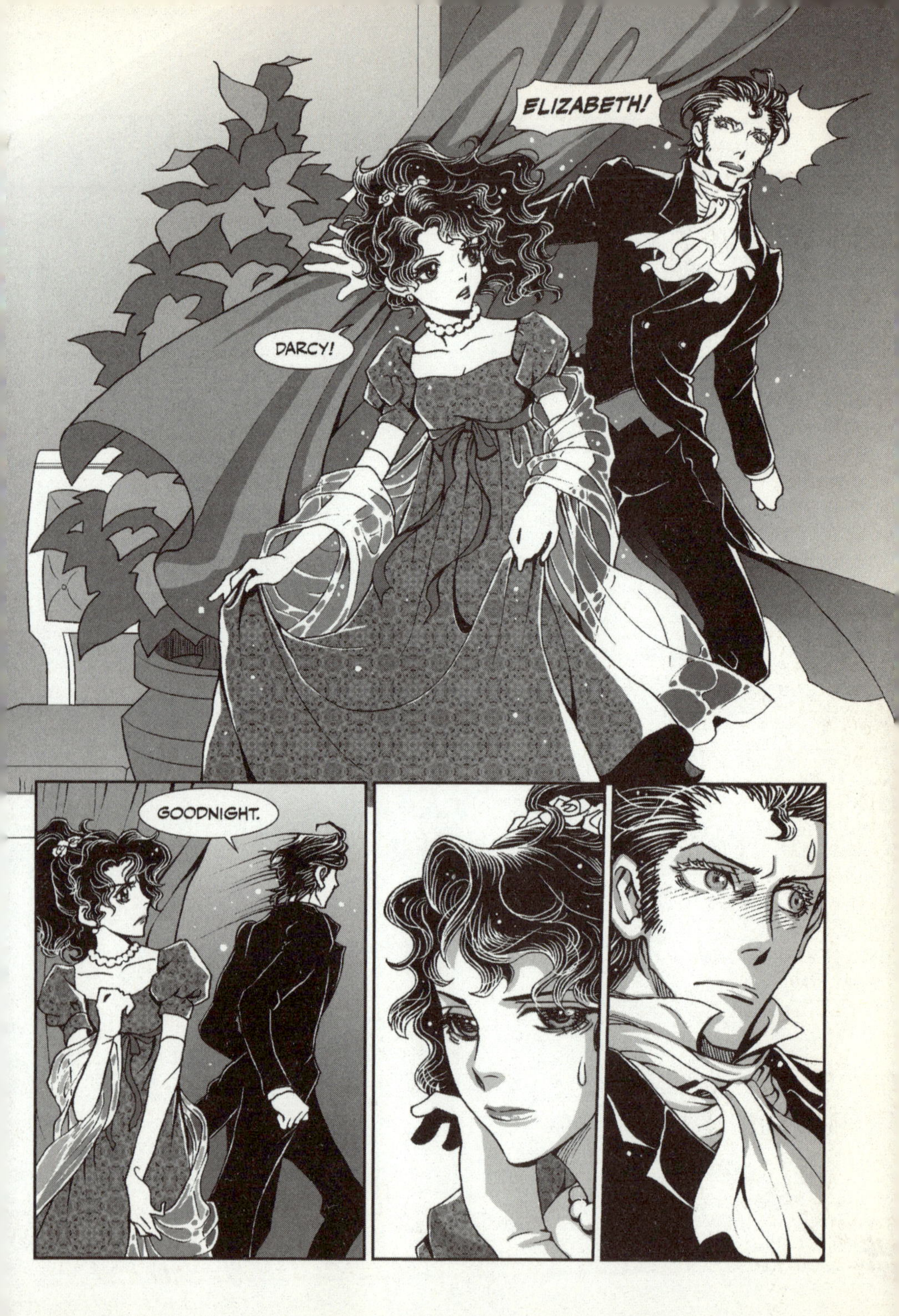
ELIZABETH!
DARCY!
GOODNIGHT.

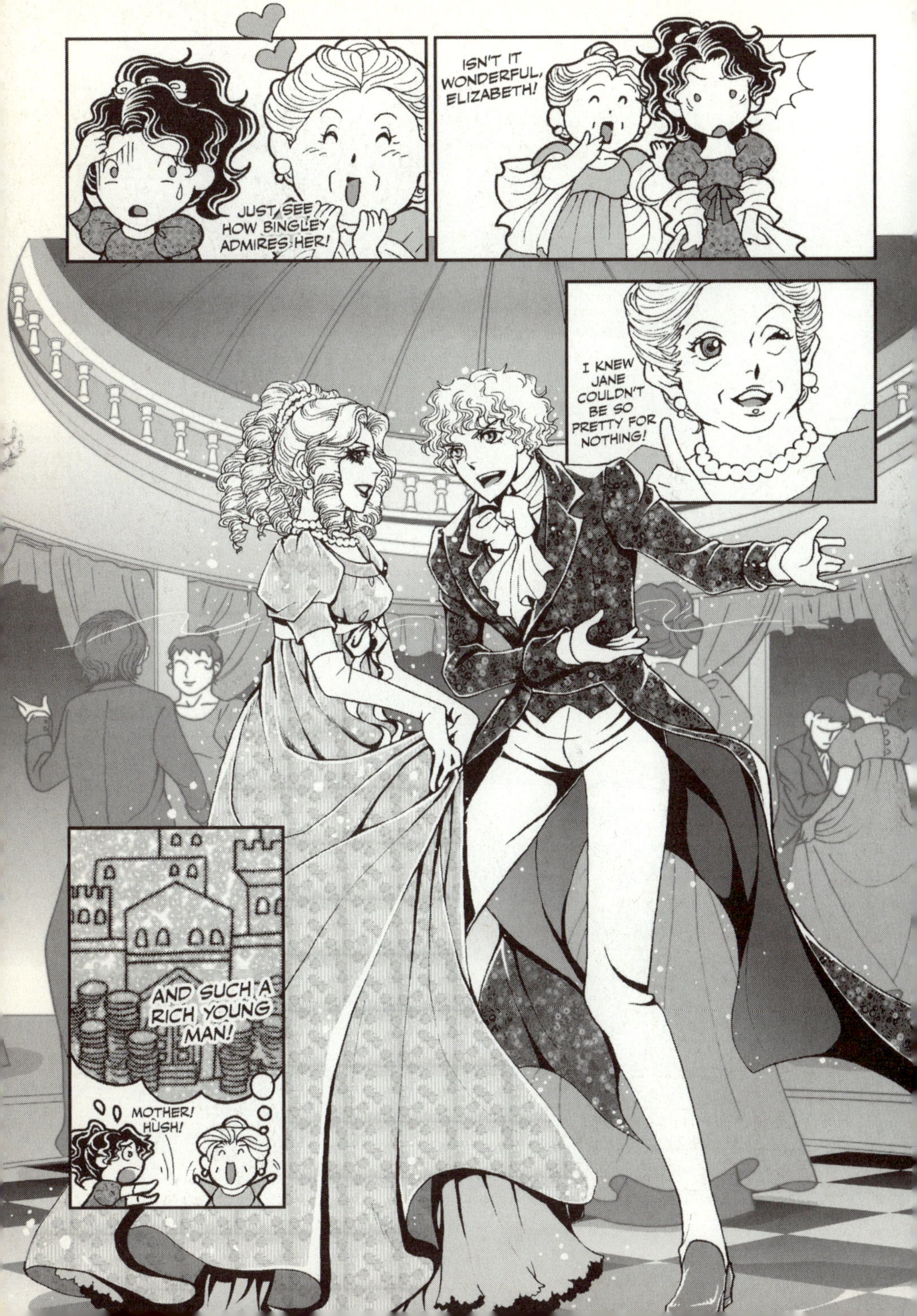
ISN'T IT WONDERFUL, ELIZABETH!
JUST SEE HOW BINGLEY ADMIRES HER!
I KNEW JANE COULDN'T BE SO PRETTY FOR NOTHING!
AND SUCH A RICH YOUNG MAN!
MOTHER! HUSH!

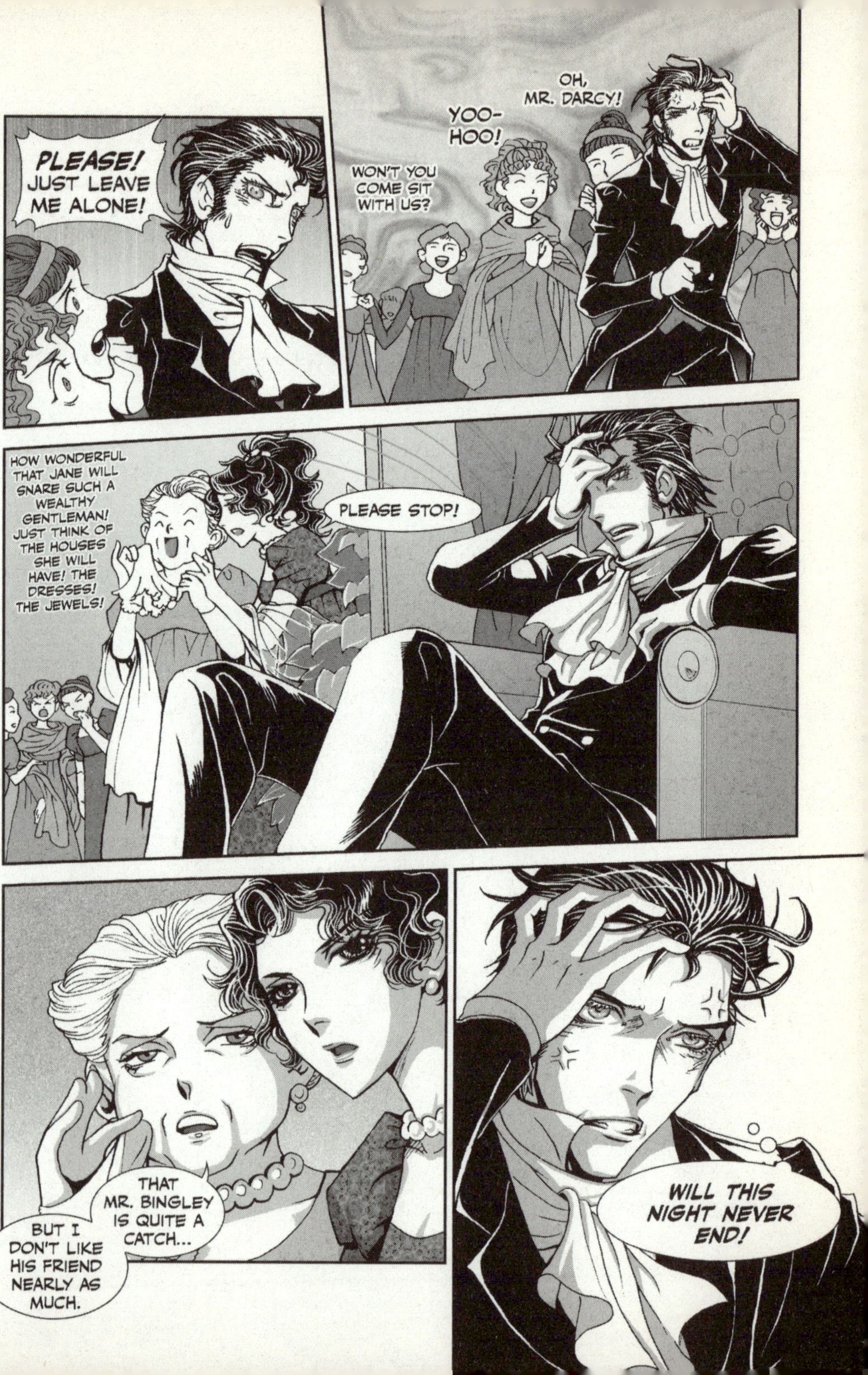
OH, MR. DARCY!
YOO-HOO!
WON'T YOU COME SIT WITH US?
PLEASE! JUST LEAVE ME ALONE!
HOW WONDERFUL THAT JANE WILL SNARE SUCH A WEALTHY GENTLEMAN! JUST THINK OF THE HOUSES SHE WILL HAVE! THE DRESSES! THE JEWELS!
PLEASE STOP!
WILL THIS NIGHT NEVER END!
THAT MR. BINGLEY IS QUITE A CATCH...
BUT I DON'T LIKE HIS FRIEND NEARLY AS MUCH.

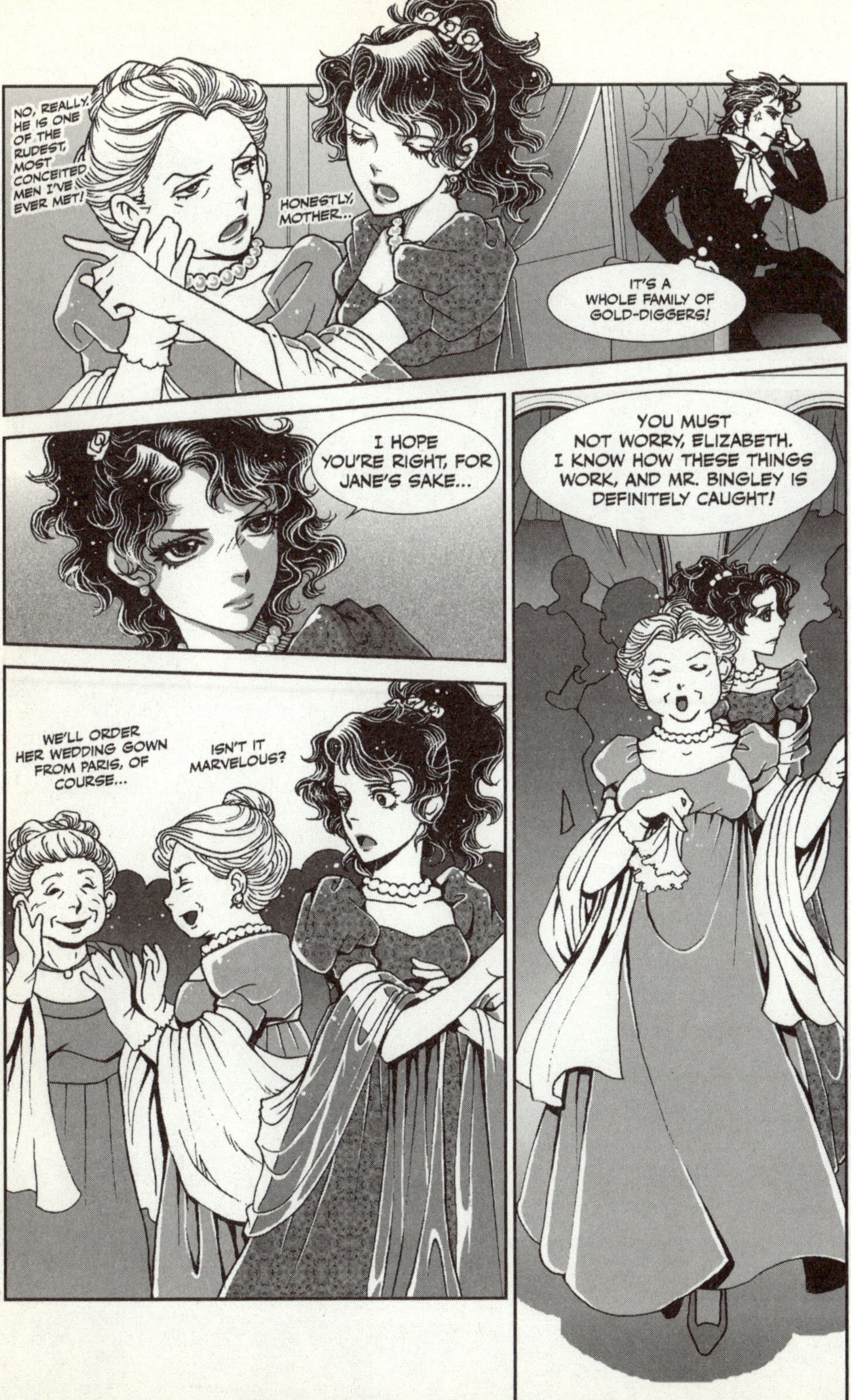
IT'S A WHOLE FAMILY OF GOLD-DIGGERS!
HONESTLY, MOTHER...
NO, REALLY. HE IS ONE OF THE RUDEST, MOST CONCEITED MEN I'VE EVER MET!
YOU MUST NOT WORRY, ELIZABETH. I KNOW HOW THESE THINGS WORK, AND MR. BINGLEY IS DEFINITELY CAUGHT!
I HOPE YOU'RE RIGHT, FOR JANE'S SAKE...
ISN'T IT MARVELOUS?
WE'LL ORDER HER WEDDING GOWN FROM PARIS, OF COURSE...

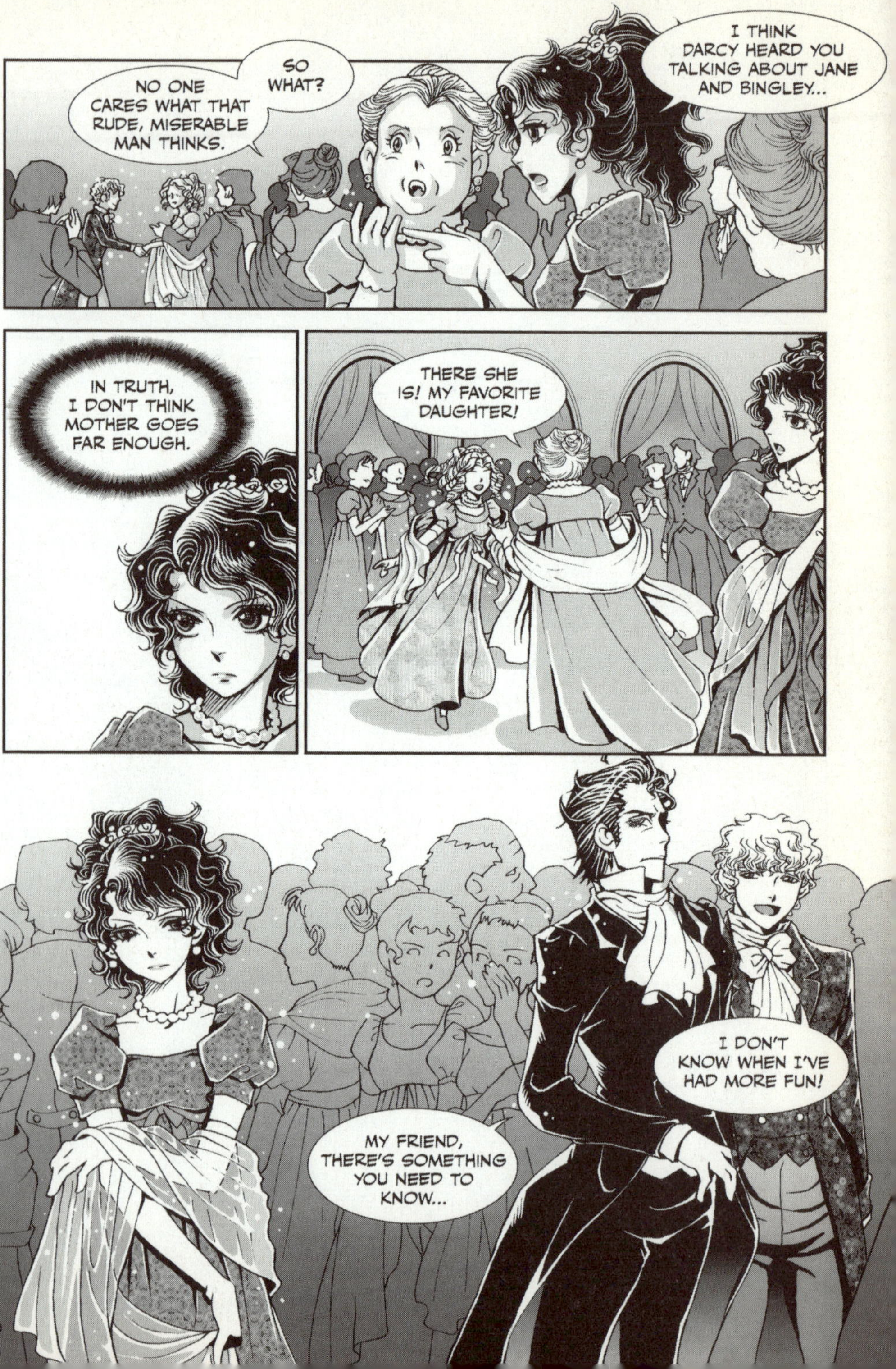
I THINK DARCY HEARD YOU TALKING ABOUT JANE AND BINGLEY...
SO WHAT?
NO ONE CARES WHAT THAT RUDE, MISERABLE MAN THINKS.
THERE SHE IS! MY FAVORITE DAUGHTER!
IN TRUTH, I DON'T THINK MOTHER GOES FAR ENOUGH.
I DON'T KNOW WHEN I'VE HAD MORE FUN!
MY FRIEND, THERE'S SOMETHING YOU NEED TO KNOW...

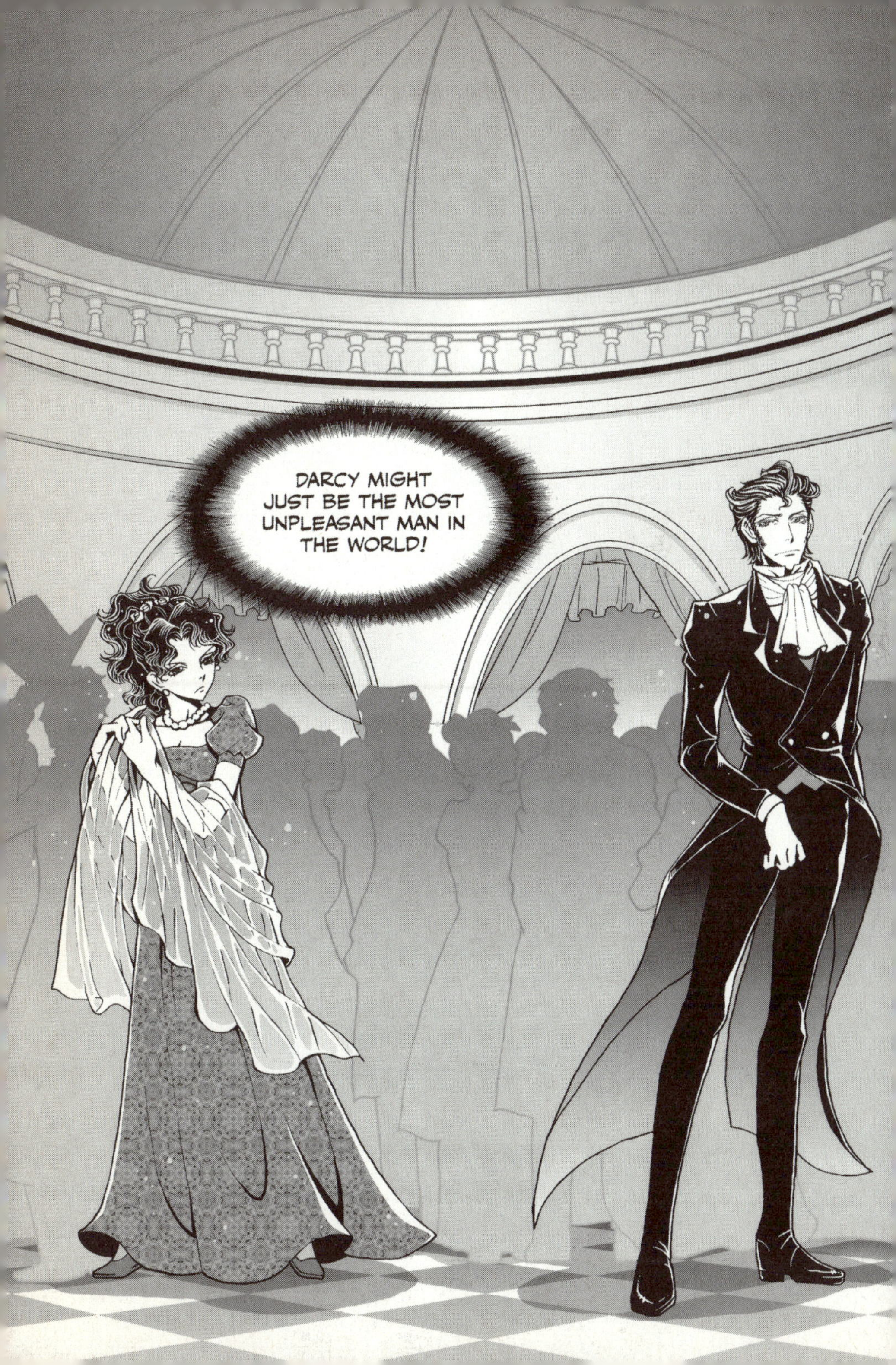
DARCY MIGHT JUST BE THE MOST UNPLEASANT MAN IN THE WORLD!

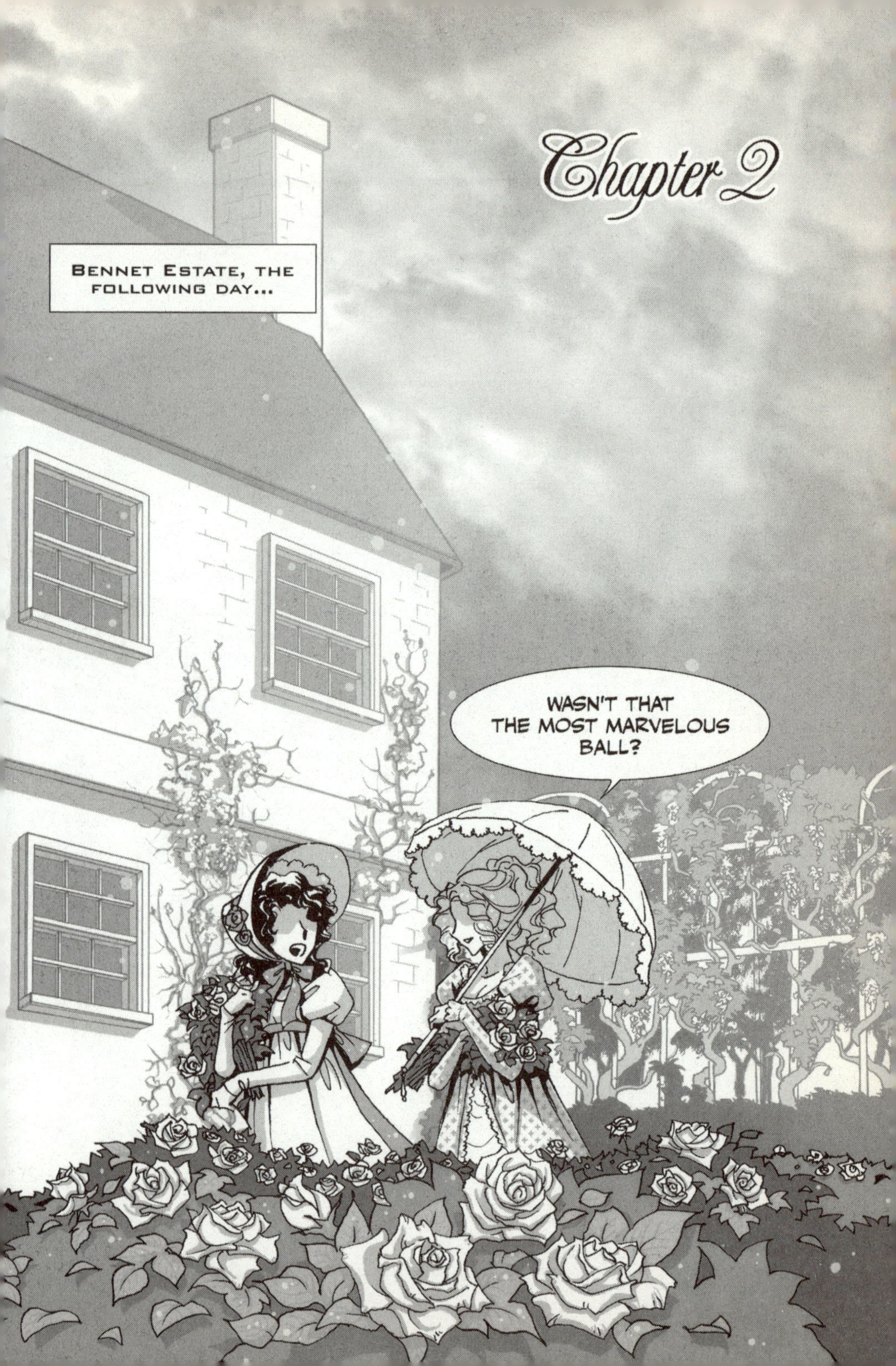
Chapter 2
BENNET ESTATE, THE FOLLOWING DAY...
WASN'T THAT THE MOST MARVELOUS BALL?

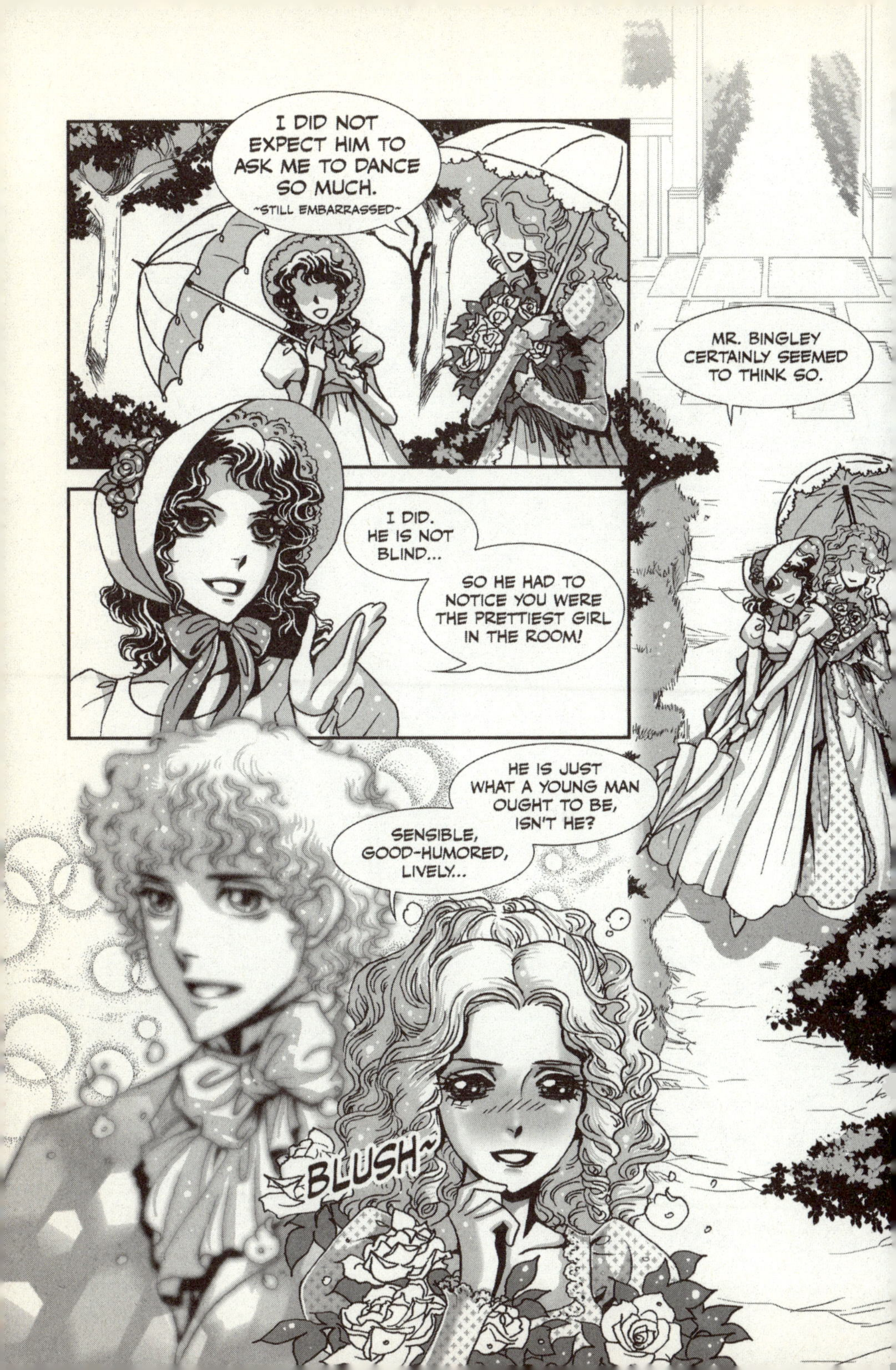
I DID NOT EXPECT HIM TO ASK ME TO DANCE SO MUCH.
~STILL EMBARRASSED~
MR. BINGLEY CERTAINLY SEEMED TO THINK SO.
I DID. HE IS NOT BLIND...
SO HE HAD TO NOTICE YOU WERE THE PRETTIEST GIRL IN THE ROOM!
HE IS JUST WHAT A YOUNG MAN OUGHT TO BE, ISN'T HE?
SENSIBLE, GOOD-HUMORED, LIVELY...
BLUSH~

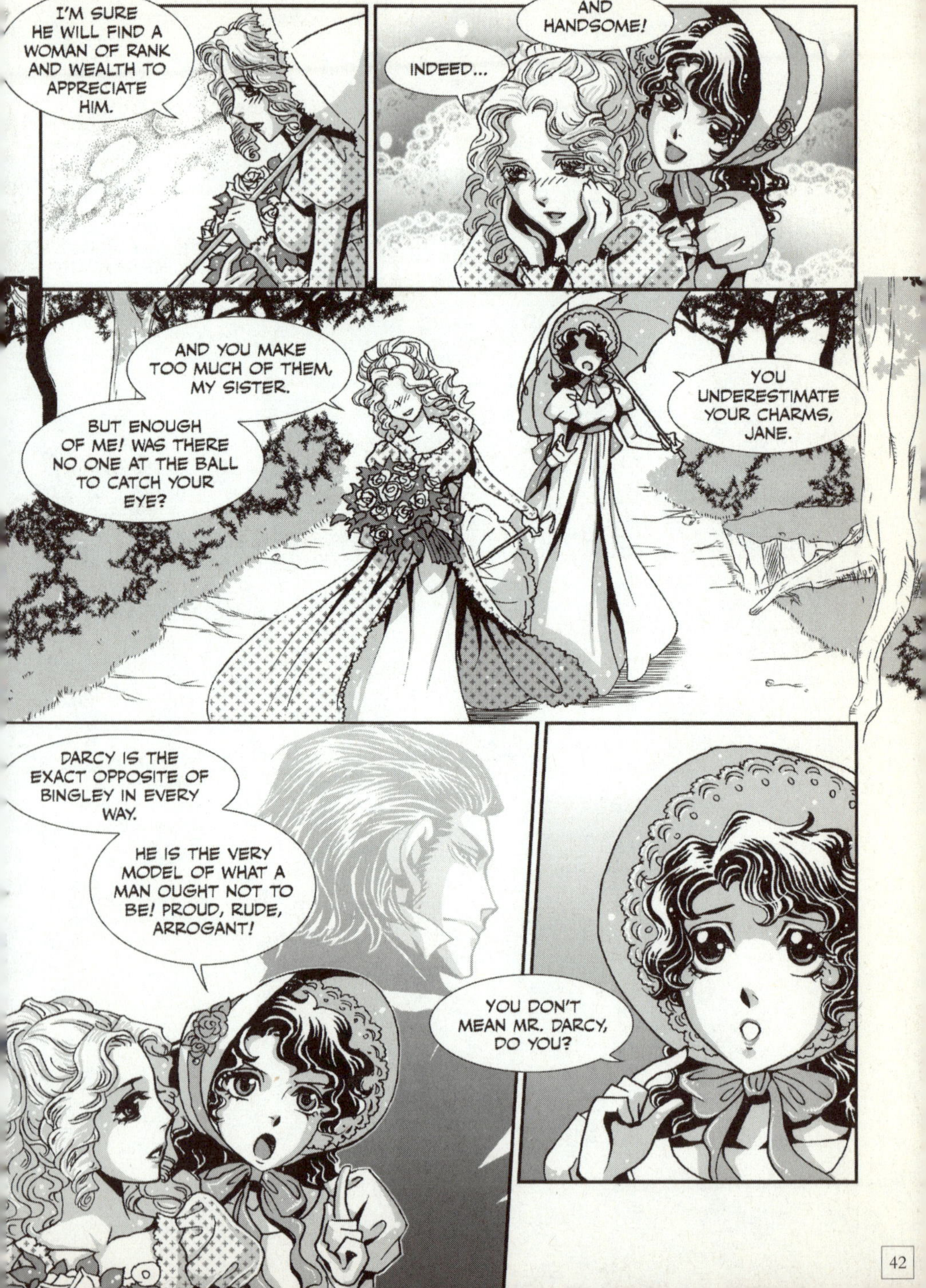
AND HANDSOME!
INDEED...
I'M SURE HE WILL FIND A WOMAN OF RANK AND WEALTH TO APPRECIATE HIM.
YOU UNDERESTIMATE YOUR CHARMS, JANE.
AND YOU MAKE TOO MUCH OF THEM, MY SISTER.
BUT ENOUGH OF ME! WAS THERE NO ONE AT THE BALL TO CATCH YOUR EYE?
YOU DON'T MEAN MR. DARCY, DO YOU?
DARCY IS THE EXACT OPPOSITE OF BINGLEY IN EVERY WAY.
HE IS THE VERY MODEL OF WHAT A MAN OUGHT NOT TO BE! PROUD, RUDE, ARROGANT!

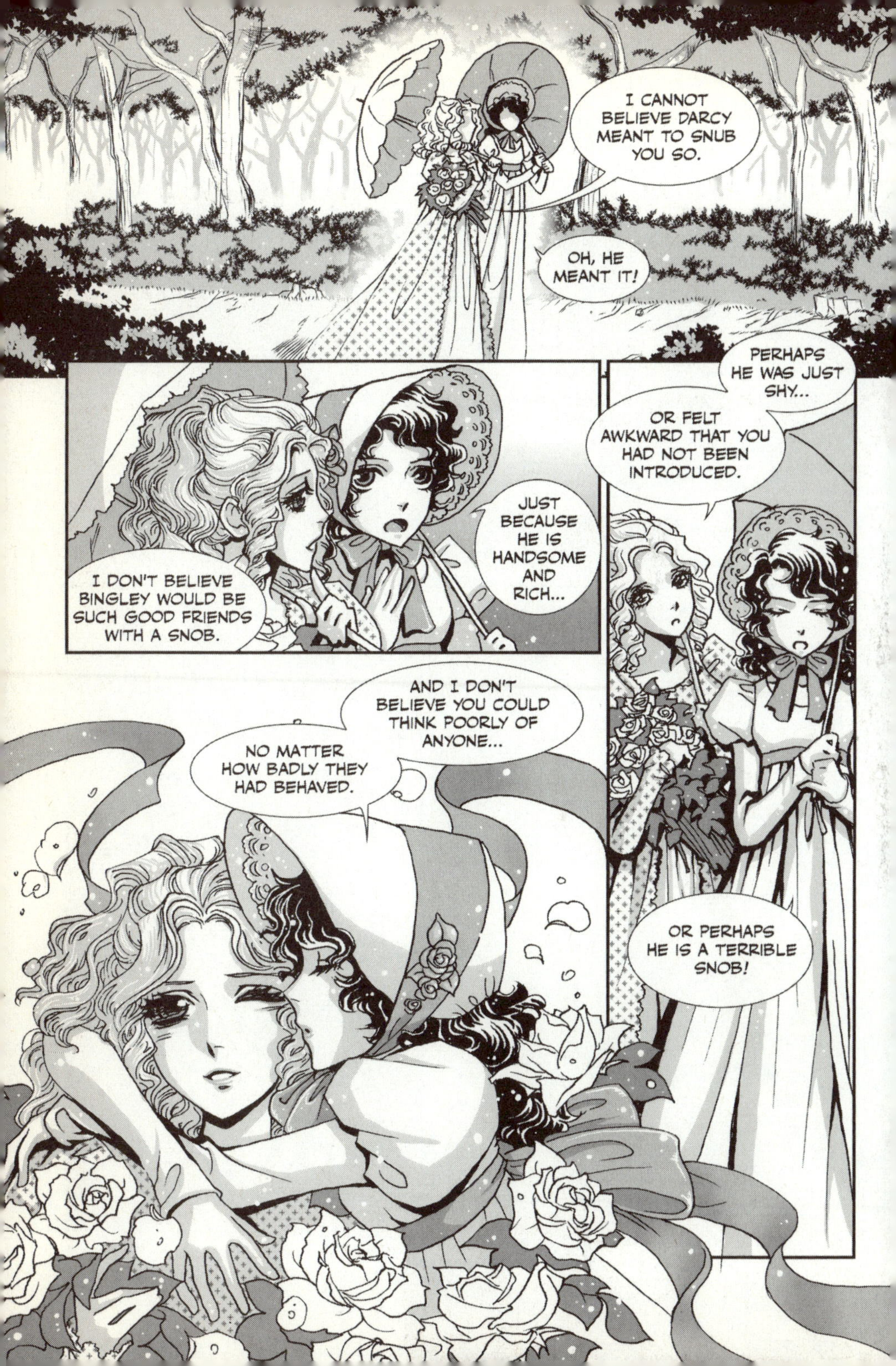
I CANNOT BELIEVE DARCY MEANT TO SNUB YOU SO.
OH, HE MEANT IT!
PERHAPS HE WAS JUST SHY...
OR FELT AWKWARD THAT YOU HAD NOT BEEN INTRODUCED.
OR PERHAPS HE IS A TERRIBLE SNOB!
JUST BECAUSE HE IS HANDSOME AND RICH...
I DON'T BELIEVE BINGLEY WOULD BE SUCH GOOD FRIENDS WITH A SNOB.
AND I DON'T BELIEVE YOU COULD THINK POORLY OF ANYONE...
NO MATTER HOW BADLY THEY HAD BEHAVED.

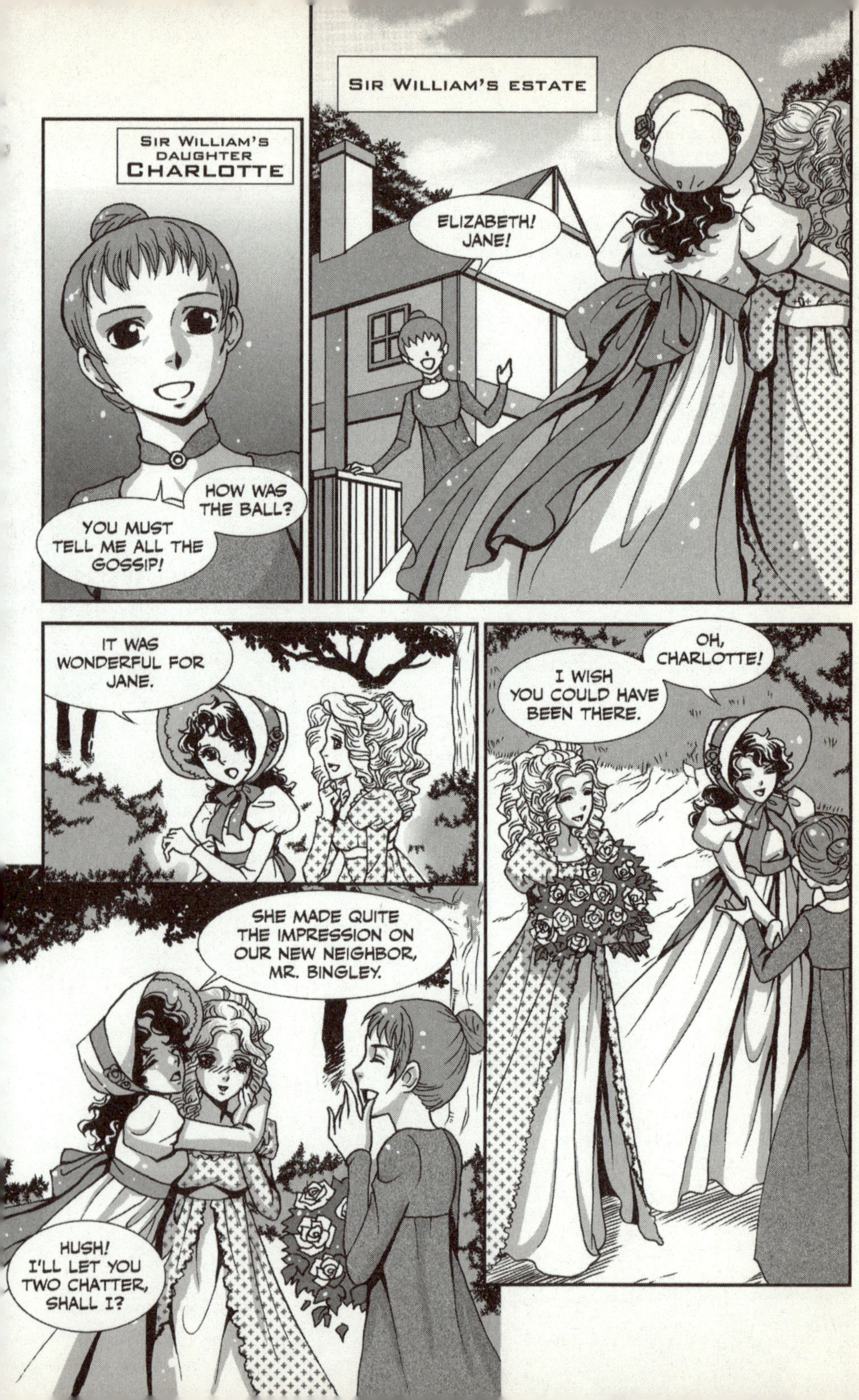
Sir William's estate
Elizabeth! Jane!
Sir William's daughter Charlotte
How was the ball?
You must tell me all the gossip!
Oh, Charlotte!
I wish you could have been there.
It was wonderful for Jane.
She made quite the impression on our new neighbor, Mr. Bingley.
Hush! I'll let you two chatter, shall I?

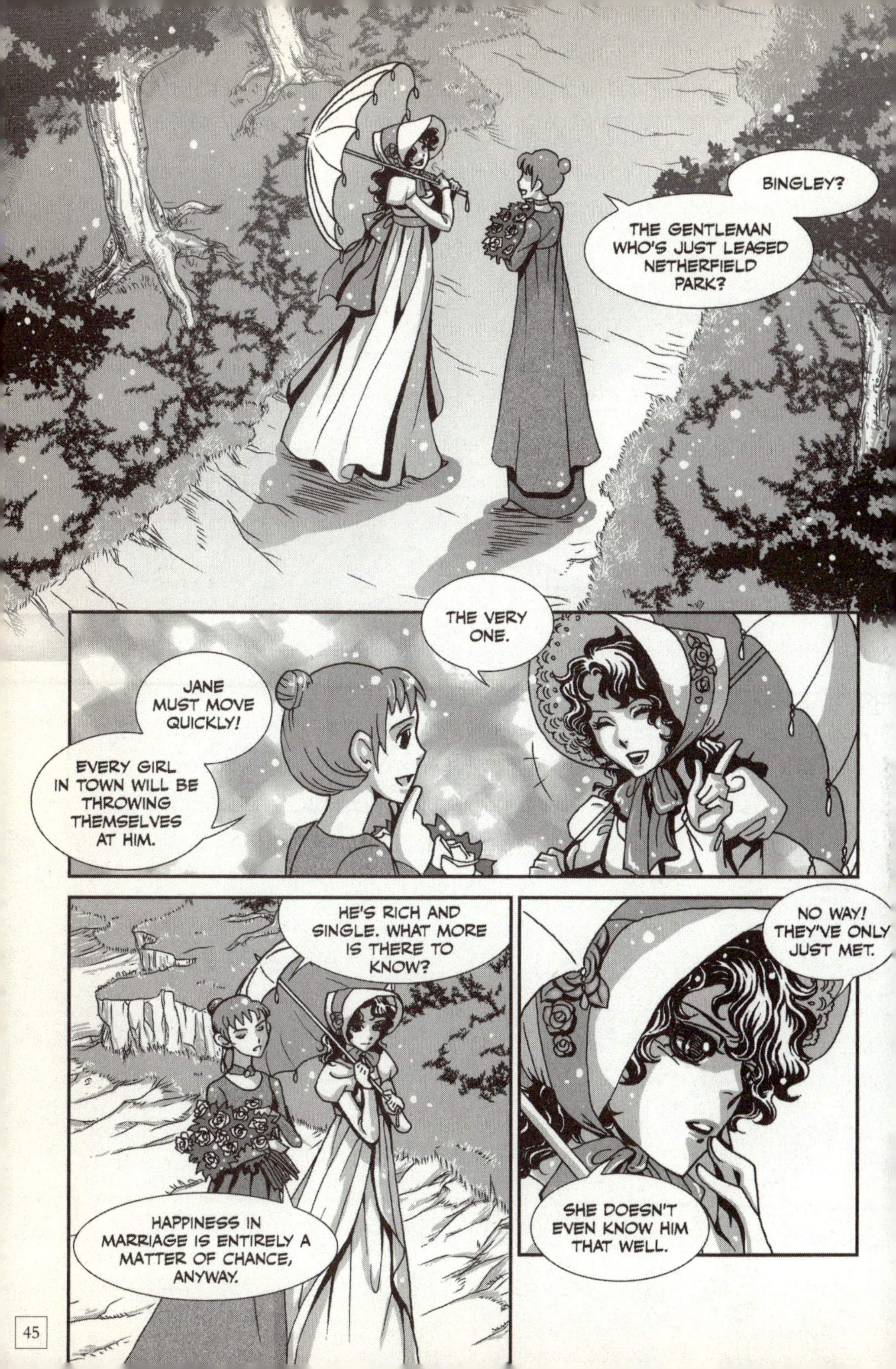
BINGLEY?
THE GENTLEMAN WHO'S JUST LEASED NETHERFIELD PARK?
THE VERY ONE.
JANE MUST MOVE QUICKLY!
EVERY GIRL IN TOWN WILL BE THROWING THEMSELVES AT HIM.
NO WAY! THEY'VE ONLY JUST MET.
SHE DOESN'T EVEN KNOW HIM THAT WELL.
HE'S RICH AND SINGLE. WHAT MORE IS THERE TO KNOW?
HAPPINESS IN MARRIAGE IS ENTIRELY A MATTER OF CHANCE, ANYWAY.

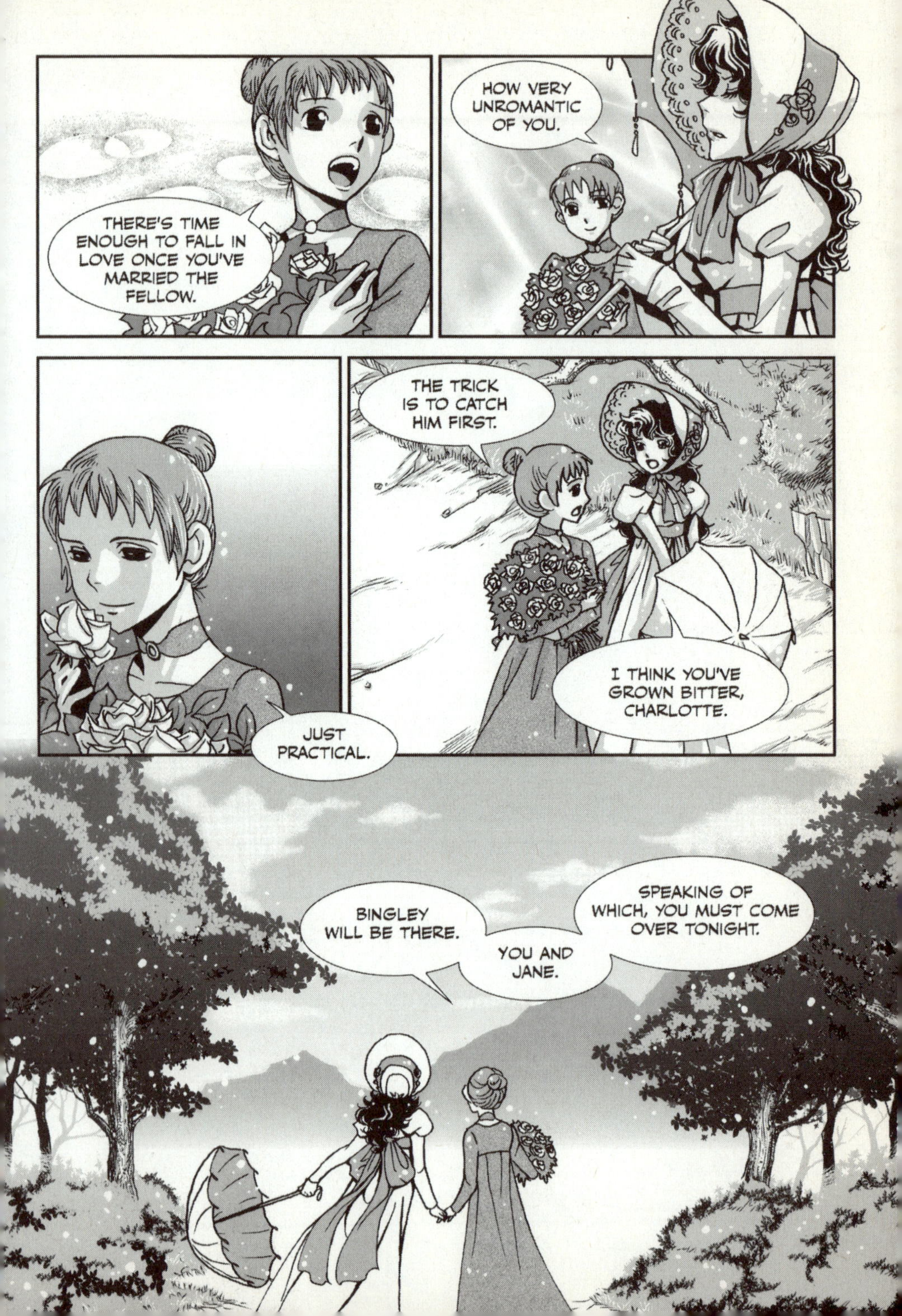
HOW VERY UNROMANTIC OF YOU.
THERE'S TIME ENOUGH TO FALL IN LOVE ONCE YOU'VE MARRIED THE FELLOW.
THE TRICK IS TO CATCH HIM FIRST.
I THINK YOU'VE GROWN BITTER, CHARLOTTE.
JUST PRACTICAL.
SPEAKING OF WHICH, YOU MUST COME OVER TONIGHT.
YOU AND JANE.
BINGLEY WILL BE THERE.

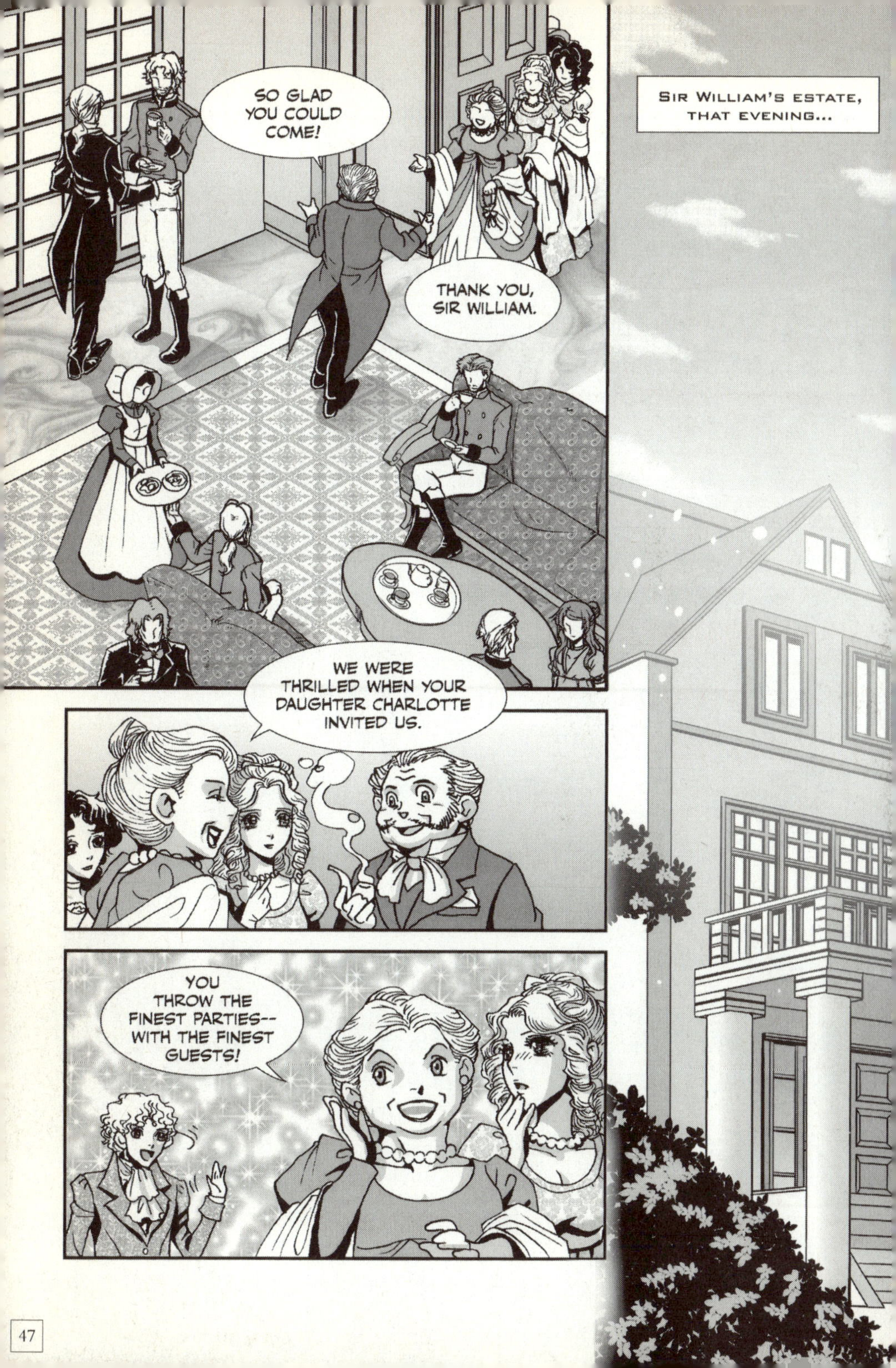
Sir William's estate, that evening...
So glad you could come!
Thank you, Sir William.
We were thrilled when your daughter Charlotte invited us.
You throw the finest parties-- with the finest guests!

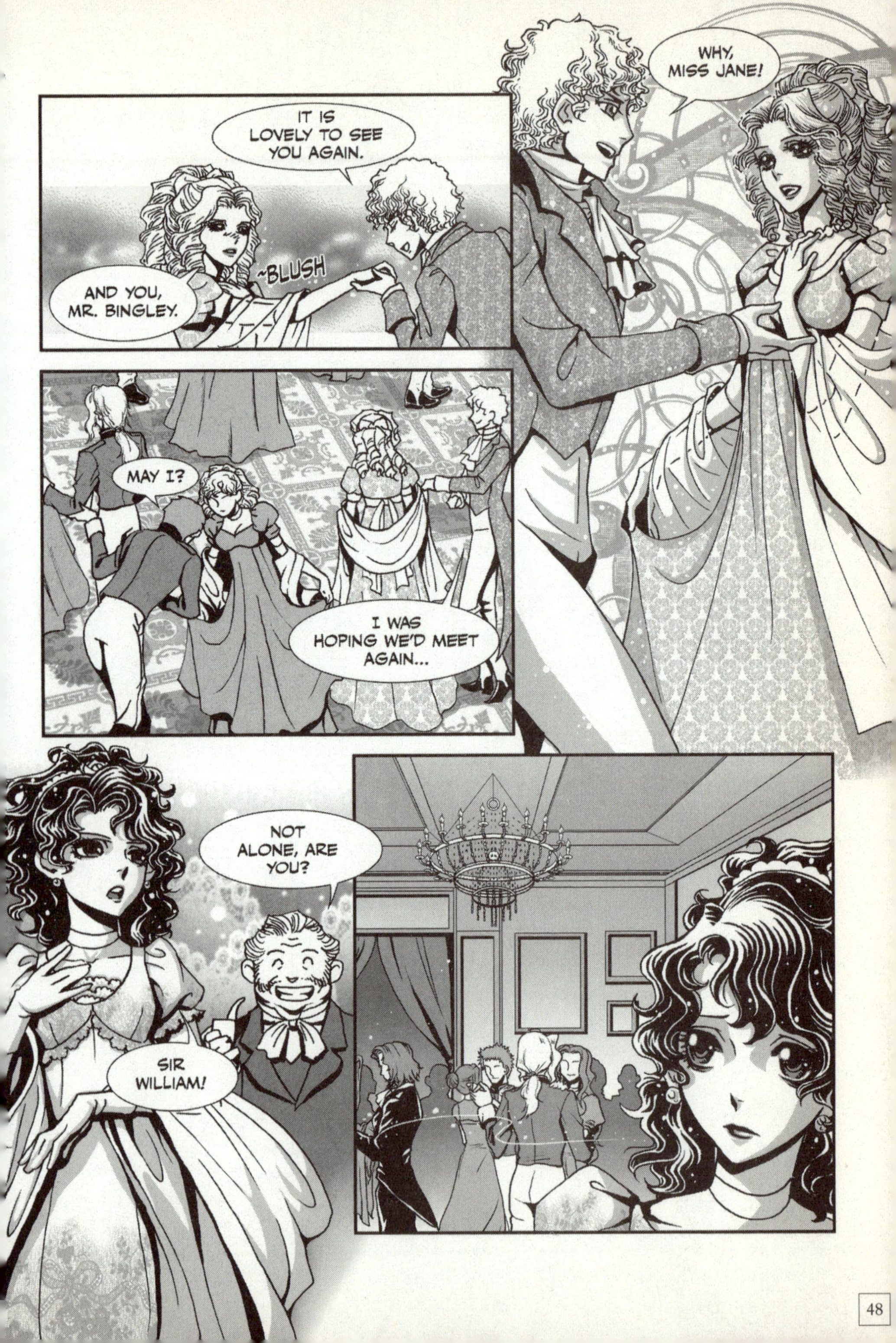
WHY, MISS JANE!
IT IS LOVELY TO SEE YOU AGAIN.
~BLUSH
AND YOU, MR. BINGLEY.
MAY I?
I WAS HOPING WE'D MEET AGAIN...
NOT ALONE, ARE YOU?
SIR WILLIAM!

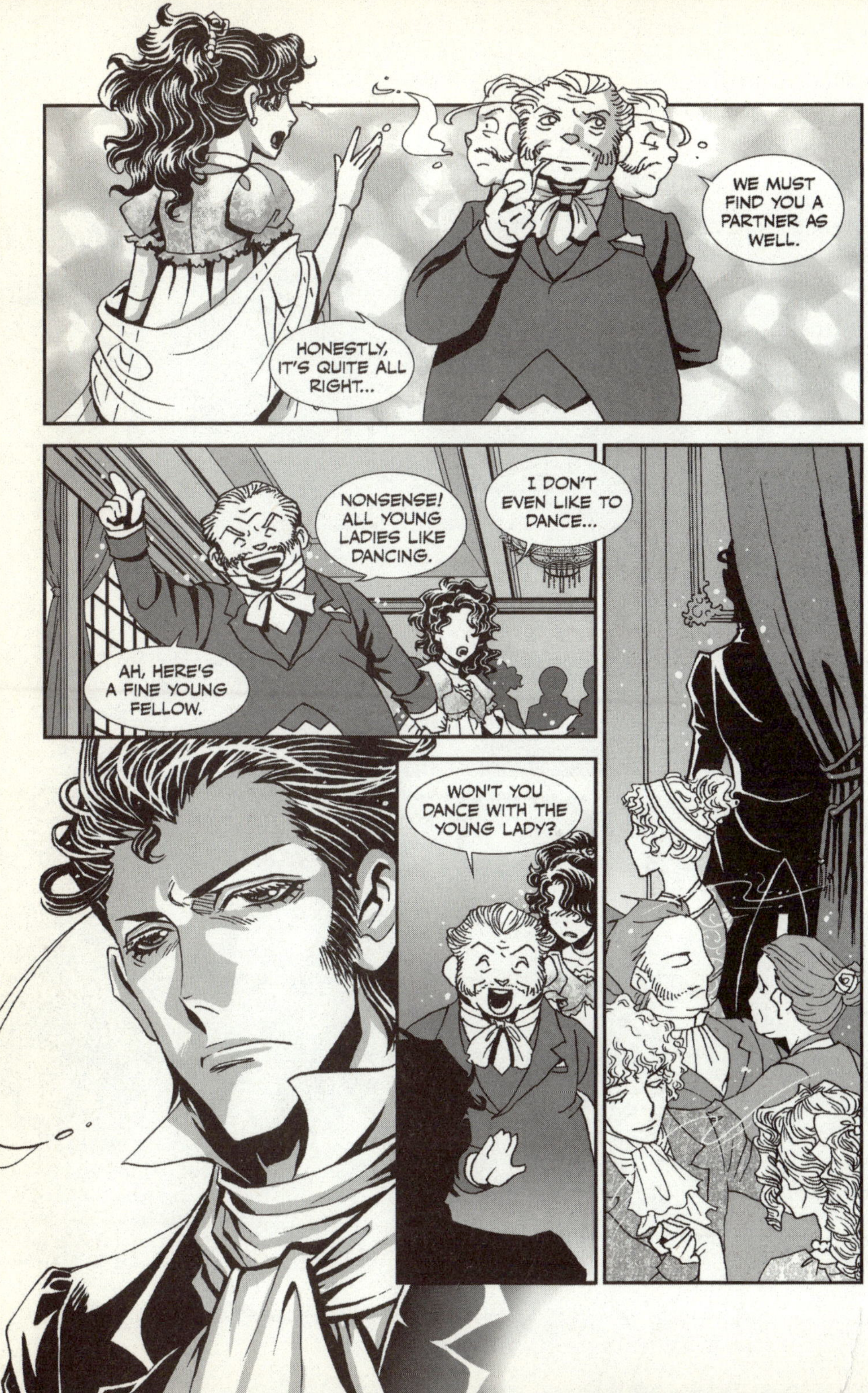
WE MUST FIND YOU A PARTNER AS WELL.
HONESTLY, IT'S QUITE ALL RIGHT...
I DON'T EVEN LIKE TO DANCE...
NONSENSE! ALL YOUNG LADIES LIKE DANCING.
AH, HERE'S A FINE YOUNG FELLOW.
WON'T YOU DANCE WITH THE YOUNG LADY?

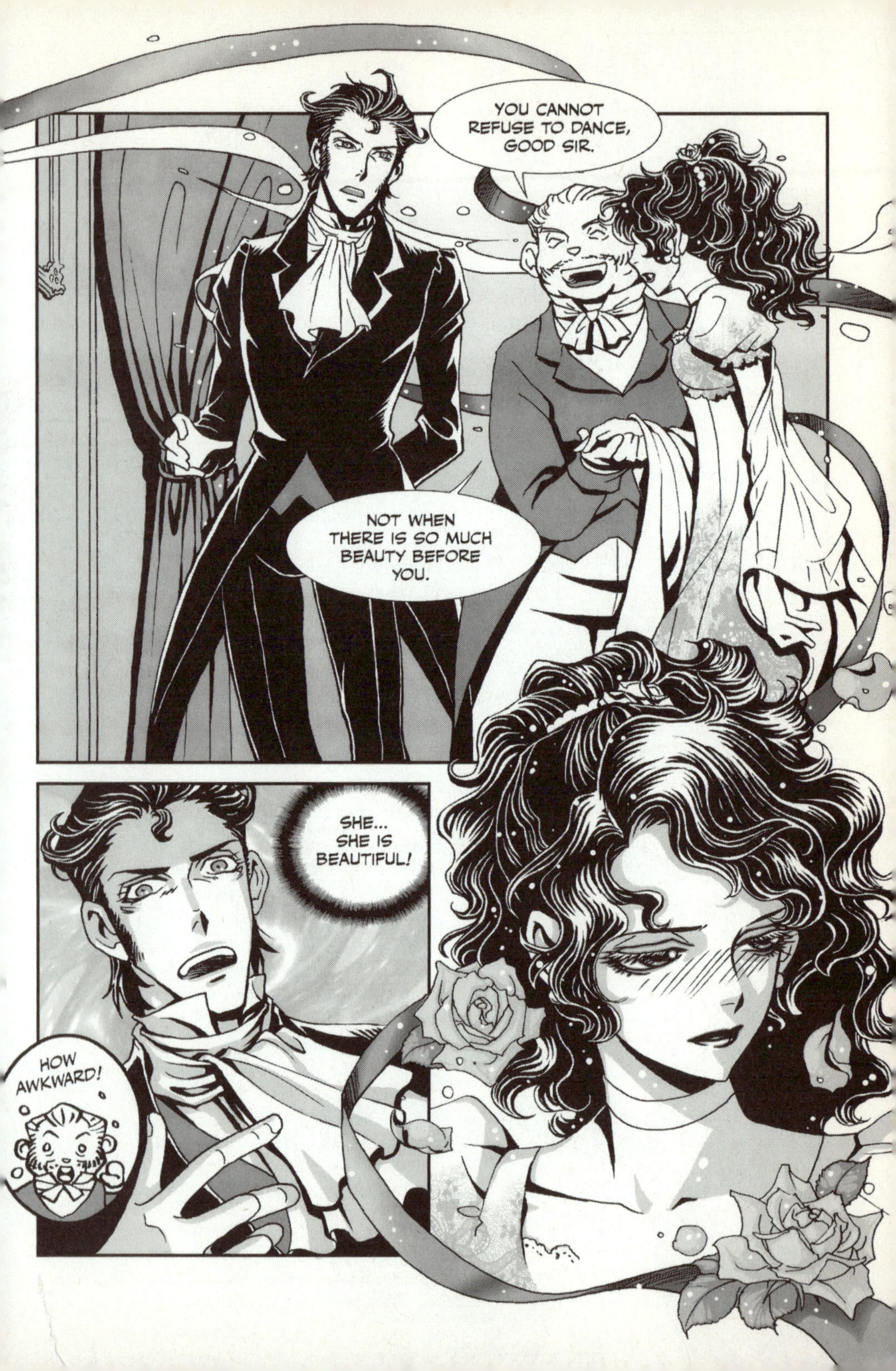
YOU CANNOT REFUSE TO DANCE, GOOD SIR.
NOT WHEN THERE IS SO MUCH BEAUTY BEFORE YOU.
SHE... SHE IS BEAUTIFUL!
HOW AWKWARD!

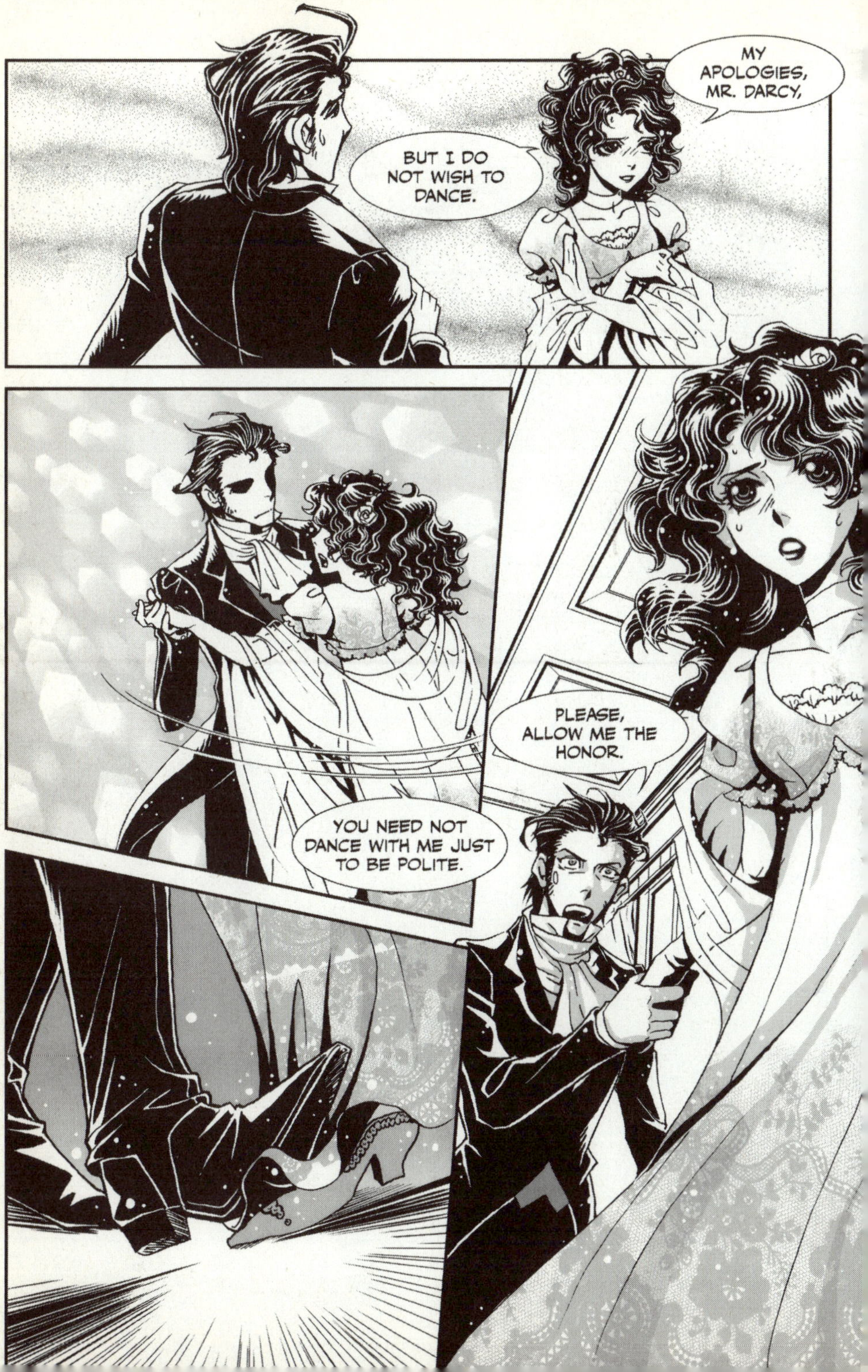
MY APOLOGIES, MR. DARCY,
BUT I DO NOT WISH TO DANCE.
PLEASE, ALLOW ME THE HONOR.
YOU NEED NOT DANCE WITH ME JUST TO BE POLITE.

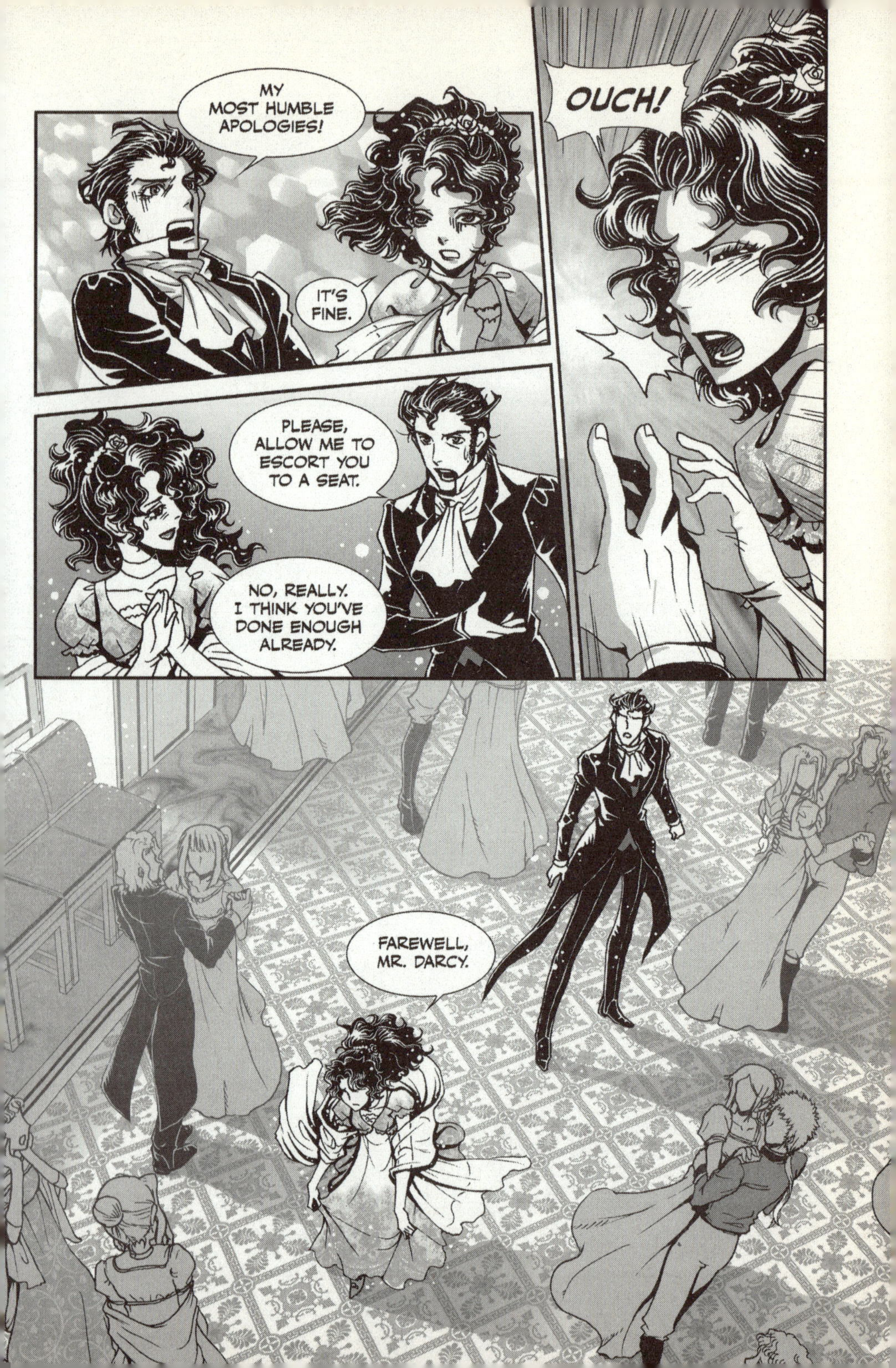
OUCH!
MY MOST HUMBLE APOLOGIES!
IT'S FINE.
PLEASE, ALLOW ME TO ESCORT YOU TO A SEAT.
NO, REALLY. I THINK YOU'VE DONE ENOUGH ALREADY.
FAREWELL, MR. DARCY.

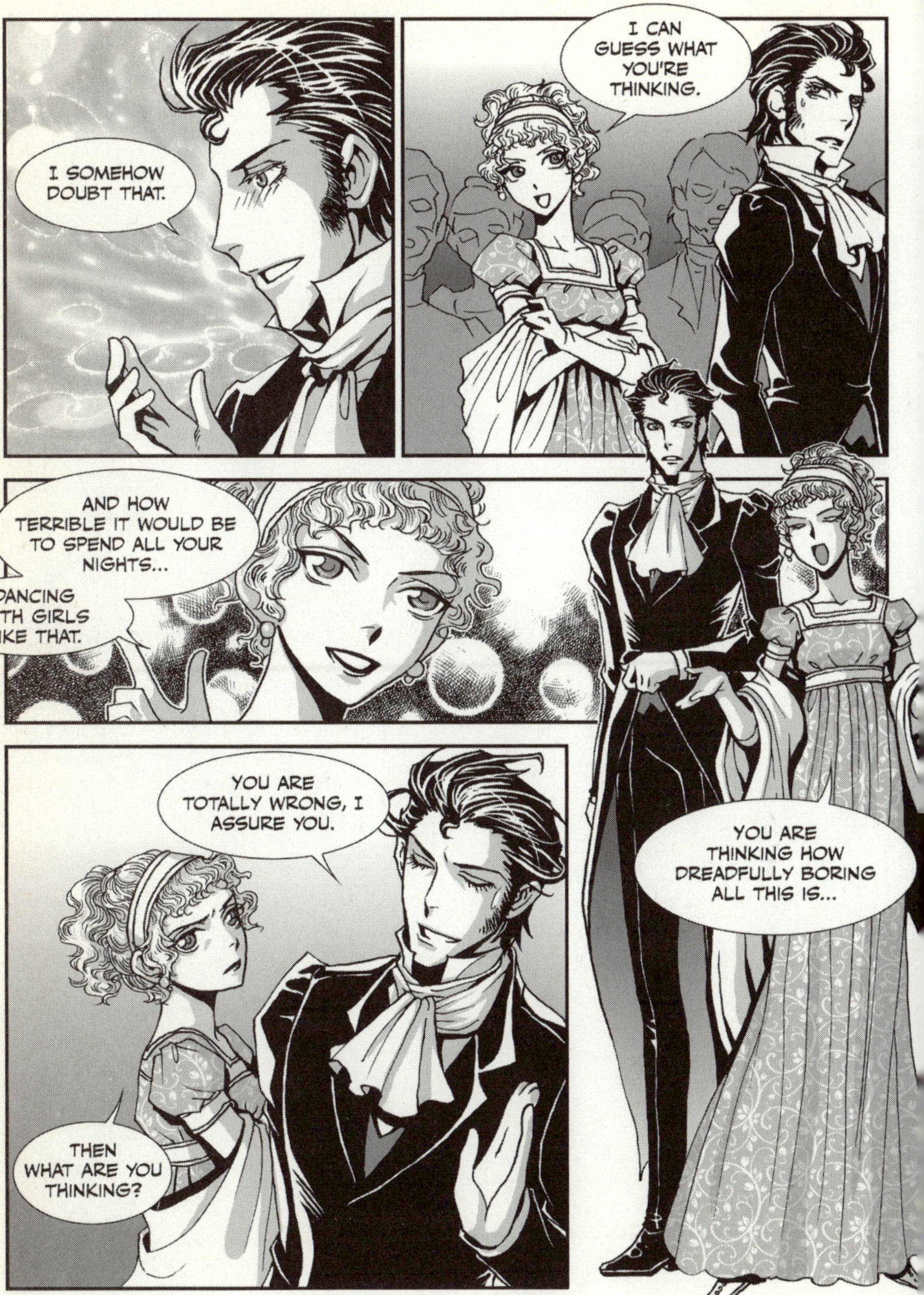
I CAN GUESS WHAT YOU'RE THINKING.
I SOMEHOW DOUBT THAT.
YOU ARE THINKING HOW DREADFULLY BORING ALL THIS IS...
AND HOW TERRIBLE IT WOULD BE TO SPEND ALL YOUR NIGHTS...
DANCING WITH GIRLS LIKE THAT.
YOU ARE TOTALLY WRONG, I ASSURE YOU.
THEN WHAT ARE YOU THINKING?

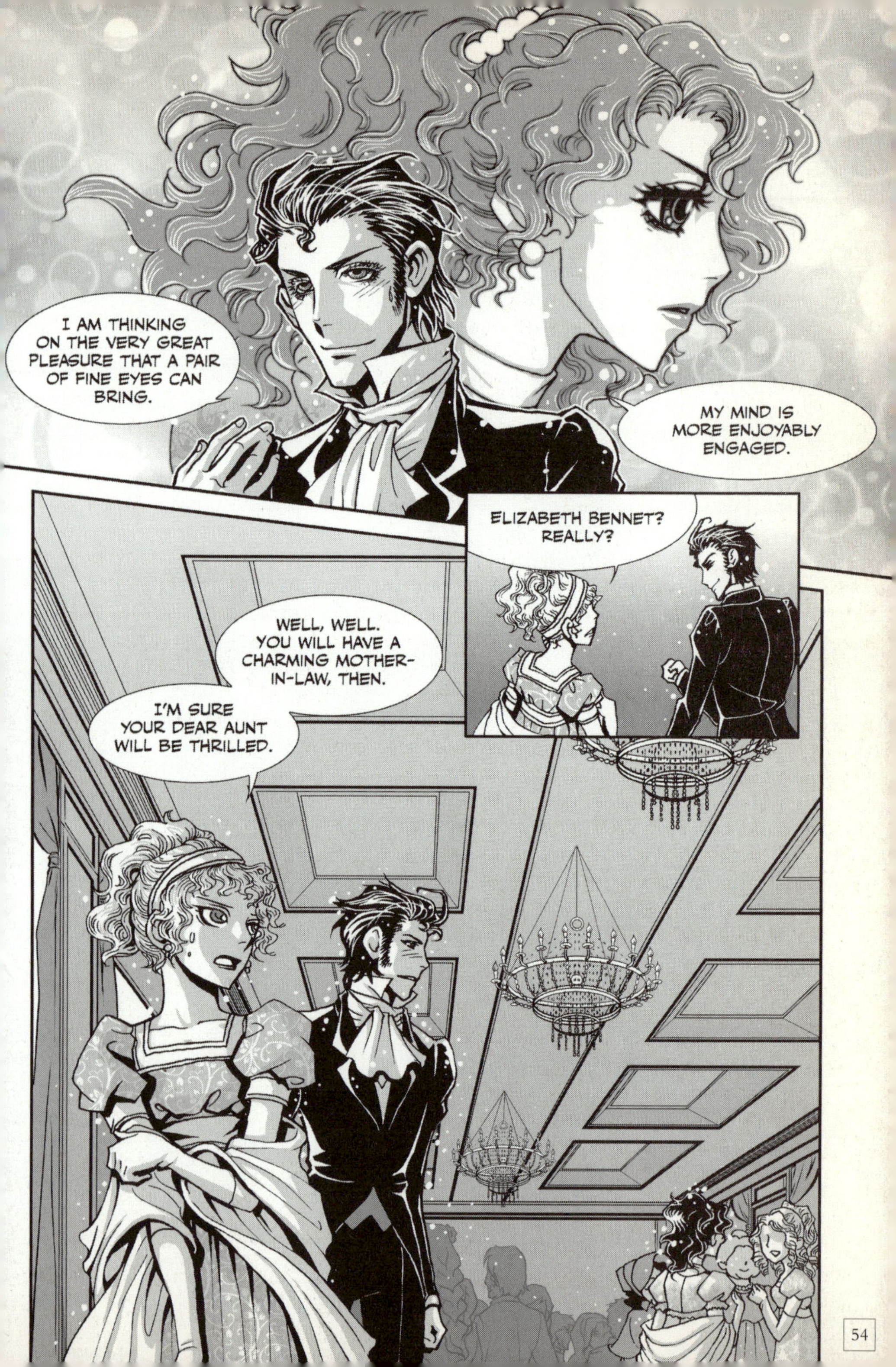
MY MIND IS MORE ENJOYABLY ENGAGED.
I AM THINKING ON THE VERY GREAT PLEASURE THAT A PAIR OF FINE EYES CAN BRING.
ELIZABETH BENNET? REALLY?
WELL, WELL. YOU WILL HAVE A CHARMING MOTHER-IN-LAW, THEN.
I'M SURE YOUR DEAR AUNT WILL BE THRILLED.

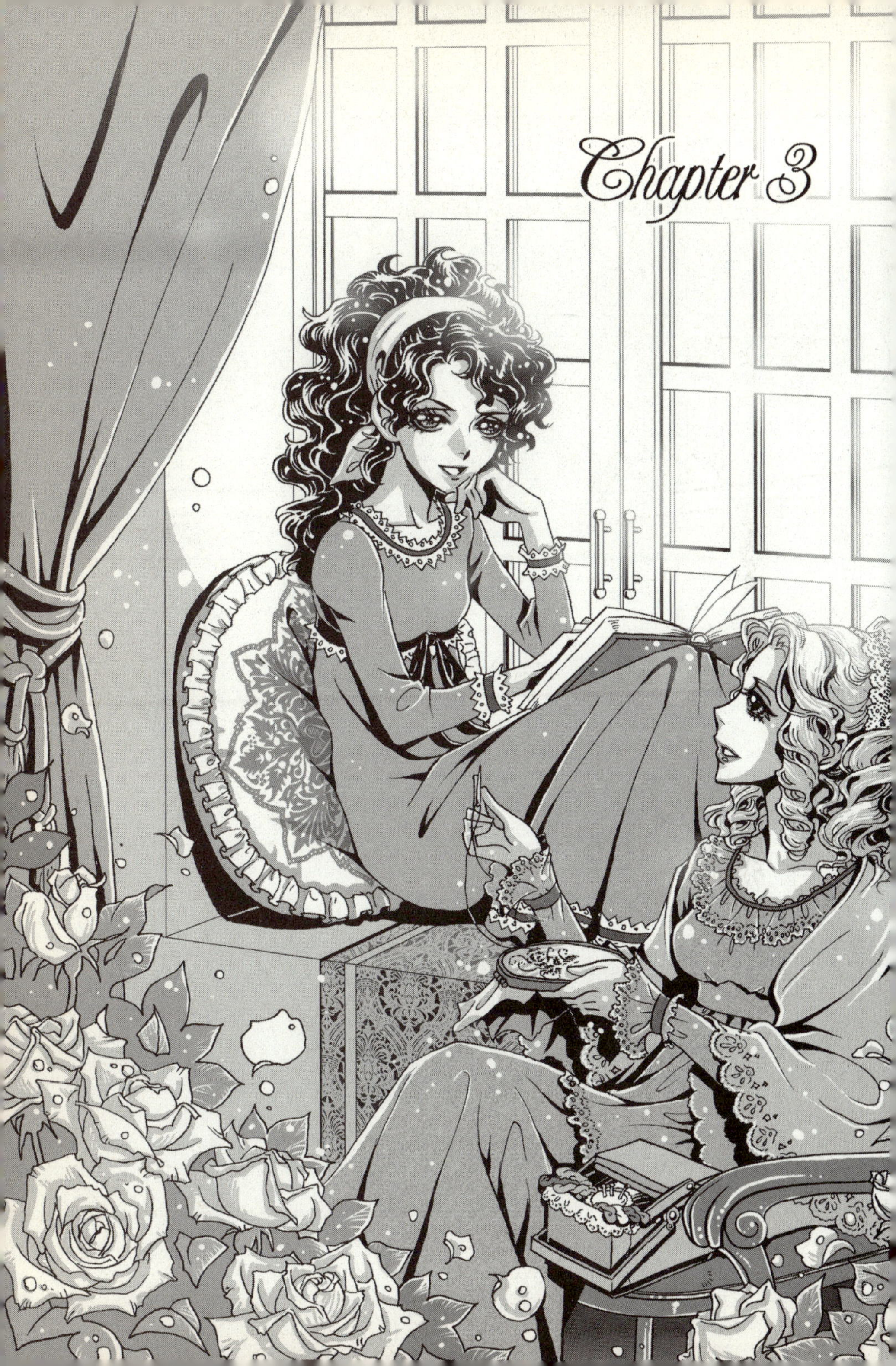
Chapter 3

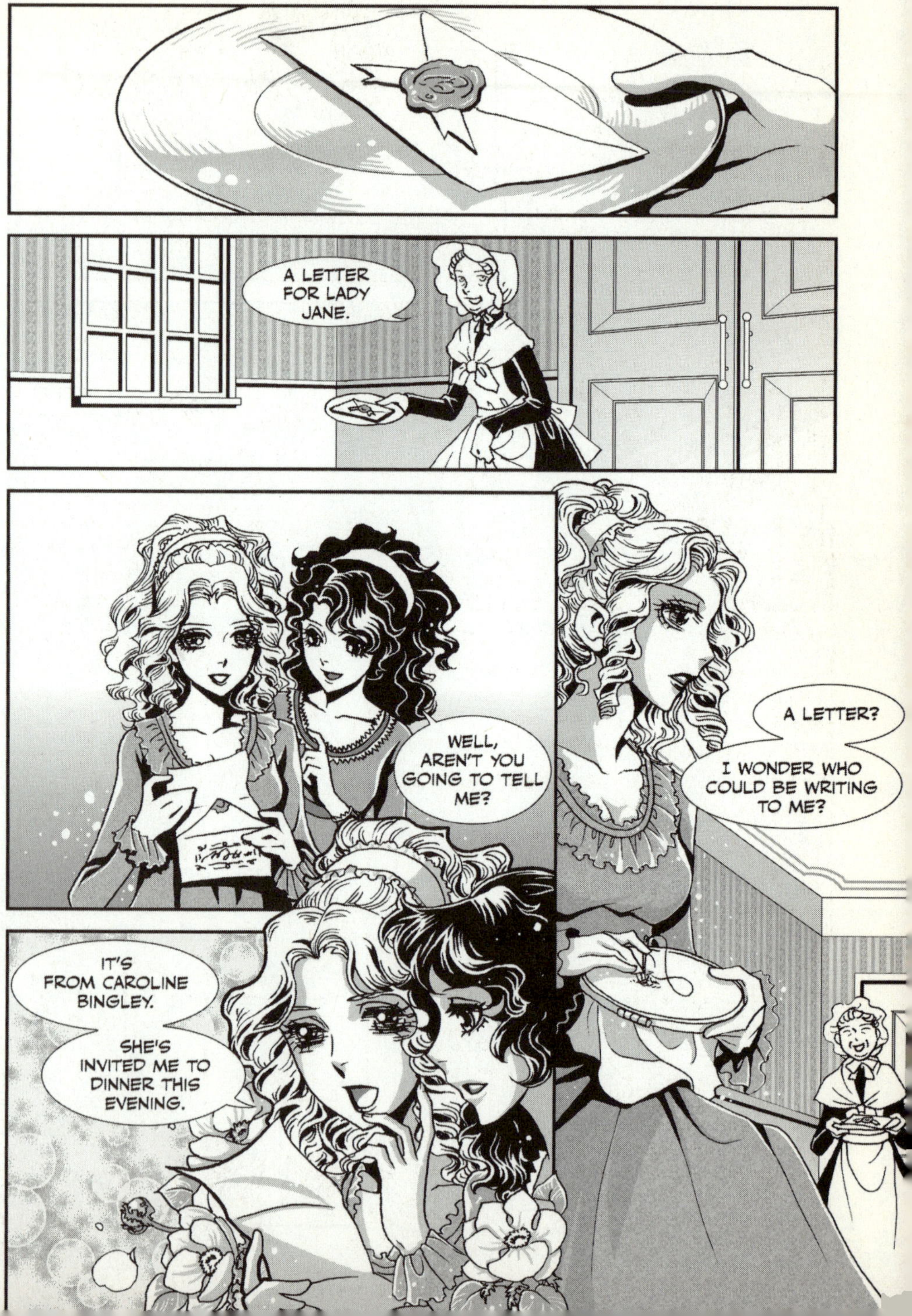
A LETTER FOR LADY JANE.
A LETTER?
I WONDER WHO COULD BE WRITING TO ME?
WELL, AREN'T YOU GOING TO TELL ME?
IT'S FROM CAROLINE BINGLEY.
SHE'S INVITED ME TO DINNER THIS EVENING.

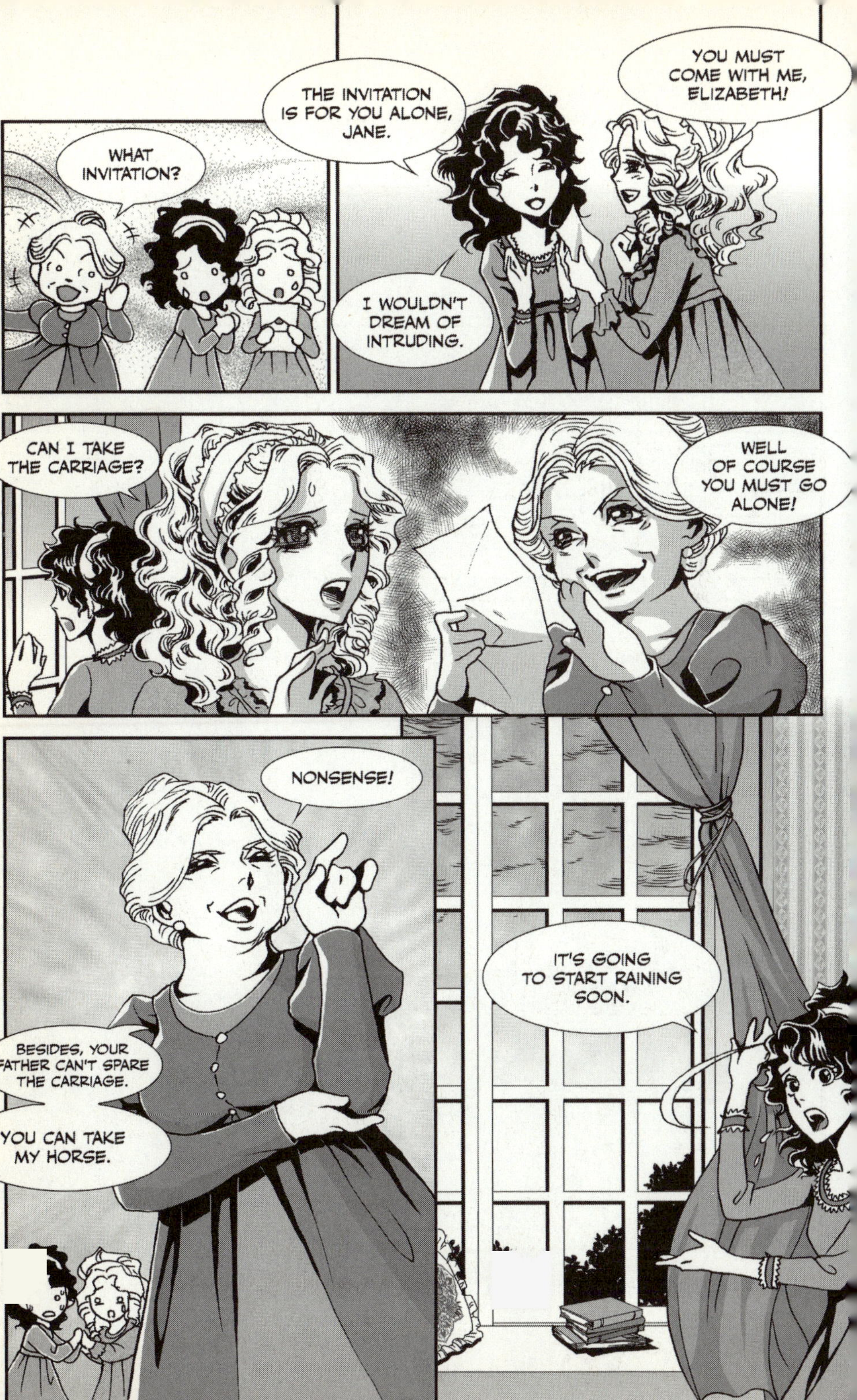
YOU MUST COME WITH ME, ELIZABETH!
THE INVITATION IS FOR YOU ALONE, JANE.
I WOULDN'T DREAM OF INTRUDING.
WHAT INVITATION?
WELL OF COURSE YOU MUST GO ALONE!
CAN I TAKE THE CARRIAGE?
IT'S GOING TO START RAINING SOON.
NONSENSE!
BESIDES, YOUR FATHER CAN'T SPARE THE CARRIAGE.
YOU CAN TAKE MY HORSE.

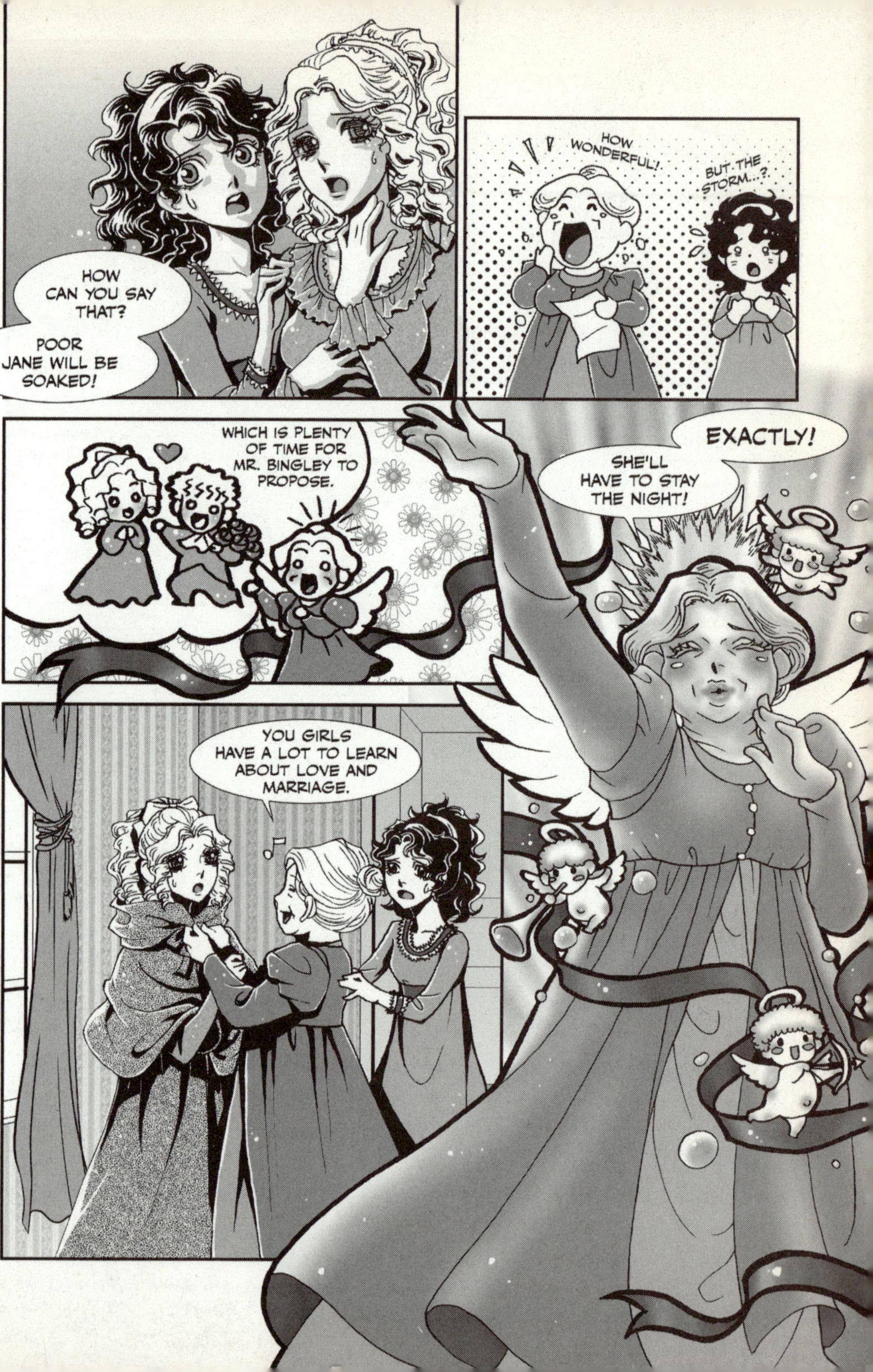
HOW WONDERFUL!
BUT THE STORM...?
HOW CAN YOU SAY THAT?
POOR JANE WILL BE SOAKED!
EXACTLY!
SHE'LL HAVE TO STAY THE NIGHT!
WHICH IS PLENTY OF TIME FOR MR. BINGLEY TO PROPOSE.
YOU GIRLS HAVE A LOT TO LEARN ABOUT LOVE AND MARRIAGE.

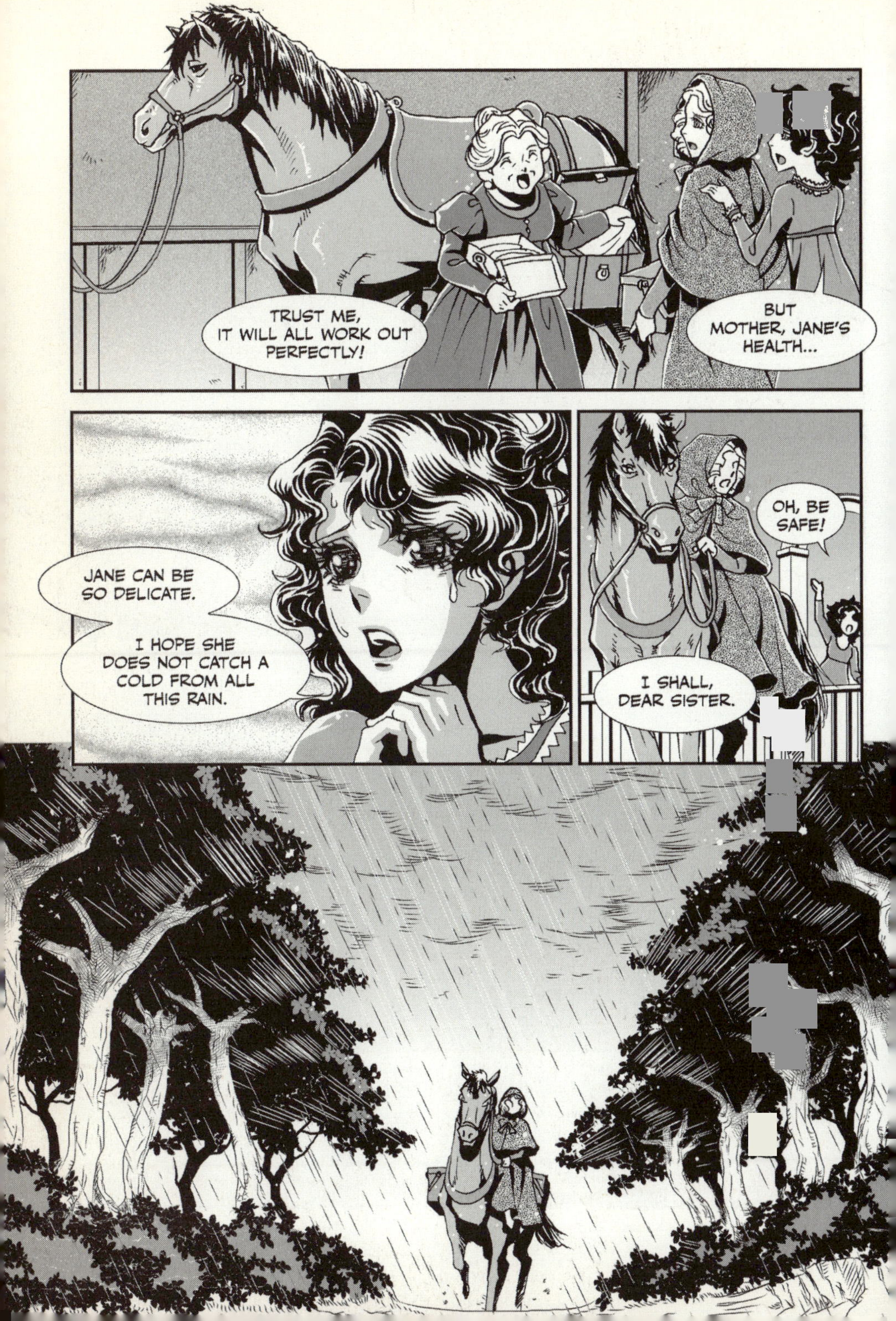
BUT MOTHER, JANE'S HEALTH...
TRUST ME, IT WILL ALL WORK OUT PERFECTLY!
OH, BE SAFE!
I SHALL, DEAR SISTER.
JANE CAN BE SO DELICATE.
I HOPE SHE DOES NOT CATCH A COLD FROM ALL THIS RAIN.

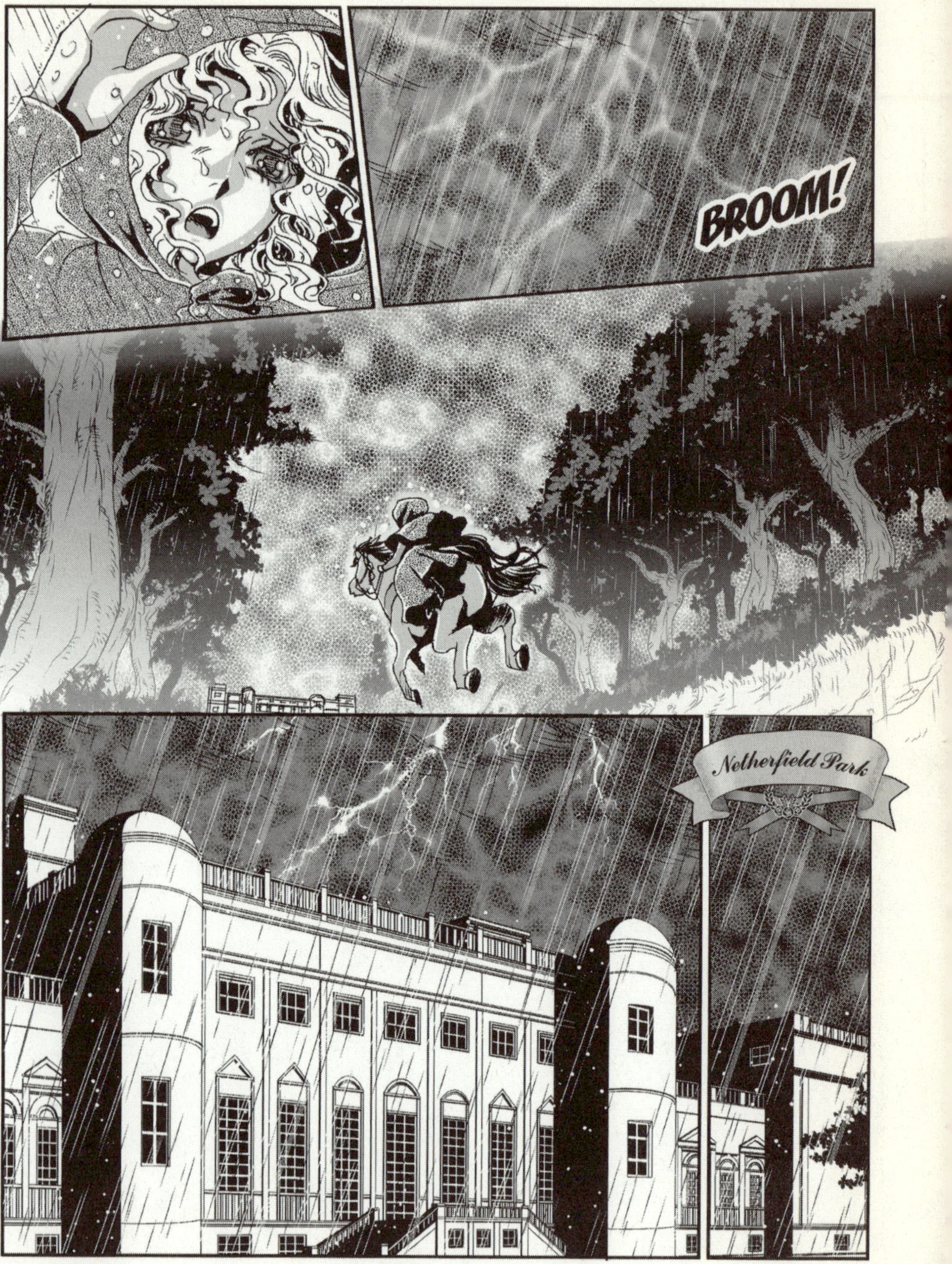
BROOM!
Netherfield Park

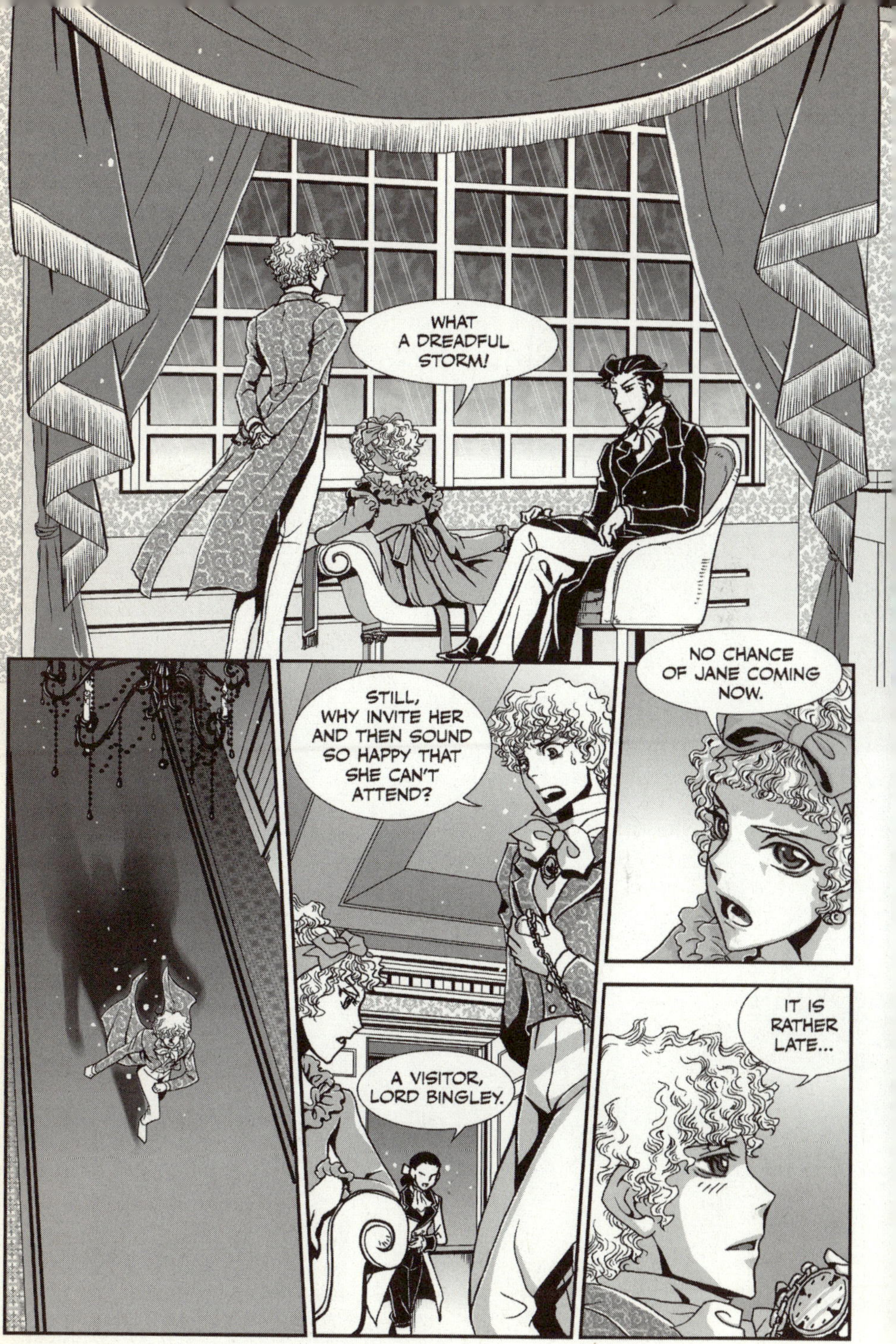
WHAT A DREADFUL STORM!
NO CHANCE OF JANE COMING NOW.
IT IS RATHER LATE...
STILL, WHY INVITE HER AND THEN SOUND SO HAPPY THAT SHE CAN'T ATTEND?
A VISITOR, LORD BINGLEY.

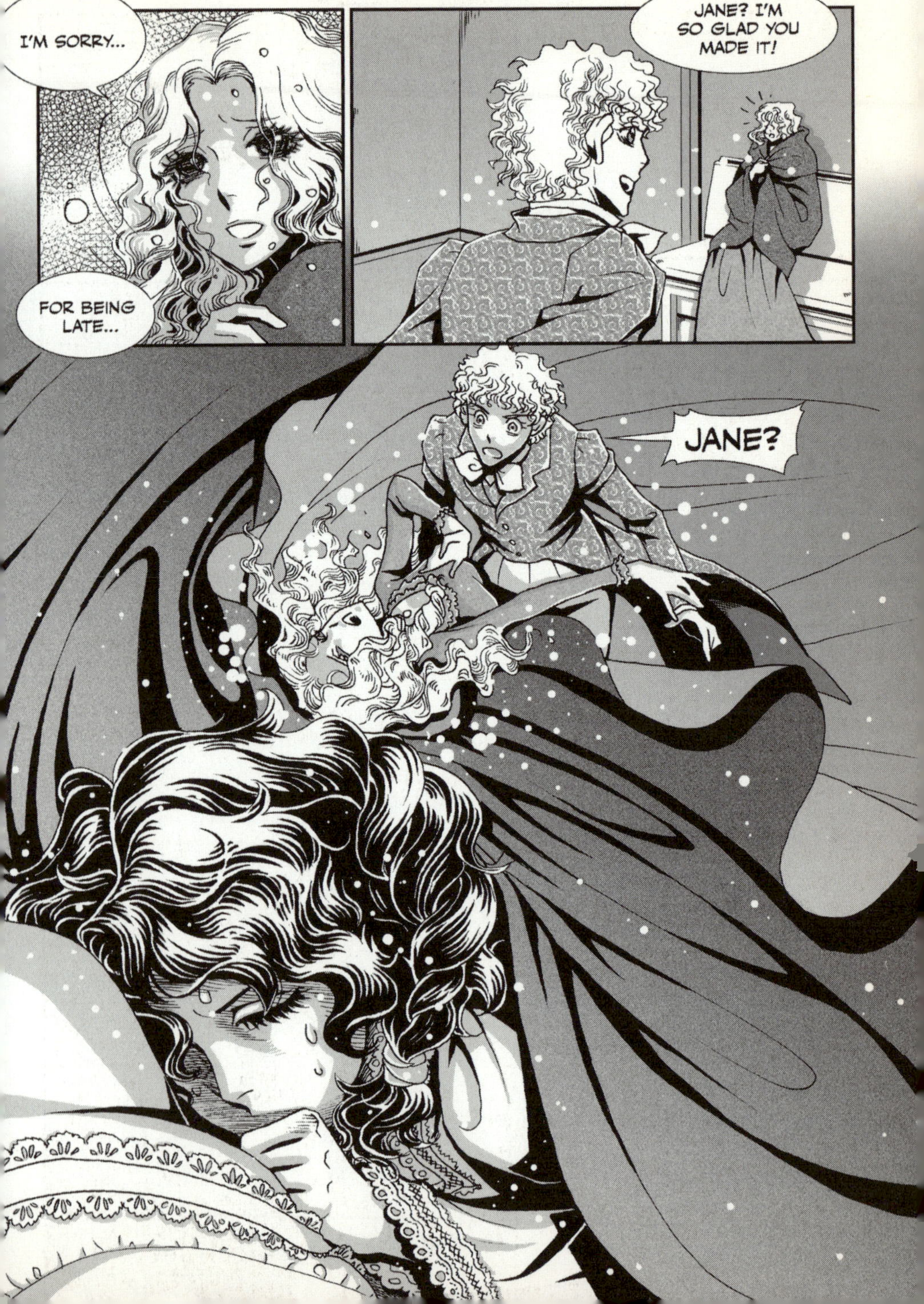
JANE? I'M SO GLAD YOU MADE IT!
I'M SORRY...
FOR BEING LATE...
JANE?

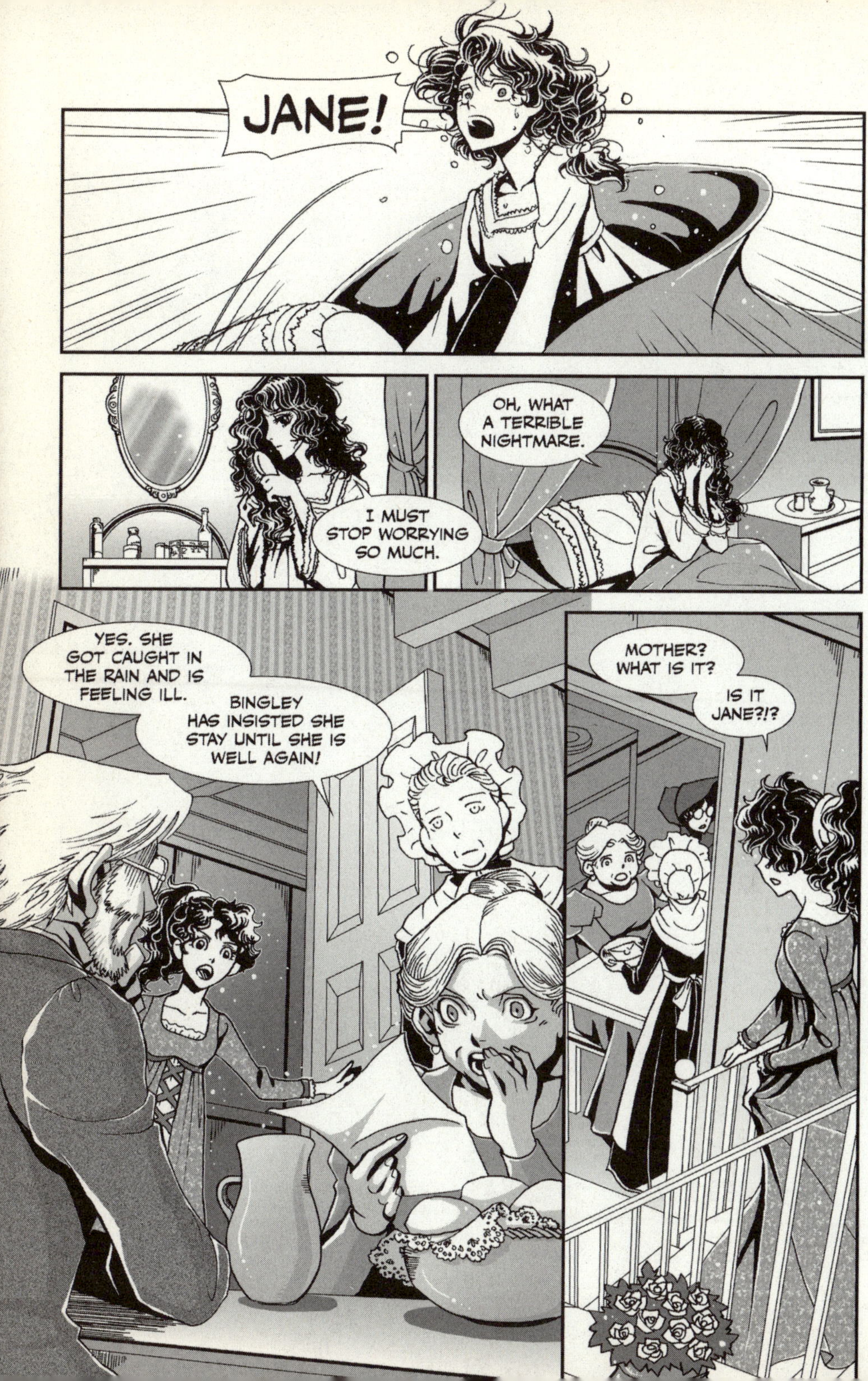
JANE!
OH, WHAT A TERRIBLE NIGHTMARE.
I MUST STOP WORRYING SO MUCH.
MOTHER? WHAT IS IT?
IS IT JANE?!?
YES. SHE GOT CAUGHT IN THE RAIN AND IS FEELING ILL.
BINGLEY HAS INSISTED SHE STAY UNTIL SHE IS WELL AGAIN!

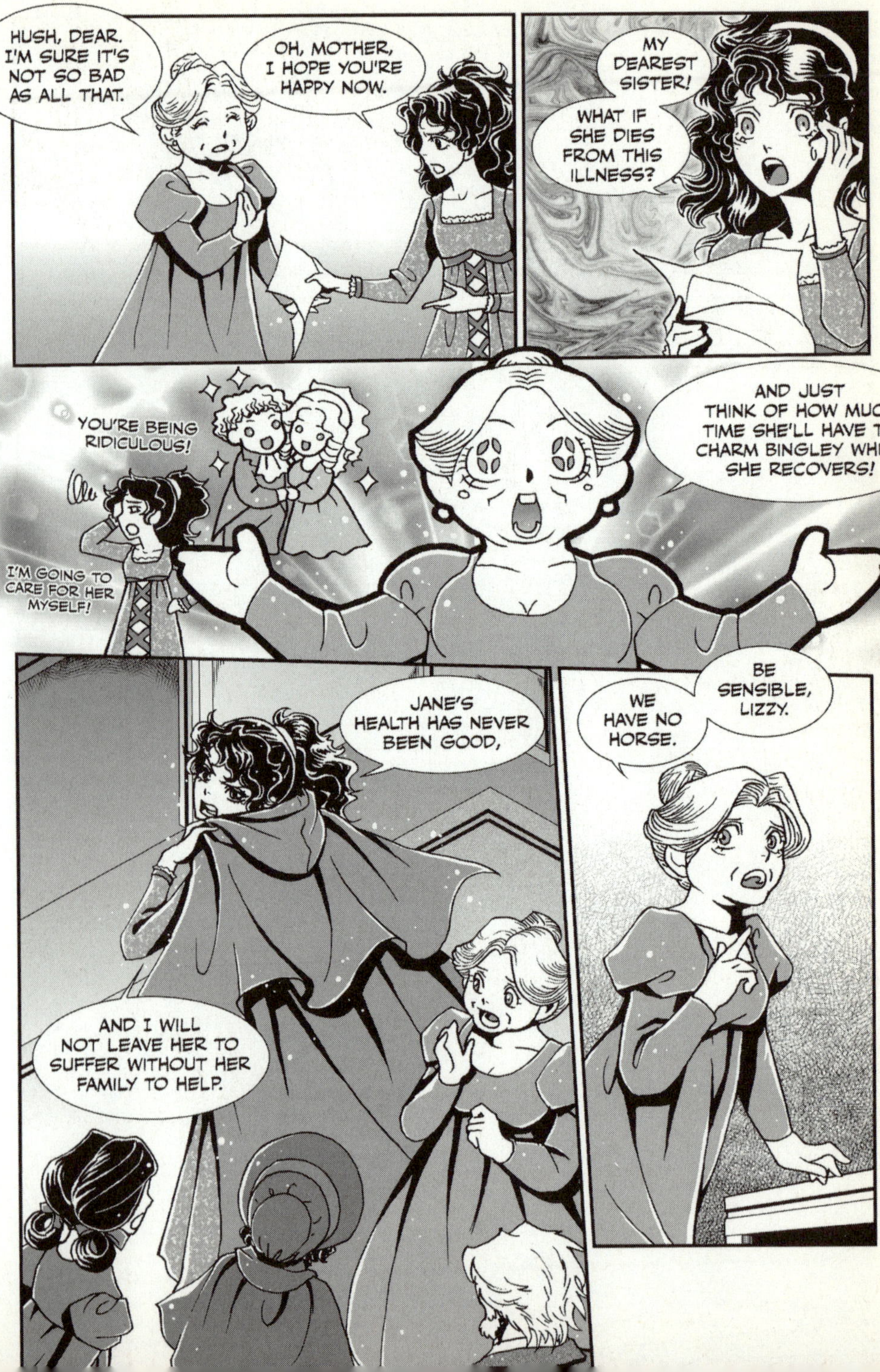
MY DEAREST SISTER!
WHAT IF SHE DIES FROM THIS ILLNESS?
OH, MOTHER, I HOPE YOU'RE HAPPY NOW.
HUSH, DEAR. I'M SURE IT'S NOT SO BAD AS ALL THAT.
AND JUST THINK OF HOW MUCH TIME SHE'LL HAVE TO CHARM BINGLEY WHILE SHE RECOVERS!
YOU'RE BEING RIDICULOUS!
I'M GOING TO CARE FOR HER MYSELF!
BE SENSIBLE, LIZZY.
WE HAVE NO HORSE.
JANE'S HEALTH HAS NEVER BEEN GOOD,
AND I WILL NOT LEAVE HER TO SUFFER WITHOUT HER FAMILY TO HELP.

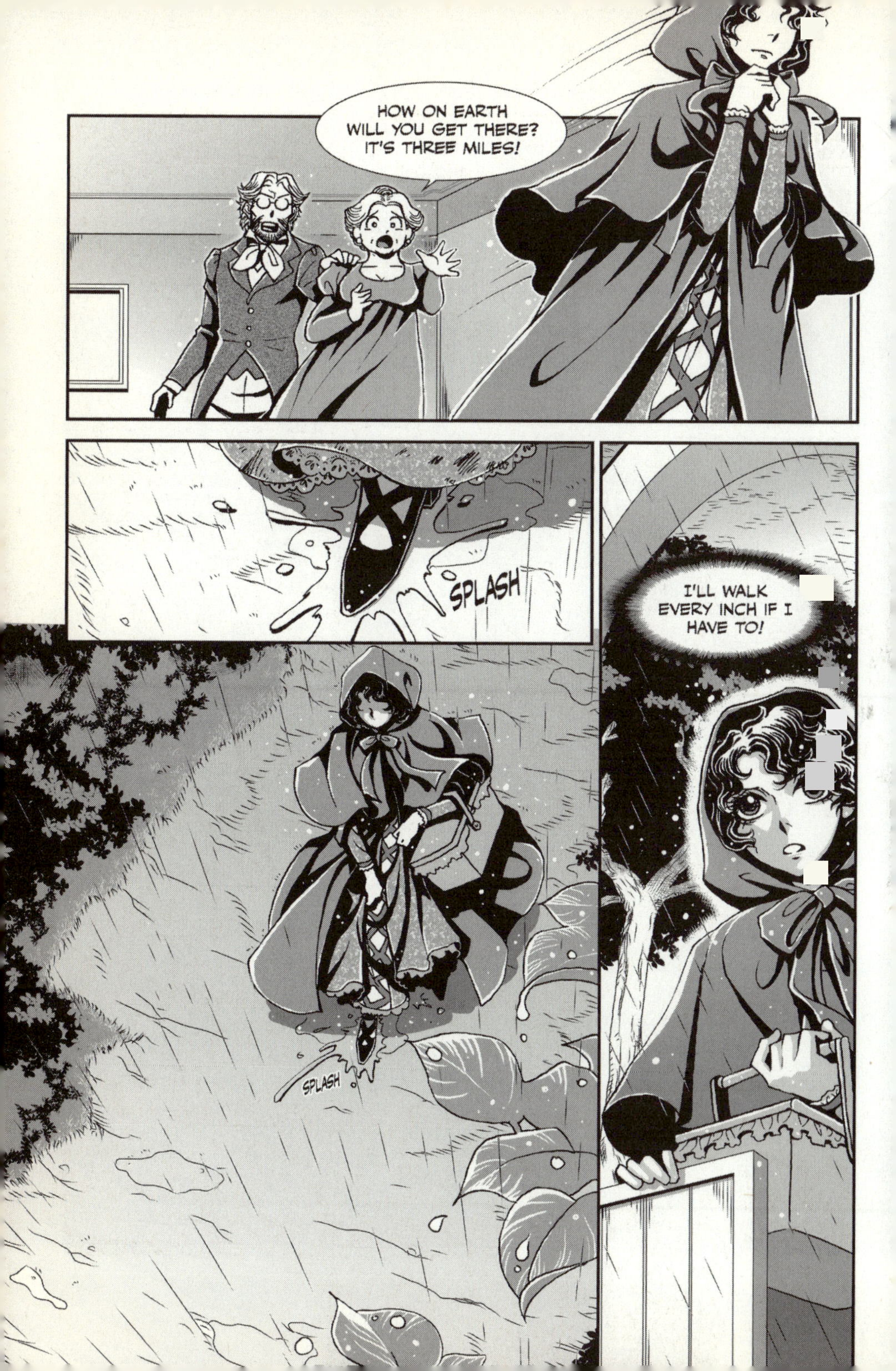
HOW ON EARTH WILL YOU GET THERE? IT'S THREE MILES!
I'LL WALK EVERY INCH IF I HAVE TO!
SPLASH
SPLASH

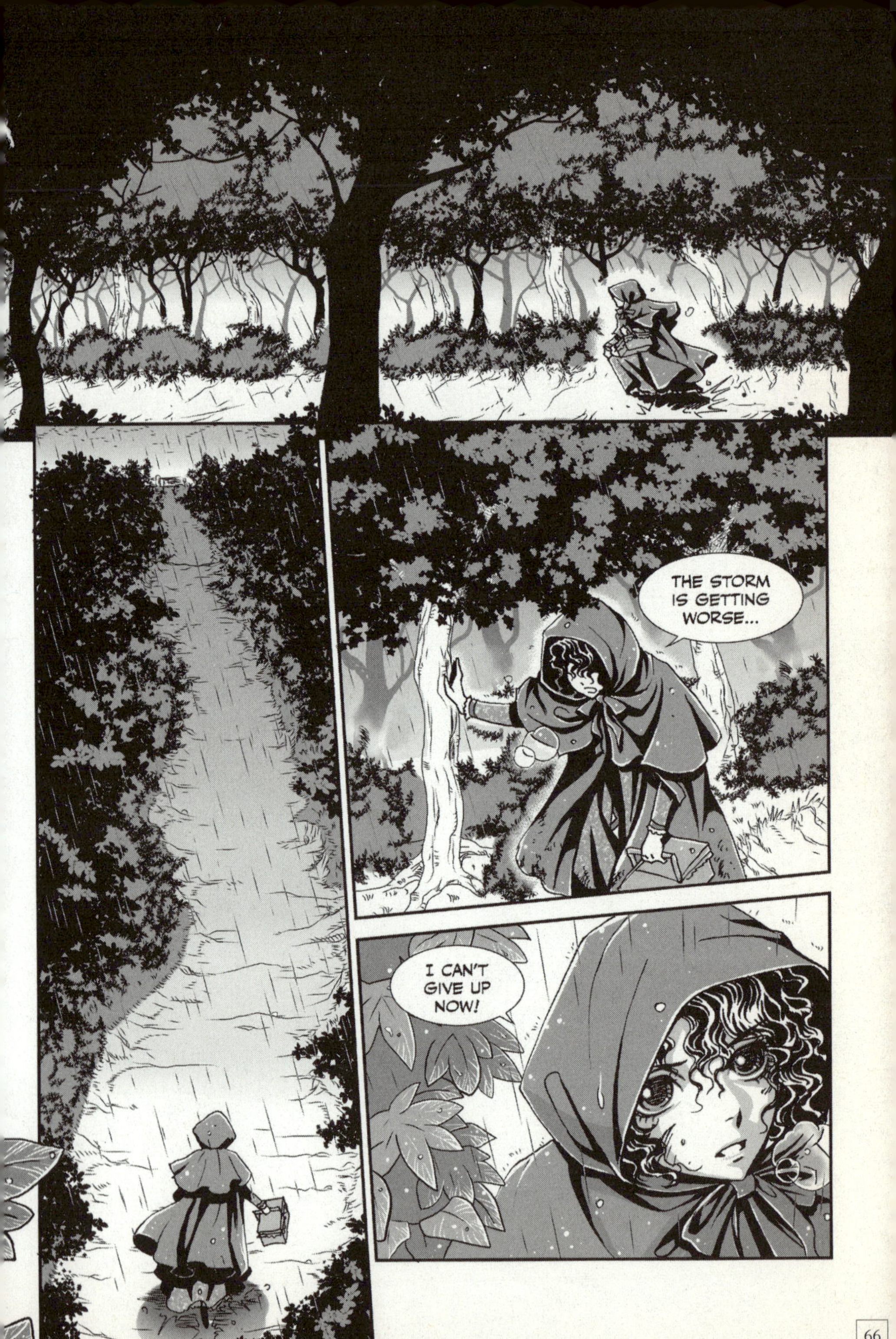
THE STORM IS GETTING WORSE...
I CAN'T GIVE UP NOW!

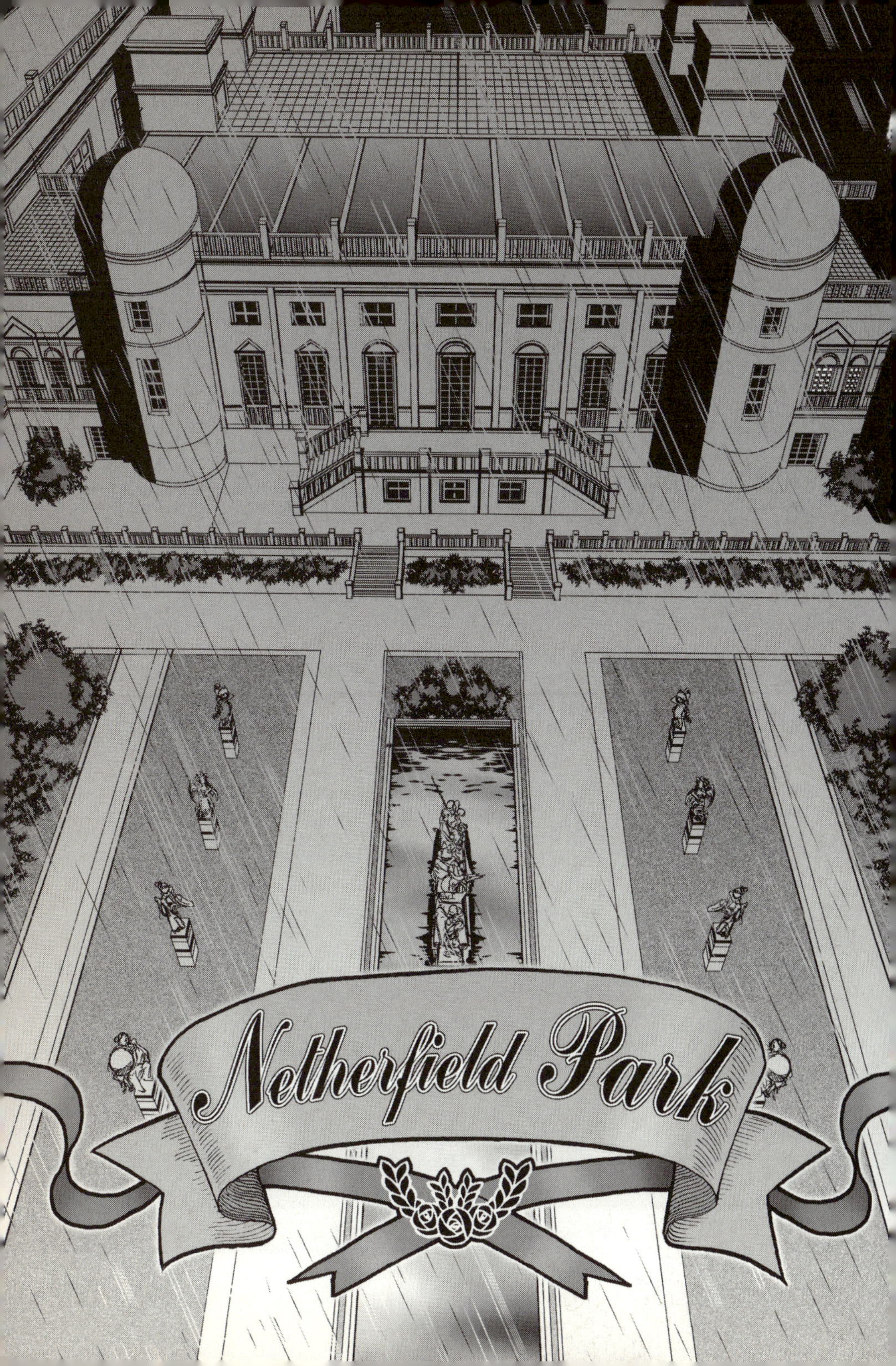
Netherfield Park

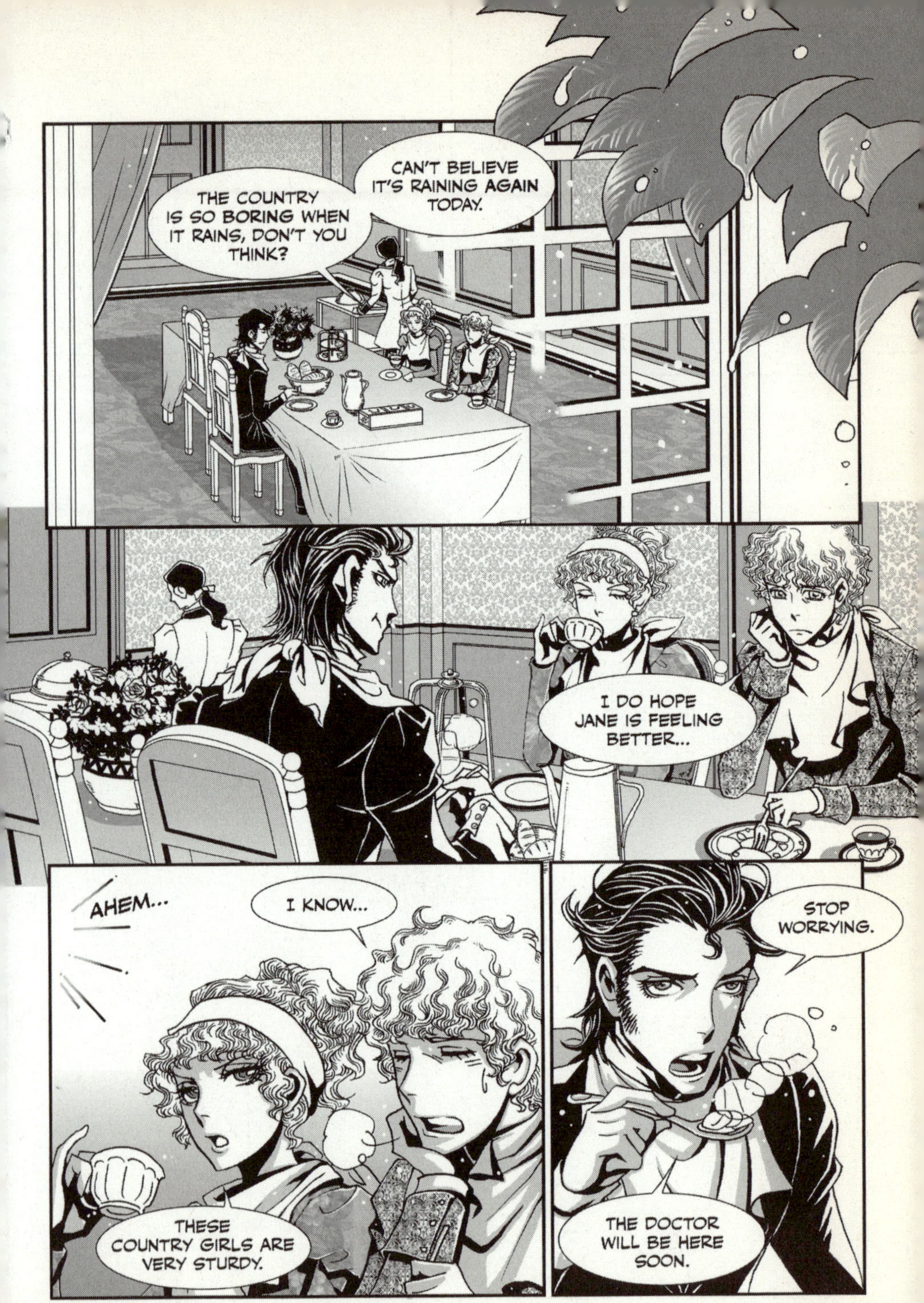
CAN'T BELIEVE IT'S RAINING AGAIN TODAY.
THE COUNTRY IS SO BORING WHEN IT RAINS, DON'T YOU THINK?
I DO HOPE JANE IS FEELING BETTER...
STOP WORRYING.
THE DOCTOR WILL BE HERE SOON.
I KNOW...
AHEM...
THESE COUNTRY GIRLS ARE VERY STURDY.

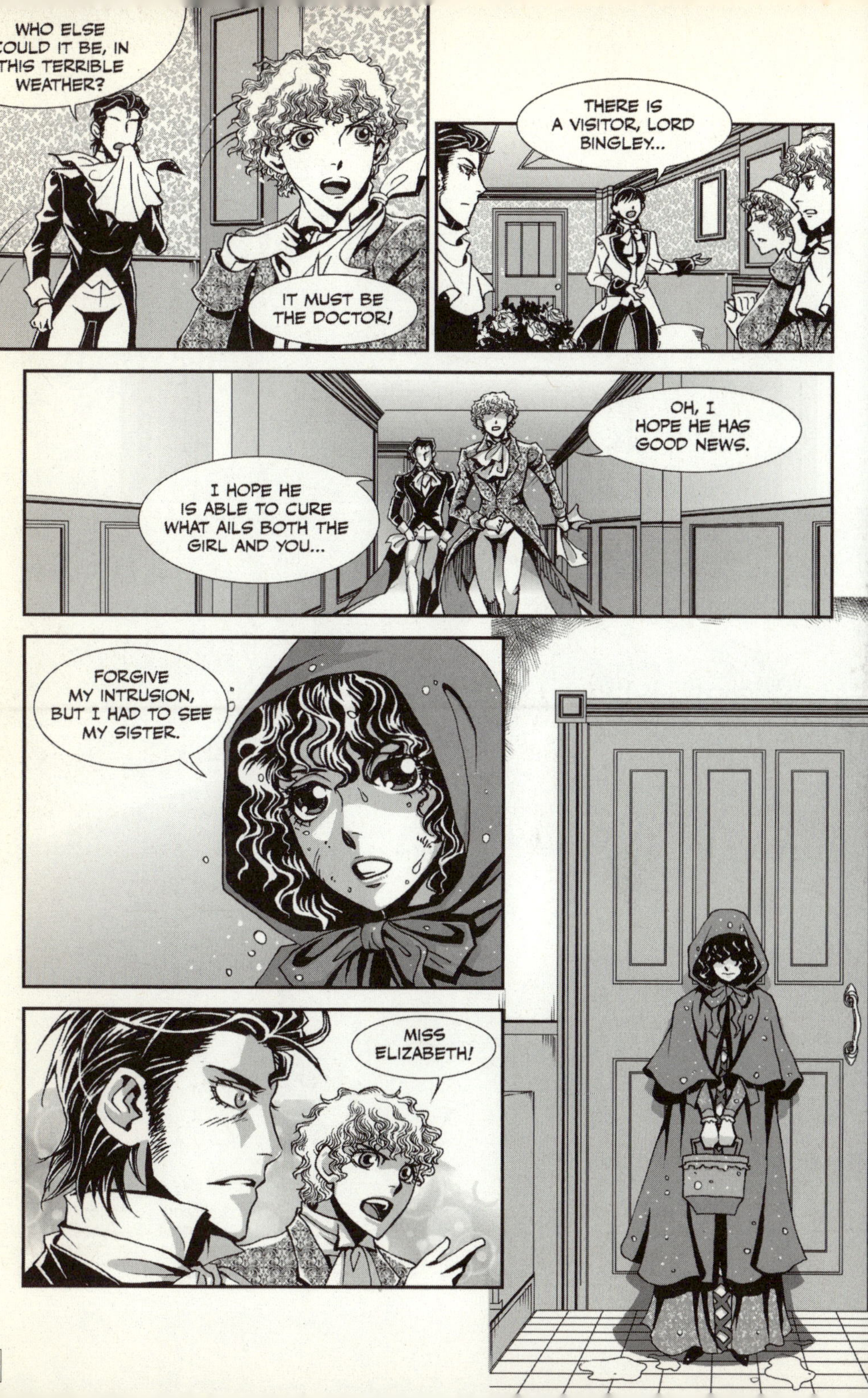
THERE IS A VISITOR, LORD BINGLEY...
WHO ELSE COULD IT BE, IN THIS TERRIBLE WEATHER?
IT MUST BE THE DOCTOR!
OH, I HOPE HE HAS GOOD NEWS.
I HOPE HE IS ABLE TO CURE WHAT AILS BOTH THE GIRL AND YOU...
FORGIVE MY INTRUSION, BUT I HAD TO SEE MY SISTER.
MISS ELIZABETH!

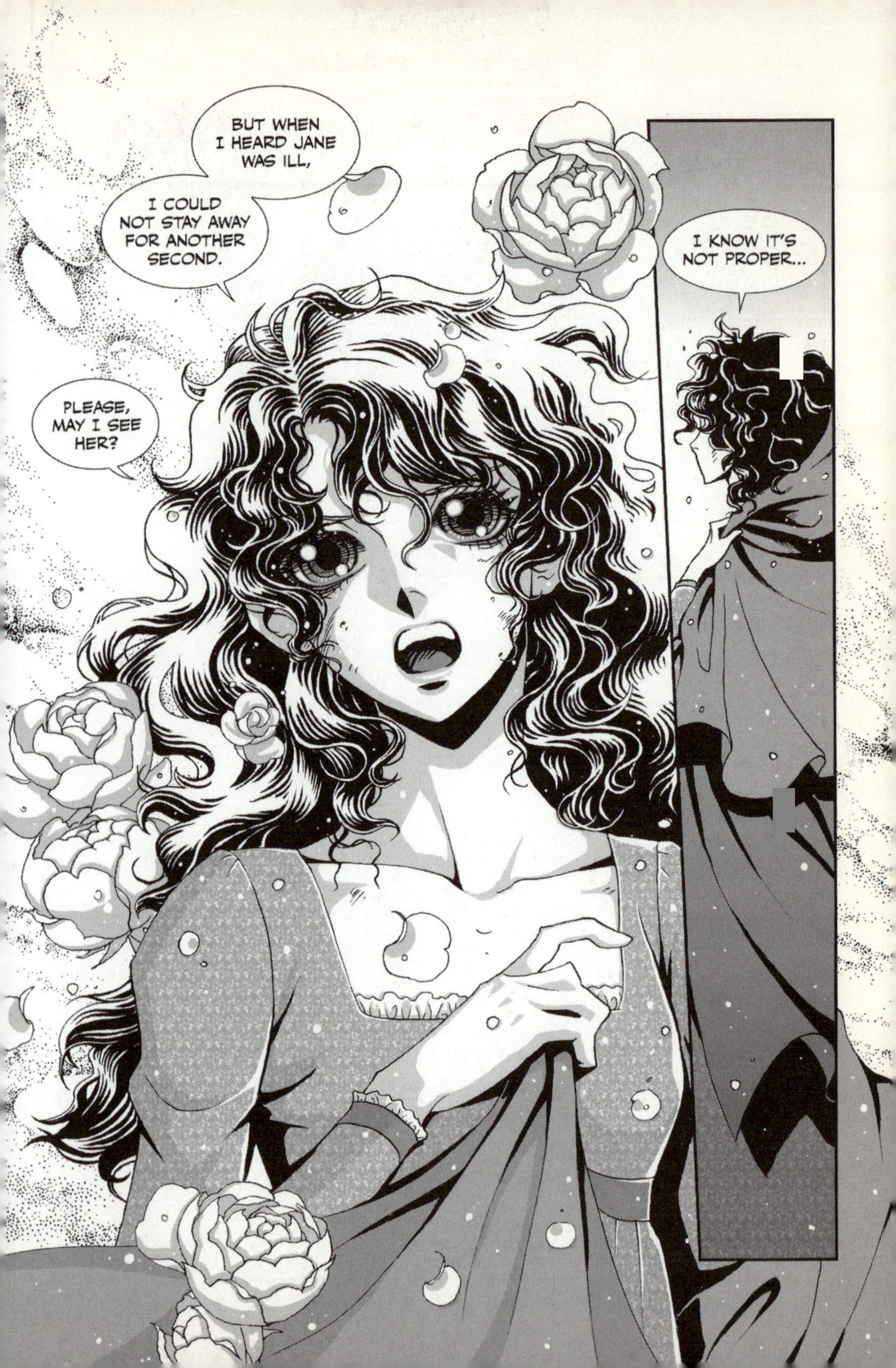
I KNOW IT'S NOT PROPER...
BUT WHEN I HEARD JANE WAS ILL,
I COULD NOT STAY AWAY FOR ANOTHER SECOND.
PLEASE, MAY I SEE HER?

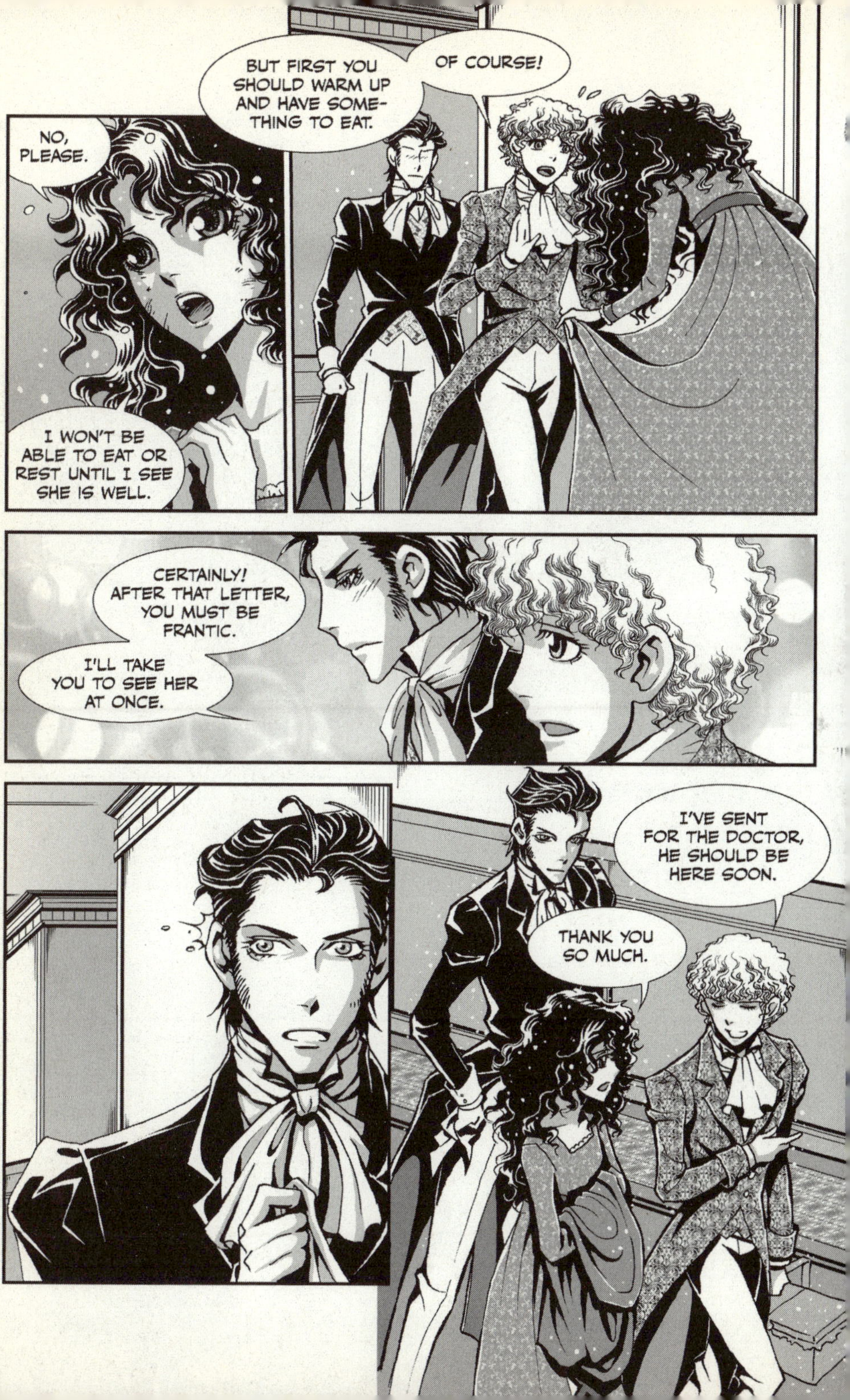
OF COURSE!
BUT FIRST YOU SHOULD WARM UP AND HAVE SOME-THING TO EAT.
NO, PLEASE.
I WON'T BE ABLE TO EAT OR REST UNTIL I SEE SHE IS WELL.
CERTAINLY! AFTER THAT LETTER, YOU MUST BE FRANTIC.
I'LL TAKE YOU TO SEE HER AT ONCE.
I'VE SENT FOR THE DOCTOR, HE SHOULD BE HERE SOON.
THANK YOU SO MUCH.

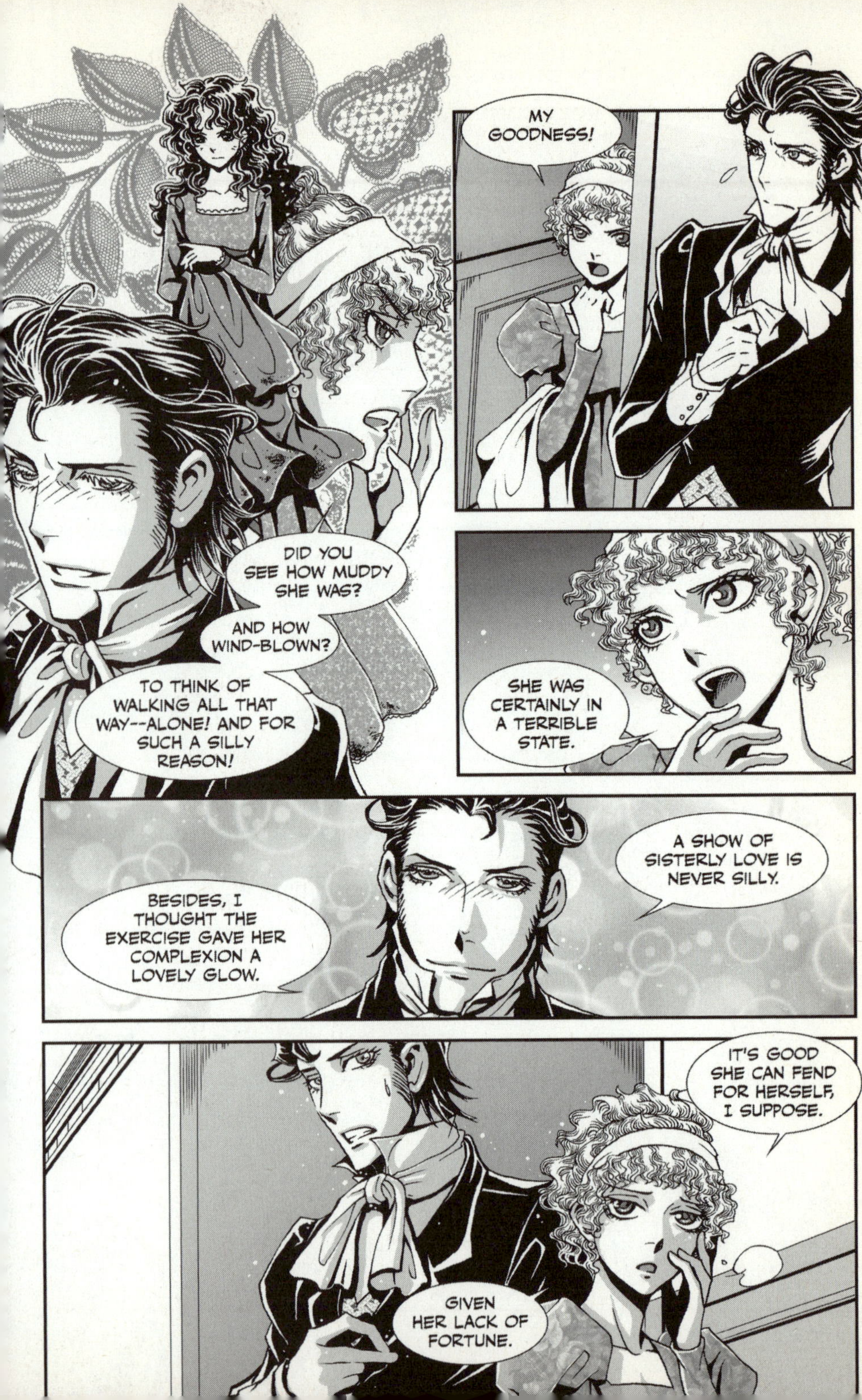
MY GOODNESS!
SHE WAS CERTAINLY IN A TERRIBLE STATE.
DID YOU SEE HOW MUDDY SHE WAS?
AND HOW WIND-BLOWN?
TO THINK OF WALKING ALL THAT WAY--ALONE! AND FOR SUCH A SILLY REASON!
A SHOW OF SISTERLY LOVE IS NEVER SILLY.
BESIDES, I THOUGHT THE EXERCISE GAVE HER COMPLEXION A LOVELY GLOW.
IT'S GOOD SHE CAN FEND FOR HERSELF, I SUPPOSE.
GIVEN HER LACK OF FORTUNE.

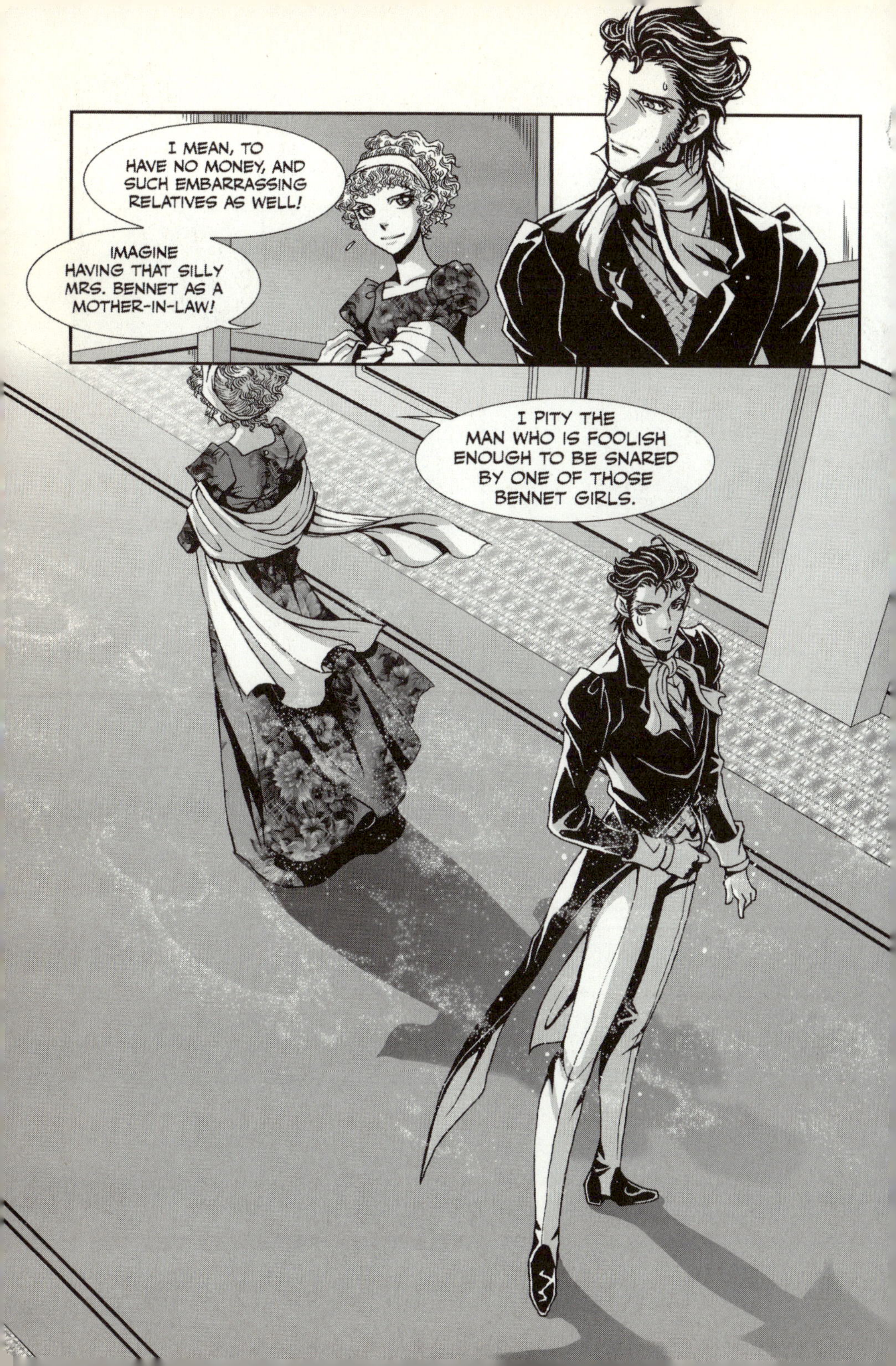
I MEAN, TO HAVE NO MONEY, AND SUCH EMBARRASSING RELATIVES AS WELL!
IMAGINE HAVING THAT SILLY MRS. BENNET AS A MOTHER-IN-LAW!
I PITY THE MAN WHO IS FOOLISH ENOUGH TO BE SNARED BY ONE OF THOSE BENNET GIRLS.

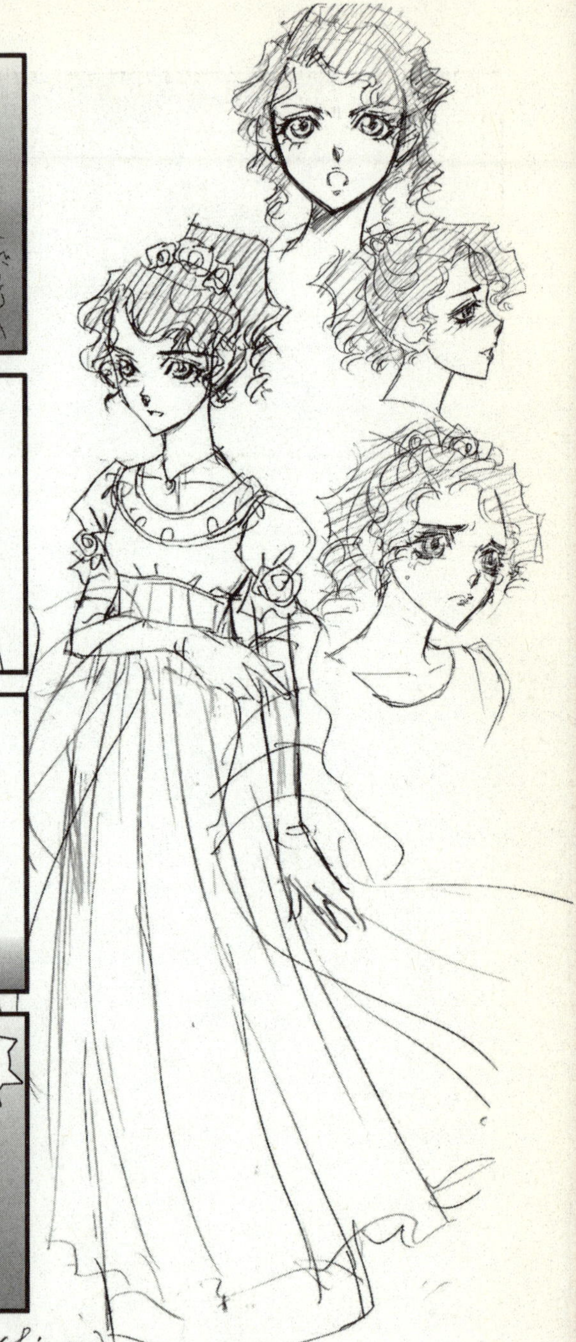

Elizabeth (Lizzy) Bennet

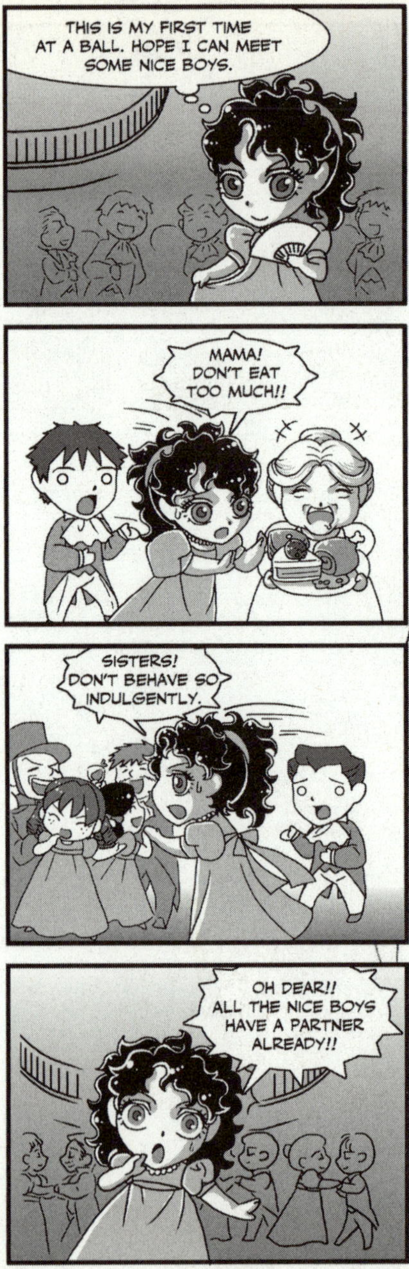

THIS IS MY FIRST TIME AT A BALL. HOPE I CAN MEET SOME NICE BOYS.
MAMA! DON'T EAT TOO MUCH!!
SISTERS! DON'T BEHAVE SO INDULGENTLY.
OH DEAR!! ALL THE NICE BOYS HAVE A PARTNER ALREADY!!

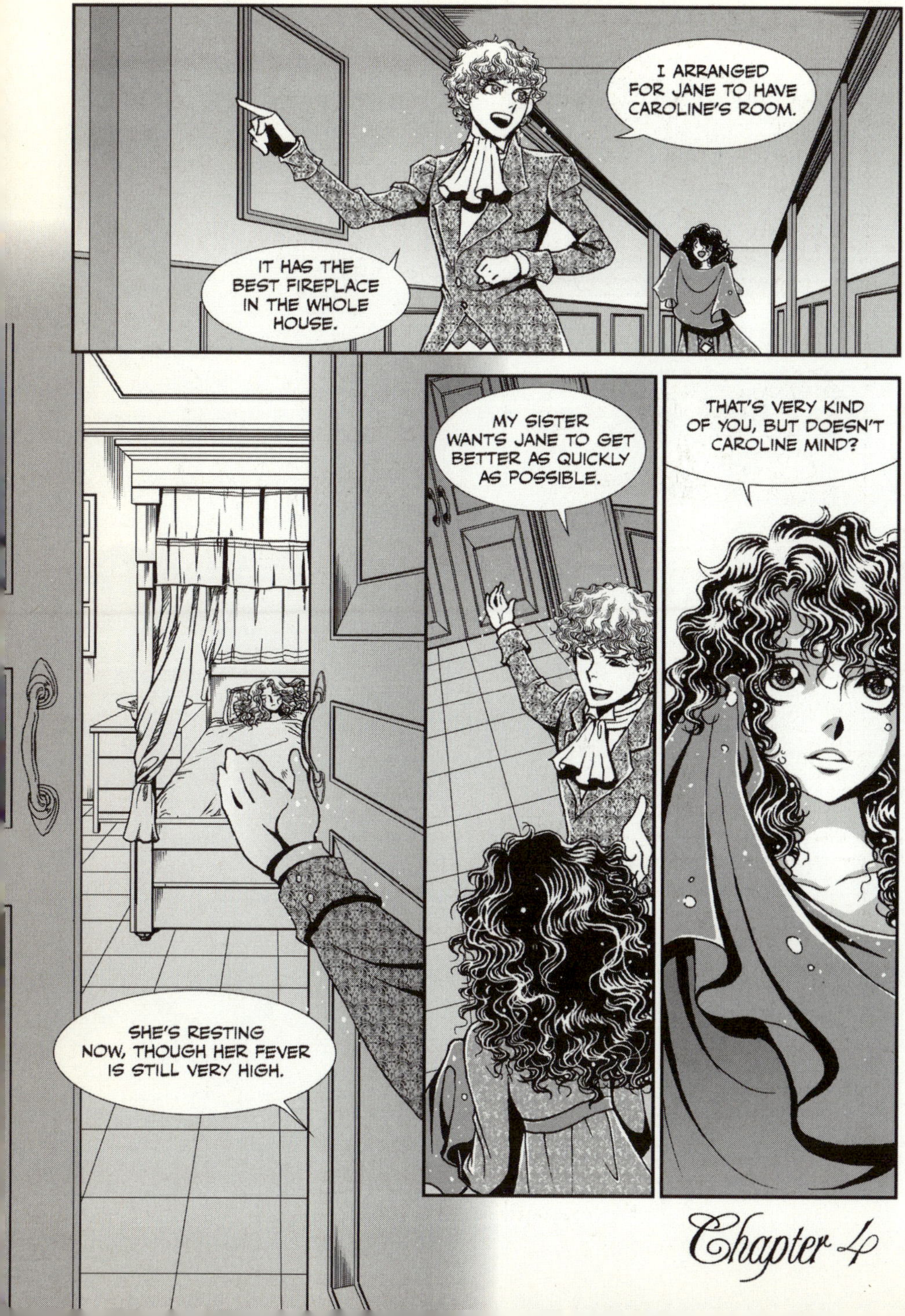
I ARRANGED FOR JANE TO HAVE CAROLINE'S ROOM.
IT HAS THE BEST FIREPLACE IN THE WHOLE HOUSE.
THAT'S VERY KIND OF YOU, BUT DOESN'T CAROLINE MIND?
MY SISTER WANTS JANE TO GET BETTER AS QUICKLY AS POSSIBLE.
SHE'S RESTING NOW, THOUGH HER FEVER IS STILL VERY HIGH.

Chapter 4

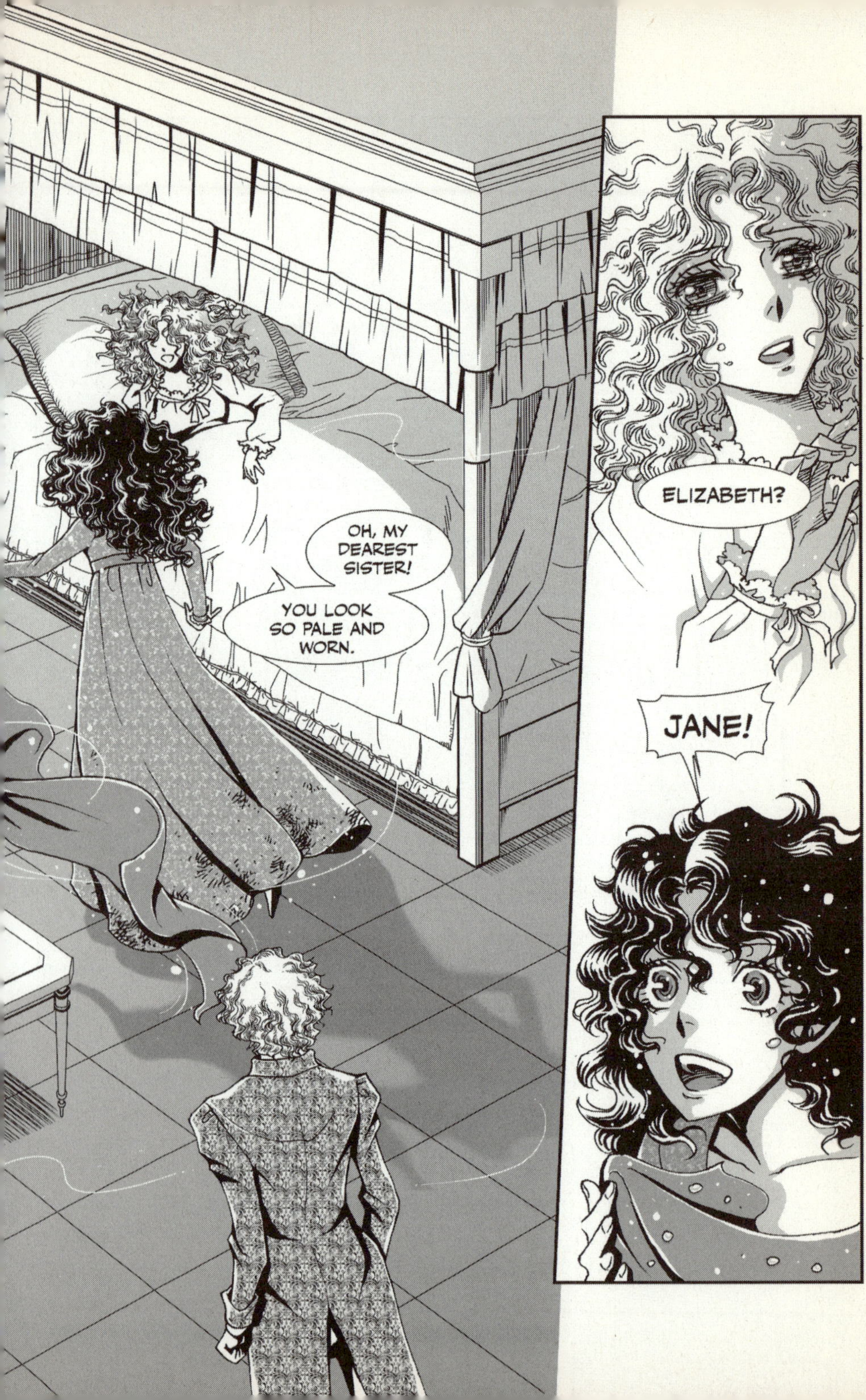
ELIZABETH?
JANE!
OH, MY DEAREST SISTER!
YOU LOOK SO PALE AND WORN.

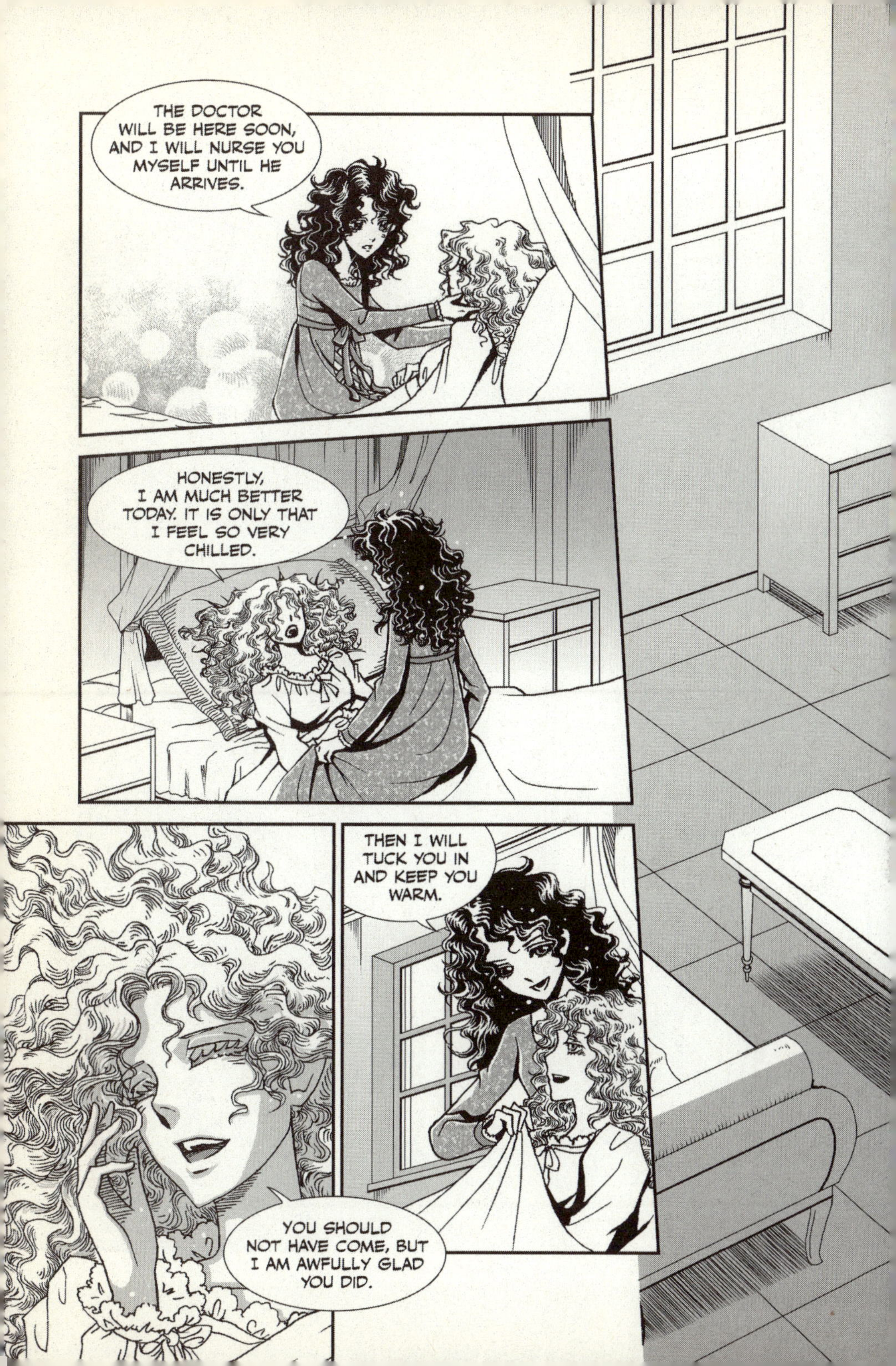
THE DOCTOR WILL BE HERE SOON, AND I WILL NURSE YOU MYSELF UNTIL HE ARRIVES.
HONESTLY, I AM MUCH BETTER TODAY. IT IS ONLY THAT I FEEL SO VERY CHILLED.
THEN I WILL TUCK YOU IN AND KEEP YOU WARM.
YOU SHOULD NOT HAVE COME, BUT I AM AWFULLY GLAD YOU DID.

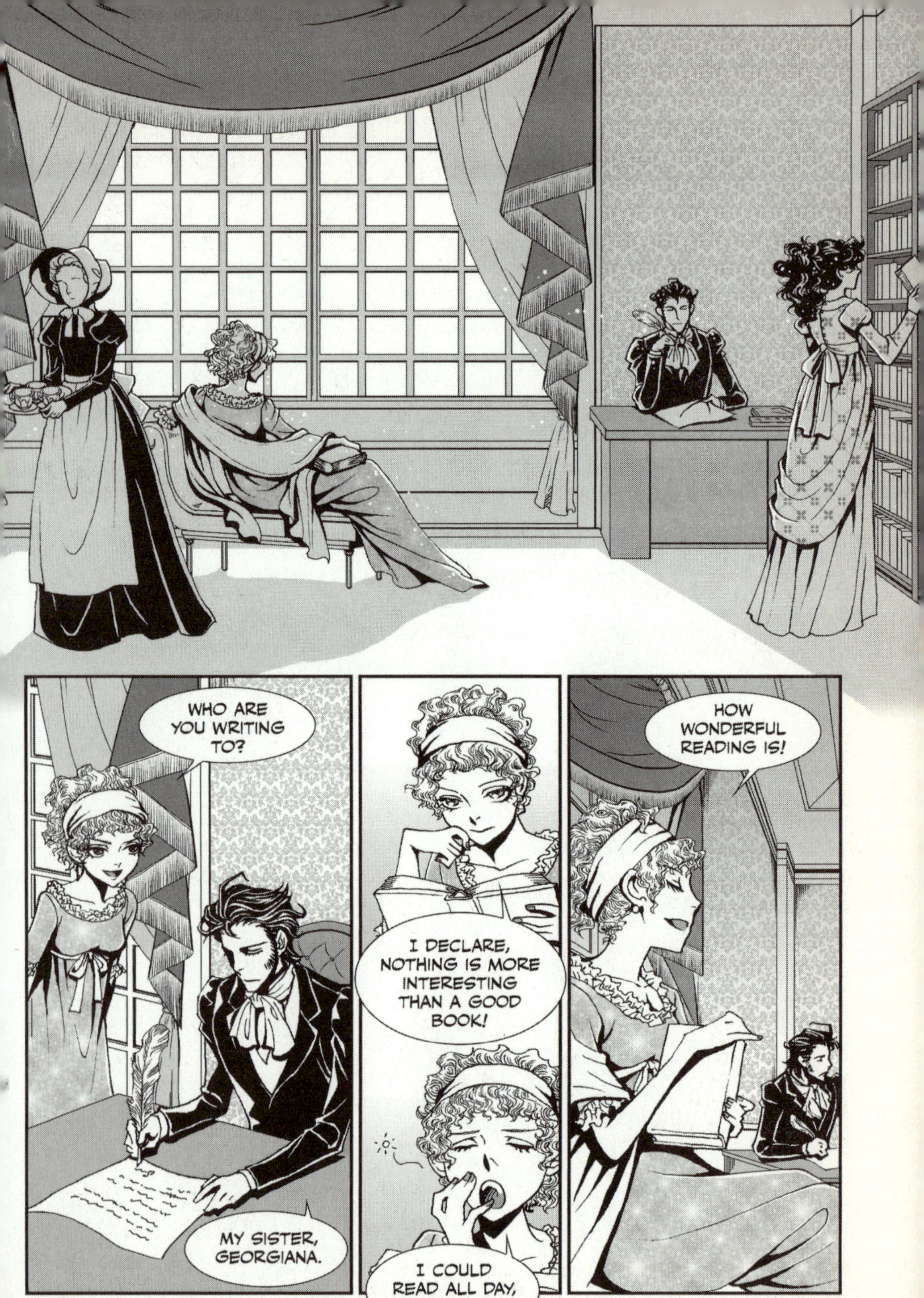
HOW WONDERFUL READING IS!
I DECLARE, NOTHING IS MORE INTERESTING THAN A GOOD BOOK!
I COULD READ ALL DAY, HONESTLY!
WHO ARE YOU WRITING TO?
MY SISTER, GEORGIANA.

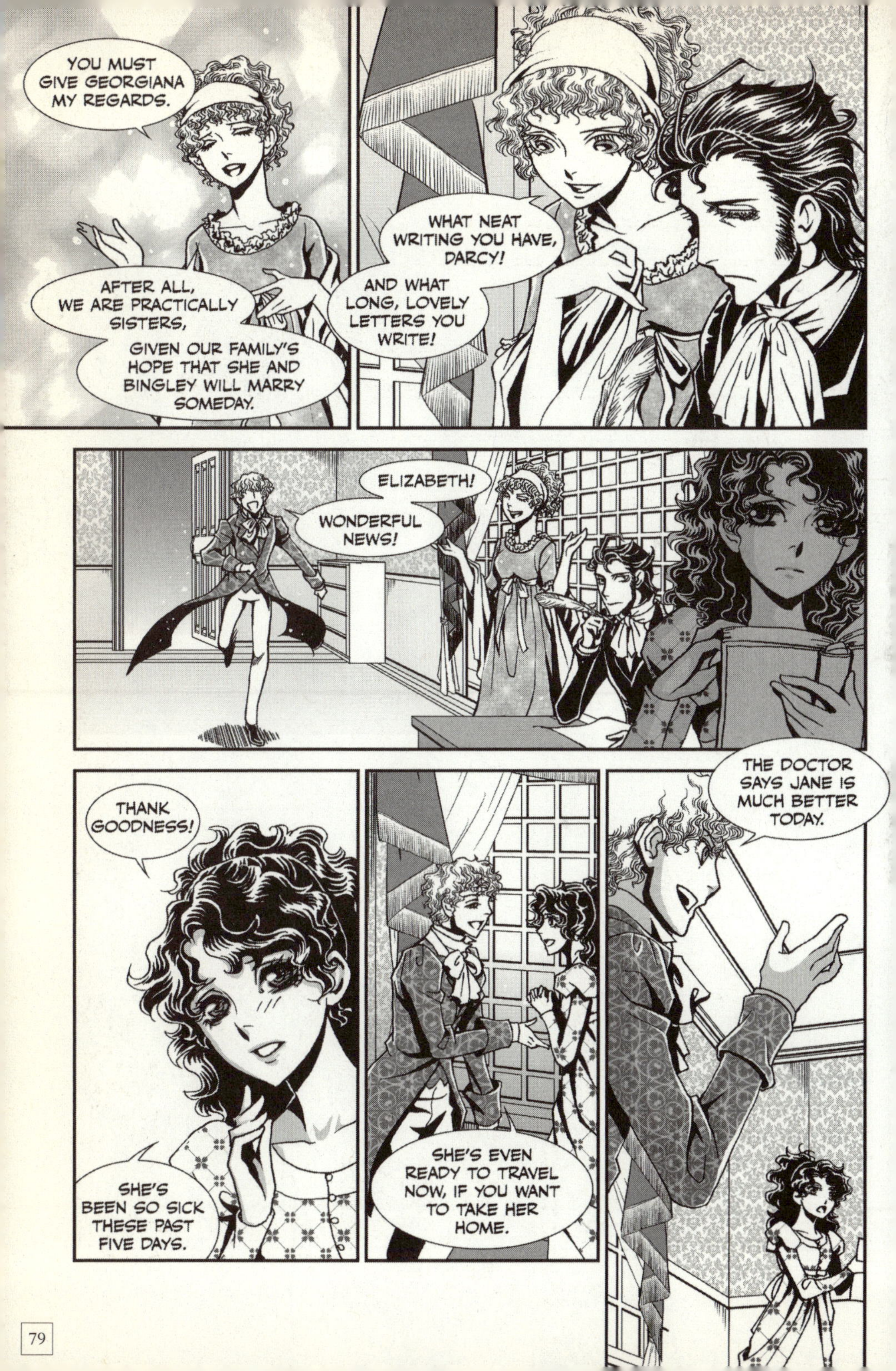
WHAT NEAT WRITING YOU HAVE, DARCY!
AND WHAT LONG, LOVELY LETTERS YOU WRITE!
YOU MUST GIVE GEORGIANA MY REGARDS.
AFTER ALL, WE ARE PRACTICALLY SISTERS,
GIVEN OUR FAMILY'S HOPE THAT SHE AND BINGLEY WILL MARRY SOMEDAY.
ELIZABETH!
WONDERFUL NEWS!
THE DOCTOR SAYS JANE IS MUCH BETTER TODAY.
SHE'S EVEN READY TO TRAVEL NOW, IF YOU WANT TO TAKE HER HOME.
THANK GOODNESS!
SHE'S BEEN SO SICK THESE PAST FIVE DAYS.

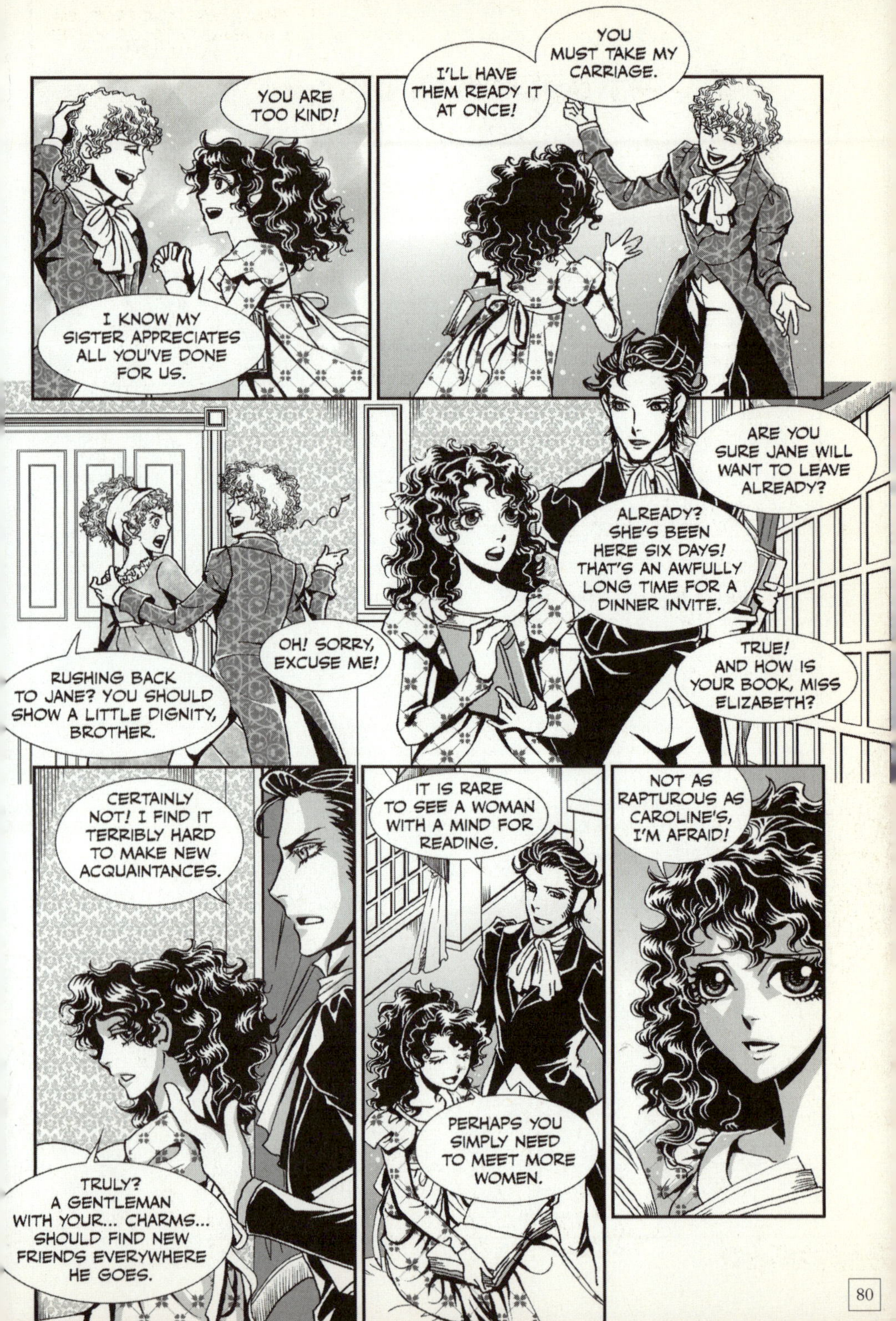
YOU MUST TAKE MY CARRIAGE.
I'LL HAVE THEM READY IT AT ONCE!
YOU ARE TOO KIND!
I KNOW MY SISTER APPRECIATES ALL YOU'VE DONE FOR US.
ARE YOU SURE JANE WILL WANT TO LEAVE ALREADY?
ALREADY? SHE'S BEEN HERE SIX DAYS! THAT'S AN AWFULLY LONG TIME FOR A DINNER INVITE.
TRUE! AND HOW IS YOUR BOOK, MISS ELIZABETH?
OH! SORRY, EXCUSE ME!
RUSHING BACK TO JANE? YOU SHOULD SHOW A LITTLE DIGNITY, BROTHER.
NOT AS RAPTUROUS AS CAROLINE'S, I'M AFRAID!
IT IS RARE TO SEE A WOMAN WITH A MIND FOR READING.
PERHAPS YOU SIMPLY NEED TO MEET MORE WOMEN.
CERTAINLY NOT! I FIND IT TERRIBLY HARD TO MAKE NEW ACQUAINTANCES.
TRULY? A GENTLEMAN WITH YOUR... CHARMS... SHOULD FIND NEW FRIENDS EVERYWHERE HE GOES.

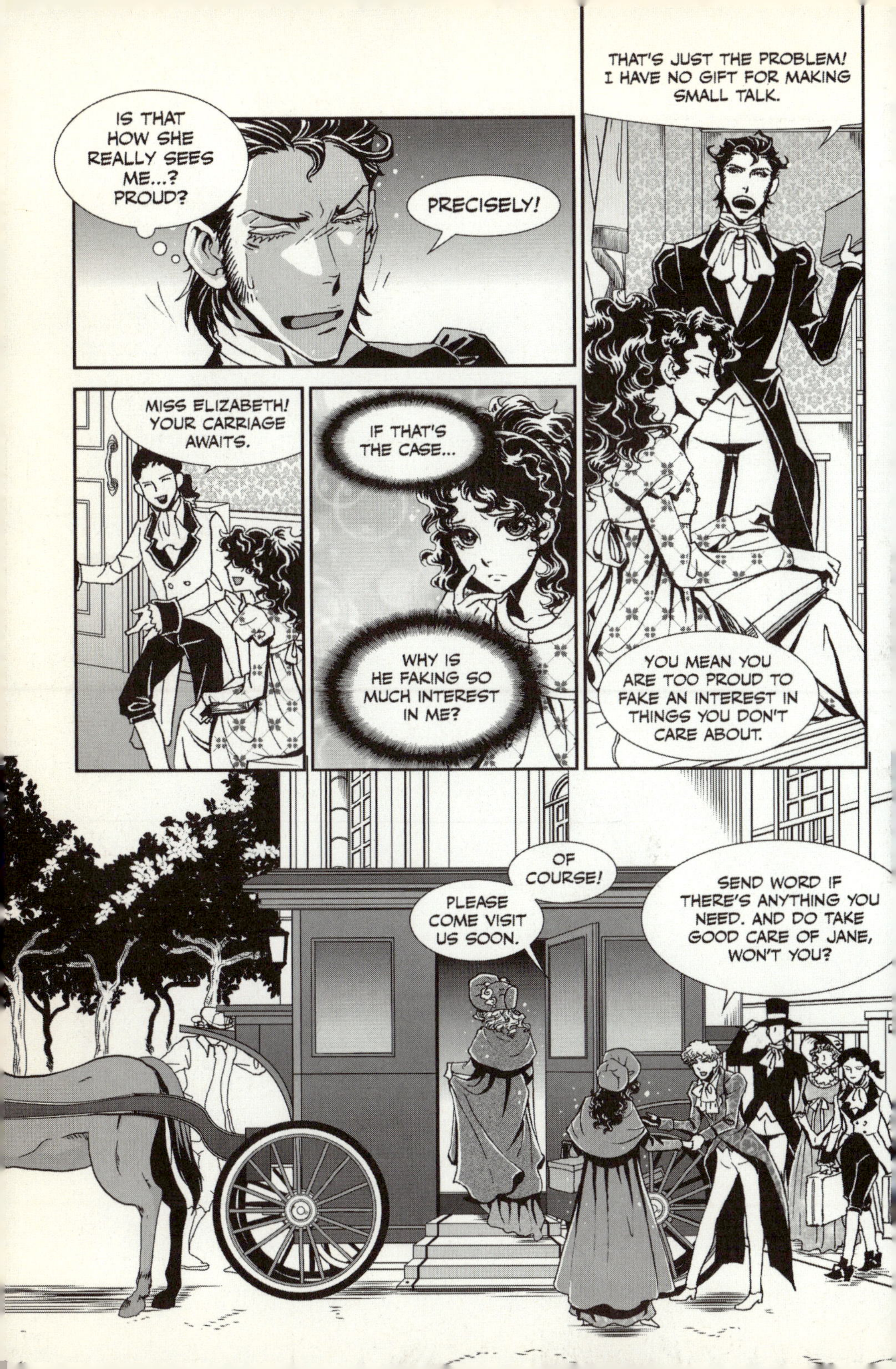
THAT'S JUST THE PROBLEM! I HAVE NO GIFT FOR MAKING SMALL TALK.
YOU MEAN YOU ARE TOO PROUD TO FAKE AN INTEREST IN THINGS YOU DON'T CARE ABOUT.
IS THAT HOW SHE REALLY SEES ME...? PROUD?
PRECISELY!
IF THAT'S THE CASE...
WHY IS HE FAKING SO MUCH INTEREST IN ME?
MISS ELIZABETH! YOUR CARRIAGE AWAITS.
SEND WORD IF THERE'S ANYTHING YOU NEED. AND DO TAKE GOOD CARE OF JANE, WON'T YOU?
OF COURSE!
PLEASE COME VISIT US SOON.

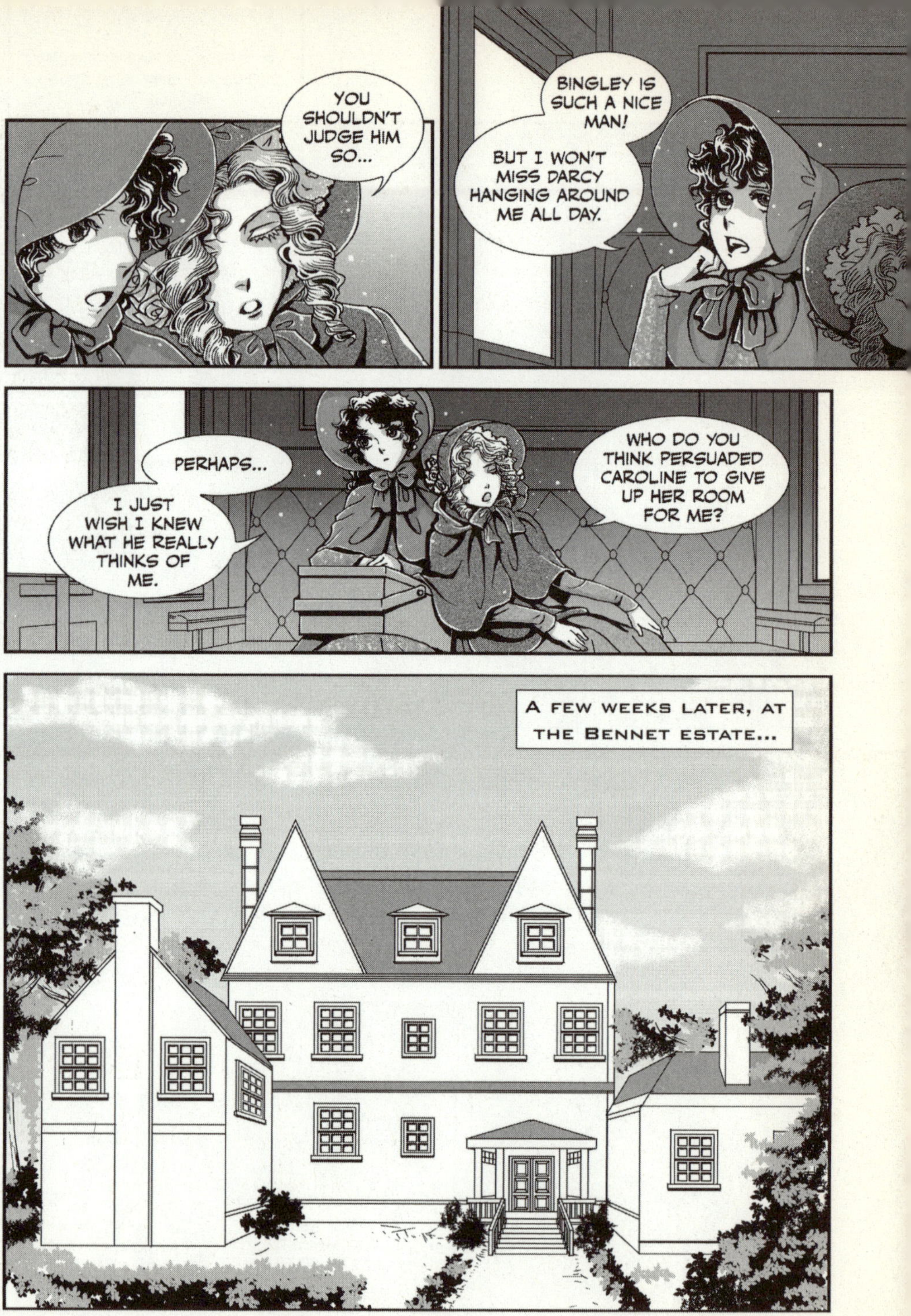
BINGLEY IS SUCH A NICE MAN!
BUT I WON'T MISS DARCY HANGING AROUND ME ALL DAY.
YOU SHOULDN'T JUDGE HIM SO...
WHO DO YOU THINK PERSUADED CAROLINE TO GIVE UP HER ROOM FOR ME?
PERHAPS...
I JUST WISH I KNEW WHAT HE REALLY THINKS OF ME.
A FEW WEEKS LATER, AT THE BENNET ESTATE...

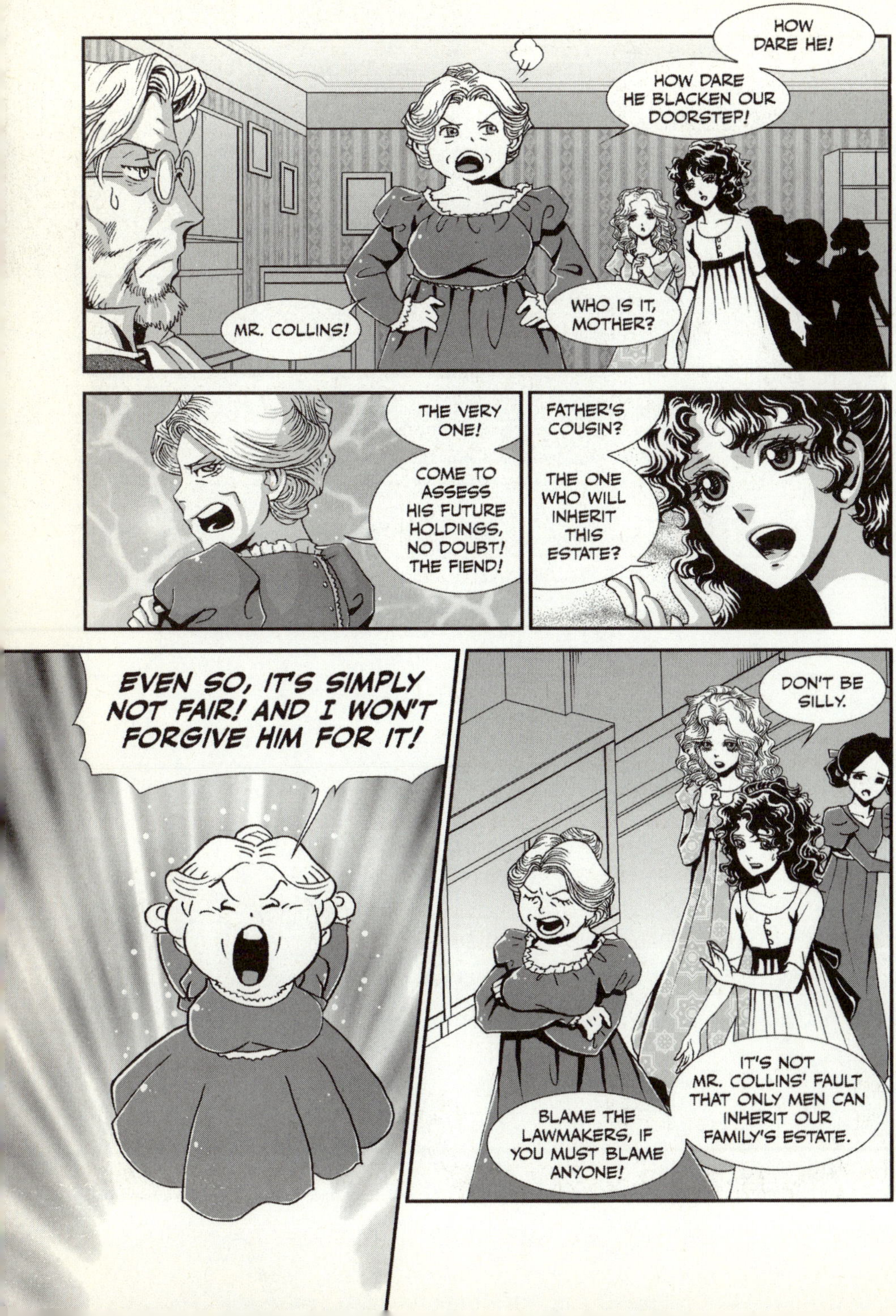

HOW DARE HE!
HOW DARE HE BLACKEN OUR DOORSTEP!
WHO IS IT, MOTHER?
MR. COLLINS!
FATHER'S COUSIN?
THE ONE WHO WILL INHERIT THIS ESTATE?
THE VERY ONE!
COME TO ASSESS HIS FUTURE HOLDINGS, NO DOUBT! THE FIEND!
DON'T BE SILLY.
IT'S NOT MR. COLLINS' FAULT THAT ONLY MEN CAN INHERIT OUR FAMILY'S ESTATE.
BLAME THE LAWMAKERS, IF YOU MUST BLAME ANYONE!
EVEN SO, IT'S SIMPLY NOT FAIR! AND I WON'T FORGIVE HIM FOR IT!

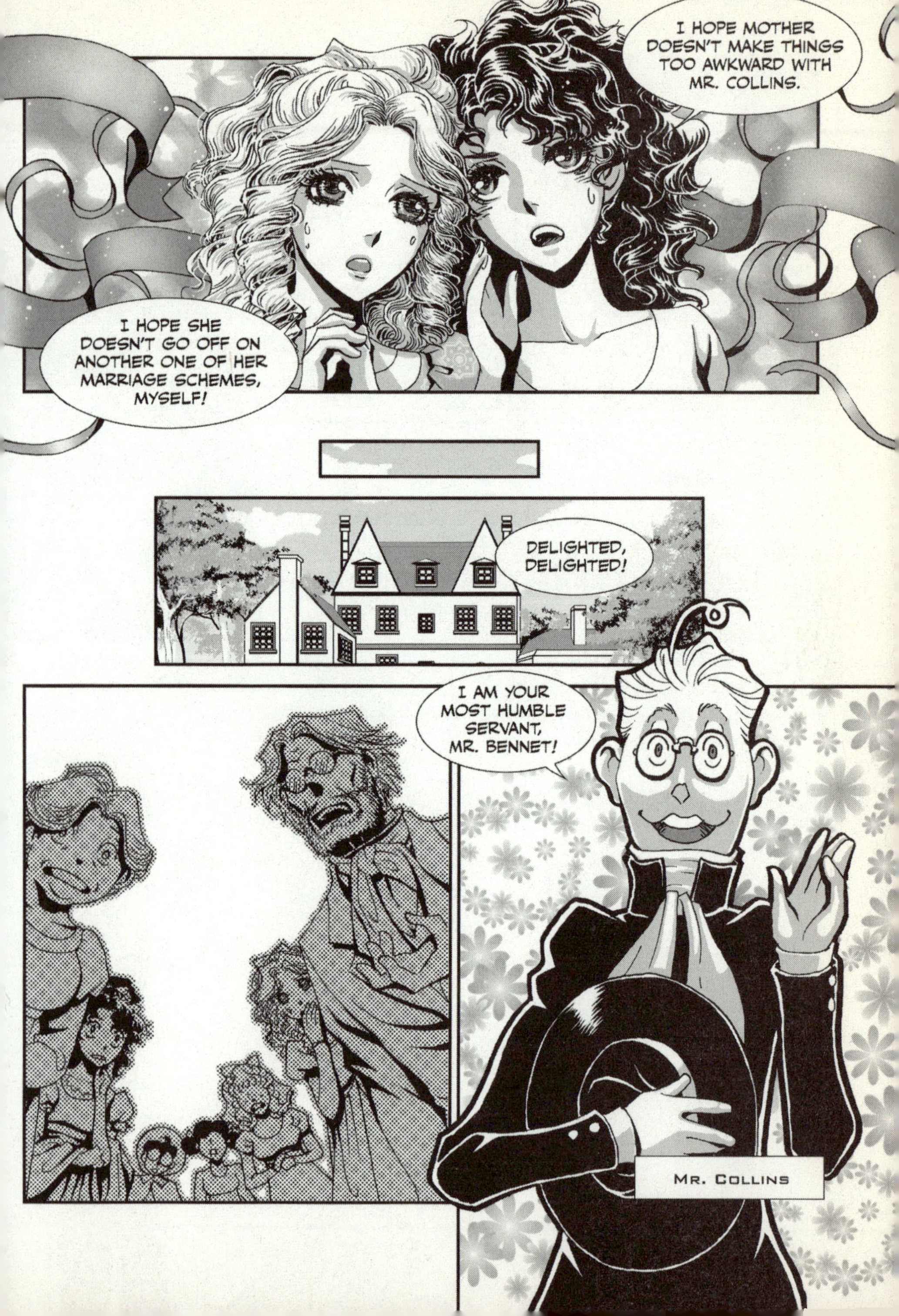
I HOPE MOTHER DOESN'T MAKE THINGS TOO AWKWARD WITH MR. COLLINS.
I HOPE SHE DOESN'T GO OFF ON ANOTHER ONE OF HER MARRIAGE SCHEMES, MYSELF!
DELIGHTED, DELIGHTED!
I AM YOUR MOST HUMBLE SERVANT, MR. BENNET!
MR. COLLINS

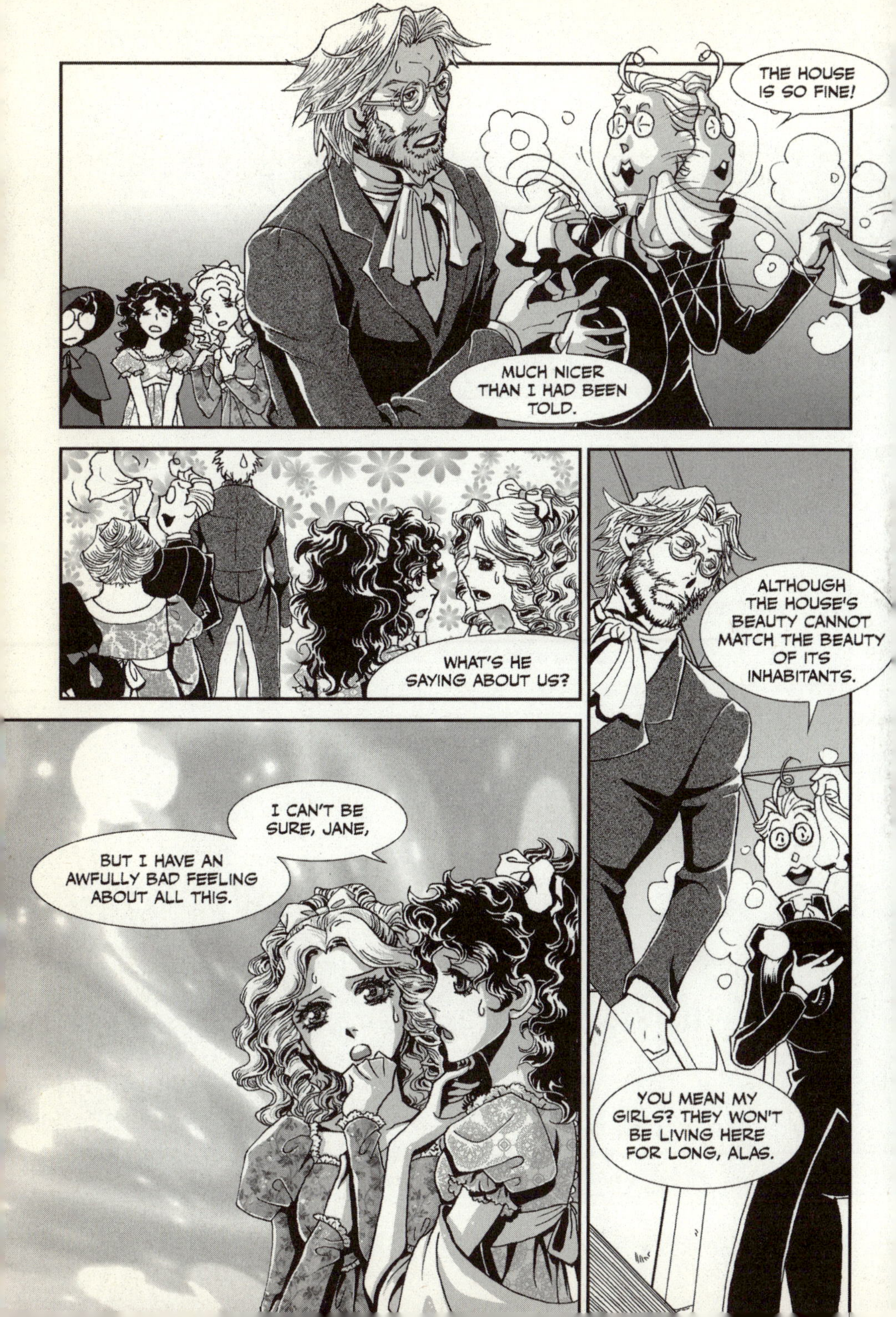
THE HOUSE IS SO FINE!
MUCH NICER THAN I HAD BEEN TOLD.
ALTHOUGH THE HOUSE'S BEAUTY CANNOT MATCH THE BEAUTY OF ITS INHABITANTS.
YOU MEAN MY GIRLS? THEY WON'T BE LIVING HERE FOR LONG, ALAS.
WHAT'S HE SAYING ABOUT US?
I CAN'T BE SURE, JANE,
BUT I HAVE AN AWFULLY BAD FEELING ABOUT ALL THIS.

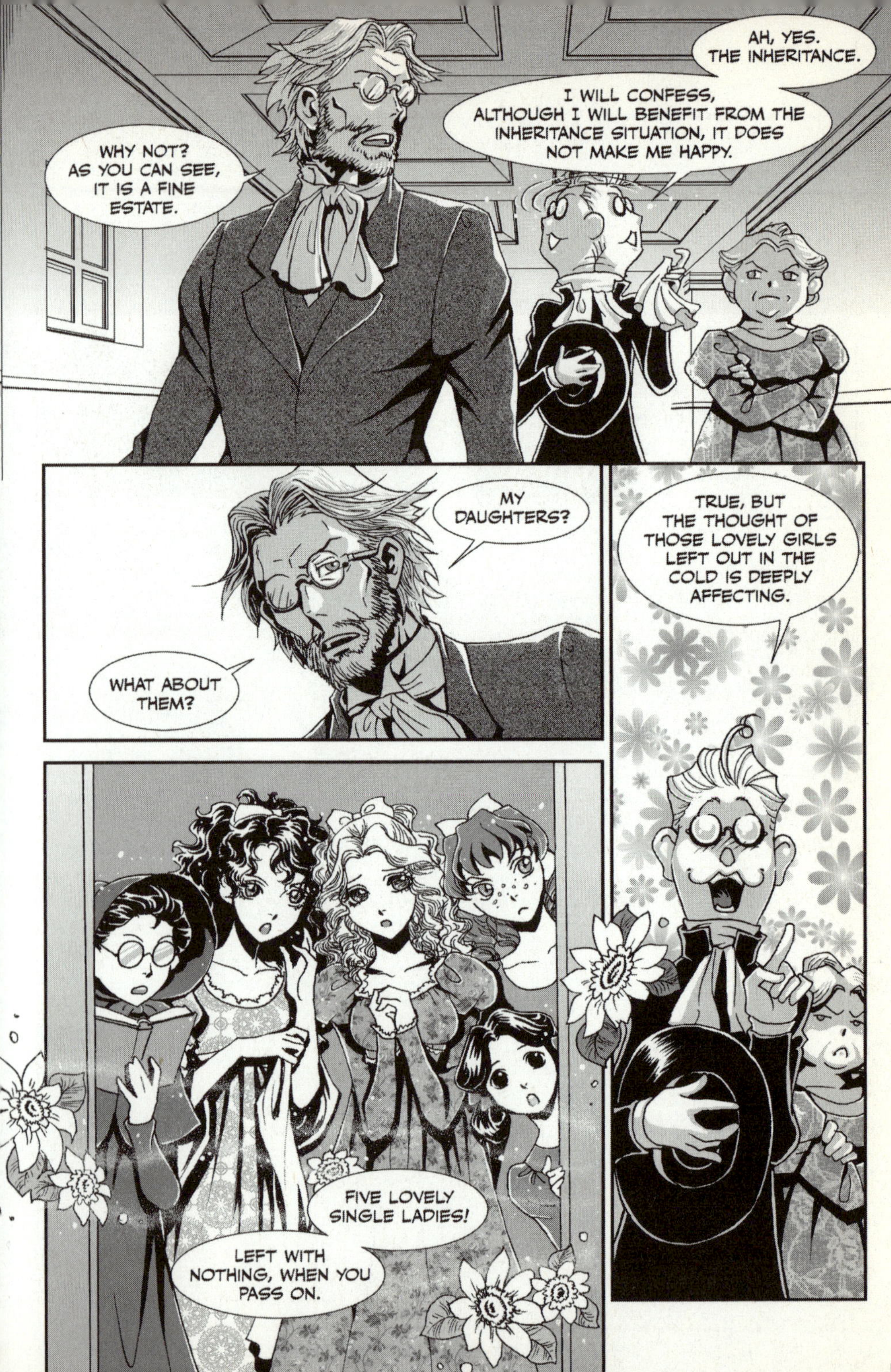
AH, YES. THE INHERITANCE.
I WILL CONFESS, ALTHOUGH I WILL BENEFIT FROM THE INHERITANCE SITUATION, IT DOES NOT MAKE ME HAPPY.
WHY NOT? AS YOU CAN SEE, IT IS A FINE ESTATE.
TRUE, BUT THE THOUGHT OF THOSE LOVELY GIRLS LEFT OUT IN THE COLD IS DEEPLY AFFECTING.
MY DAUGHTERS?
WHAT ABOUT THEM?
FIVE LOVELY SINGLE LADIES!
LEFT WITH NOTHING, WHEN YOU PASS ON.

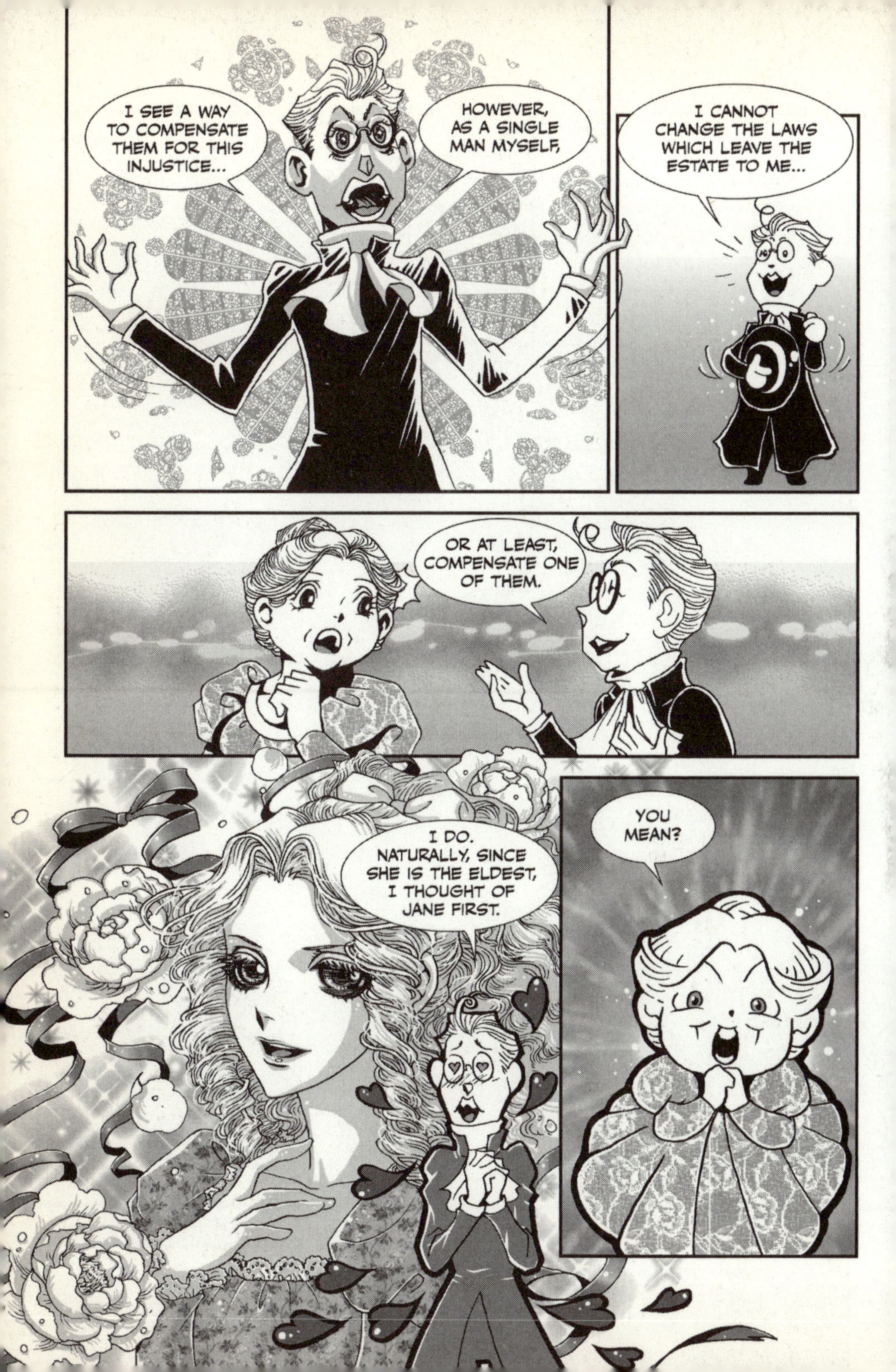
I CANNOT CHANGE THE LAWS WHICH LEAVE THE ESTATE TO ME...
HOWEVER, AS A SINGLE MAN MYSELF,
I SEE A WAY TO COMPENSATE THEM FOR THIS INJUSTICE...
OR AT LEAST, COMPENSATE ONE OF THEM.
YOU MEAN?
I DO. NATURALLY, SINCE SHE IS THE ELDEST, I THOUGHT OF JANE FIRST.

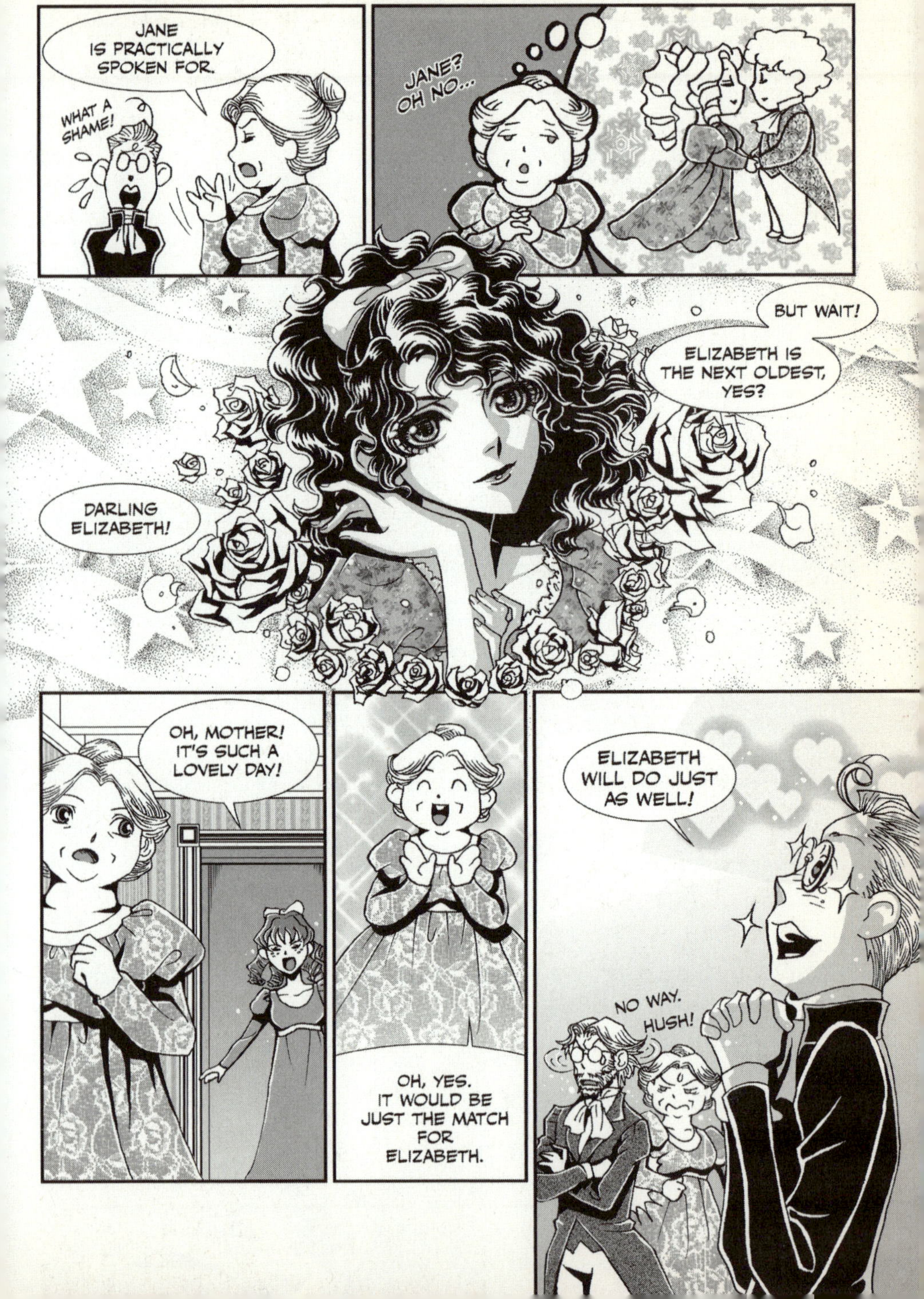
JANE? OH NO...
JANE IS PRACTICALLY SPOKEN FOR.
WHAT A SHAME!
BUT WAIT!
ELIZABETH IS THE NEXT OLDEST, YES?
DARLING ELIZABETH!
ELIZABETH WILL DO JUST AS WELL!
NO WAY.
HUSH!
OH, YES. IT WOULD BE JUST THE MATCH FOR ELIZABETH.
OH, MOTHER! IT'S SUCH A LOVELY DAY!

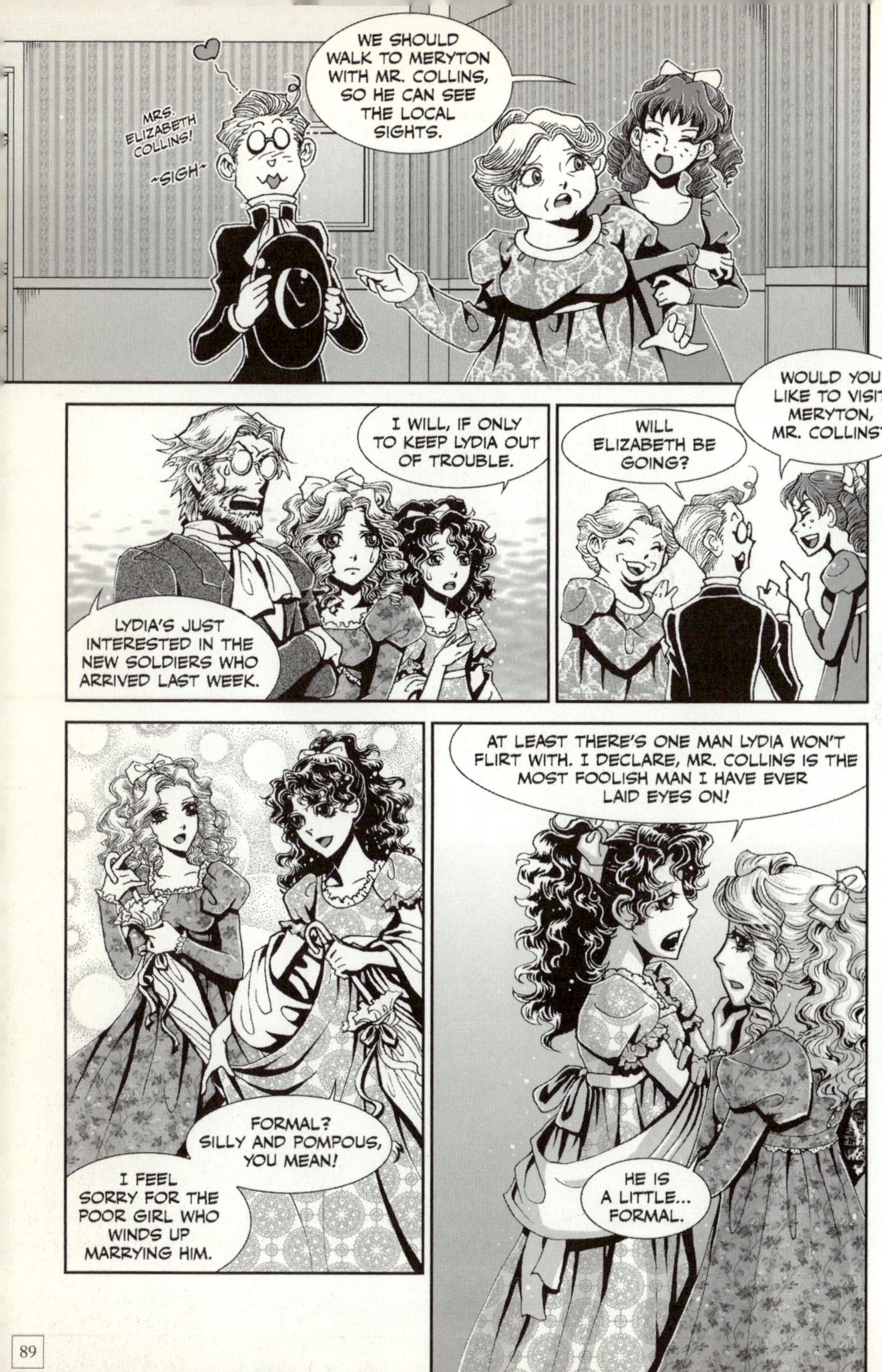
WE SHOULD WALK TO MERYTON WITH MR. COLLINS, SO HE CAN SEE THE LOCAL SIGHTS.
MRS. ELIZABETH COLLINS!
~SIGH~
WOULD YOU LIKE TO VISIT MERYTON, MR. COLLINS?
WILL ELIZABETH BE GOING?
I WILL, IF ONLY TO KEEP LYDIA OUT OF TROUBLE.
LYDIA'S JUST INTERESTED IN THE NEW SOLDIERS WHO ARRIVED LAST WEEK.
AT LEAST THERE'S ONE MAN LYDIA WON'T FLIRT WITH. I DECLARE, MR. COLLINS IS THE MOST FOOLISH MAN I HAVE EVER LAID EYES ON!
HE IS A LITTLE... FORMAL.
FORMAL? SILLY AND POMPOUS, YOU MEAN!
I FEEL SORRY FOR THE POOR GIRL WHO WINDS UP MARRYING HIM.

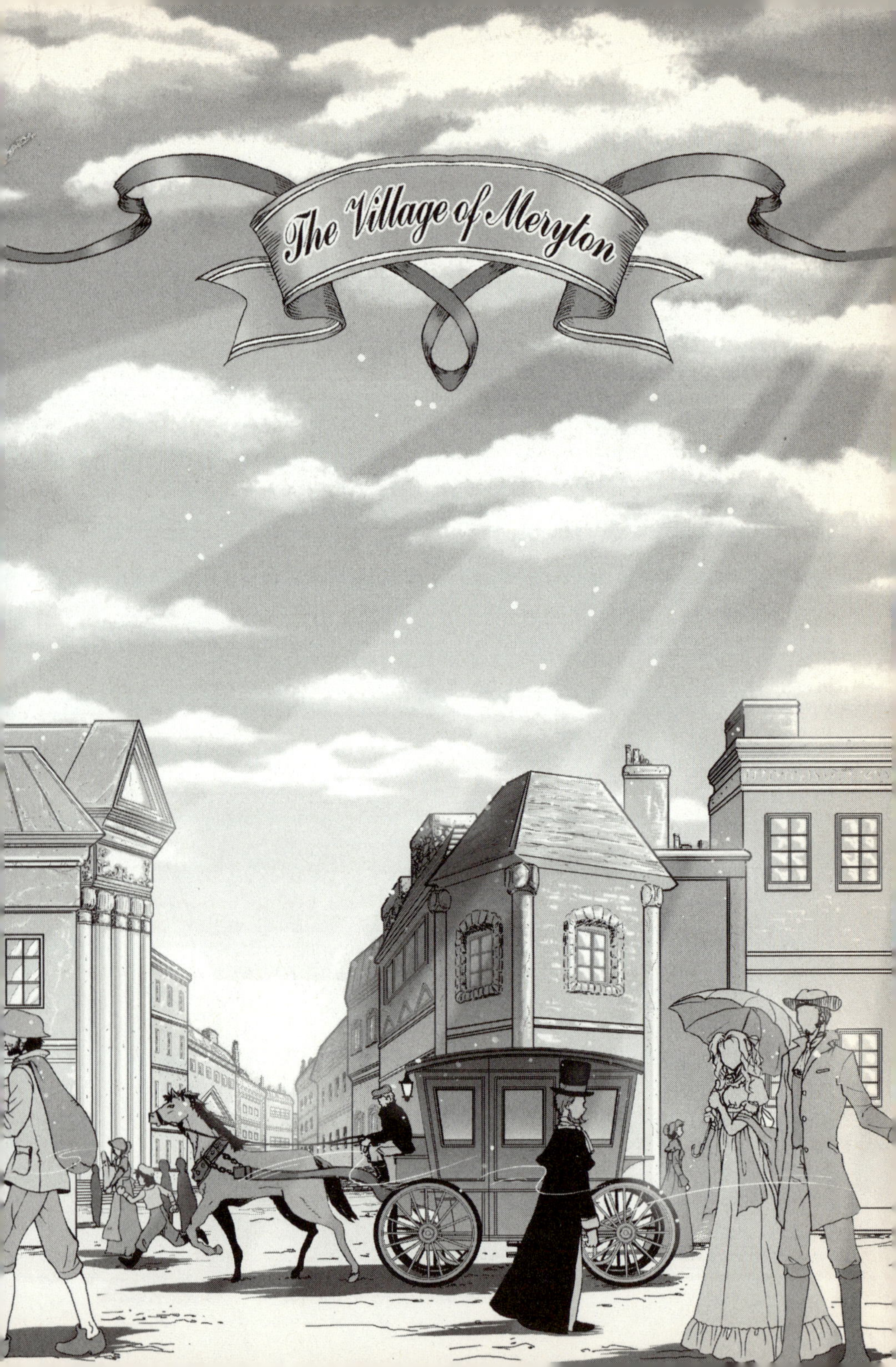
The Village of Meryton

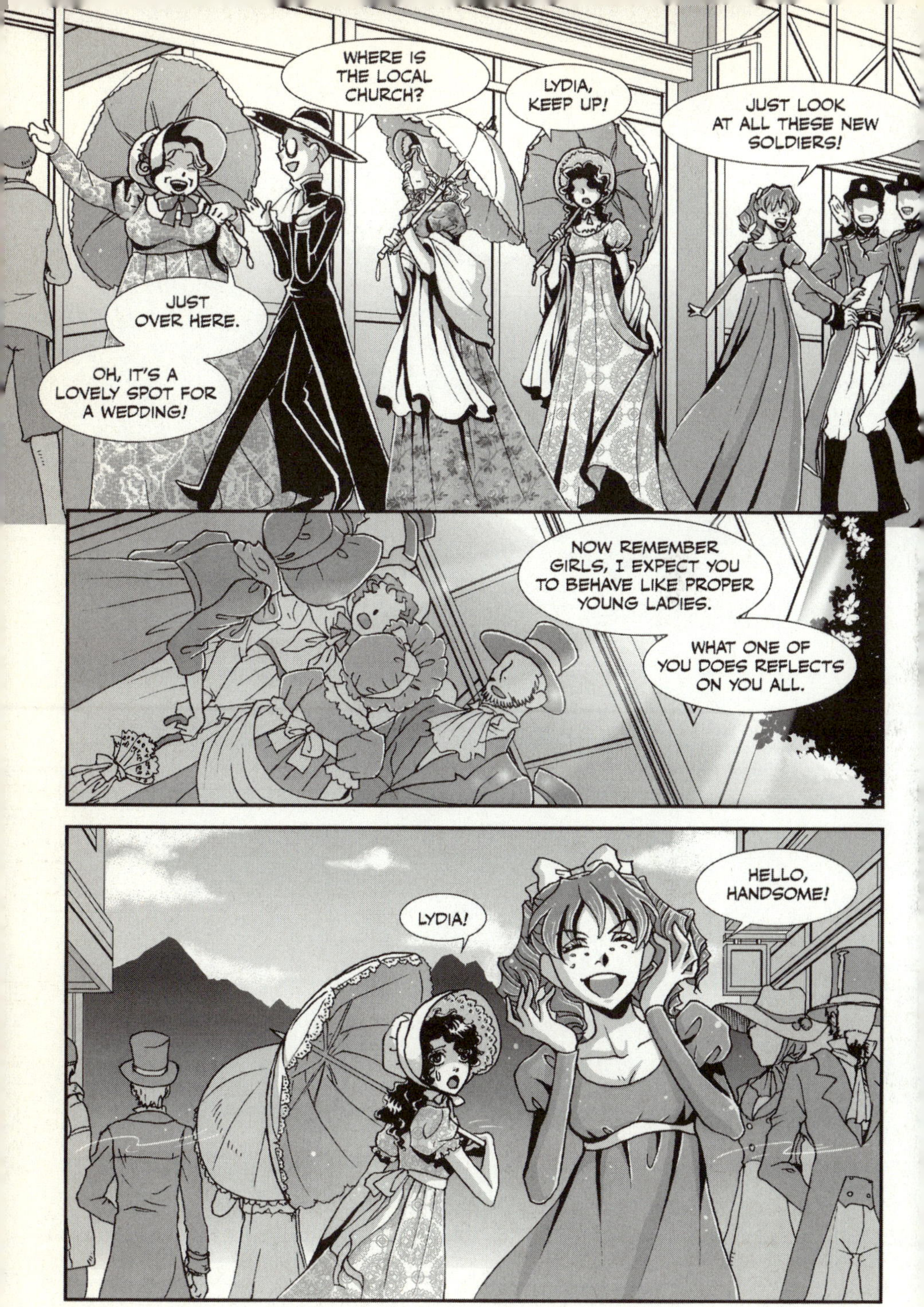
JUST LOOK AT ALL THESE NEW SOLDIERS!
LYDIA, KEEP UP!
WHERE IS THE LOCAL CHURCH?
JUST OVER HERE.
OH, IT'S A LOVELY SPOT FOR A WEDDING!
NOW REMEMBER GIRLS, I EXPECT YOU TO BEHAVE LIKE PROPER YOUNG LADIES.
WHAT ONE OF YOU DOES REFLECTS ON YOU ALL.
HELLO, HANDSOME!
LYDIA!

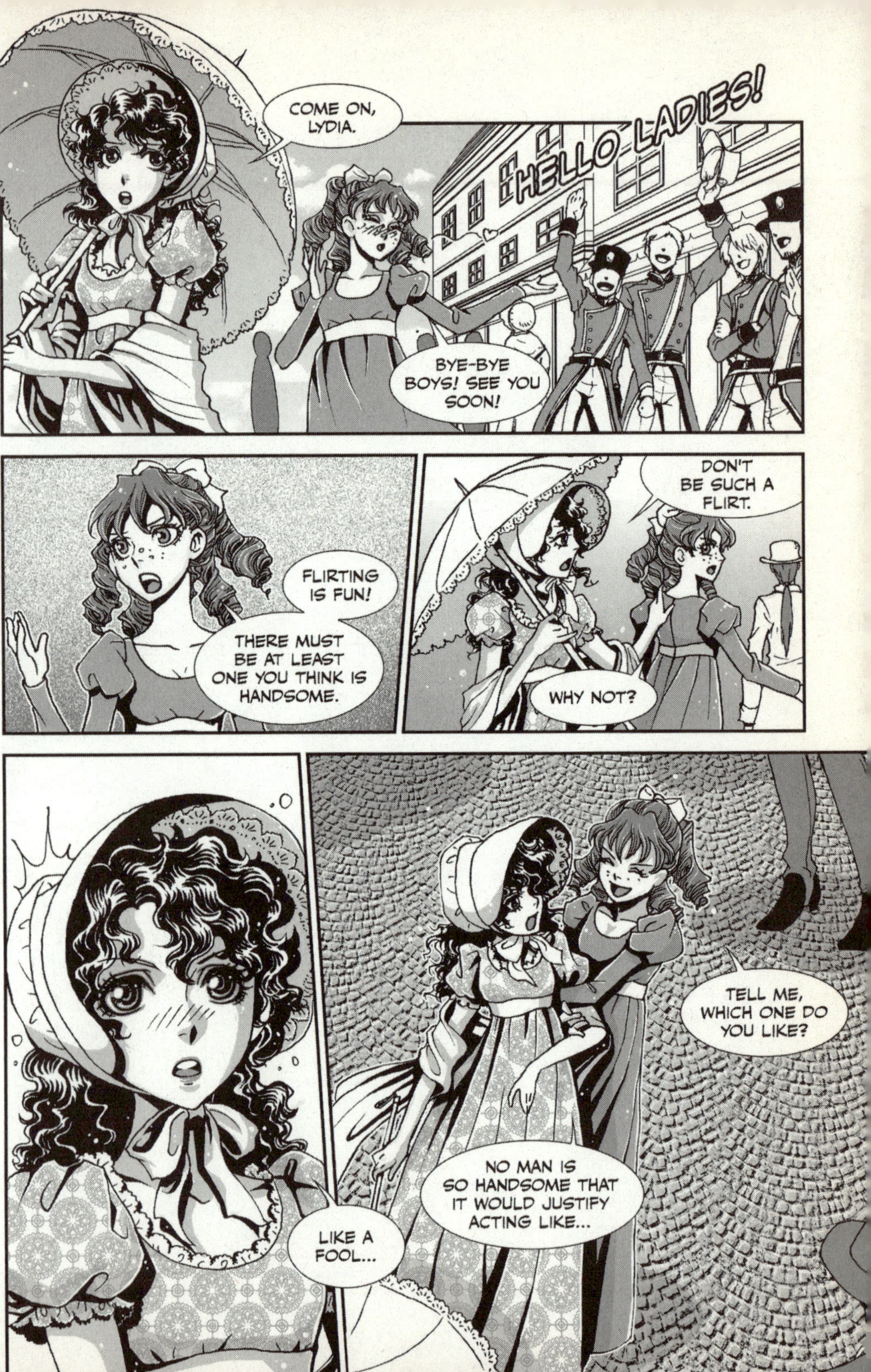
HELLO LADIES!
COME ON, LYDIA.
BYE-BYE BOYS! SEE YOU SOON!
DON'T BE SUCH A FLIRT.
WHY NOT?
FLIRTING IS FUN!
THERE MUST BE AT LEAST ONE YOU THINK IS HANDSOME.
TELL ME, WHICH ONE DO YOU LIKE?
NO MAN IS SO HANDSOME THAT IT WOULD JUSTIFY ACTING LIKE...
LIKE A FOOL...

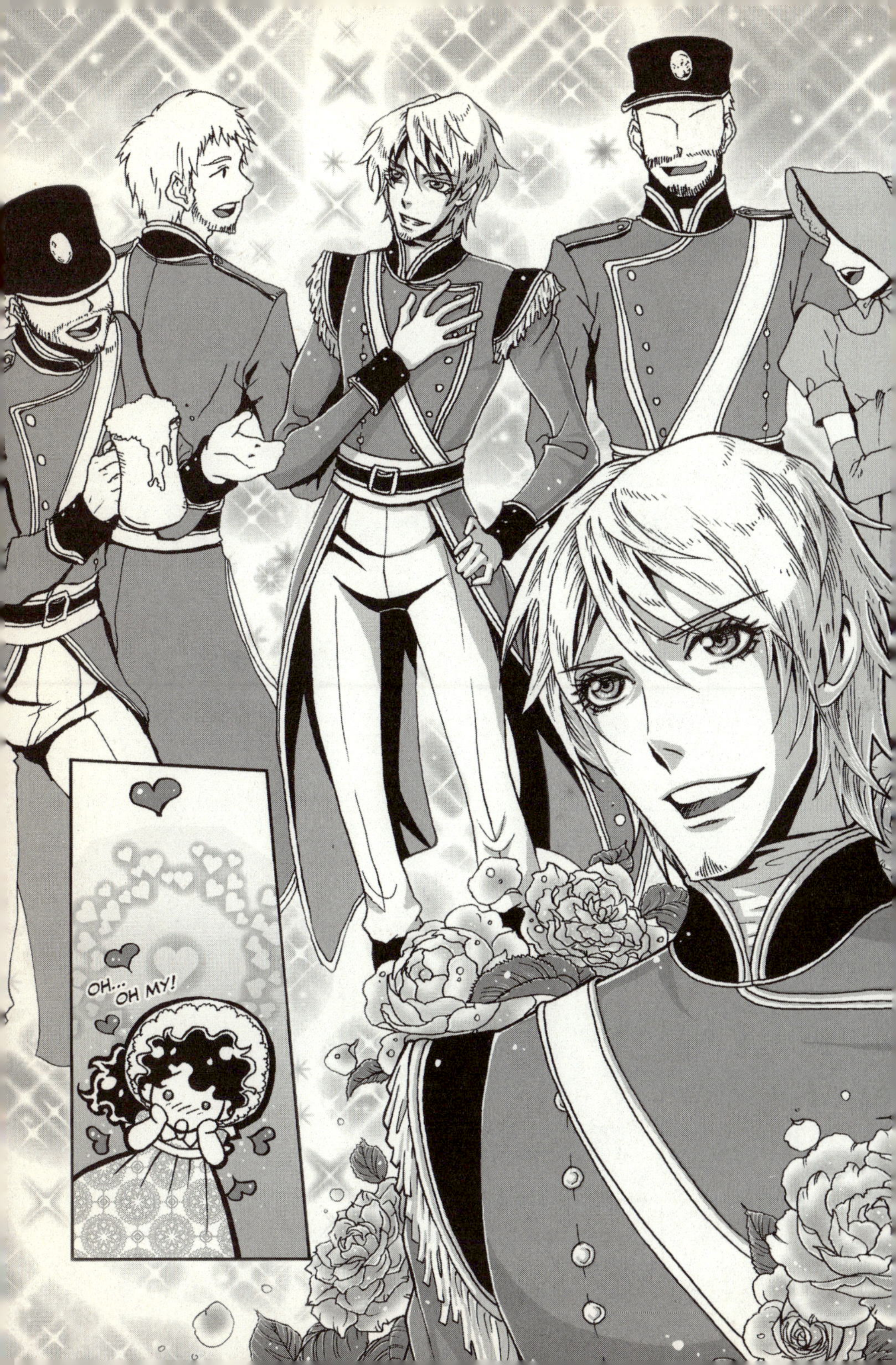
OH... OH MY!

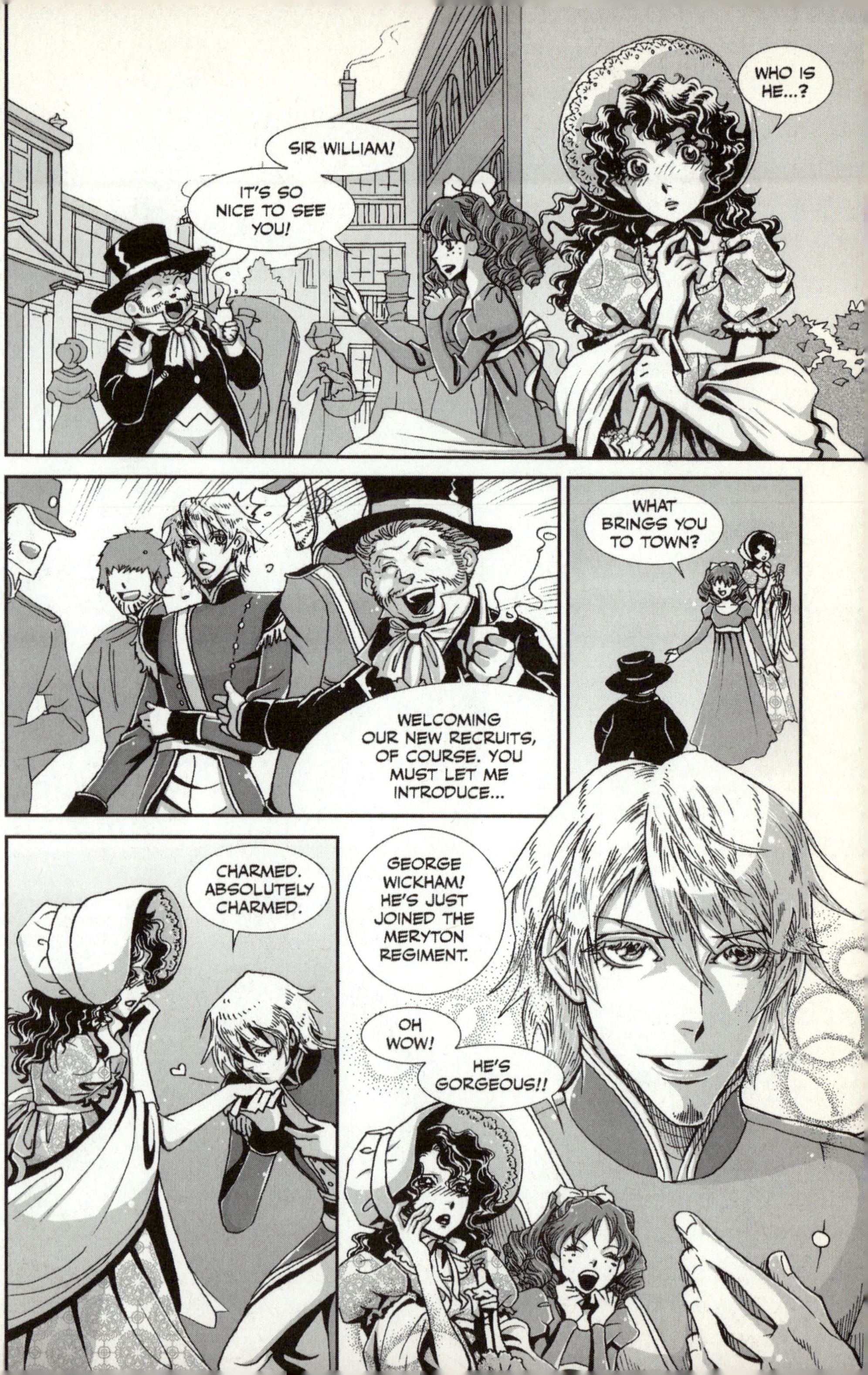
WHO IS HE...?
SIR WILLIAM!
IT'S SO NICE TO SEE YOU!
WHAT BRINGS YOU TO TOWN?
WELCOMING OUR NEW RECRUITS, OF COURSE. YOU MUST LET ME INTRODUCE...
GEORGE WICKHAM! HE'S JUST JOINED THE MERYTON REGIMENT.
OH WOW!
HE'S GORGEOUS!!
CHARMED. ABSOLUTELY CHARMED.

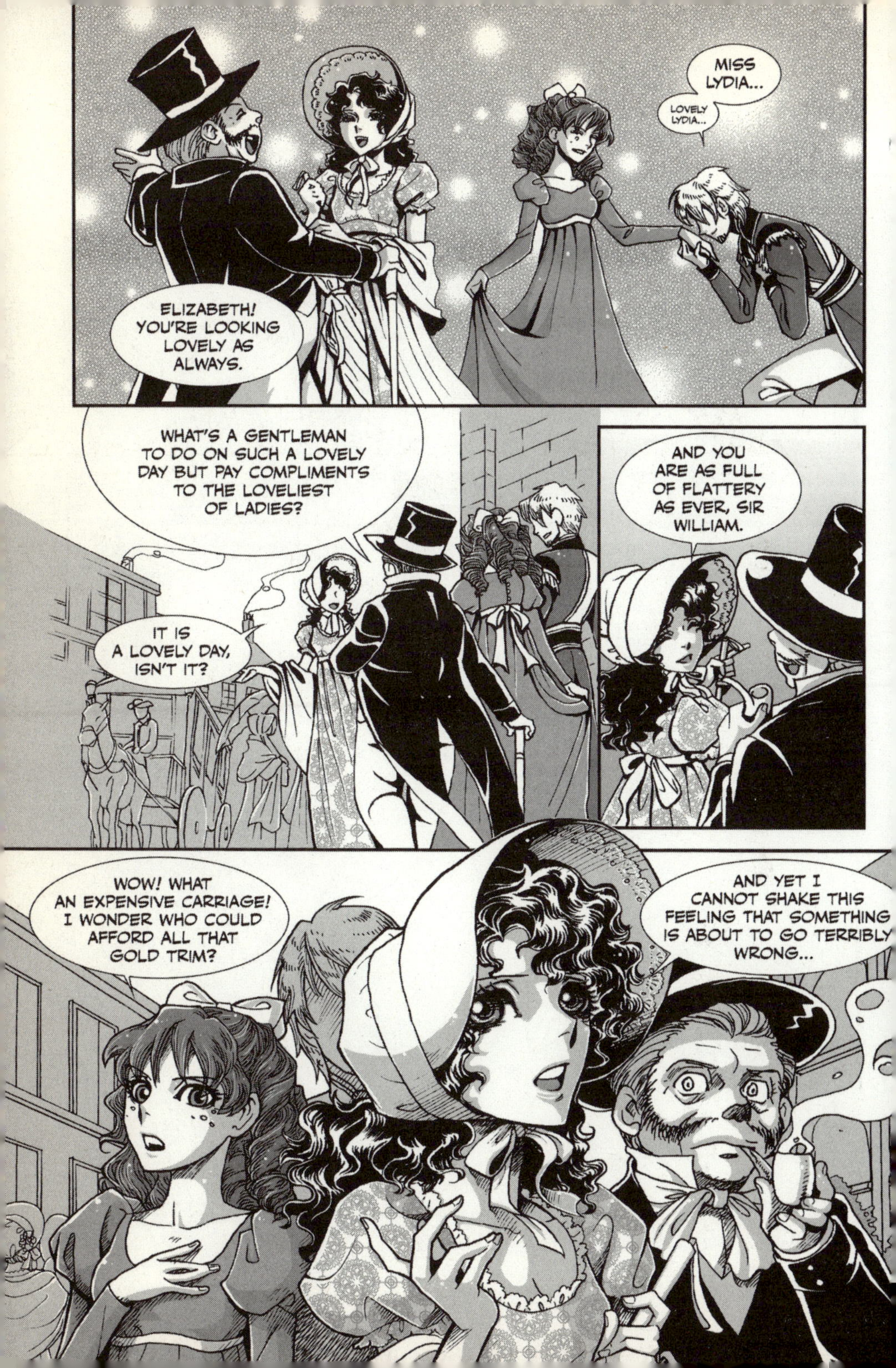
MISS LYDIA...
LOVELY LYDIA...
ELIZABETH! YOU'RE LOOKING LOVELY AS ALWAYS.
AND YOU ARE AS FULL OF FLATTERY AS EVER, SIR WILLIAM.
WHAT'S A GENTLEMAN TO DO ON SUCH A LOVELY DAY BUT PAY COMPLIMENTS TO THE LOVELIEST OF LADIES?
IT IS A LOVELY DAY, ISN'T IT?
AND YET I CANNOT SHAKE THIS FEELING THAT SOMETHING IS ABOUT TO GO TERRIBLY WRONG...
WOW! WHAT AN EXPENSIVE CARRIAGE! I WONDER WHO COULD AFFORD ALL THAT GOLD TRIM?

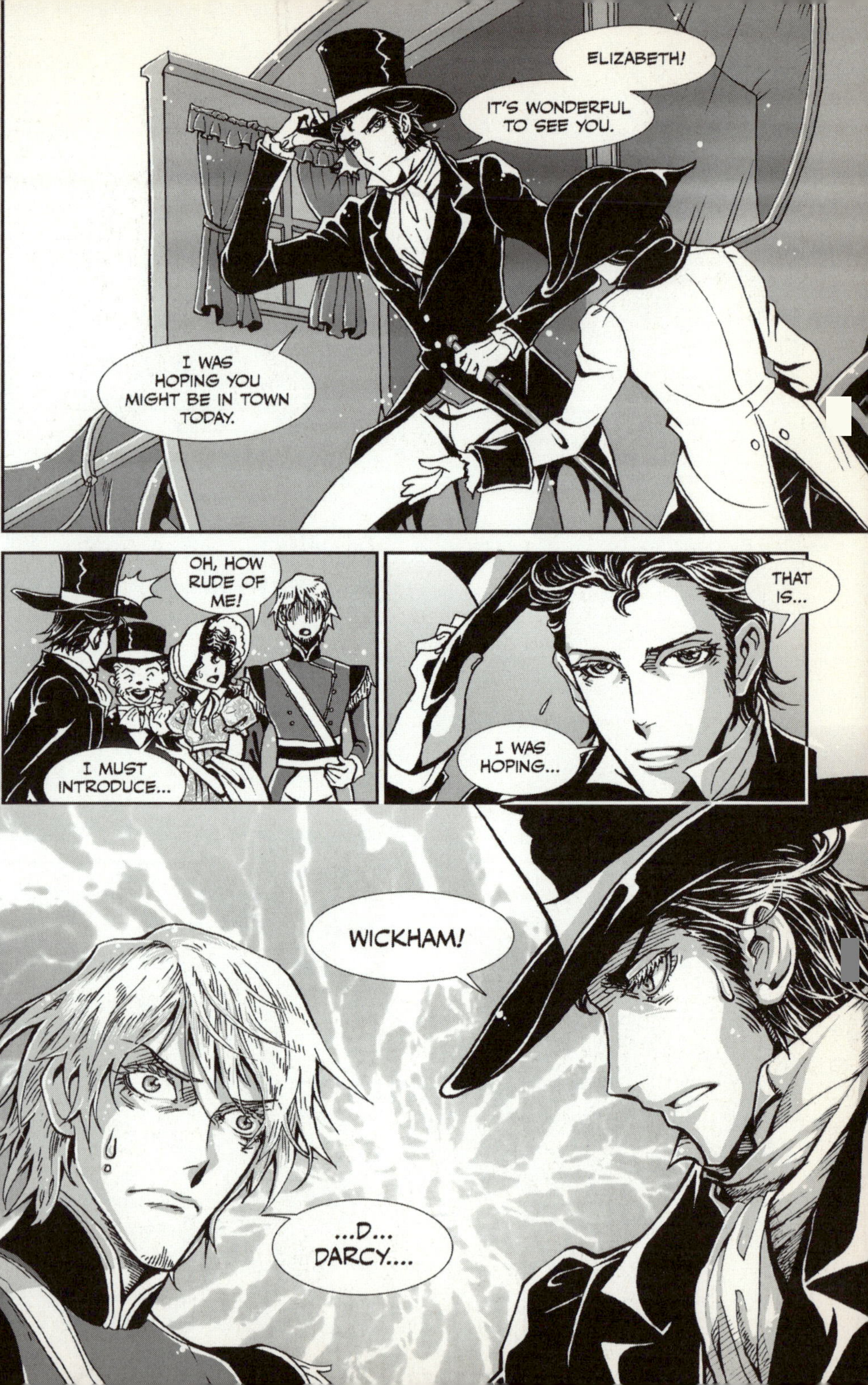
ELIZABETH!
IT'S WONDERFUL TO SEE YOU.
I WAS HOPING YOU MIGHT BE IN TOWN TODAY.
THAT IS...
I WAS HOPING...
OH, HOW RUDE OF ME!
I MUST INTRODUCE...
WICKHAM!
...D... DARCY....

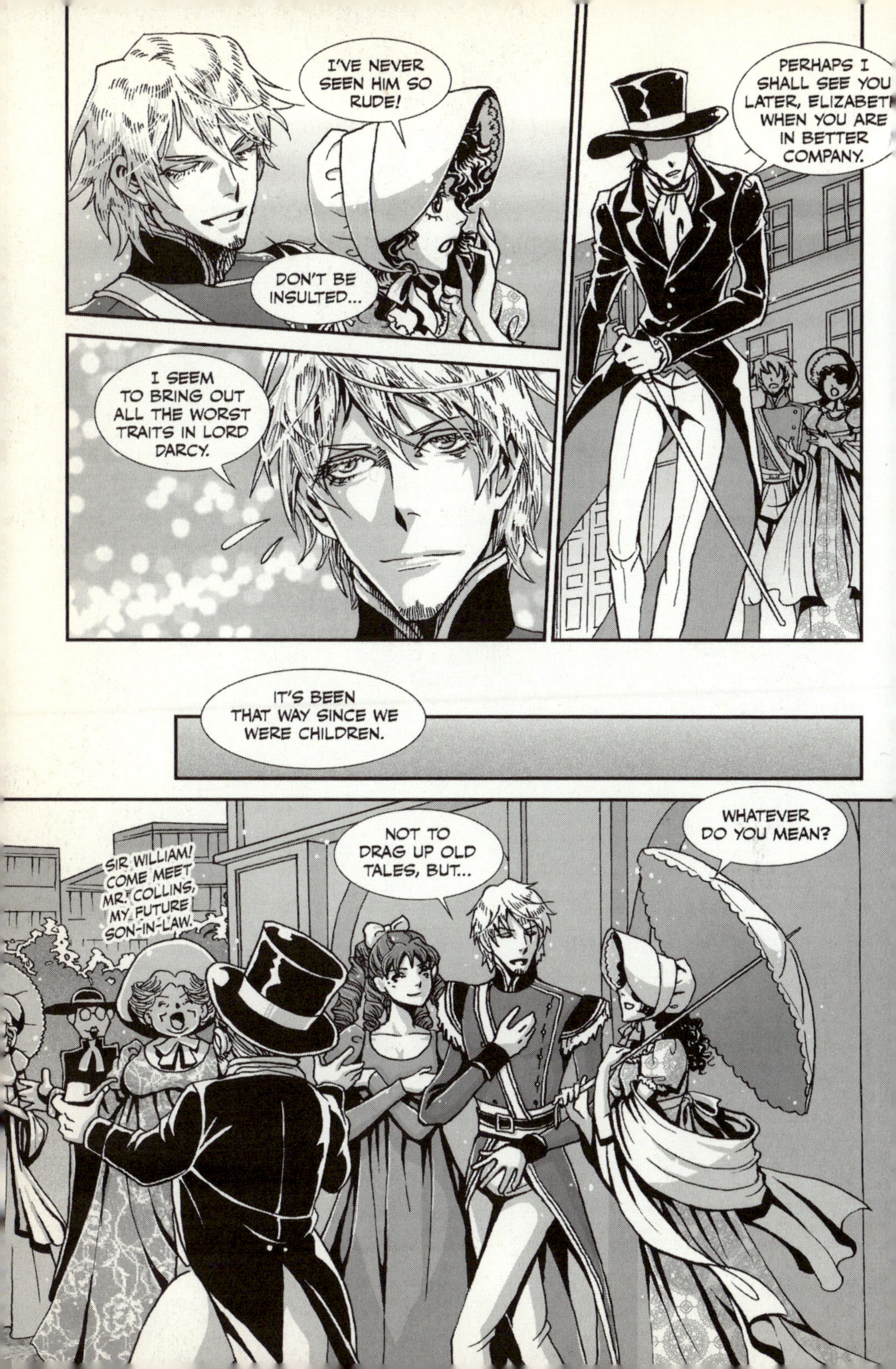
PERHAPS I SHALL SEE YOU LATER, ELIZABETH, WHEN YOU ARE IN BETTER COMPANY.
I'VE NEVER SEEN HIM SO RUDE!
DON'T BE INSULTED...
I SEEM TO BRING OUT ALL THE WORST TRAITS IN LORD DARCY.
IT'S BEEN THAT WAY SINCE WE WERE CHILDREN.
WHATEVER DO YOU MEAN?
NOT TO DRAG UP OLD TALES, BUT...
SIR WILLIAM! COME MEET MR. COLLINS, MY FUTURE SON-IN-LAW.

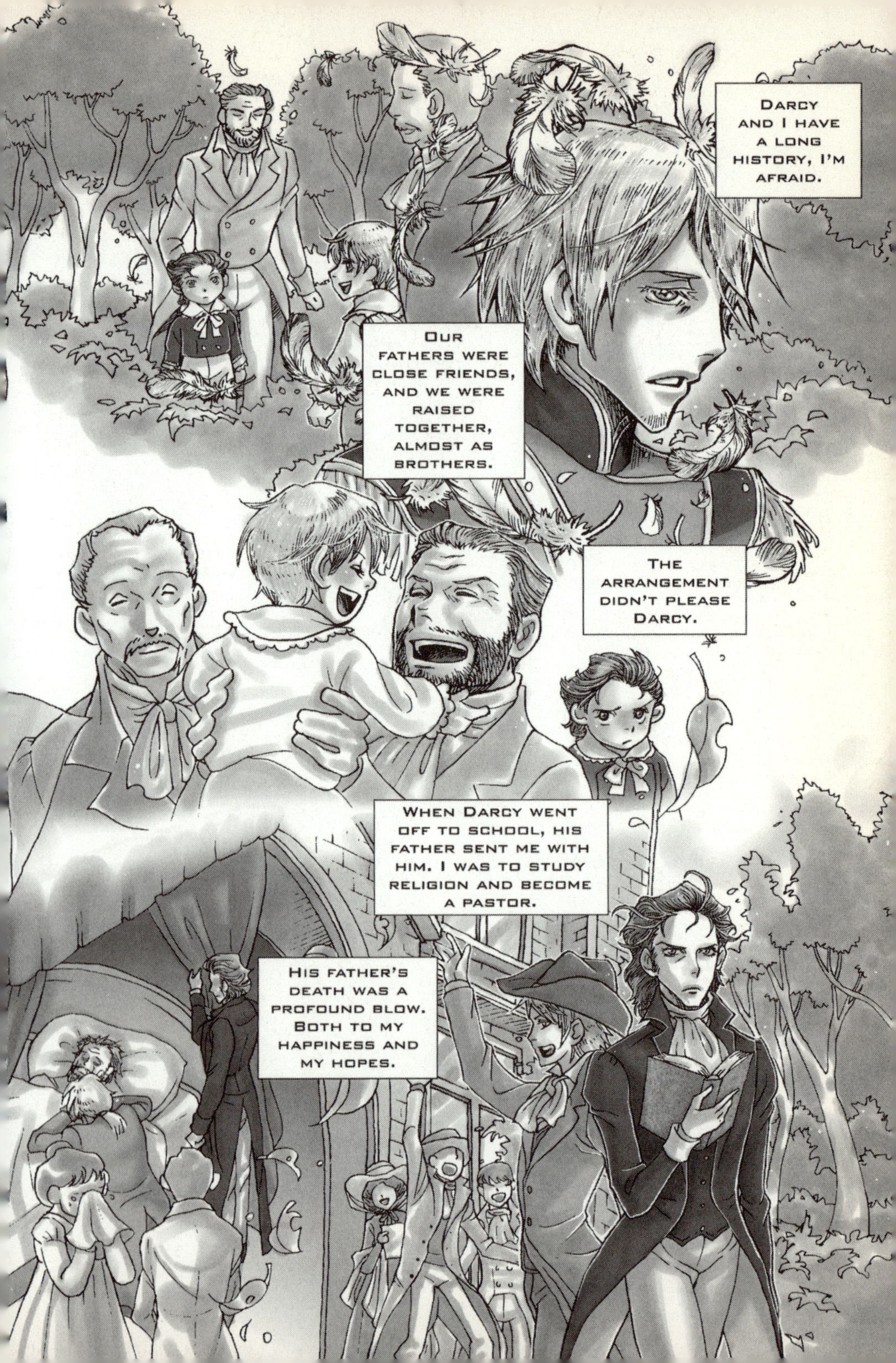
Darcy and I have a long history, I'm afraid.
Our fathers were close friends, and we were raised together, almost as brothers.
The arrangement didn't please Darcy.
When Darcy went off to school, his father sent me with him. I was to study religion and become a pastor.
His father's death was a profound blow. Both to my happiness and my hopes.

Darcy's father left me a small parish in his will. It was enough for me to make an honest living and do some good.
But...Darcy denied his father's last wishes and blocked my advancement!
He did everything in his power to keep me from getting the parish I was promised.
I was left out in the cold.
Without any other means of earning a living, I was forced to join the army. It's an honourable job, but I can never forget what I ought to have had.

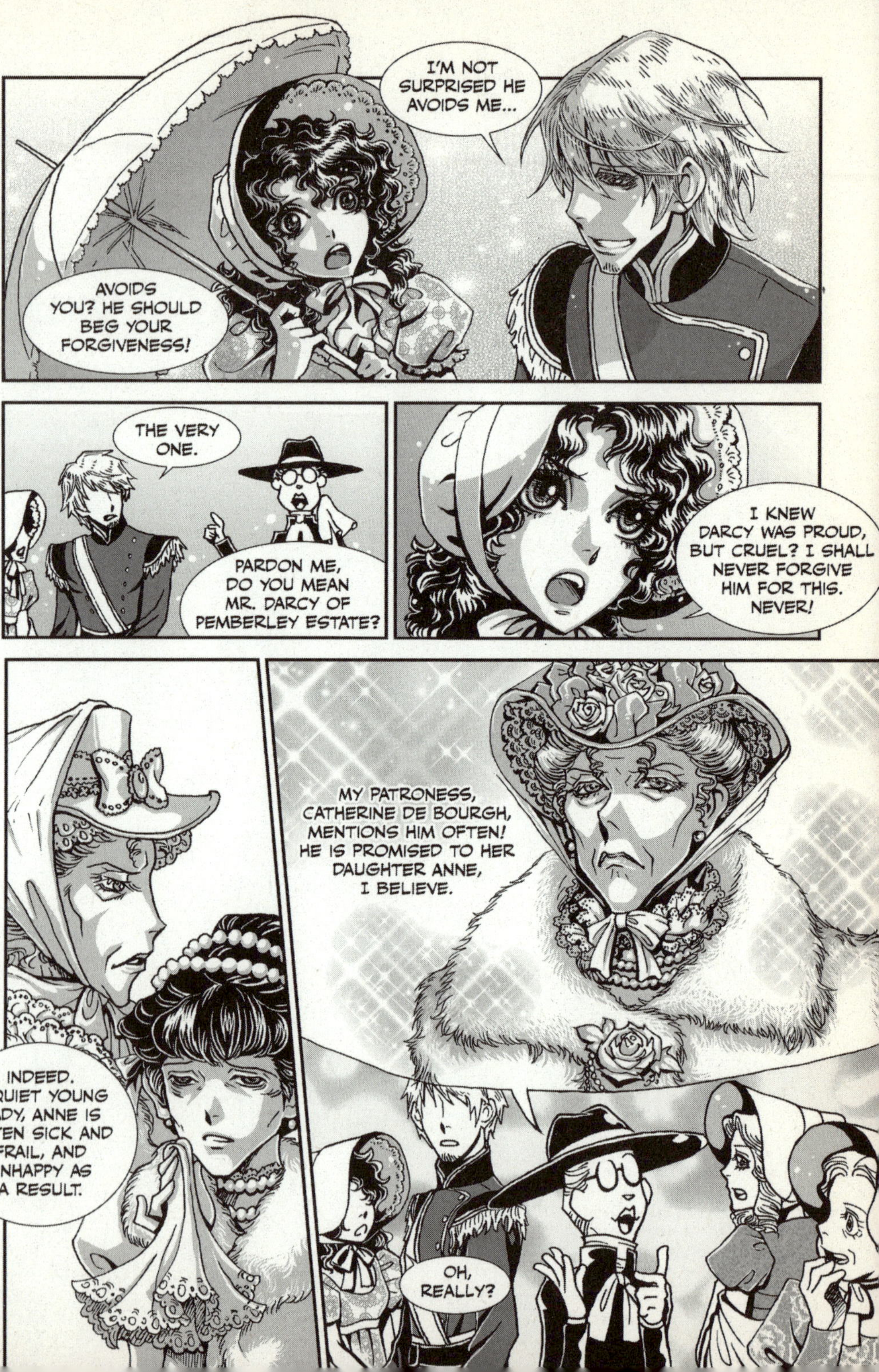
I'M NOT SURPRISED HE AVOIDS ME...
AVOIDS YOU? HE SHOULD BEG YOUR FORGIVENESS!
I KNEW DARCY WAS PROUD, BUT CRUEL? I SHALL NEVER FORGIVE HIM FOR THIS. NEVER!
PARDON ME, DO YOU MEAN MR. DARCY OF PEMBERLEY ESTATE?
THE VERY ONE.
MY PATRONESS, CATHERINE DE BOURGH, MENTIONS HIM OFTEN! HE IS PROMISED TO HER DAUGHTER ANNE, I BELIEVE.
OH, REALLY?
INDEED. A QUIET YOUNG LADY, ANNE IS OFTEN SICK AND FRAIL, AND UNHAPPY AS A RESULT.

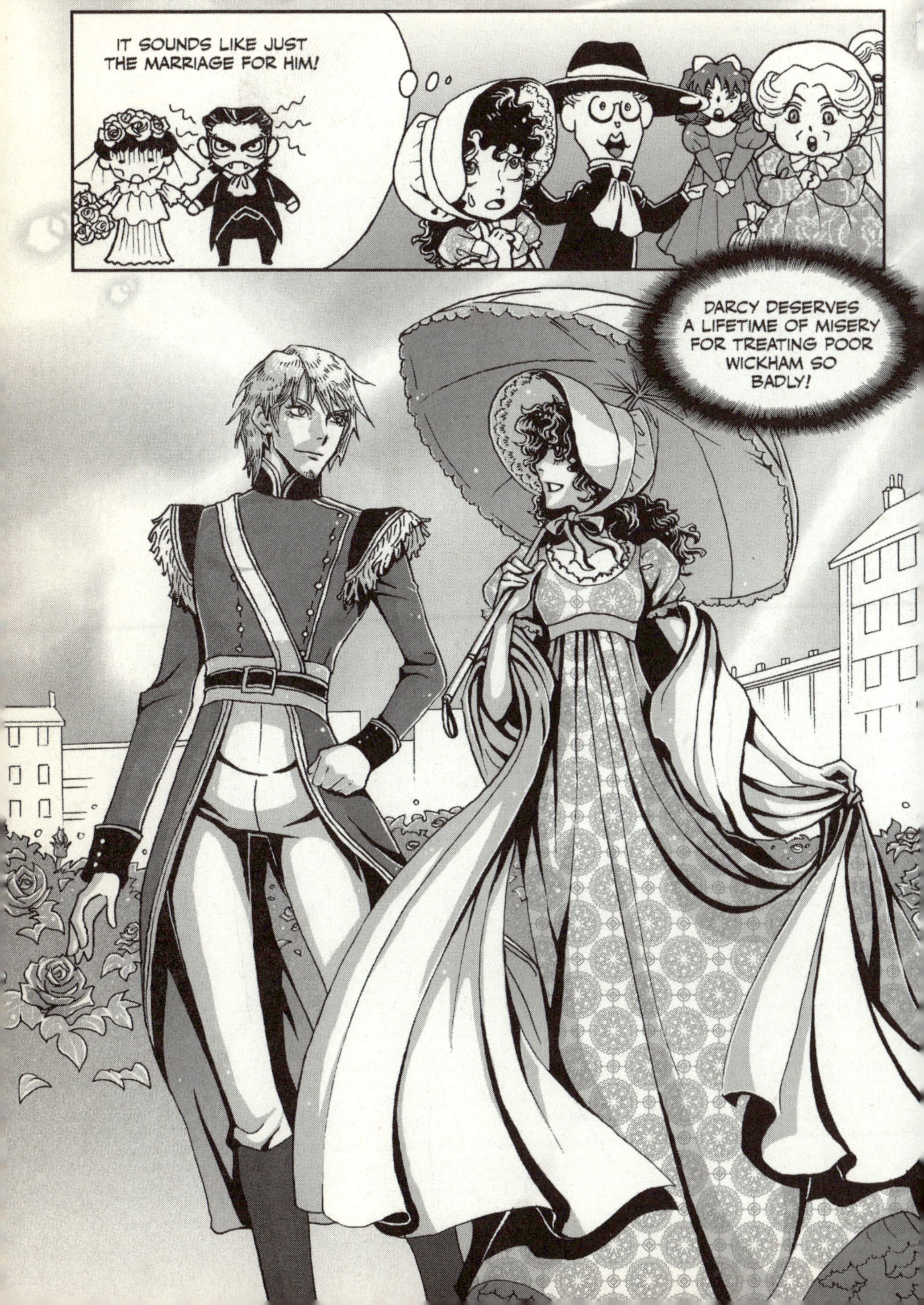
IT SOUNDS LIKE JUST THE MARRIAGE FOR HIM!
DARCY DESERVES A LIFETIME OF MISERY FOR TREATING POOR WICKHAM SO BADLY!

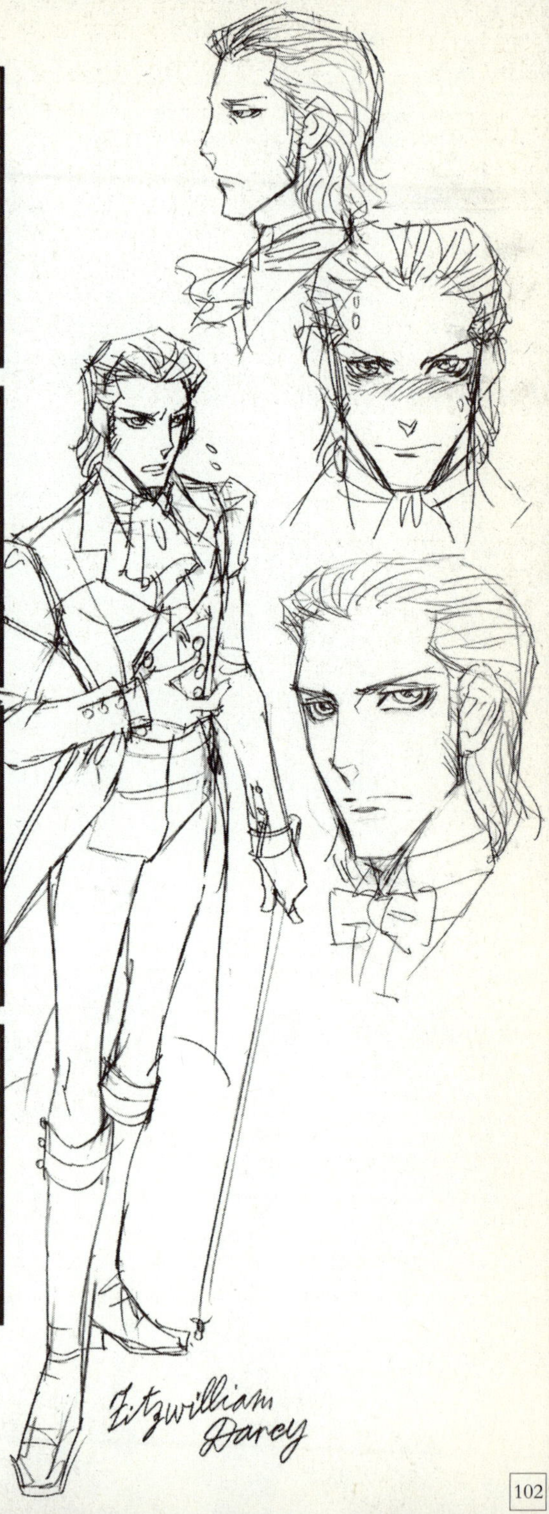
Fitzwilliam Darcy

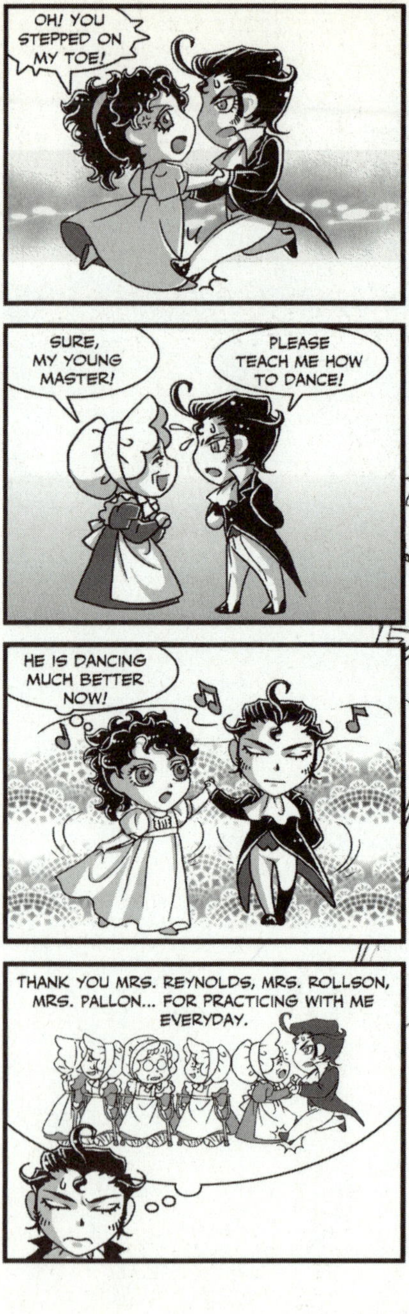
OH! YOU STEPPED ON MY TOE!
SURE, MY YOUNG MASTER!
PLEASE TEACH ME HOW TO DANCE!
HE IS DANCING MUCH BETTER NOW!
THANK YOU MRS. REYNOLDS, MRS. ROLLSON, MRS. PALLON... FOR PRACTICING WITH ME EVERYDAY.

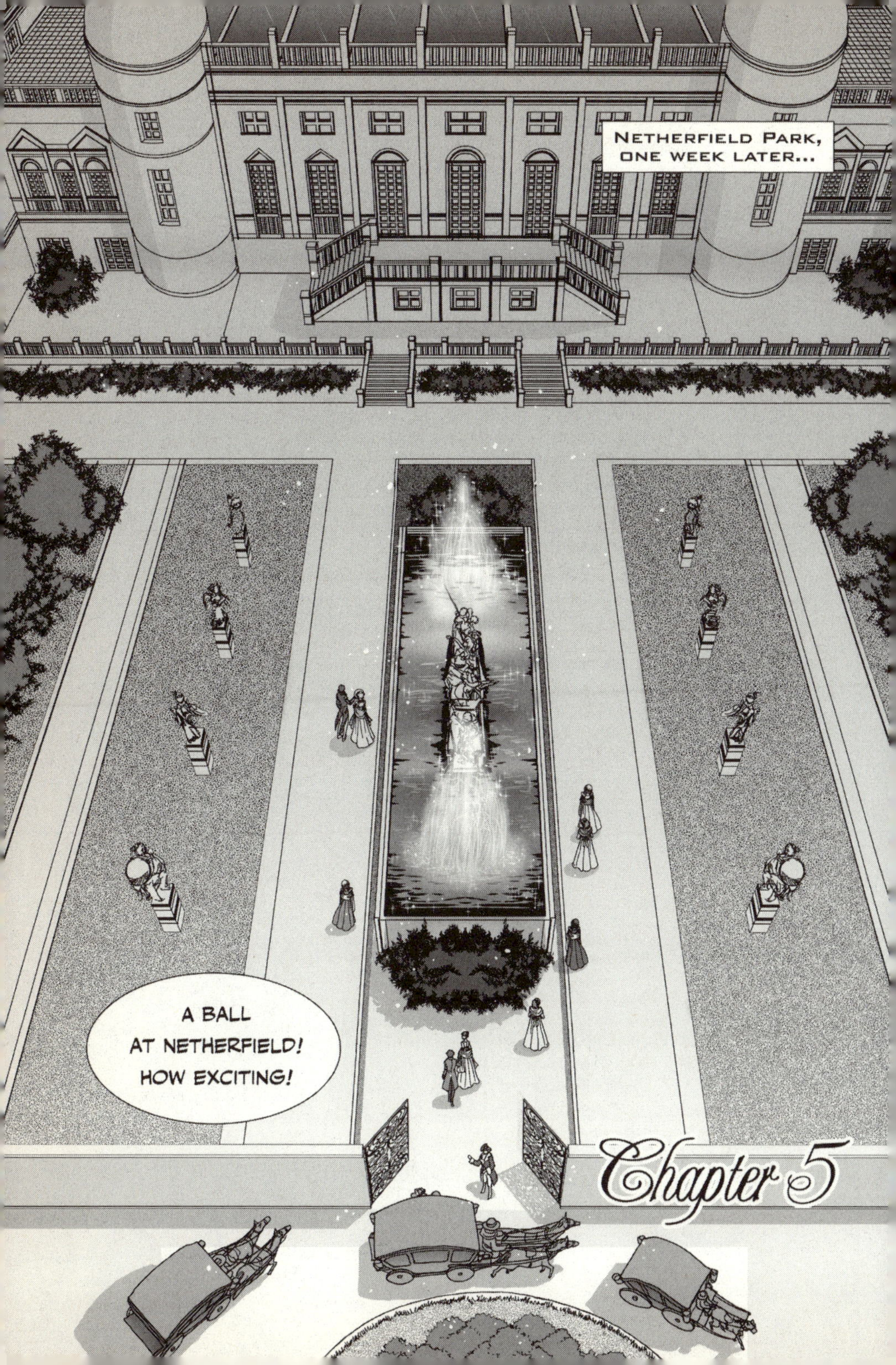
Netherfield Park, one week later...
A ball at Netherfield! How exciting!
Chapter 5

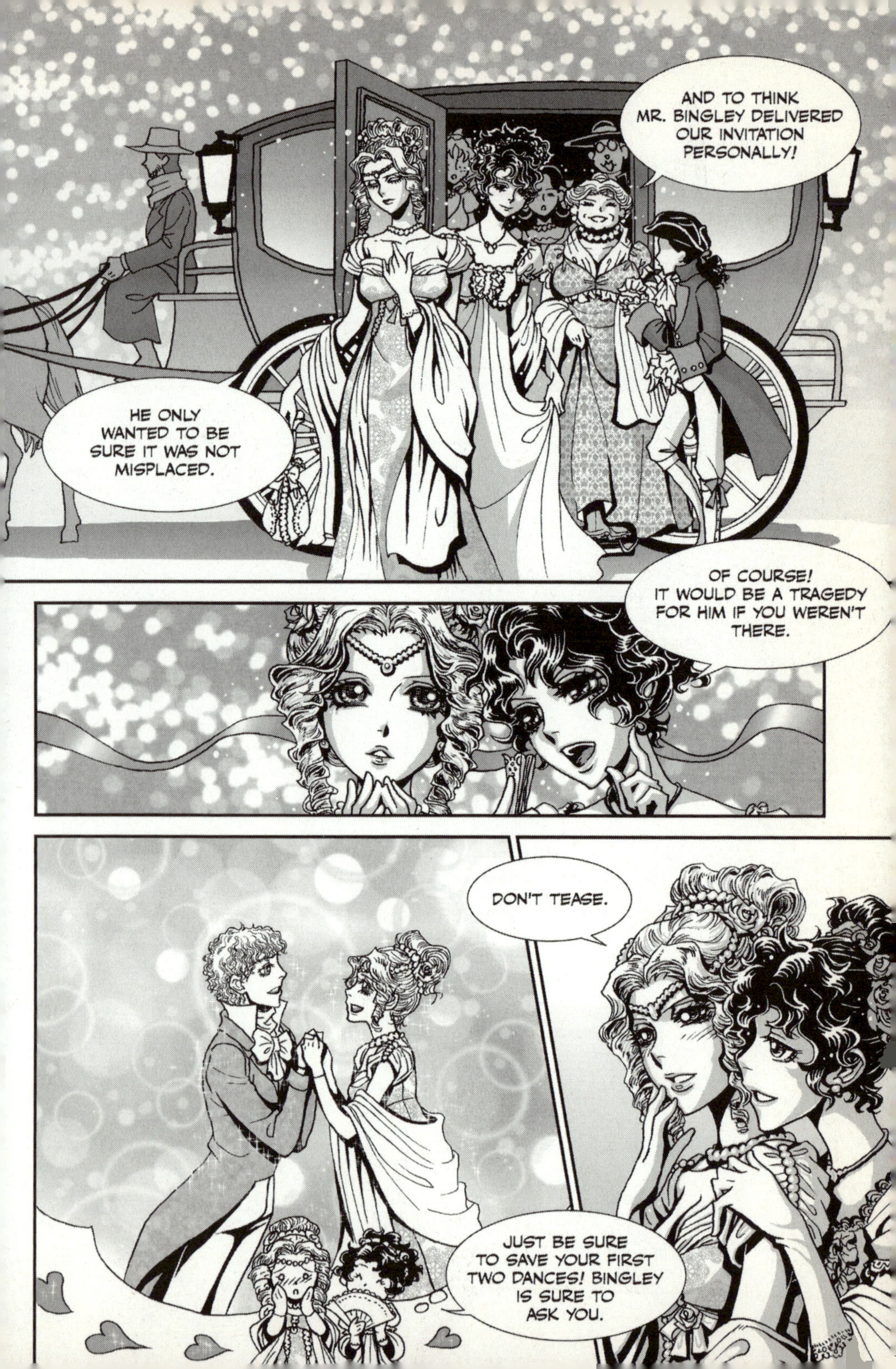
AND TO THINK MR. BINGLEY DELIVERED OUR INVITATION PERSONALLY!
HE ONLY WANTED TO BE SURE IT WAS NOT MISPLACED.
OF COURSE! IT WOULD BE A TRAGEDY FOR HIM IF YOU WEREN'T THERE.
DON'T TEASE.
JUST BE SURE TO SAVE YOUR FIRST TWO DANCES! BINGLEY IS SURE TO ASK YOU.

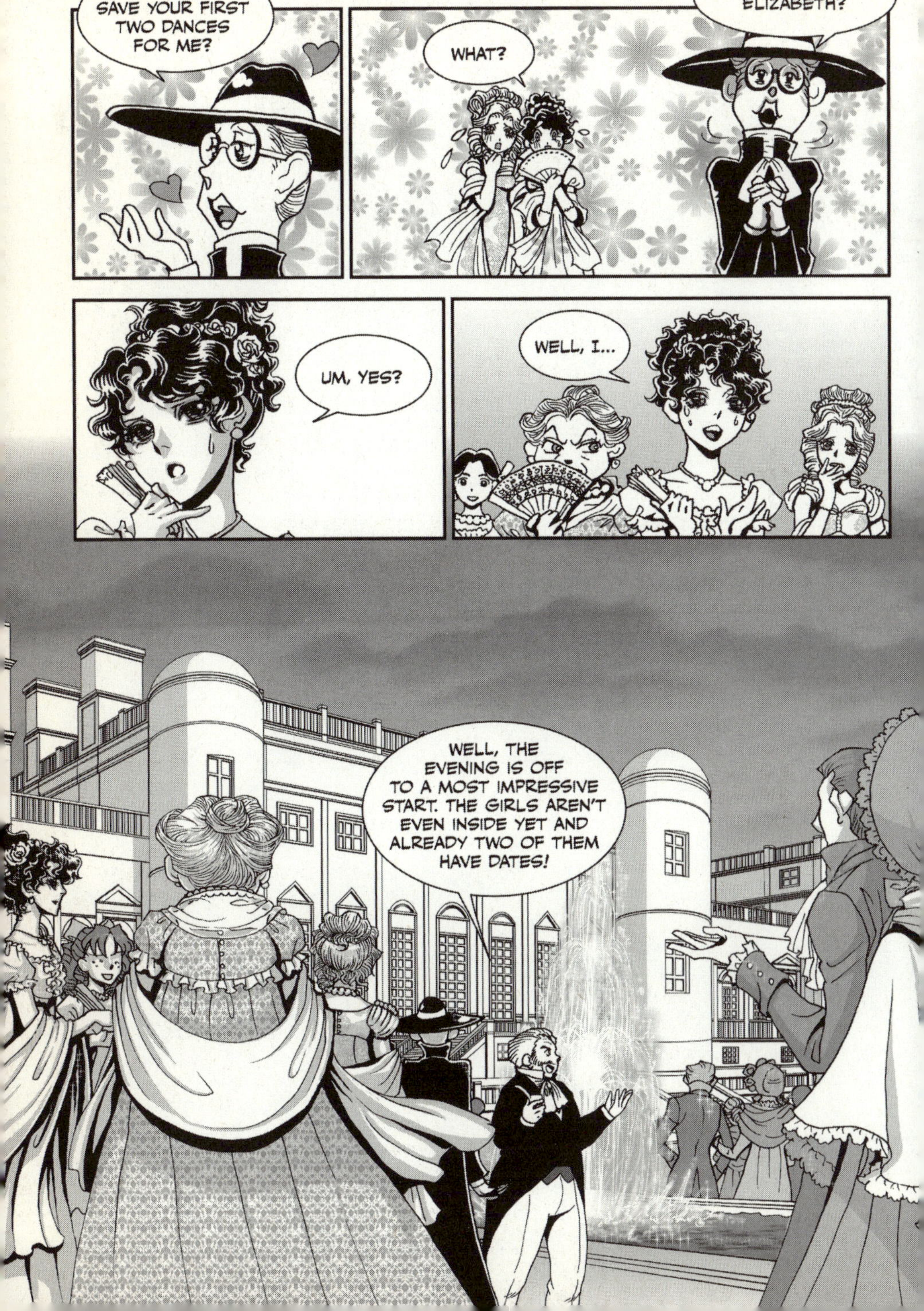
WILL YOU SAVE YOUR FIRST TWO DANCES FOR ME?
WHAT?
AND YOU, ELIZABETH?
UM, YES?
WELL, I...
WELL, THE EVENING IS OFF TO A MOST IMPRESSIVE START. THE GIRLS AREN'T EVEN INSIDE YET AND ALREADY TWO OF THEM HAVE DATES!

DARN COLLINS! HE CAUGHT ME OFF-GUARD. I MEANT TO SAVE THOSE DANCES FOR WICKHAM.
SPEAKING OF WICKHAM, I WONDER WHERE HE IS...?

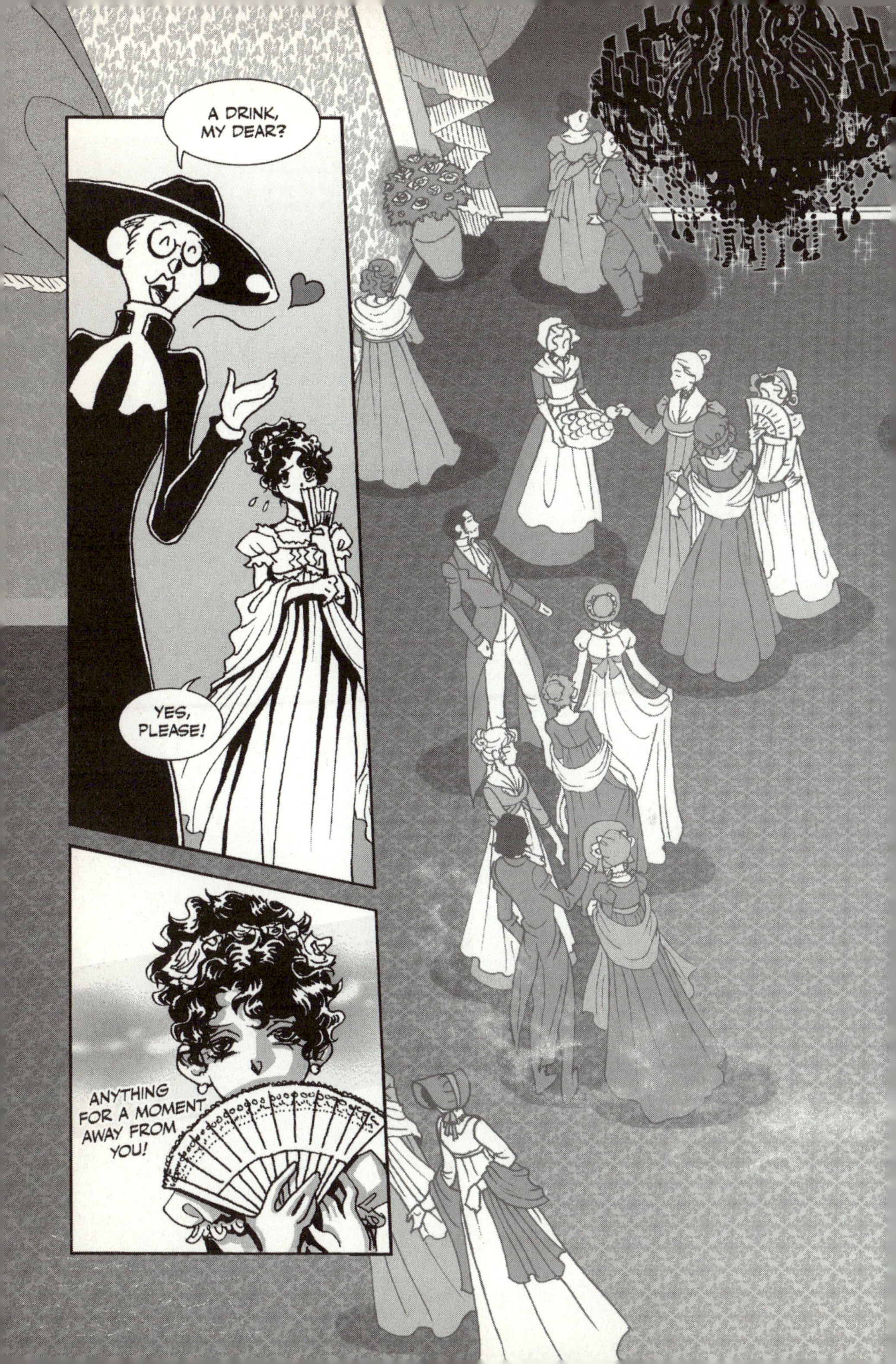
A DRINK, MY DEAR?
YES, PLEASE!
ANYTHING FOR A MOMENT AWAY FROM YOU!

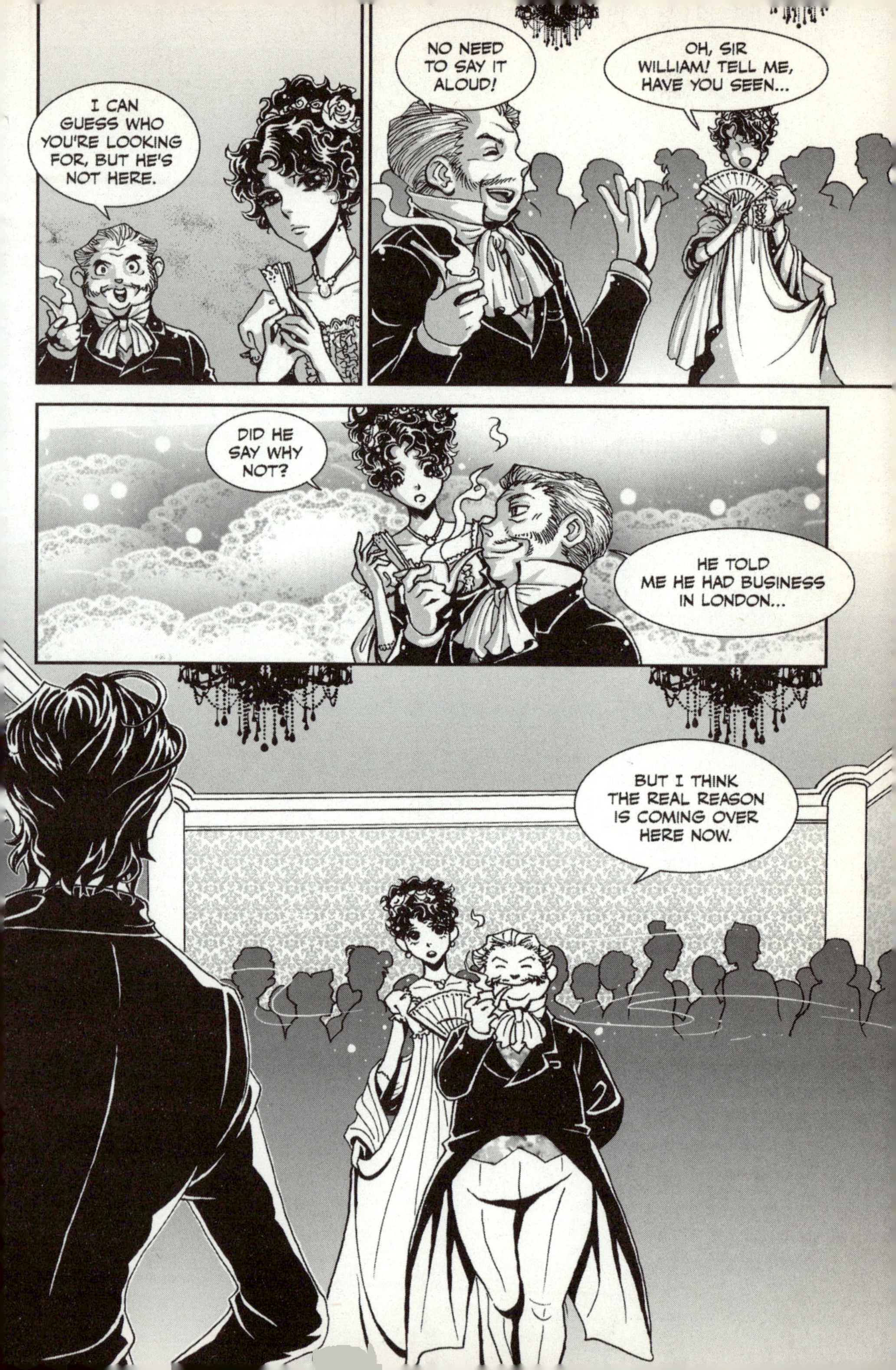
OH, SIR WILLIAM! TELL ME, HAVE YOU SEEN...
NO NEED TO SAY IT ALOUD!
I CAN GUESS WHO YOU'RE LOOKING FOR, BUT HE'S NOT HERE.
DID HE SAY WHY NOT?
HE TOLD ME HE HAD BUSINESS IN LONDON...
BUT I THINK THE REAL REASON IS COMING OVER HERE NOW.

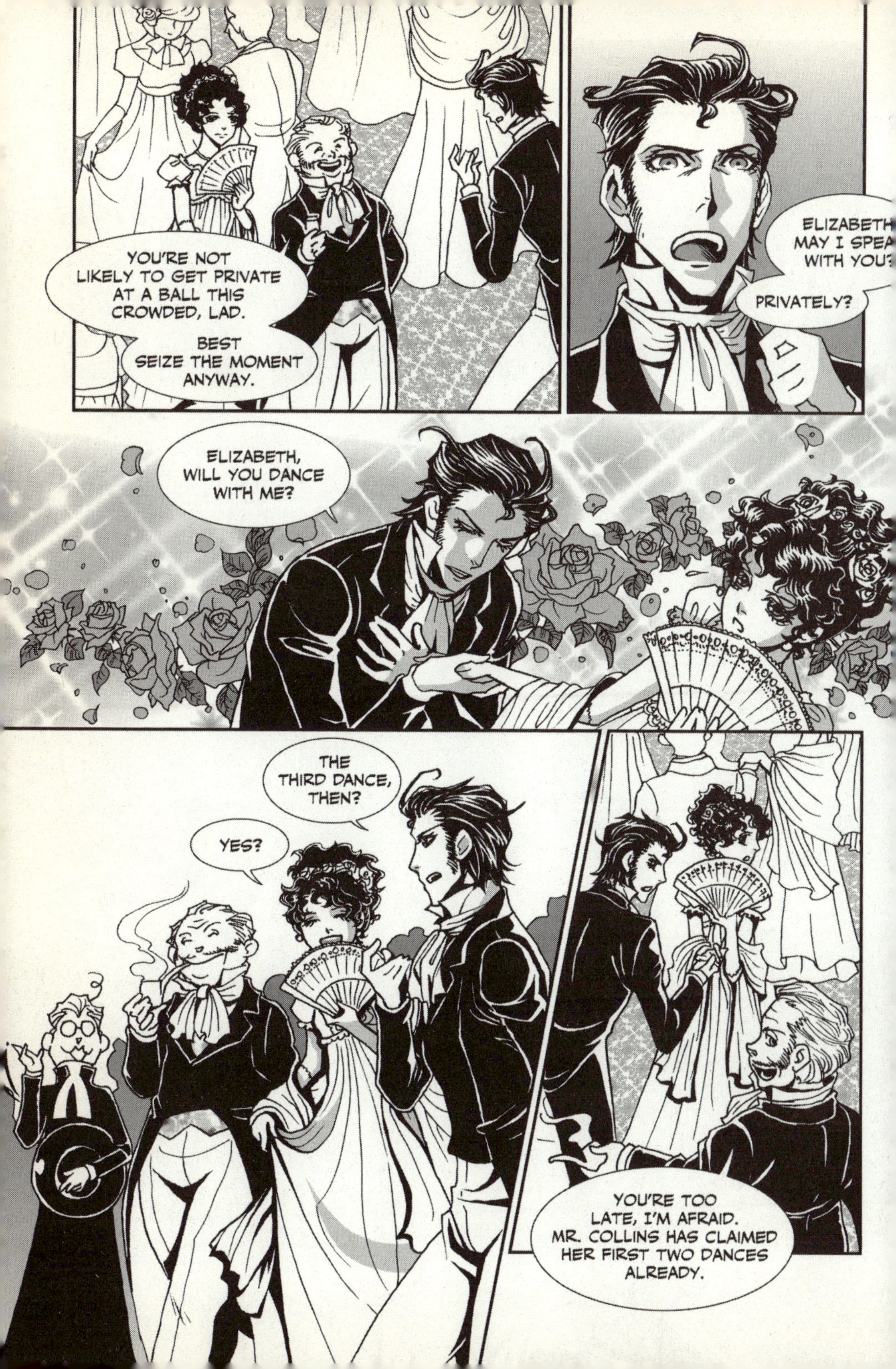
ELIZABETH MAY I SPEA WITH YOU?
PRIVATELY?
YOU'RE NOT LIKELY TO GET PRIVATE AT A BALL THIS CROWDED, LAD.
BEST SEIZE THE MOMENT ANYWAY.
ELIZABETH, WILL YOU DANCE WITH ME?
YOU'RE TOO LATE, I'M AFRAID. MR. COLLINS HAS CLAIMED HER FIRST TWO DANCES ALREADY.
THE THIRD DANCE, THEN?
YES?

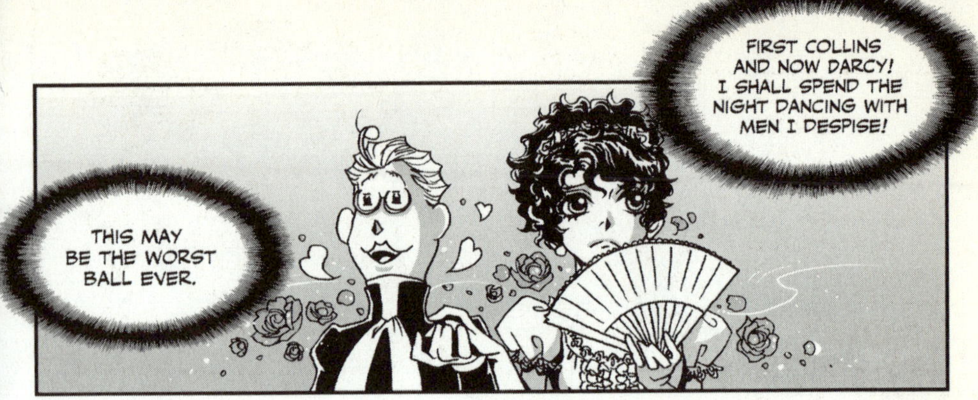
FIRST COLLINS AND NOW DARCY! I SHALL SPEND THE NIGHT DANCING WITH MEN I DESPISE!
THIS MAY BE THE WORST BALL EVER.
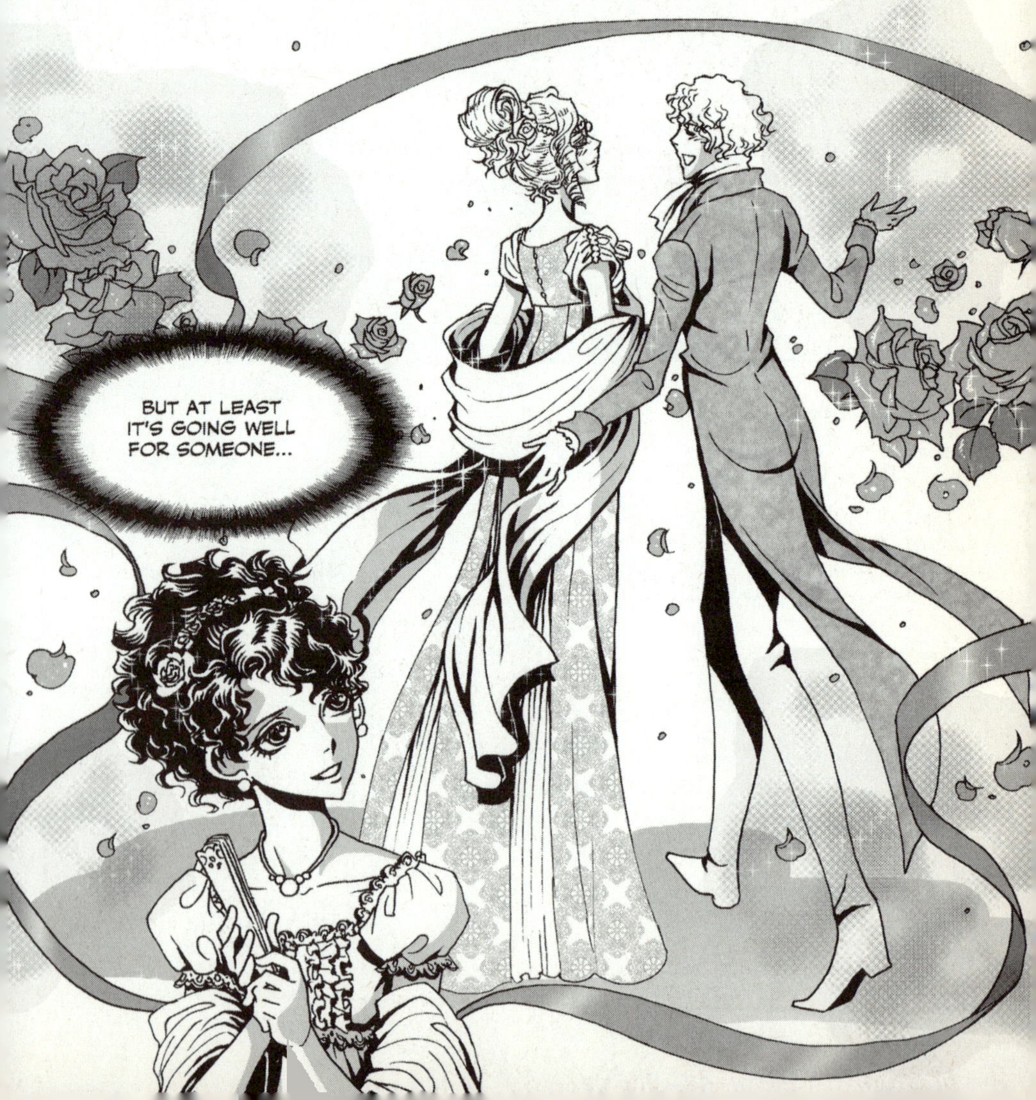
BUT AT LEAST IT'S GOING WELL FOR SOMEONE...

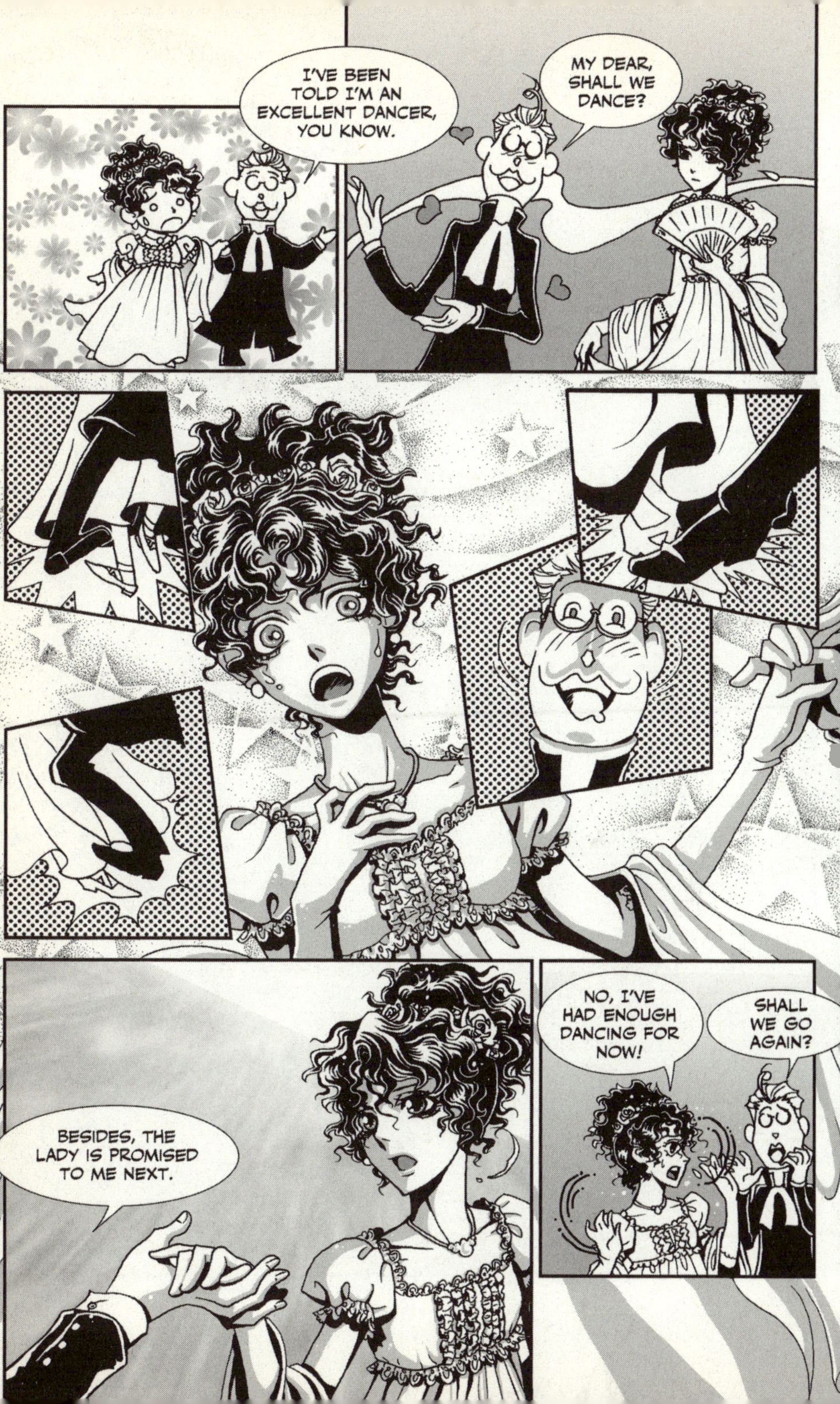
MY DEAR, SHALL WE DANCE?
I'VE BEEN TOLD I'M AN EXCELLENT DANCER, YOU KNOW.
SHALL WE GO AGAIN?
NO, I'VE HAD ENOUGH DANCING FOR NOW!
BESIDES, THE LADY IS PROMISED TO ME NEXT.

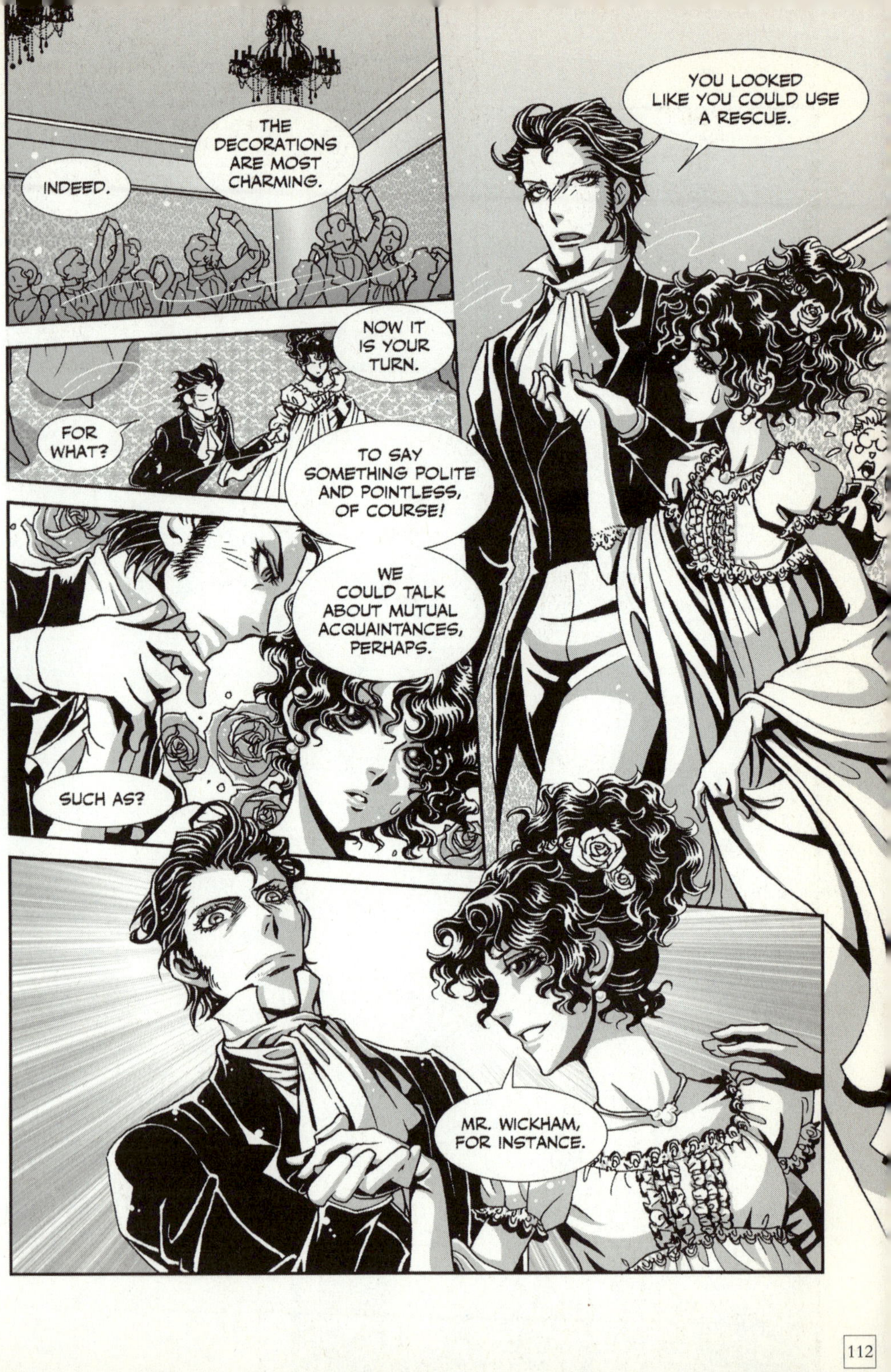
YOU LOOKED LIKE YOU COULD USE A RESCUE.
THE DECORATIONS ARE MOST CHARMING.
INDEED.
NOW IT IS YOUR TURN.
FOR WHAT?
TO SAY SOMETHING POLITE AND POINTLESS, OF COURSE!
WE COULD TALK ABOUT MUTUAL ACQUAINTANCES, PERHAPS.
SUCH AS?
MR. WICKHAM, FOR INSTANCE.

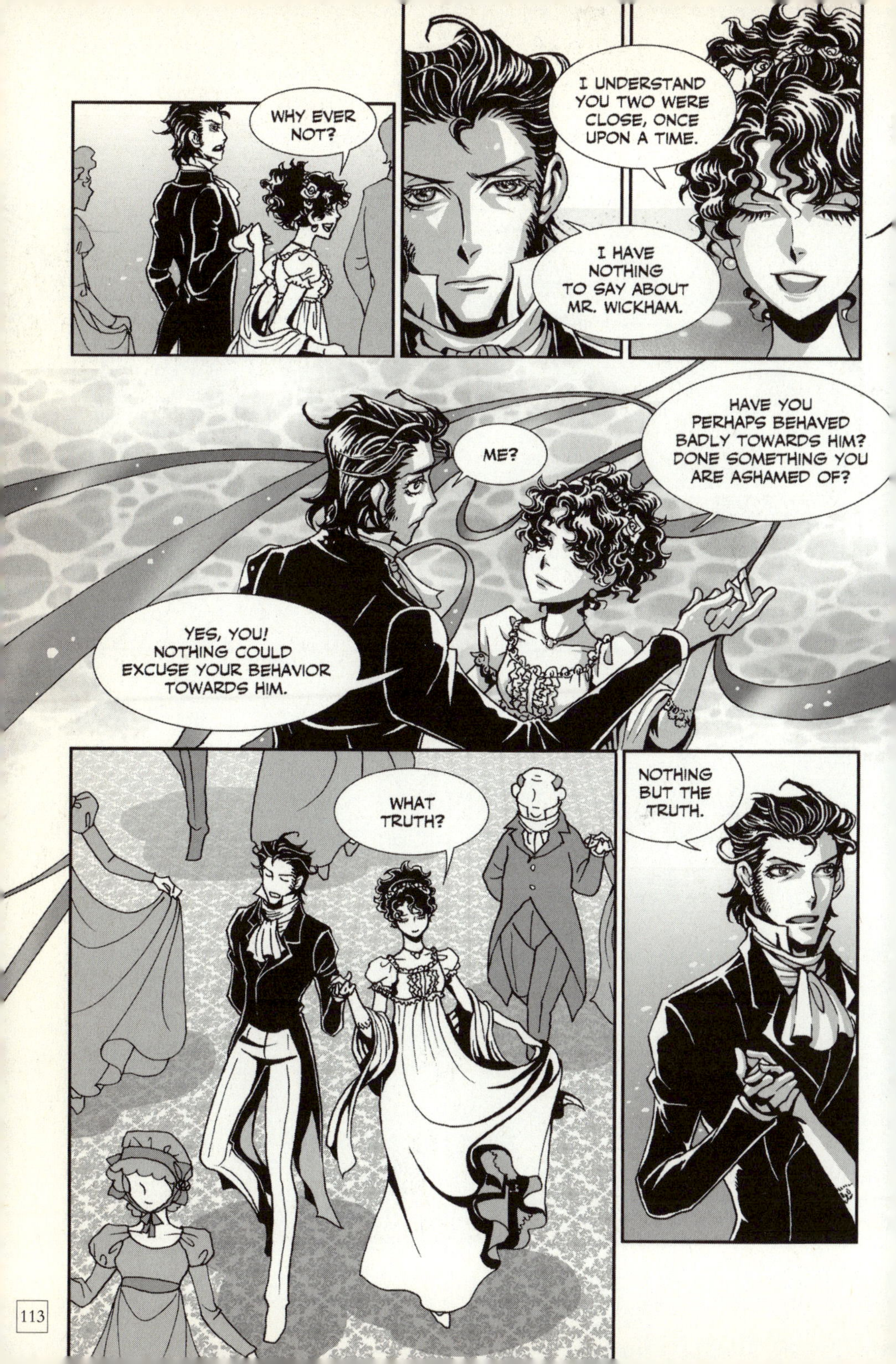
I UNDERSTAND YOU TWO WERE CLOSE, ONCE UPON A TIME.
I HAVE NOTHING TO SAY ABOUT MR. WICKHAM.
WHY EVER NOT?
HAVE YOU PERHAPS BEHAVED BADLY TOWARDS HIM? DONE SOMETHING YOU ARE ASHAMED OF?
ME?
YES, YOU! NOTHING COULD EXCUSE YOUR BEHAVIOR TOWARDS HIM.
NOTHING BUT THE TRUTH.
WHAT TRUTH?

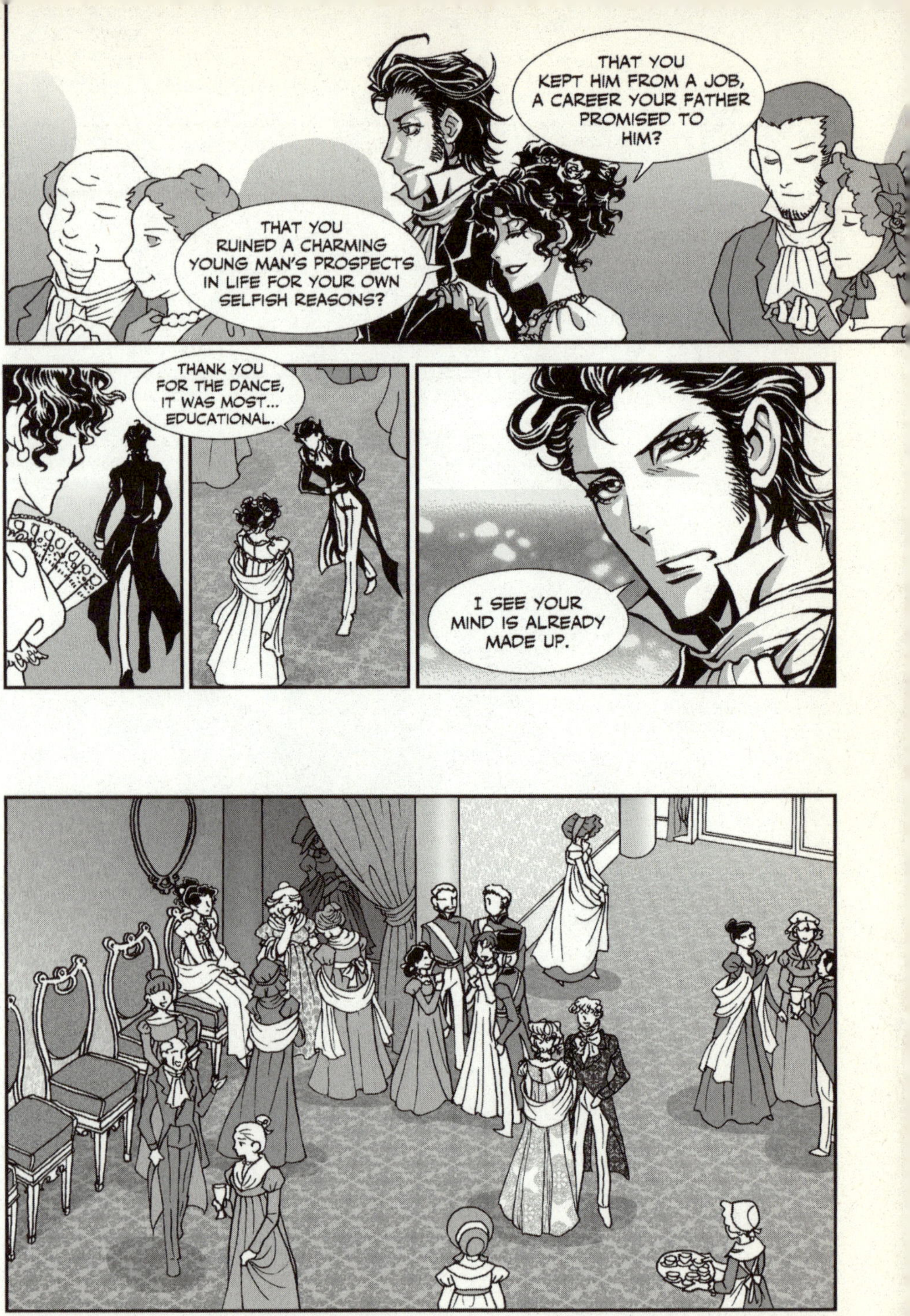
THAT YOU KEPT HIM FROM A JOB, A CAREER YOUR FATHER PROMISED TO HIM?
THAT YOU RUINED A CHARMING YOUNG MAN'S PROSPECTS IN LIFE FOR YOUR OWN SELFISH REASONS?
I SEE YOUR MIND IS ALREADY MADE UP.
THANK YOU FOR THE DANCE, IT WAS MOST... EDUCATIONAL.

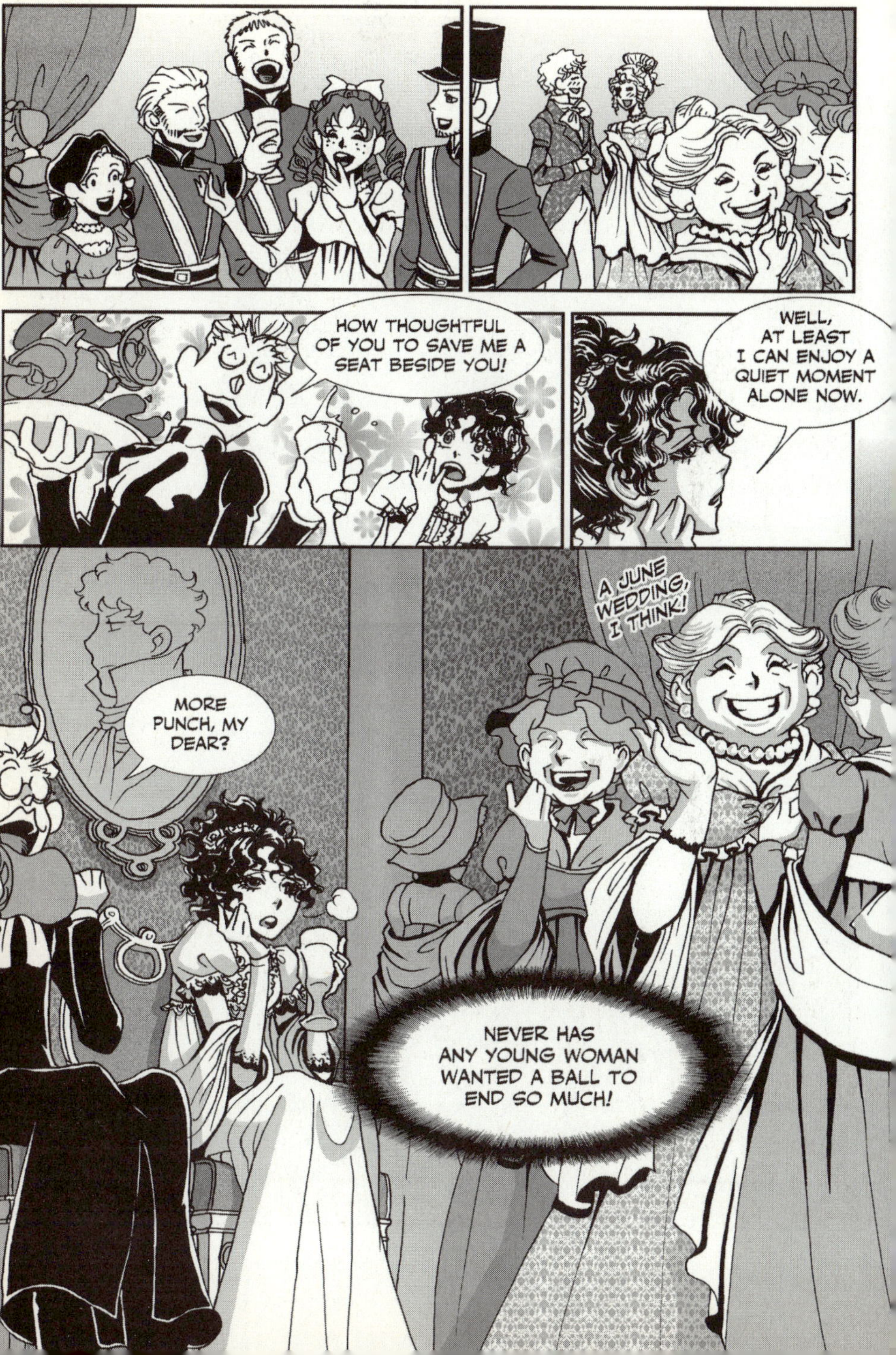
WELL, AT LEAST I CAN ENJOY A QUIET MOMENT ALONE NOW.
HOW THOUGHTFUL OF YOU TO SAVE ME A SEAT BESIDE YOU!
A JUNE WEDDING, I THINK!
MORE PUNCH, MY DEAR?
NEVER HAS ANY YOUNG WOMAN WANTED A BALL TO END SO MUCH!

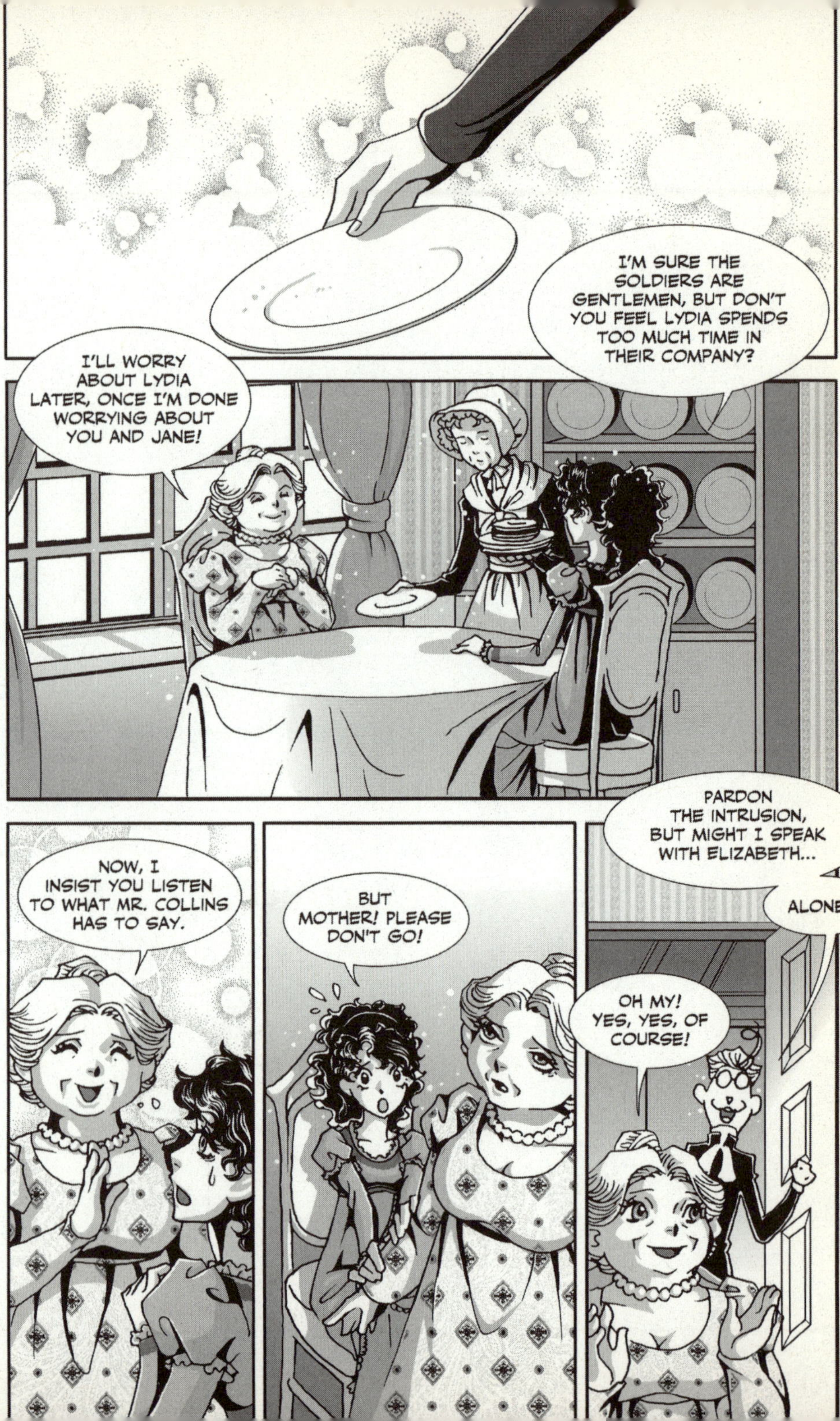
I'M SURE THE SOLDIERS ARE GENTLEMEN, BUT DON'T YOU FEEL LYDIA SPENDS TOO MUCH TIME IN THEIR COMPANY?
I'LL WORRY ABOUT LYDIA LATER, ONCE I'M DONE WORRYING ABOUT YOU AND JANE!
PARDON THE INTRUSION, BUT MIGHT I SPEAK WITH ELIZABETH...
ALONE?
OH MY! YES, YES, OF COURSE!
BUT MOTHER! PLEASE DON'T GO!
NOW, I INSIST YOU LISTEN TO WHAT MR. COLLINS HAS TO SAY.

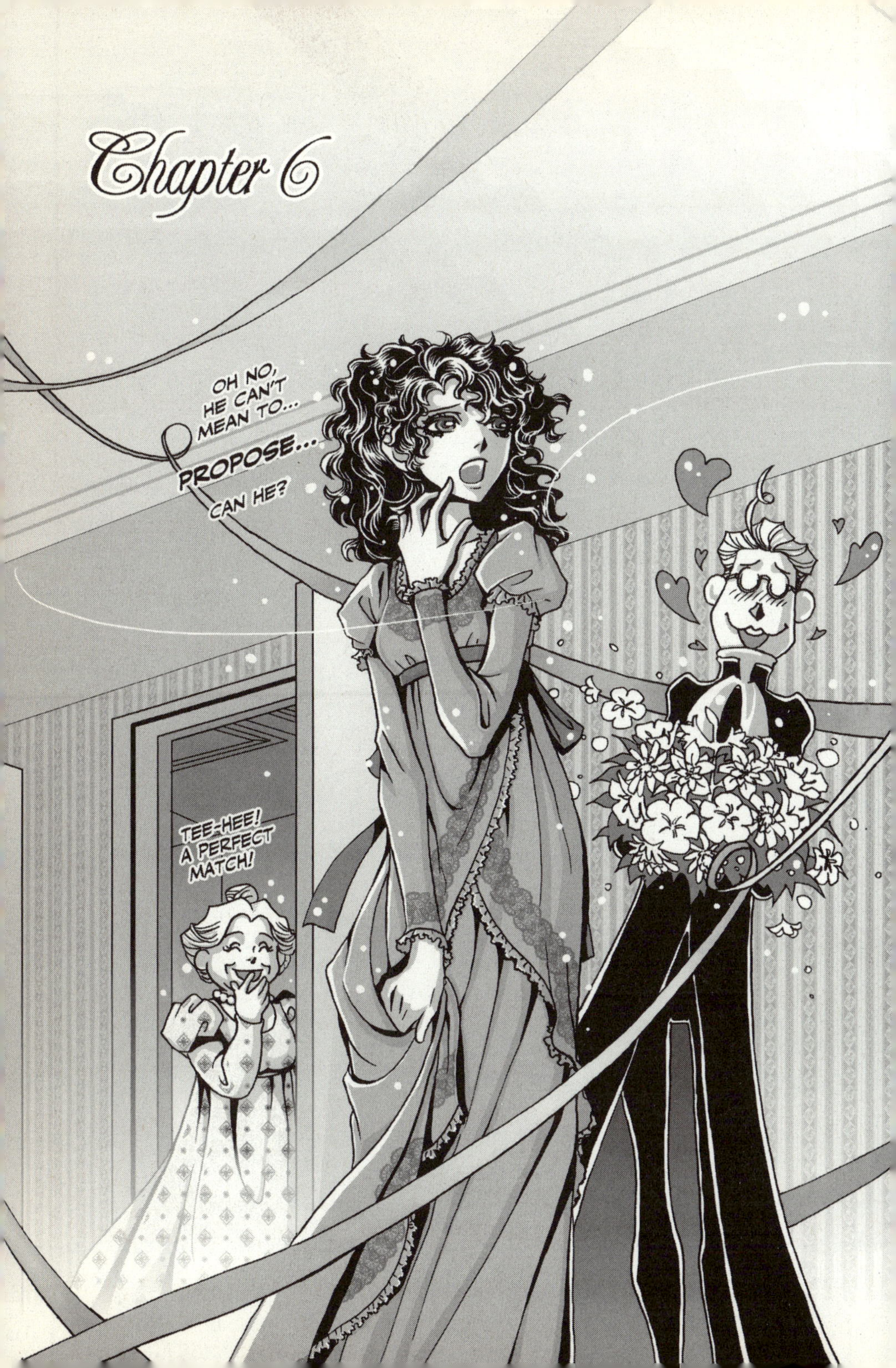
Chapter 6
OH NO, HE CAN'T MEAN TO... PROPOSE... CAN HE?
TEE-HEE! A PERFECT MATCH!

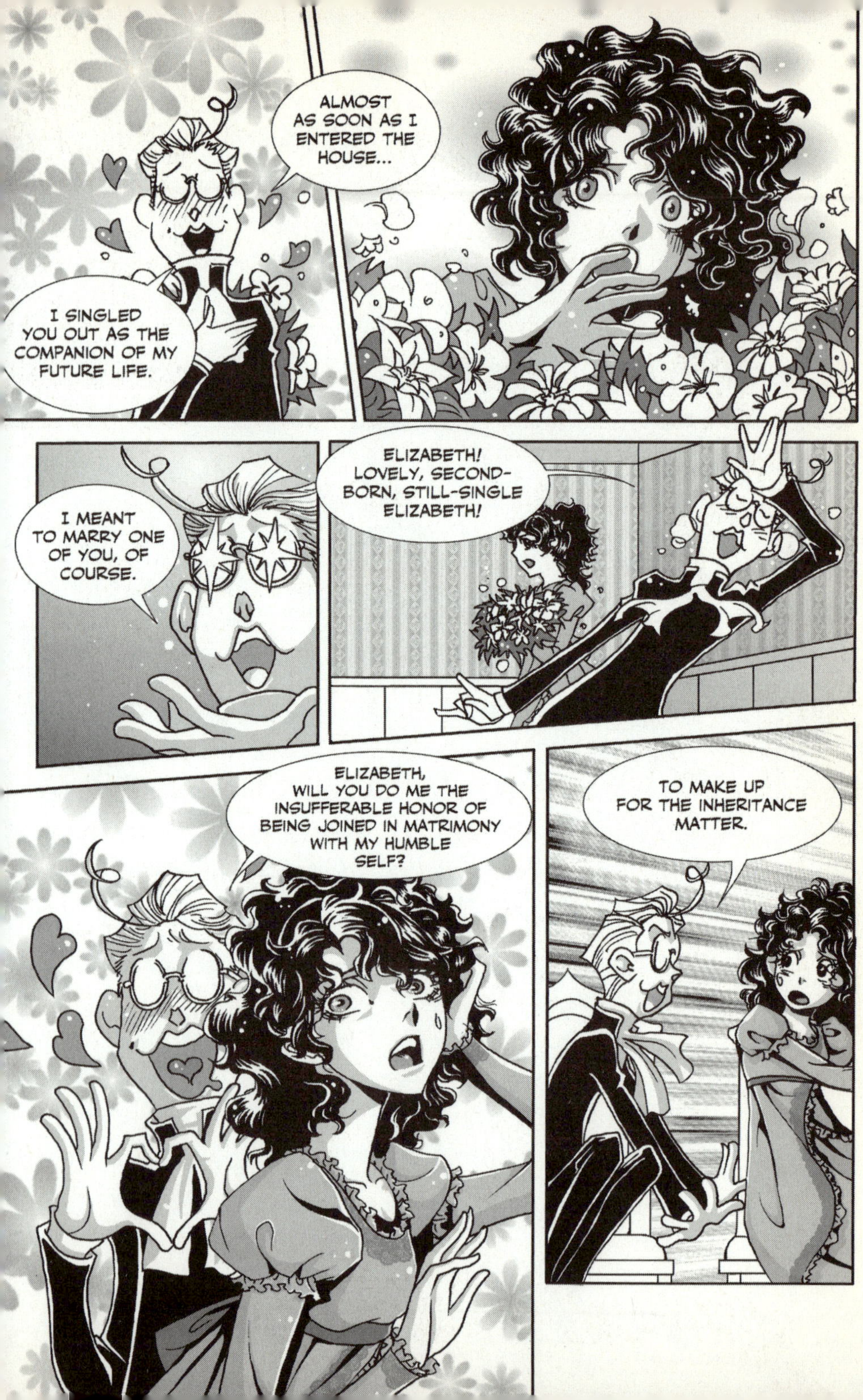
ALMOST AS SOON AS I ENTERED THE HOUSE...
I SINGLED YOU OUT AS THE COMPANION OF MY FUTURE LIFE.
ELIZABETH! LOVELY, SECOND-BORN, STILL-SINGLE ELIZABETH!
I MEANT TO MARRY ONE OF YOU, OF COURSE.
TO MAKE UP FOR THE INHERITANCE MATTER.
ELIZABETH, WILL YOU DO ME THE INSUFFERABLE HONOR OF BEING JOINED IN MATRIMONY WITH MY HUMBLE SELF?

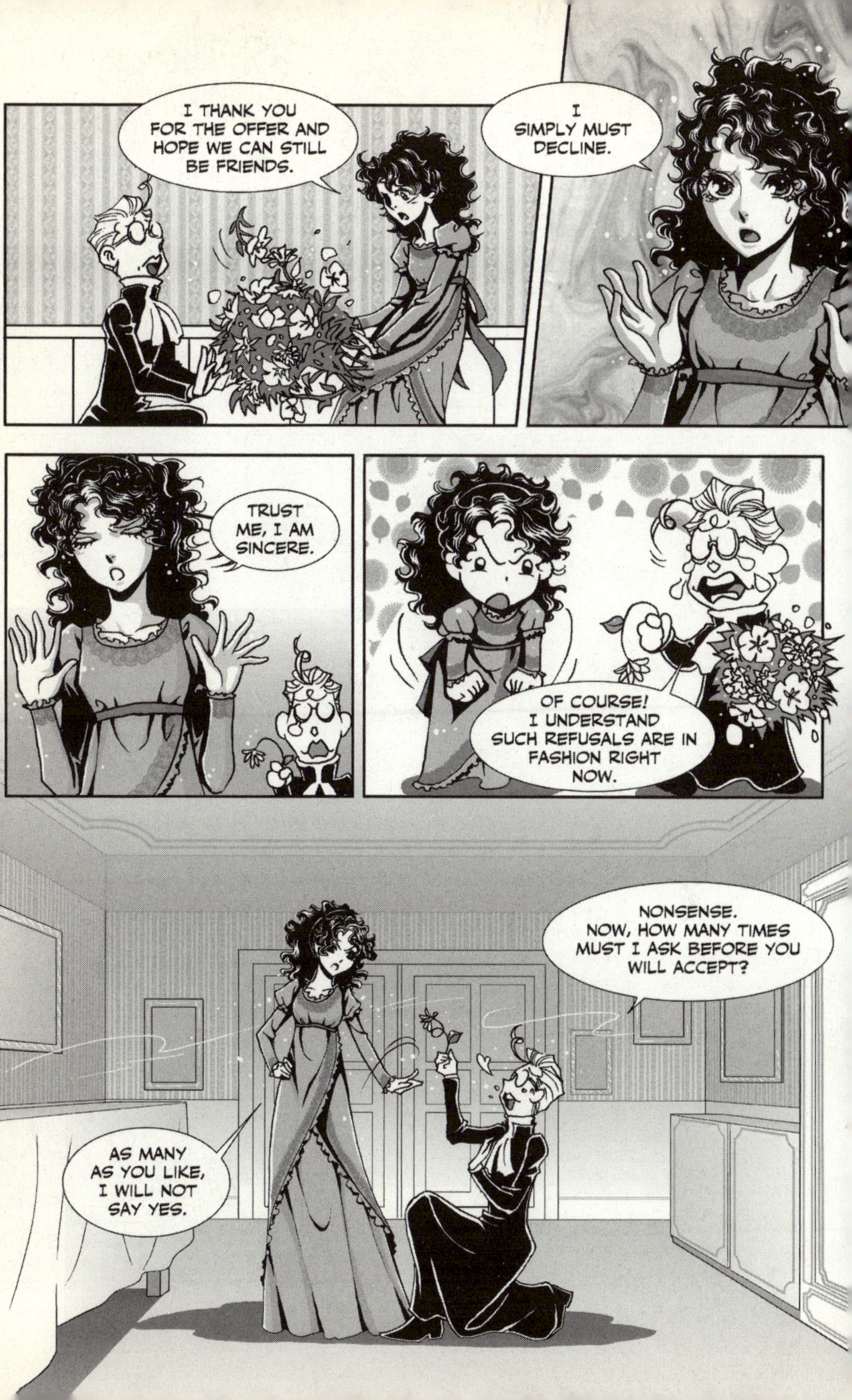

I SIMPLY MUST DECLINE.
I THANK YOU FOR THE OFFER AND HOPE WE CAN STILL BE FRIENDS.
OF COURSE! I UNDERSTAND SUCH REFUSALS ARE IN FASHION RIGHT NOW.
TRUST ME, I AM SINCERE.
NONSENSE. NOW, HOW MANY TIMES MUST I ASK BEFORE YOU WILL ACCEPT?
AS MANY AS YOU LIKE, I WILL NOT SAY YES.

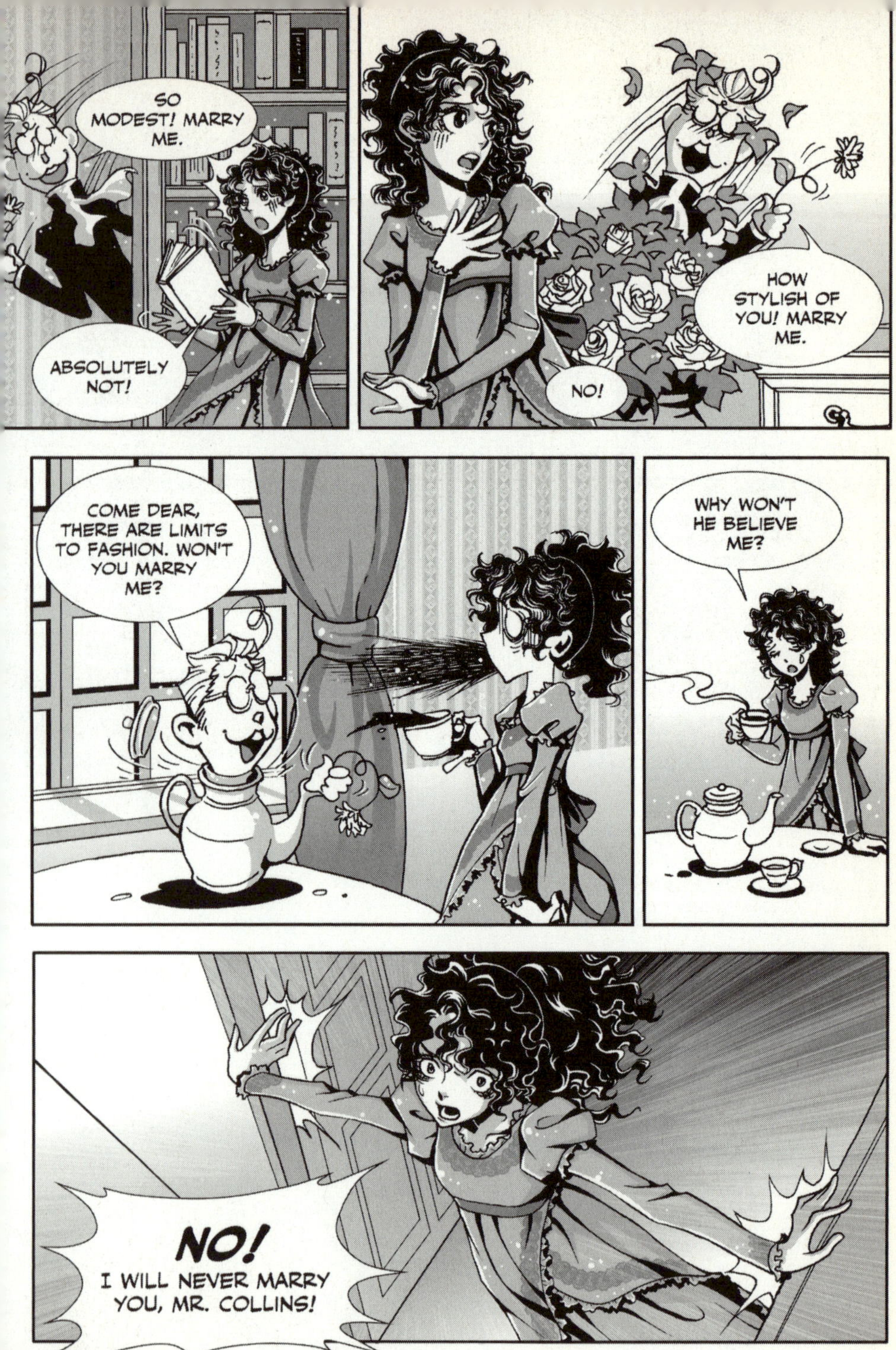
HOW STYLISH OF YOU! MARRY ME.
NO!
SO MODEST! MARRY ME.
ABSOLUTELY NOT!
WHY WON'T HE BELIEVE ME?
COME DEAR, THERE ARE LIMITS TO FASHION. WON'T YOU MARRY ME?
NO!
I WILL NEVER MARRY YOU, MR. COLLINS!

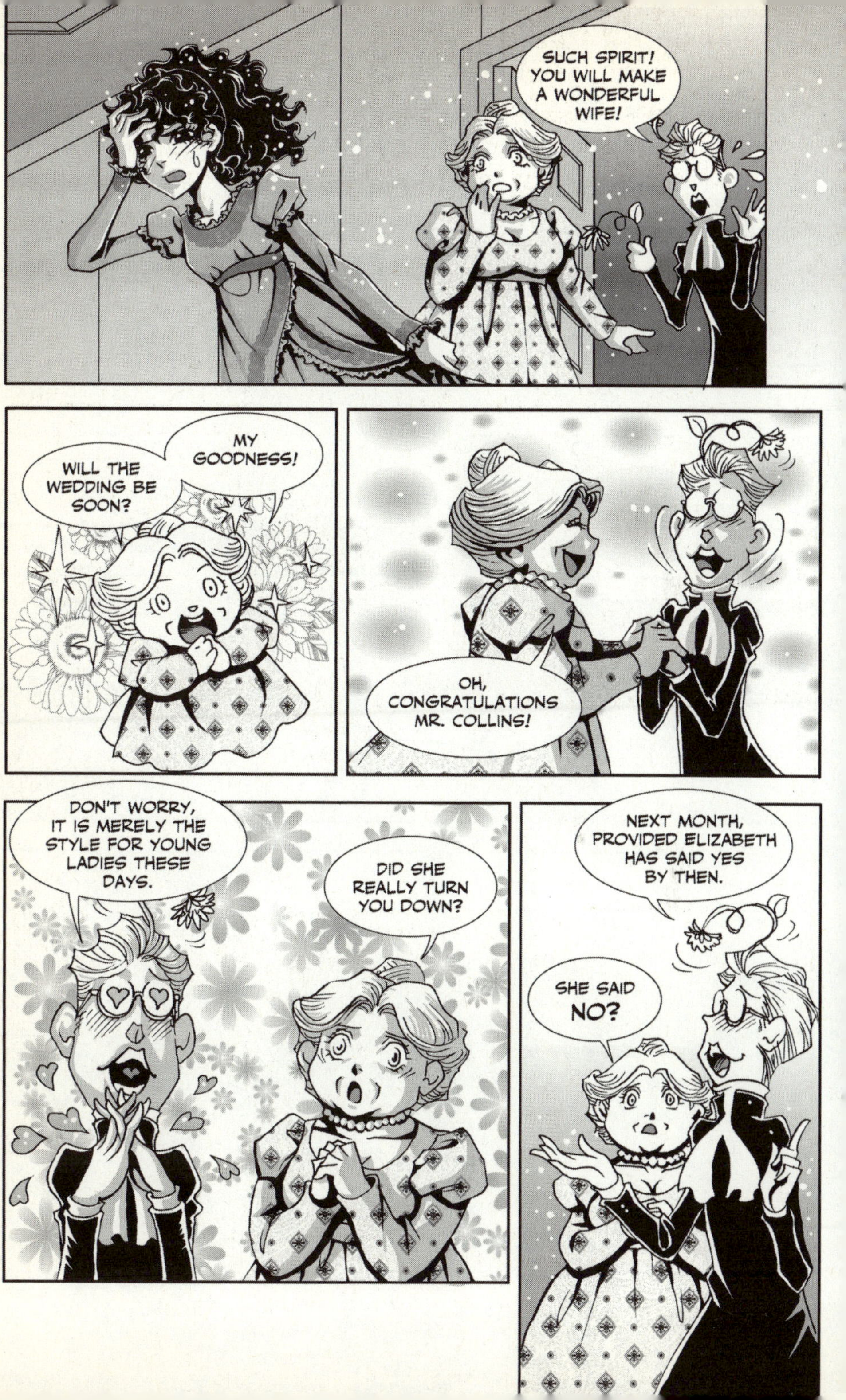
SUCH SPIRIT! YOU WILL MAKE A WONDERFUL WIFE!
OH, CONGRATULATIONS MR. COLLINS!
MY GOODNESS!
WILL THE WEDDING BE SOON?
NEXT MONTH, PROVIDED ELIZABETH HAS SAID YES BY THEN.
SHE SAID NO?
DID SHE REALLY TURN YOU DOWN?
DON'T WORRY, IT IS MERELY THE STYLE FOR YOUNG LADIES THESE DAYS.

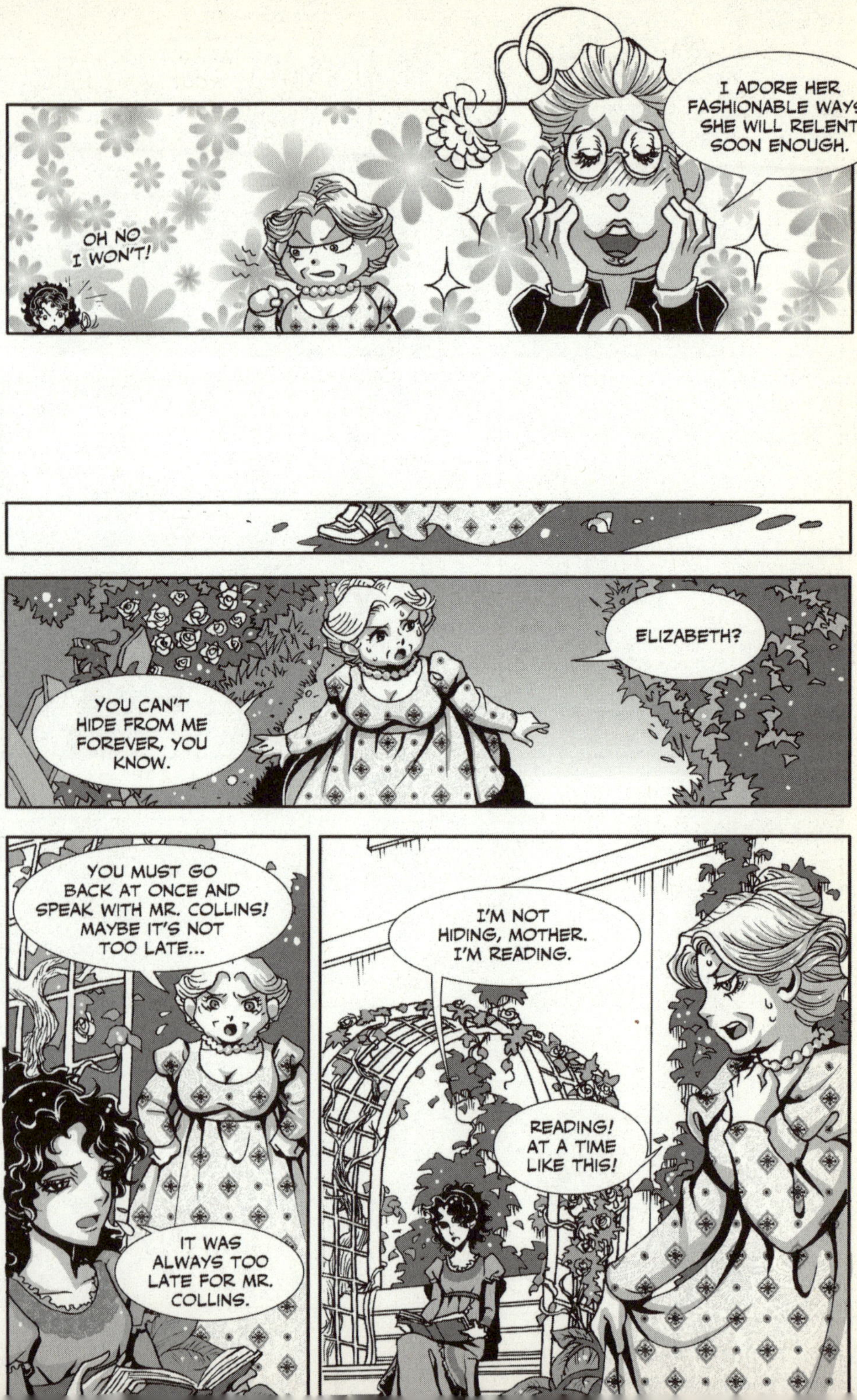
I ADORE HER FASHIONABLE WAYS! SHE WILL RELENT SOON ENOUGH.
OH NO I WON'T!
ELIZABETH?
YOU CAN'T HIDE FROM ME FOREVER, YOU KNOW.
I'M NOT HIDING, MOTHER. I'M READING.
READING! AT A TIME LIKE THIS!
YOU MUST GO BACK AT ONCE AND SPEAK WITH MR. COLLINS! MAYBE IT'S NOT TOO LATE...
IT WAS ALWAYS TOO LATE FOR MR. COLLINS.

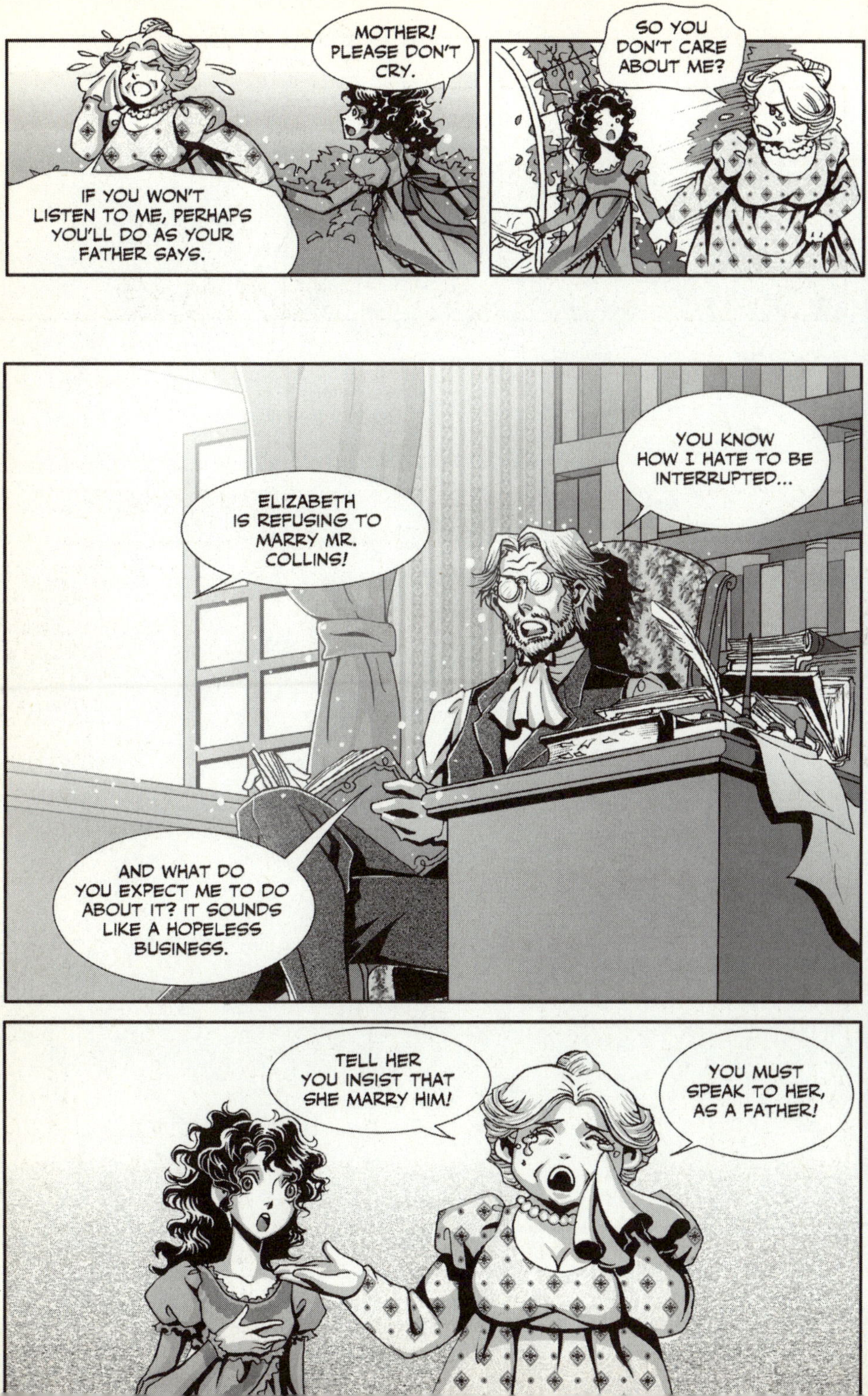
SO YOU DON'T CARE ABOUT ME?
MOTHER! PLEASE DON'T CRY.
IF YOU WON'T LISTEN TO ME, PERHAPS YOU'LL DO AS YOUR FATHER SAYS.
YOU KNOW HOW I HATE TO BE INTERRUPTED...
ELIZABETH IS REFUSING TO MARRY MR. COLLINS!
AND WHAT DO YOU EXPECT ME TO DO ABOUT IT? IT SOUNDS LIKE A HOPELESS BUSINESS.
YOU MUST SPEAK TO HER, AS A FATHER!
TELL HER YOU INSIST THAT SHE MARRY HIM!

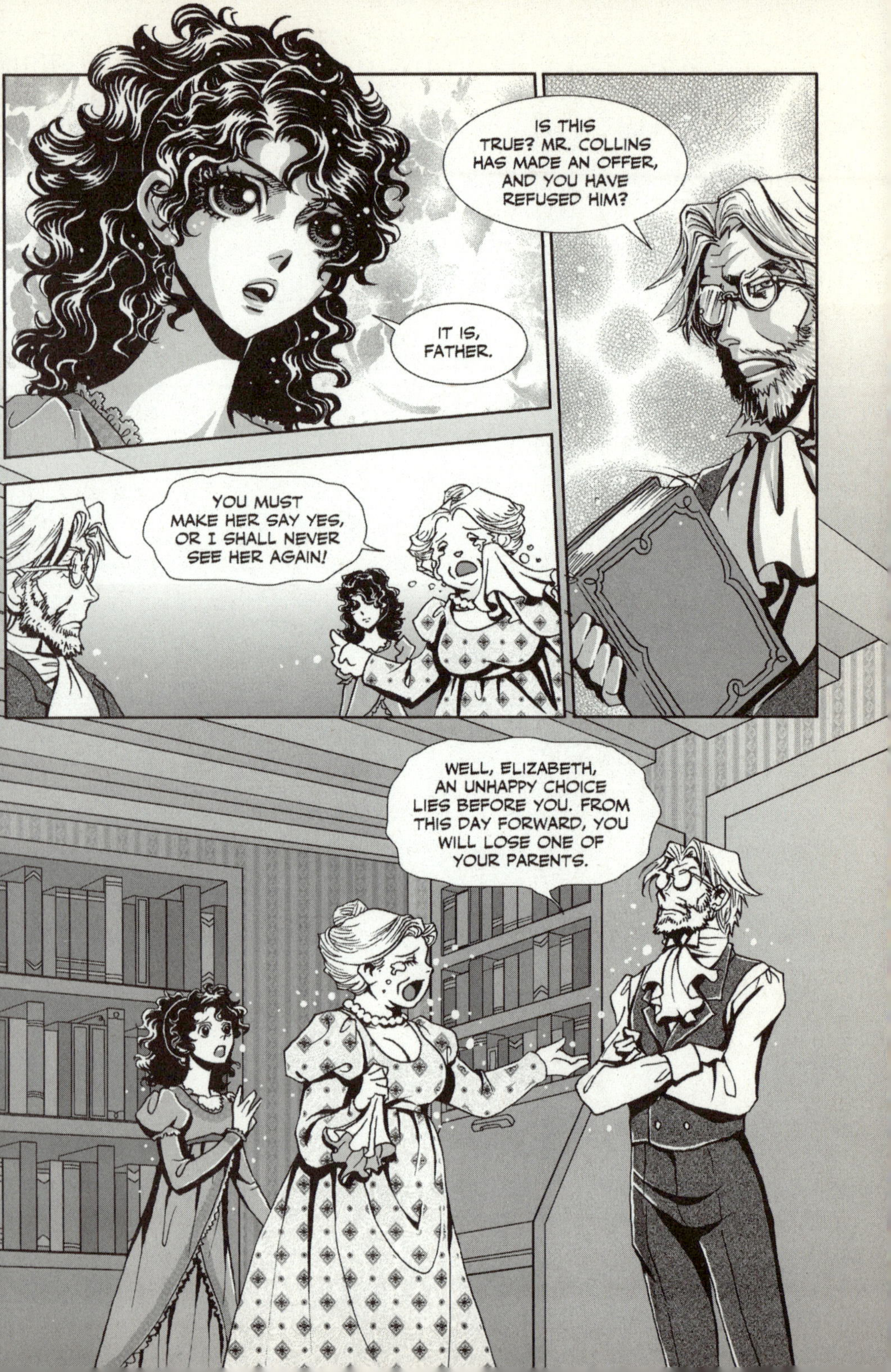
IS THIS TRUE? MR. COLLINS HAS MADE AN OFFER, AND YOU HAVE REFUSED HIM?
IT IS, FATHER.
YOU MUST MAKE HER SAY YES, OR I SHALL NEVER SEE HER AGAIN!
WELL, ELIZABETH, AN UNHAPPY CHOICE LIES BEFORE YOU. FROM THIS DAY FORWARD, YOU WILL LOSE ONE OF YOUR PARENTS.

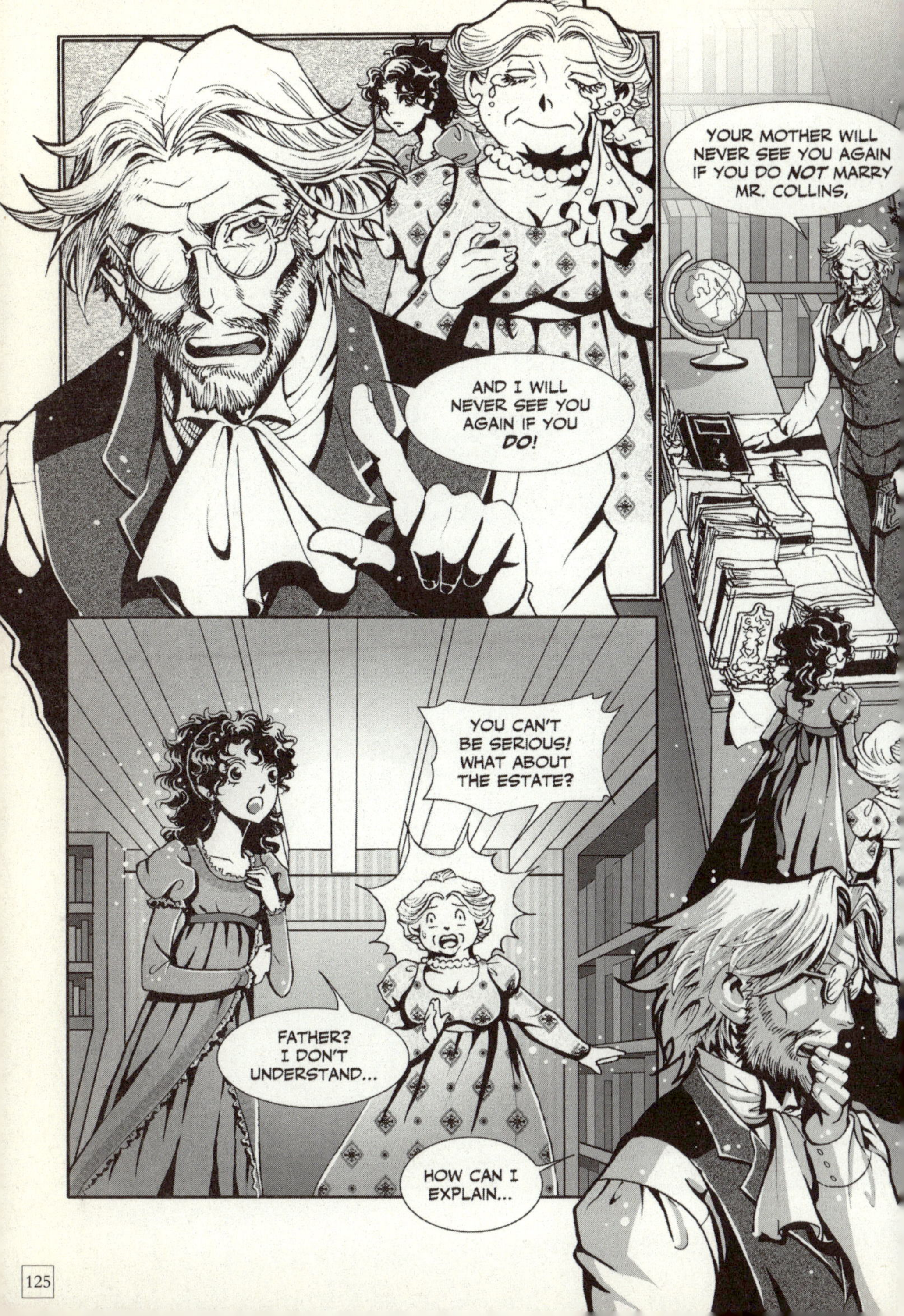
YOUR MOTHER WILL NEVER SEE YOU AGAIN IF YOU DO *NOT* MARRY MR. COLLINS,
AND I WILL NEVER SEE YOU AGAIN IF YOU *DO*!
YOU CAN'T BE SERIOUS! WHAT ABOUT THE ESTATE?
FATHER? I DON'T UNDERSTAND...
HOW CAN I EXPLAIN...

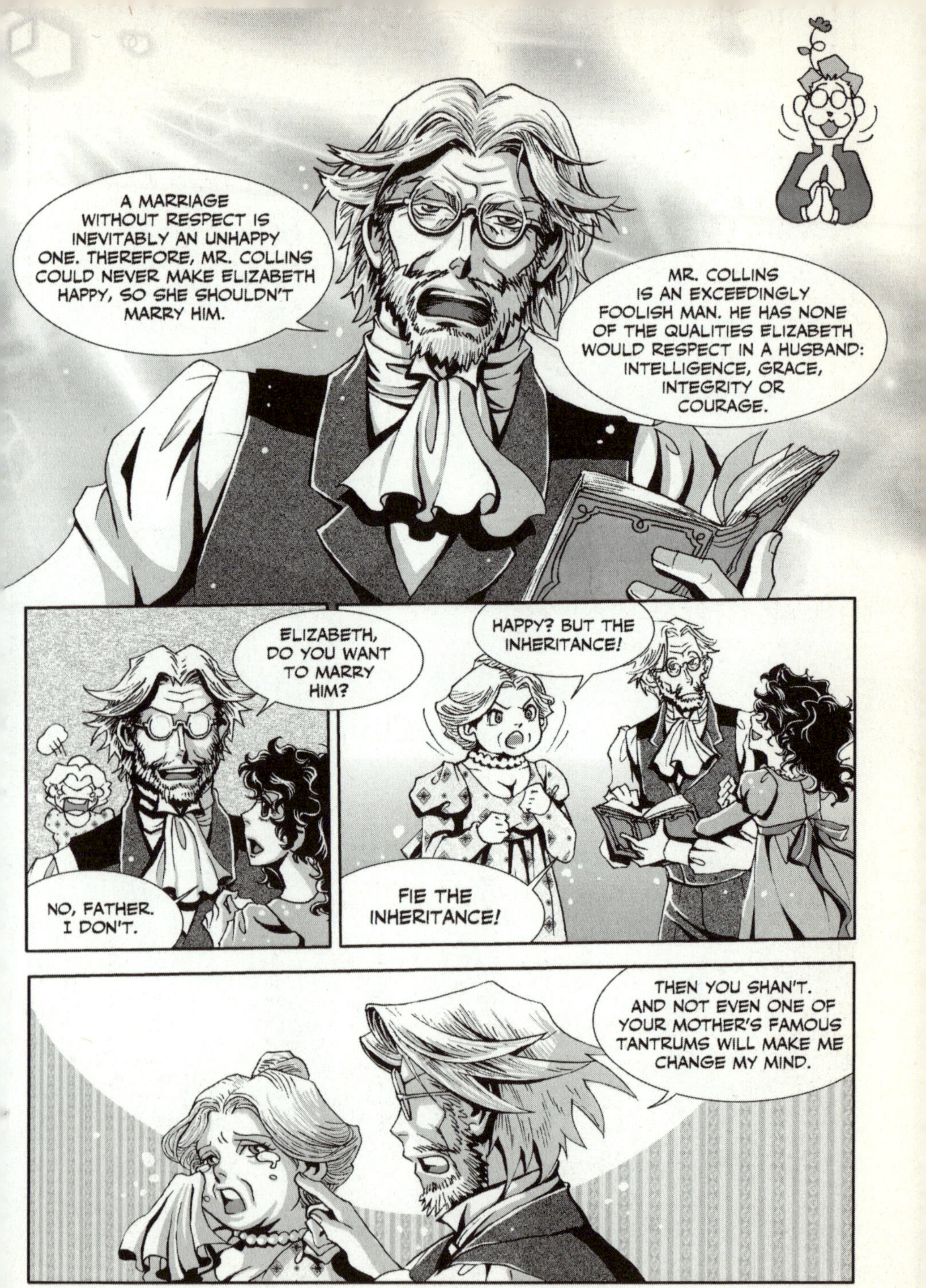
MR. COLLINS IS AN EXCEEDINGLY FOOLISH MAN. HE HAS NONE OF THE QUALITIES ELIZABETH WOULD RESPECT IN A HUSBAND: INTELLIGENCE, GRACE, INTEGRITY OR COURAGE.
A MARRIAGE WITHOUT RESPECT IS INEVITABLY AN UNHAPPY ONE. THEREFORE, MR. COLLINS COULD NEVER MAKE ELIZABETH HAPPY, SO SHE SHOULDN'T MARRY HIM.
HAPPY? BUT THE INHERITANCE!
FIE THE INHERITANCE!
ELIZABETH, DO YOU WANT TO MARRY HIM?
NO, FATHER. I DON'T.
THEN YOU SHAN'T. AND NOT EVEN ONE OF YOUR MOTHER'S FAMOUS TANTRUMS WILL MAKE ME CHANGE MY MIND.

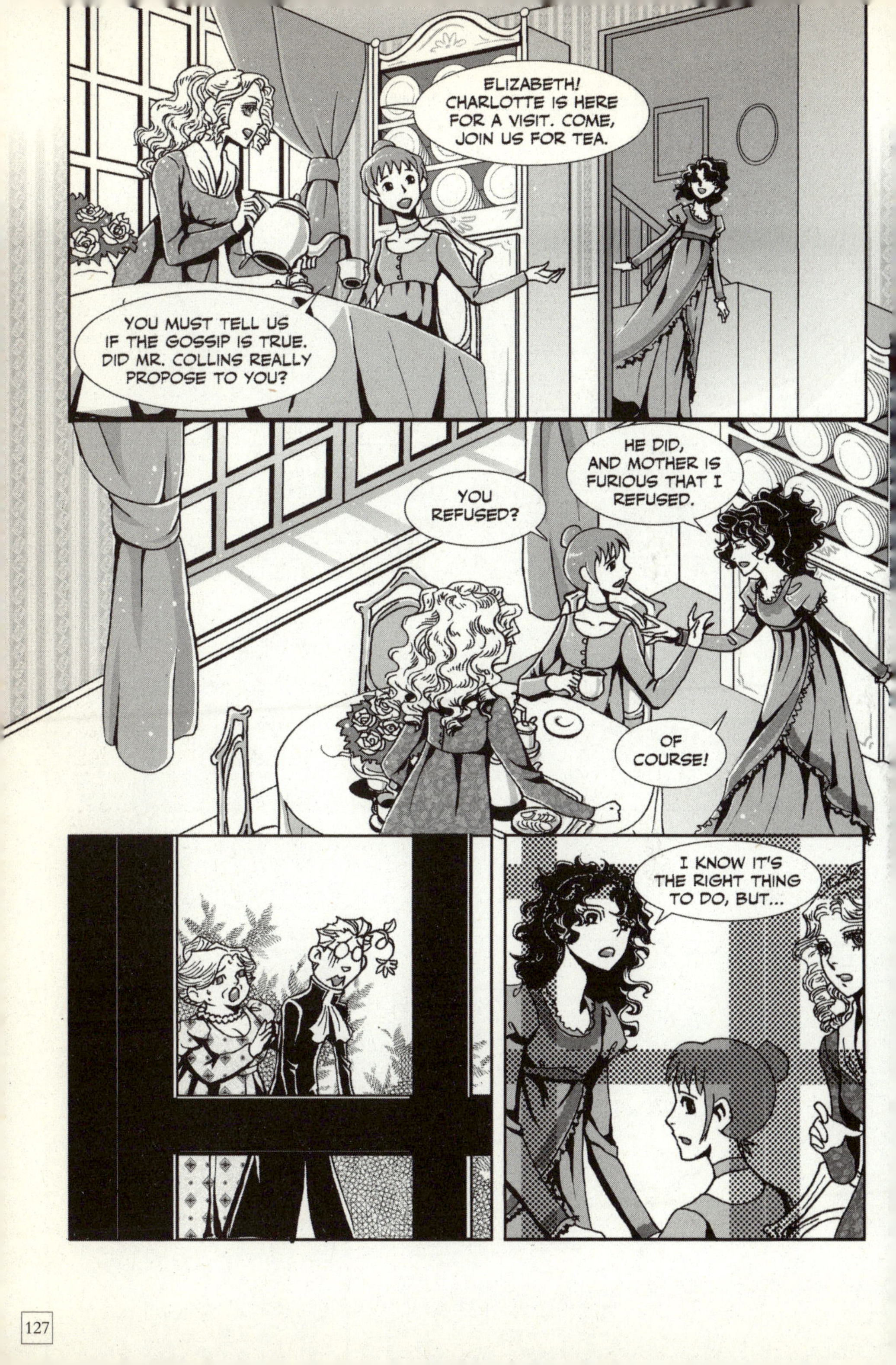
ELIZABETH! CHARLOTTE IS HERE FOR A VISIT. COME, JOIN US FOR TEA.
YOU MUST TELL US IF THE GOSSIP IS TRUE. DID MR. COLLINS REALLY PROPOSE TO YOU?
HE DID, AND MOTHER IS FURIOUS THAT I REFUSED.
YOU REFUSED?
OF COURSE!
I KNOW IT'S THE RIGHT THING TO DO, BUT...

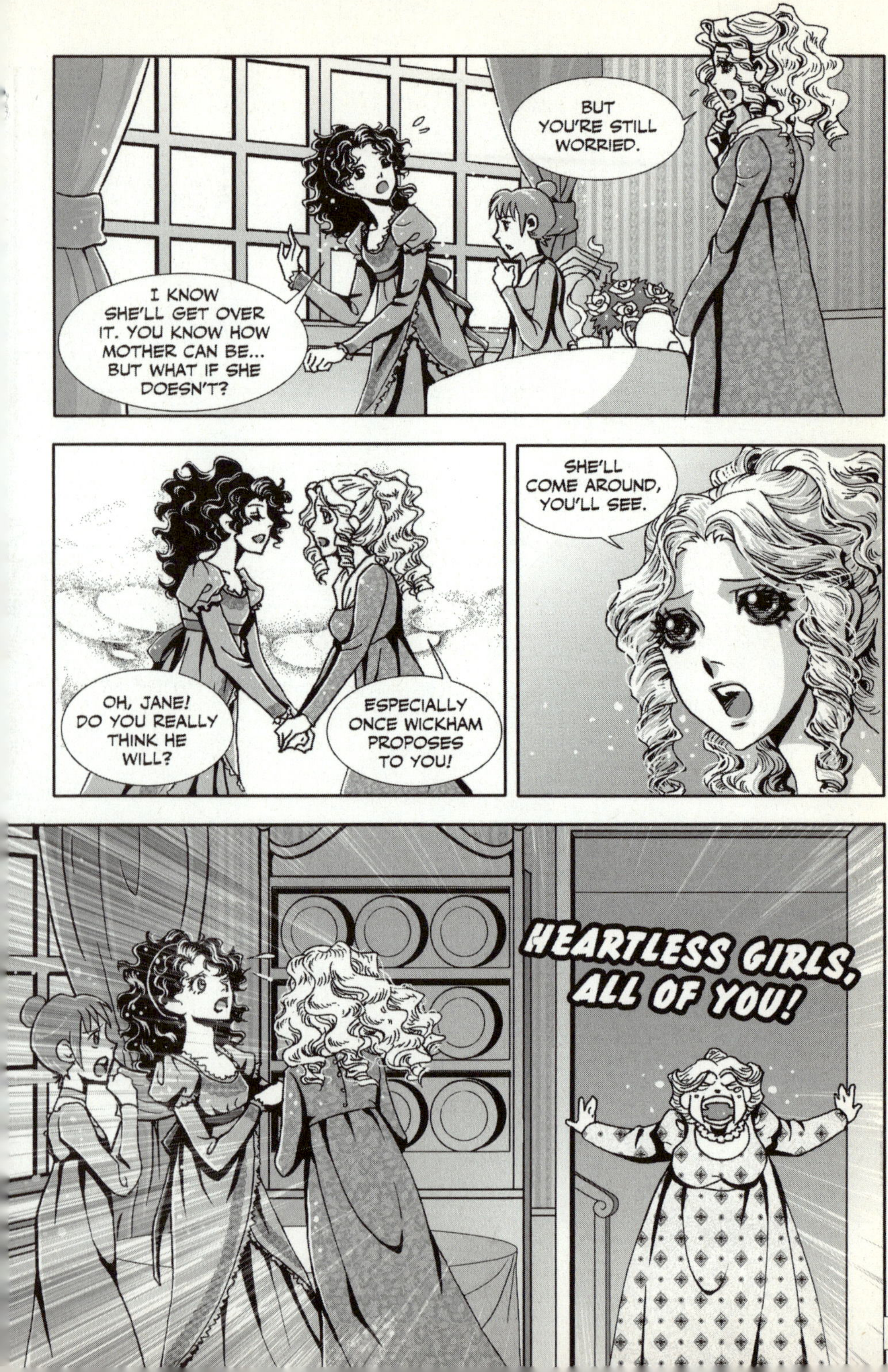
BUT YOU'RE STILL WORRIED.
I KNOW SHE'LL GET OVER IT. YOU KNOW HOW MOTHER CAN BE... BUT WHAT IF SHE DOESN'T?
SHE'LL COME AROUND, YOU'LL SEE.
ESPECIALLY ONCE WICKHAM PROPOSES TO YOU!
OH, JANE! DO YOU REALLY THINK HE WILL?
HEARTLESS GIRLS, ALL OF YOU!

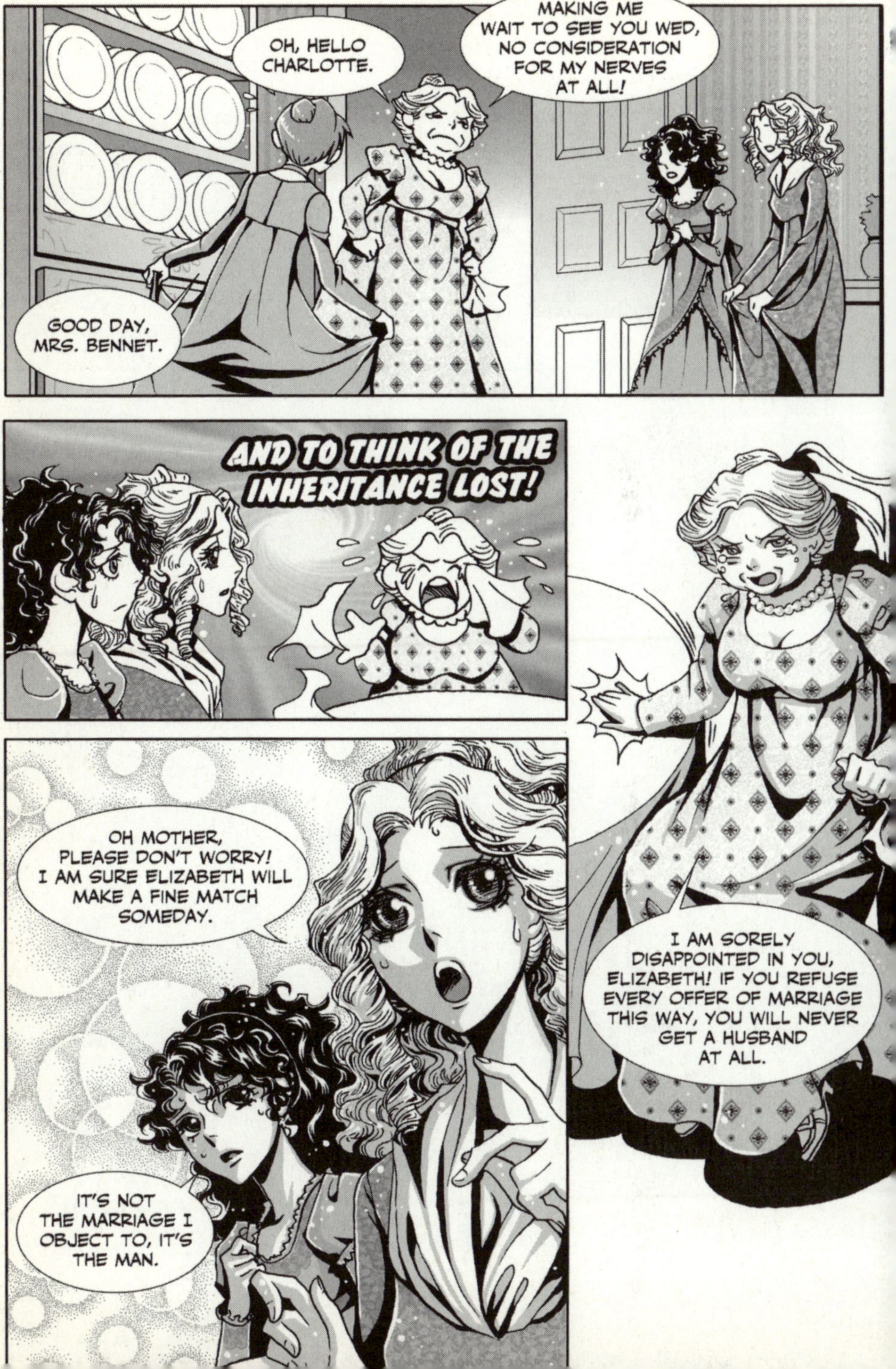
MAKING ME WAIT TO SEE YOU WED, NO CONSIDERATION FOR MY NERVES AT ALL!
OH, HELLO CHARLOTTE.
GOOD DAY, MRS. BENNET.
I AM SORELY DISAPPOINTED IN YOU, ELIZABETH! IF YOU REFUSE EVERY OFFER OF MARRIAGE THIS WAY, YOU WILL NEVER GET A HUSBAND AT ALL.
AND TO THINK OF THE INHERITANCE LOST!
OH MOTHER, PLEASE DON'T WORRY! I AM SURE ELIZABETH WILL MAKE A FINE MATCH SOMEDAY.
IT'S NOT THE MARRIAGE I OBJECT TO, IT'S THE MAN.

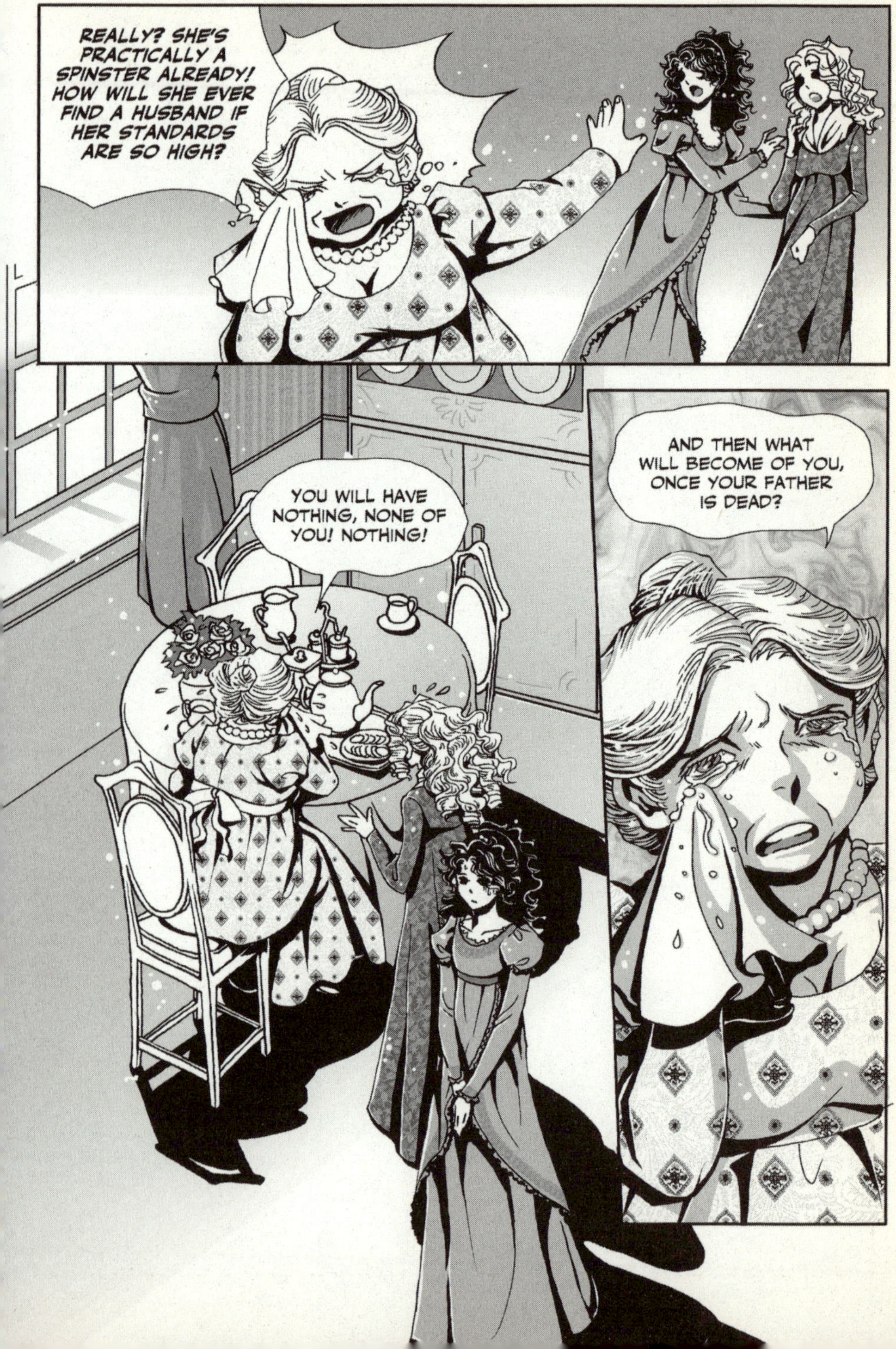
REALLY? SHE'S PRACTICALLY A SPINSTER ALREADY! HOW WILL SHE EVER FIND A HUSBAND IF HER STANDARDS ARE SO HIGH?
AND THEN WHAT WILL BECOME OF YOU, ONCE YOUR FATHER IS DEAD?
YOU WILL HAVE NOTHING, NONE OF YOU! NOTHING!

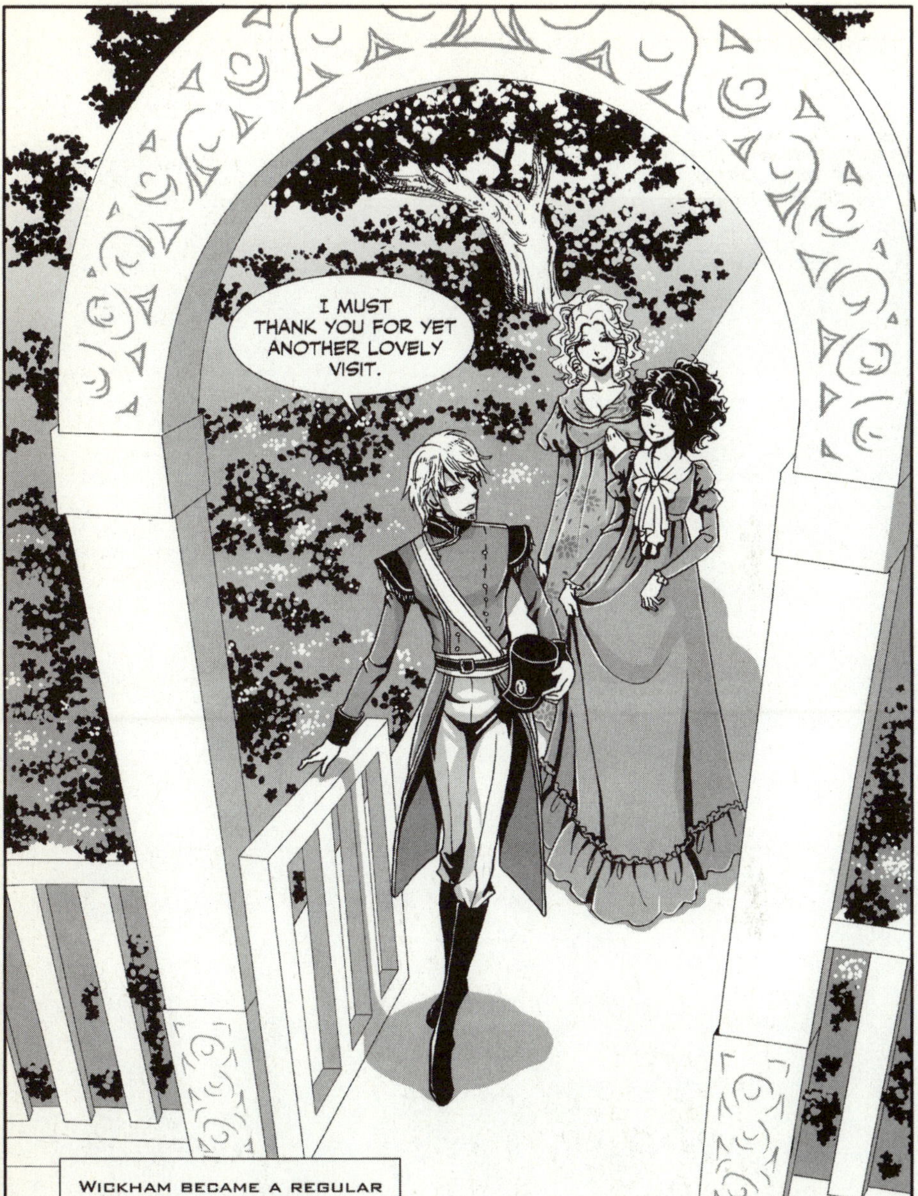
I MUST THANK YOU FOR YET ANOTHER LOVELY VISIT.
WICKHAM BECAME A REGULAR VISITOR AT THE BENNET ESTATE DURING THE NEXT FEW WEEKS, MUCH TO THE DELIGHT OF ELIZABETH AND HER SISTER.
Chapter 7

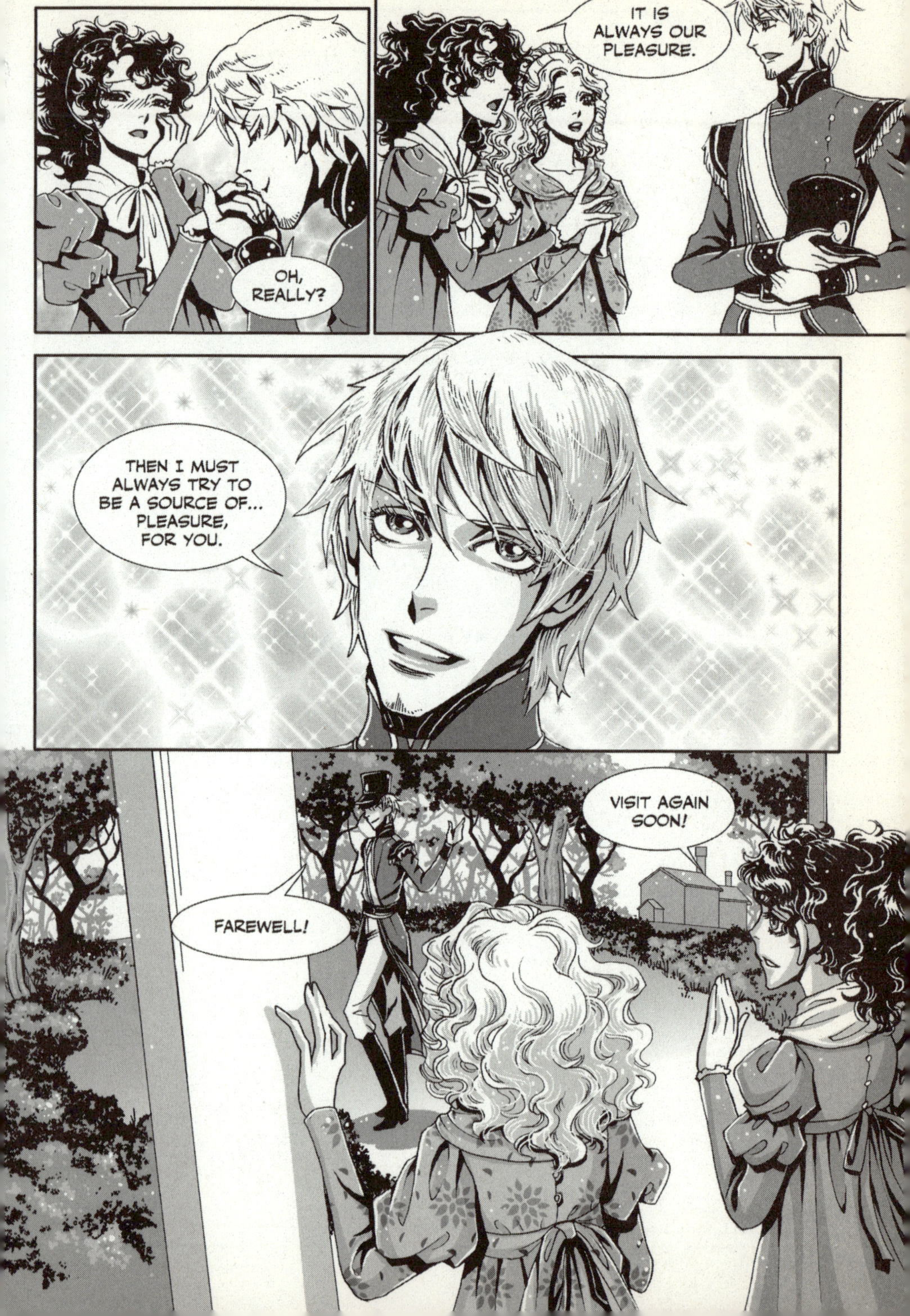
IT IS ALWAYS OUR PLEASURE.
OH, REALLY?
THEN I MUST ALWAYS TRY TO BE A SOURCE OF... PLEASURE, FOR YOU.
VISIT AGAIN SOON!
FAREWELL!

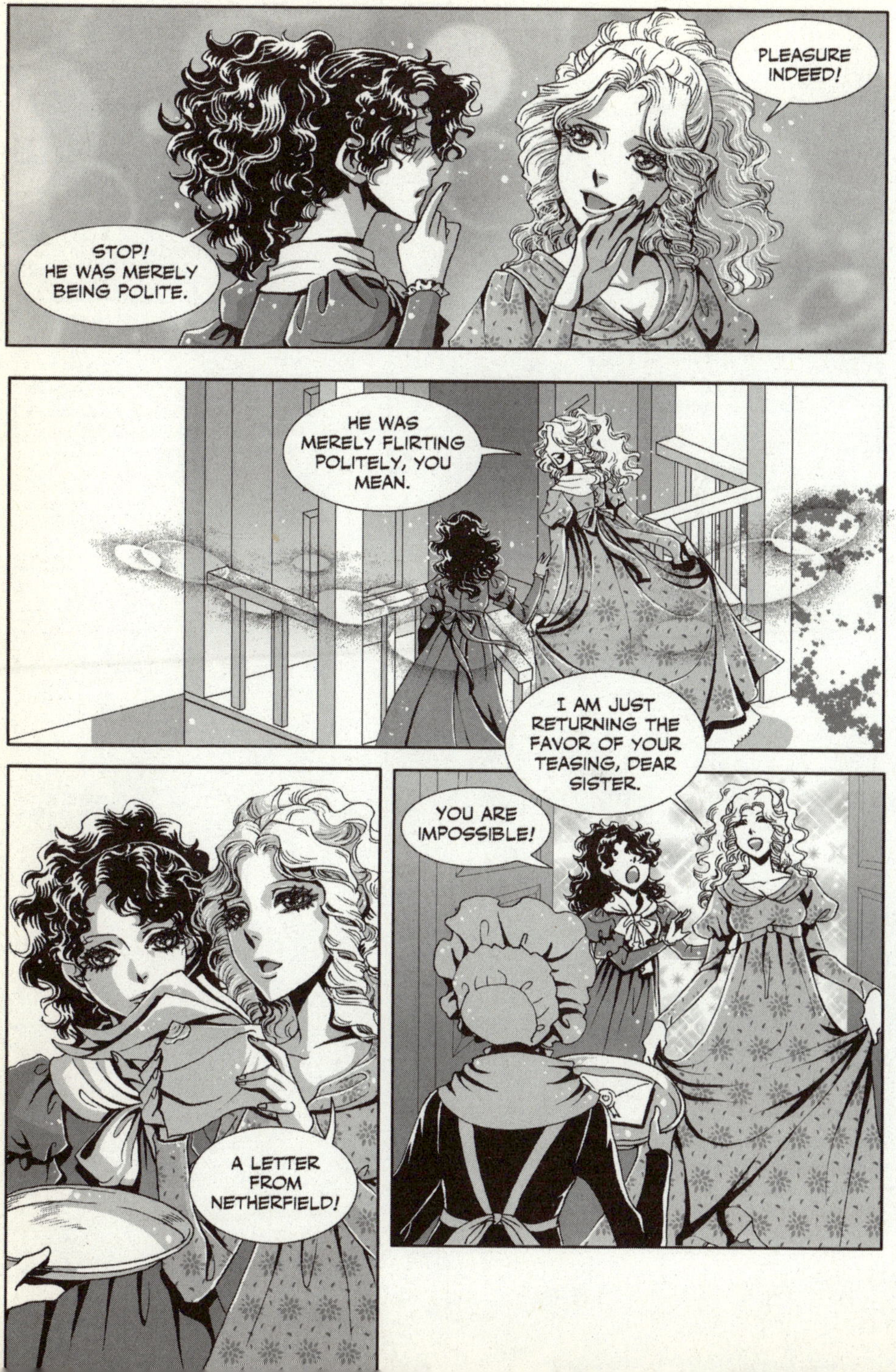
PLEASURE INDEED!
STOP! HE WAS MERELY BEING POLITE.
HE WAS MERELY FLIRTING POLITELY, YOU MEAN.
I AM JUST RETURNING THE FAVOR OF YOUR TEASING, DEAR SISTER.
YOU ARE IMPOSSIBLE!
A LETTER FROM NETHERFIELD!

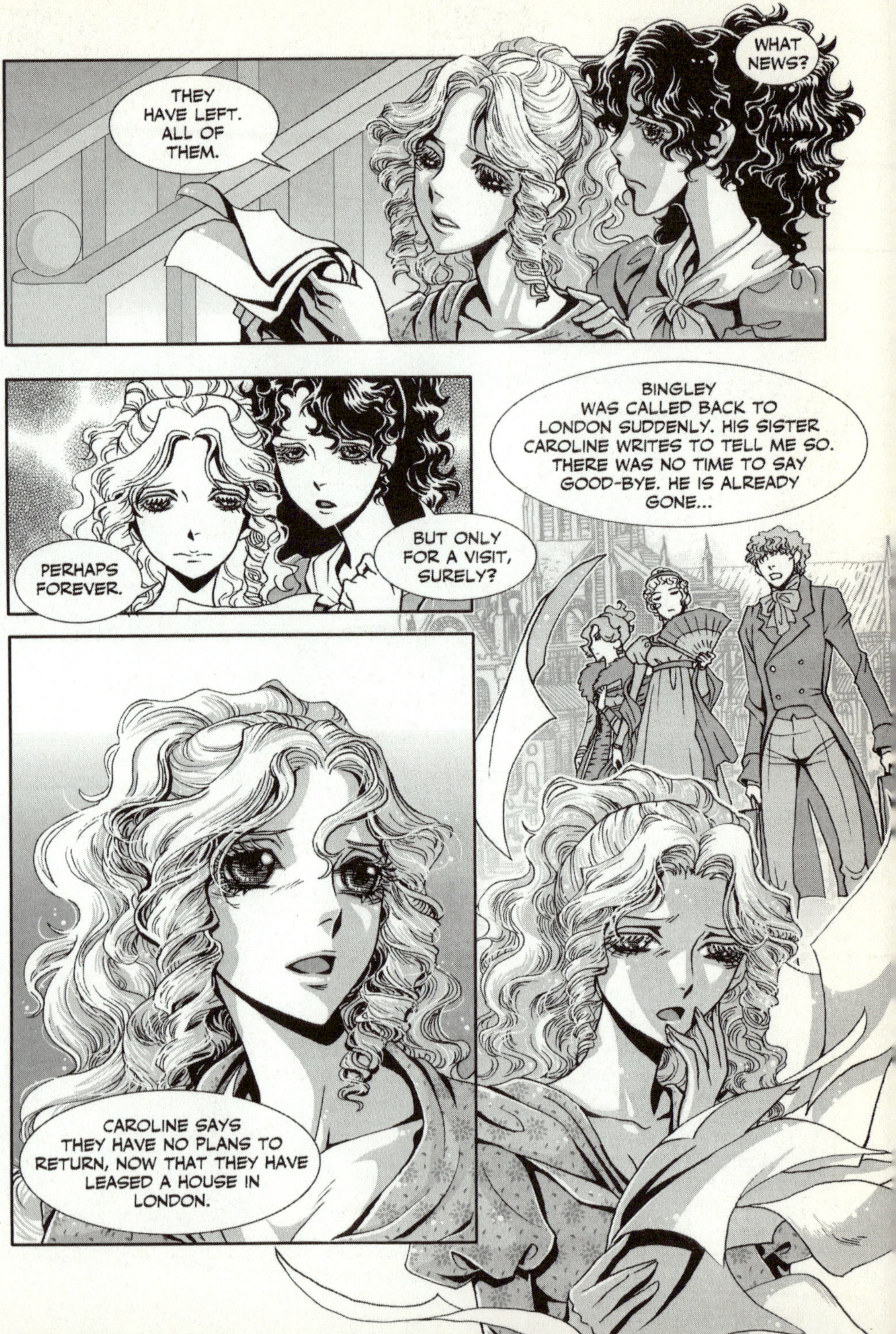
WHAT NEWS?
THEY HAVE LEFT. ALL OF THEM.
BINGLEY WAS CALLED BACK TO LONDON SUDDENLY. HIS SISTER CAROLINE WRITES TO TELL ME SO. THERE WAS NO TIME TO SAY GOOD-BYE. HE IS ALREADY GONE...
BUT ONLY FOR A VISIT, SURELY?
PERHAPS FOREVER.
CAROLINE SAYS THEY HAVE NO PLANS TO RETURN, NOW THAT THEY HAVE LEASED A HOUSE IN LONDON.

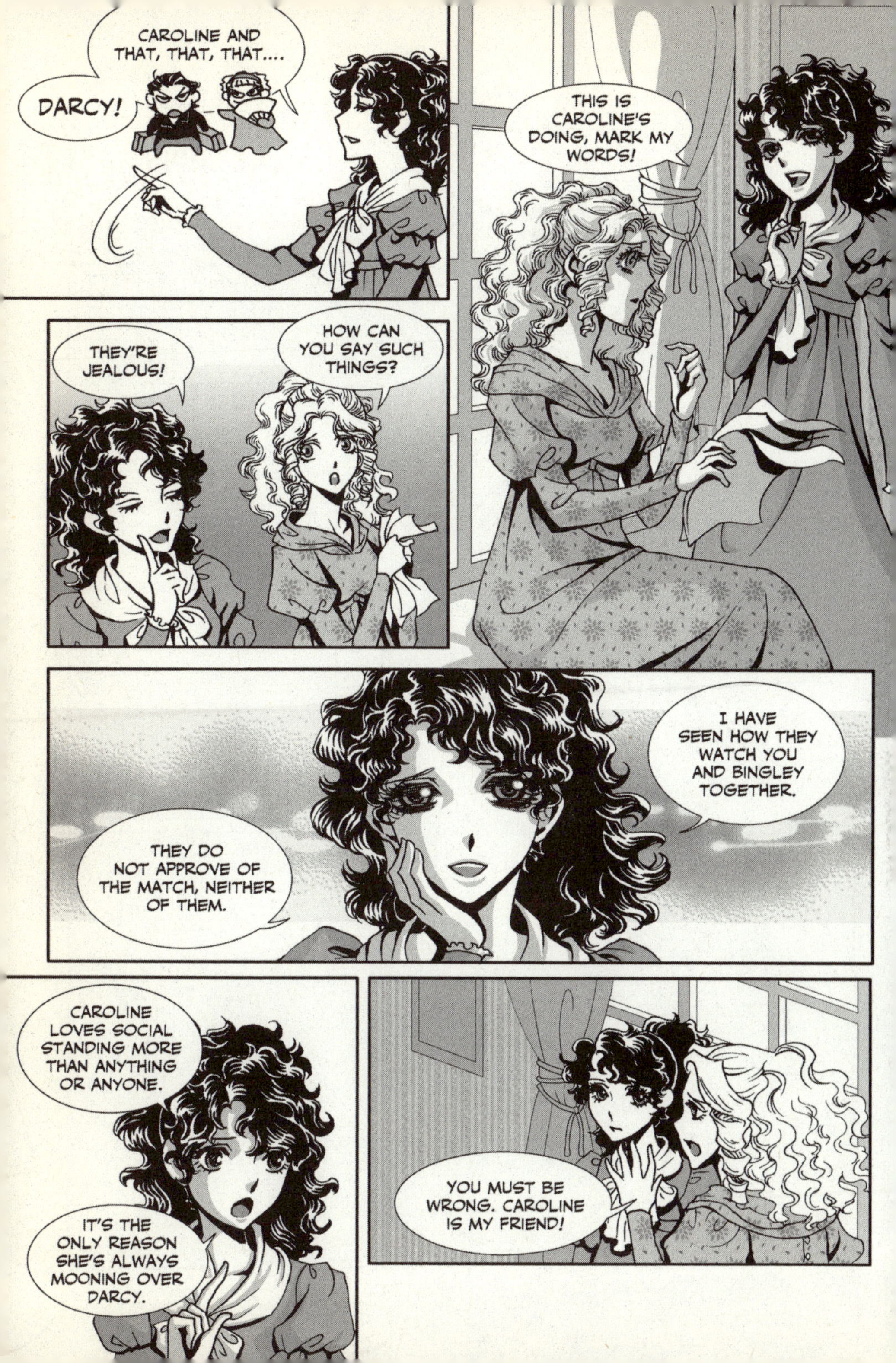
THIS IS CAROLINE'S DOING, MARK MY WORDS!
CAROLINE AND THAT, THAT, THAT....
DARCY!
HOW CAN YOU SAY SUCH THINGS?
THEY'RE JEALOUS!
I HAVE SEEN HOW THEY WATCH YOU AND BINGLEY TOGETHER.
THEY DO NOT APPROVE OF THE MATCH, NEITHER OF THEM.
YOU MUST BE WRONG. CAROLINE IS MY FRIEND!
CAROLINE LOVES SOCIAL STANDING MORE THAN ANYTHING OR ANYONE.
IT'S THE ONLY REASON SHE'S ALWAYS MOONING OVER DARCY.

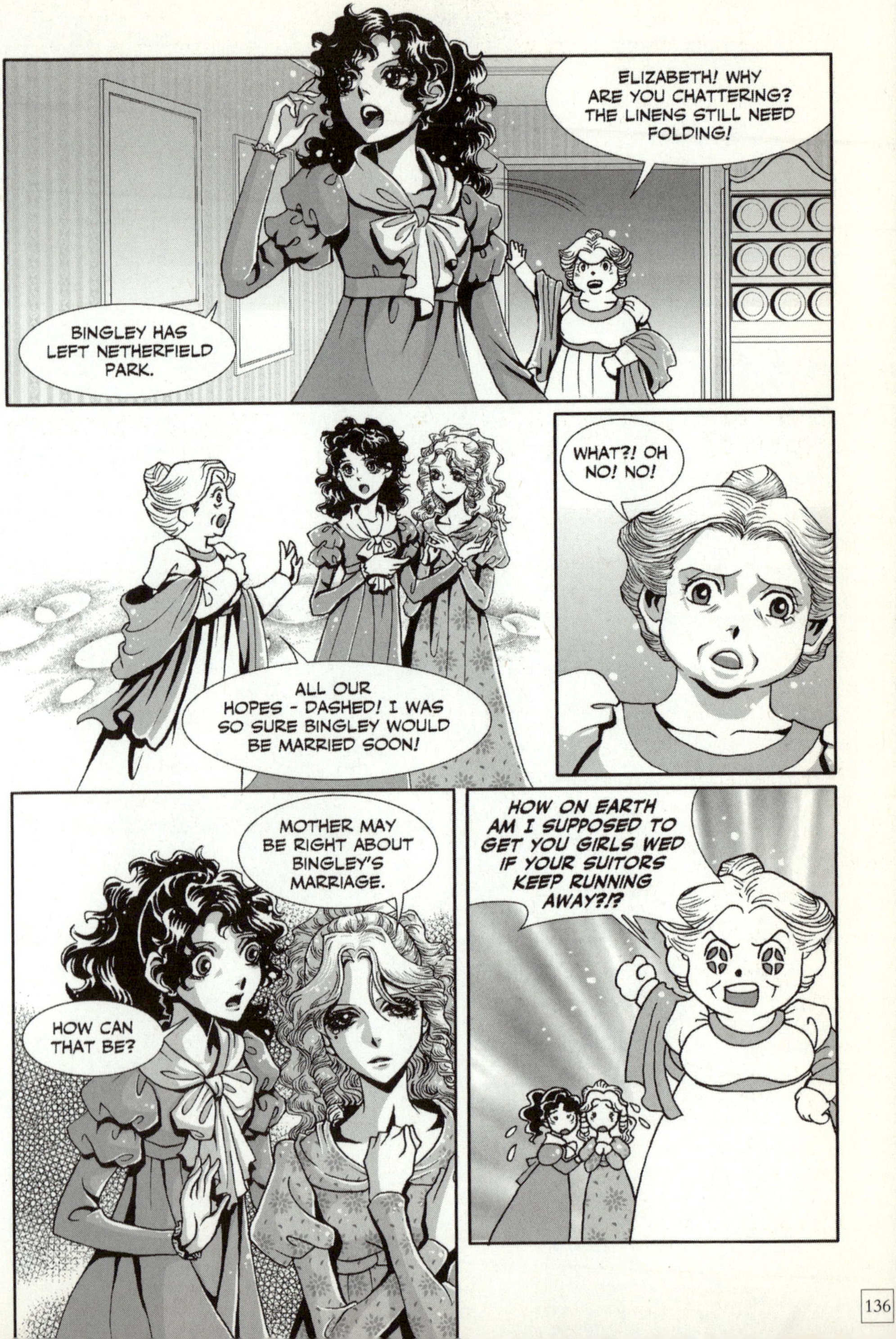
ELIZABETH! WHY ARE YOU CHATTERING? THE LINENS STILL NEED FOLDING!
BINGLEY HAS LEFT NETHERFIELD PARK.
WHAT?! OH NO! NO!
ALL OUR HOPES - DASHED! I WAS SO SURE BINGLEY WOULD BE MARRIED SOON!
HOW ON EARTH AM I SUPPOSED TO GET YOU GIRLS WED IF YOUR SUITORS KEEP RUNNING AWAY?!?
MOTHER MAY BE RIGHT ABOUT BINGLEY'S MARRIAGE.
HOW CAN THAT BE?

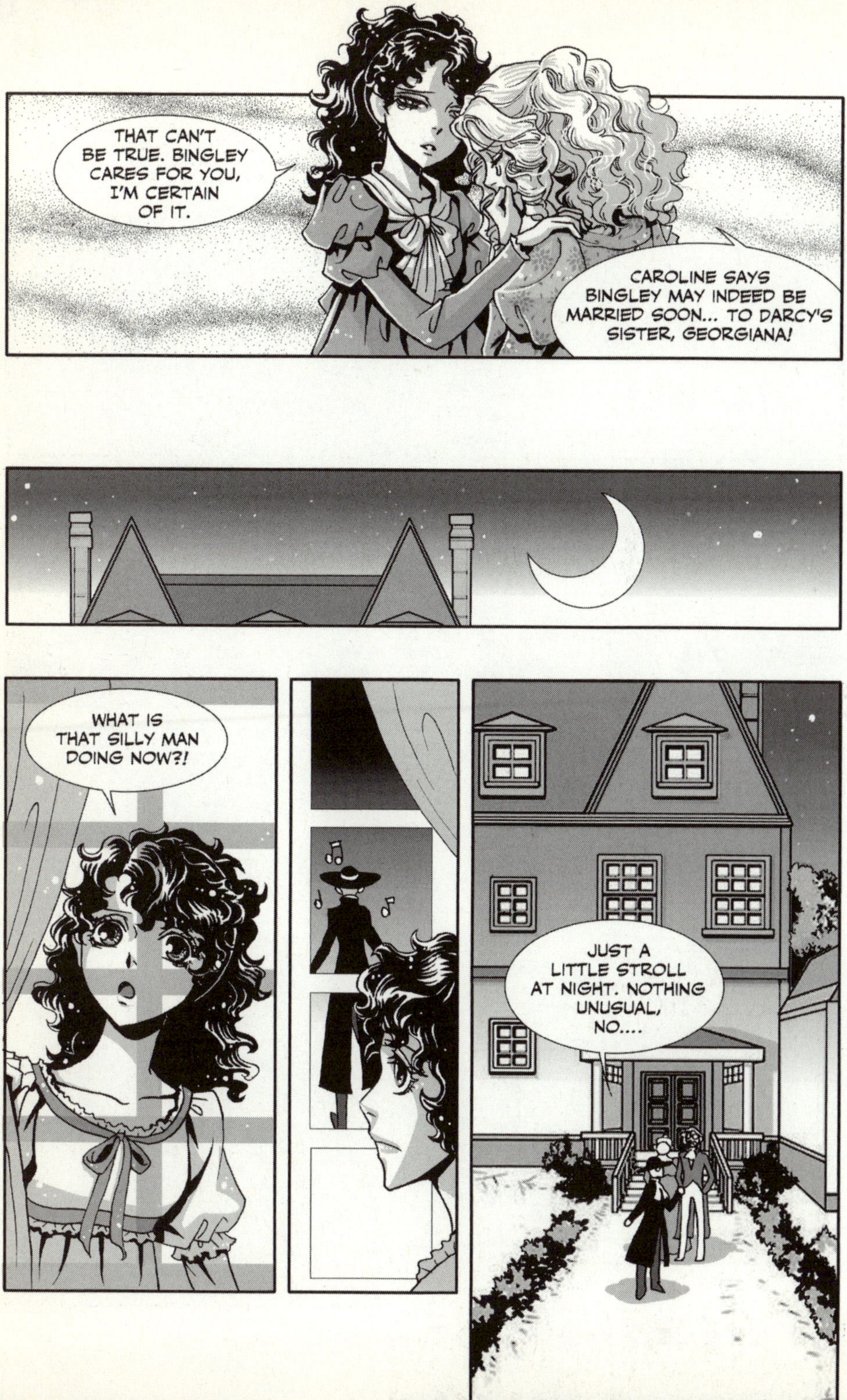
CAROLINE SAYS BINGLEY MAY INDEED BE MARRIED SOON... TO DARCY'S SISTER, GEORGIANA!
THAT CAN'T BE TRUE. BINGLEY CARES FOR YOU, I'M CERTAIN OF IT.
JUST A LITTLE STROLL AT NIGHT. NOTHING UNUSUAL, NO....
WHAT IS THAT SILLY MAN DOING NOW?!

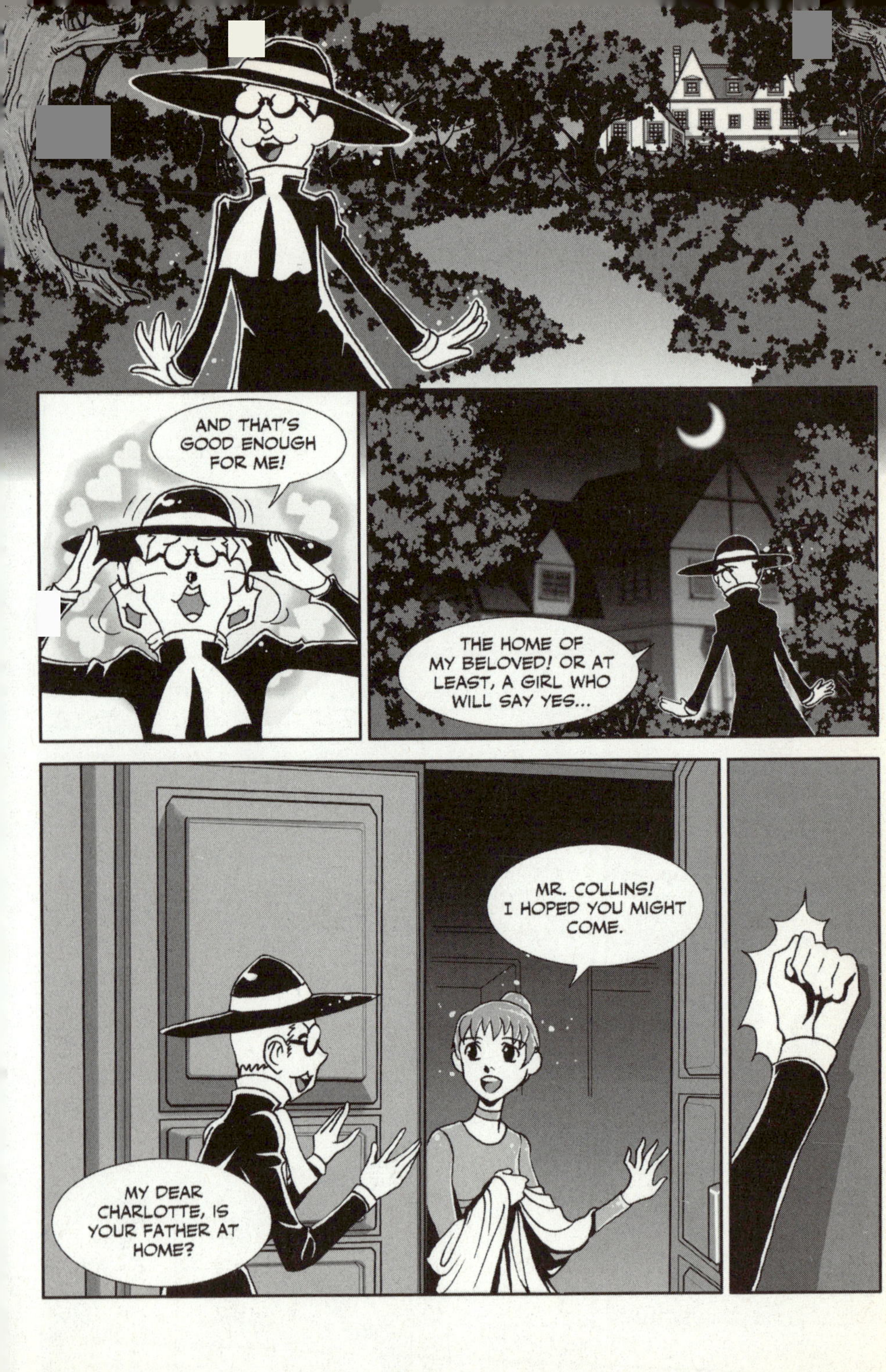
THE HOME OF MY BELOVED! OR AT LEAST, A GIRL WHO WILL SAY YES...
AND THAT'S GOOD ENOUGH FOR ME!
MR. COLLINS! I HOPED YOU MIGHT COME.
MY DEAR CHARLOTTE, IS YOUR FATHER AT HOME?

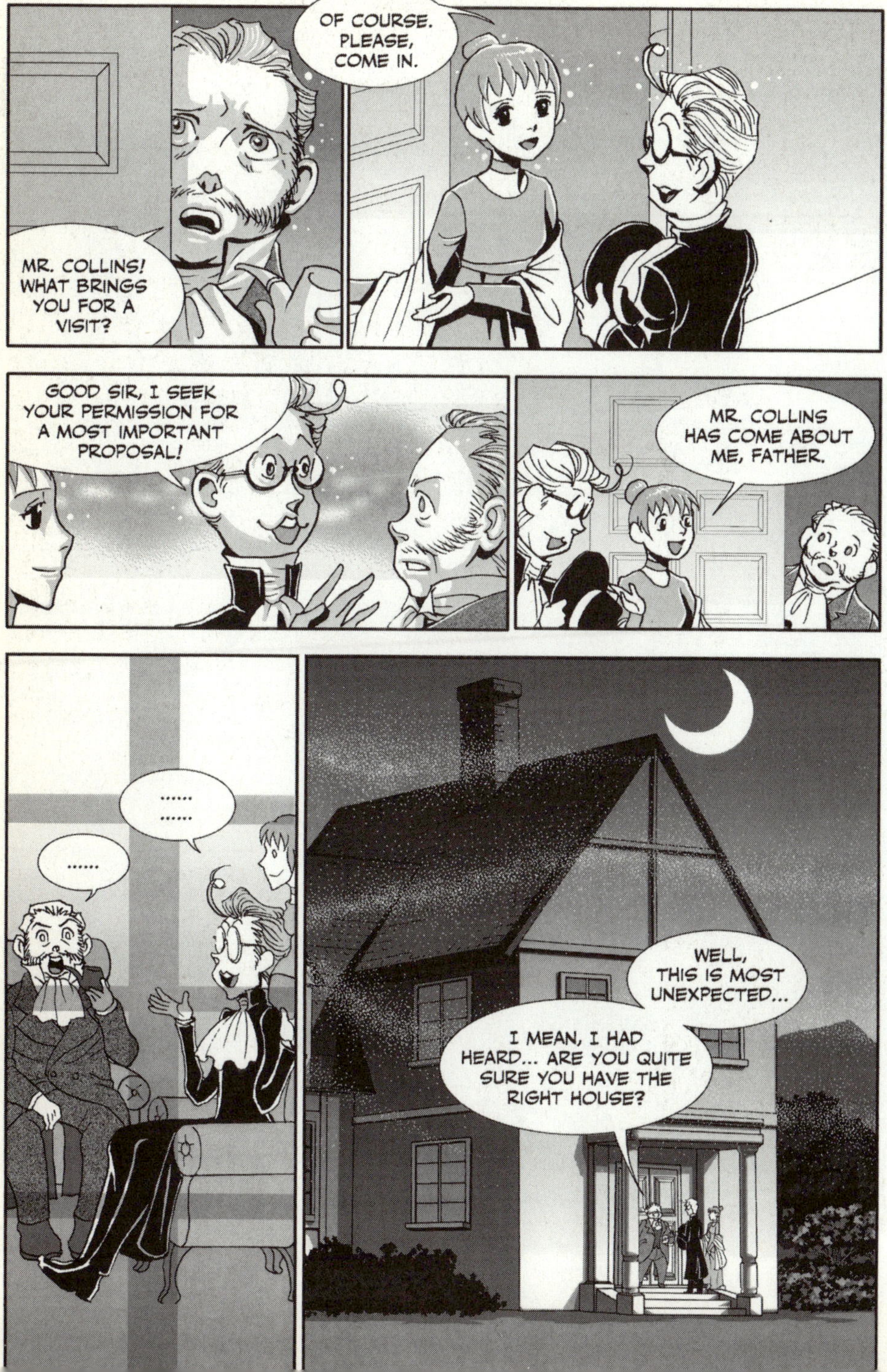
OF COURSE. PLEASE, COME IN.
MR. COLLINS! WHAT BRINGS YOU FOR A VISIT?
MR. COLLINS HAS COME ABOUT ME, FATHER.
GOOD SIR, I SEEK YOUR PERMISSION FOR A MOST IMPORTANT PROPOSAL!
WELL, THIS IS MOST UNEXPECTED...
I MEAN, I HAD HEARD... ARE YOU QUITE SURE YOU HAVE THE RIGHT HOUSE?
....
......

THE NEXT MORNING...

ENGAGED! TO MR. COLLINS!

WHY IMPOSSIBLE?

MY DEAR CHARLOTTE, IT'S IMPOSSIBLE!

DID YOU REALLY THINK NO ONE WOULD MARRY HIM, JUST BECAUSE YOU REFUSED?

MR. COLLINS IS KIND, PROSPEROUS AND WELL-CONNECTED.

WHY NOT? I AM NOT A ROMANTIC, YOU KNOW.

HE CAN PROVIDE A GOOD HOME, AND I CAN PROVIDE TOLERANCE FOR ALL HIS QUIRKS.

OUR CHANCE OF HAPPINESS IS AS GOOD AS ANYONE'S, I WAGER.

YOU TALK OF MONEY AND CONNECTIONS. ARE THOSE THE FOUNDATIONS OF A HEALTHY MARRIAGE TO YOU?

HE IS ALSO FOOLISH, VAIN, ALTOGETHER PREPOSTEROUS!

HOW CAN SUCH A MAN MAKE YOU HAPPY?

I BELIEVE IT IS A BET I HAVE ALREADY WON.

THEN I WISH YOU A HAPPY GAMBLE.

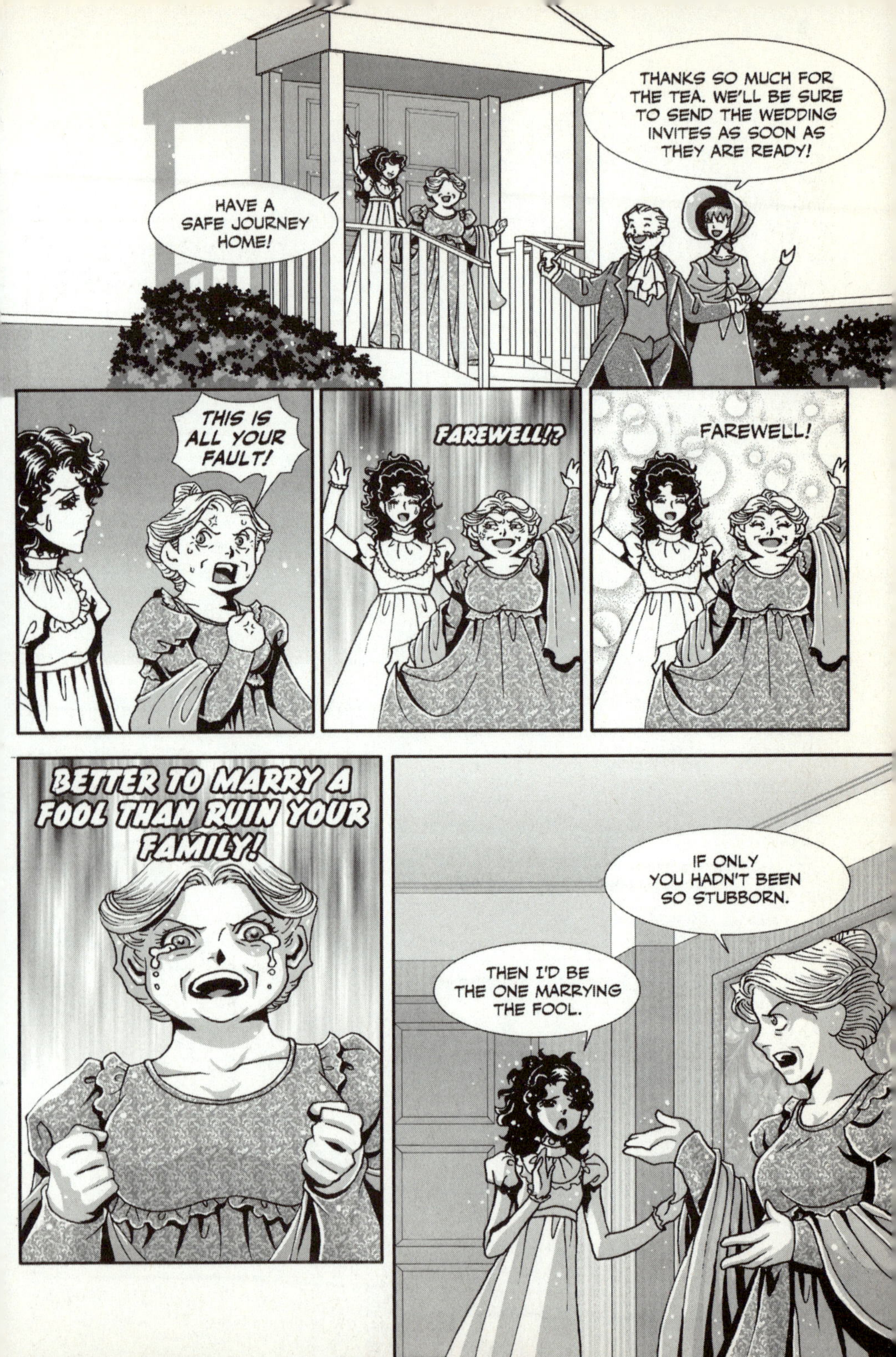
THANKS SO MUCH FOR THE TEA. WE'LL BE SURE TO SEND THE WEDDING INVITES AS SOON AS THEY ARE READY!
HAVE A SAFE JOURNEY HOME!
FAREWELL!
FAREWELL!?
THIS IS ALL YOUR FAULT!
IF ONLY YOU HADN'T BEEN SO STUBBORN.
THEN I'D BE THE ONE MARRYING THE FOOL.
BETTER TO MARRY A FOOL THAN RUIN YOUR FAMILY!

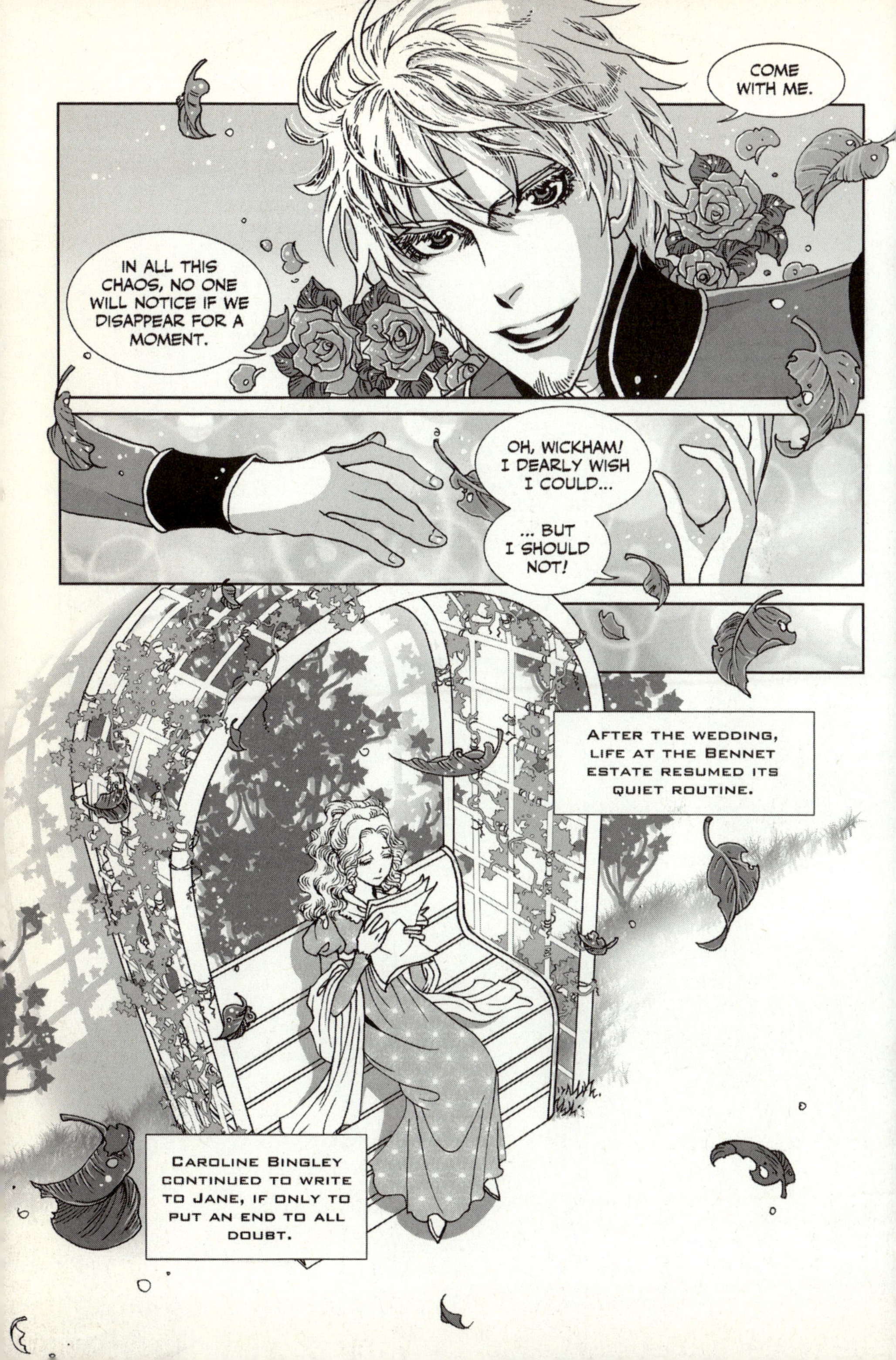
COME WITH ME.
IN ALL THIS CHAOS, NO ONE WILL NOTICE IF WE DISAPPEAR FOR A MOMENT.
OH, WICKHAM! I DEARLY WISH I COULD...
... BUT I SHOULD NOT!
AFTER THE WEDDING, LIFE AT THE BENNET ESTATE RESUMED ITS QUIET ROUTINE.
CAROLINE BINGLEY CONTINUED TO WRITE TO JANE, IF ONLY TO PUT AN END TO ALL DOUBT.

146

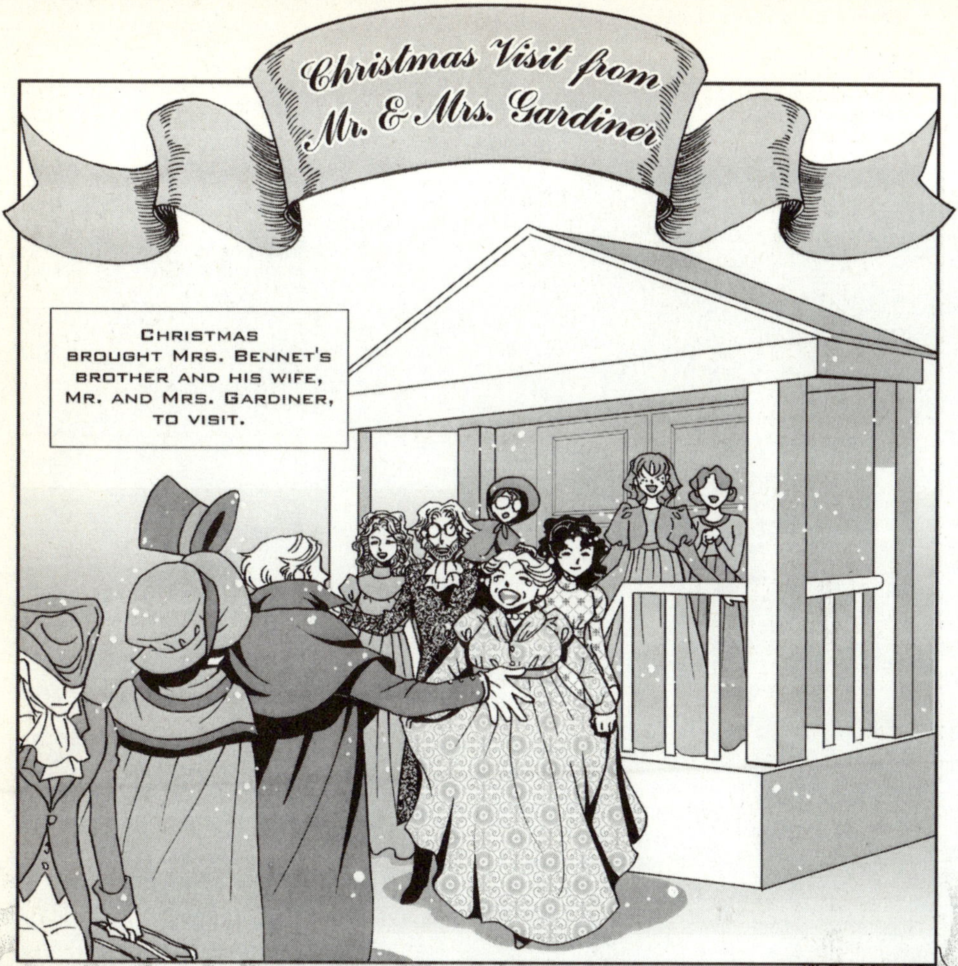
Christmas Visit from Mr. & Mrs. Gardiner
CHRISTMAS BROUGHT MRS. BENNET'S BROTHER AND HIS WIFE, MR. AND MRS. GARDINER, TO VISIT.

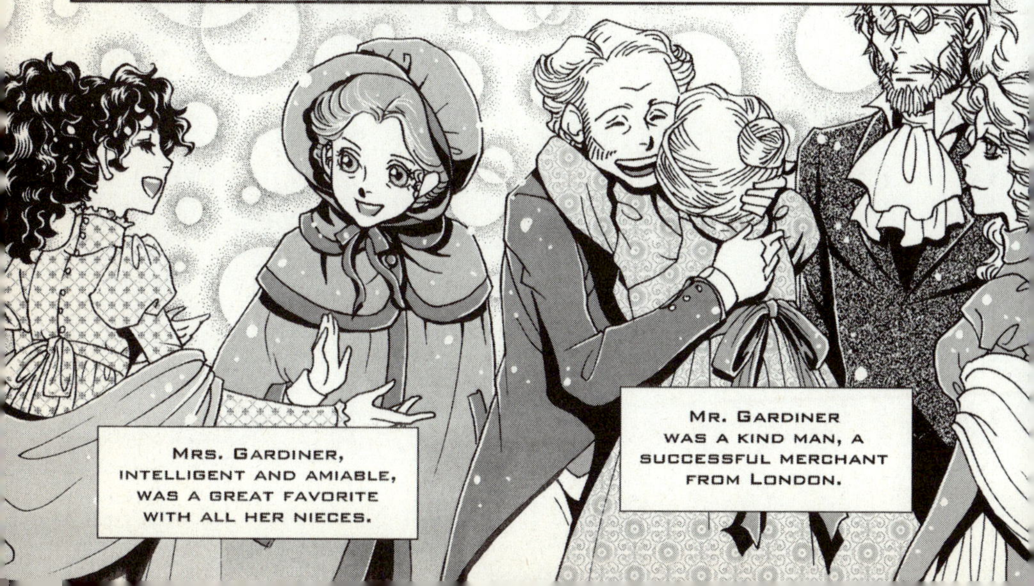
MR. GARDINER WAS A KIND MAN, A SUCCESSFUL MERCHANT FROM LONDON.
MRS. GARDINER, INTELLIGENT AND AMIABLE, WAS A GREAT FAVORITE WITH ALL HER NIECES.

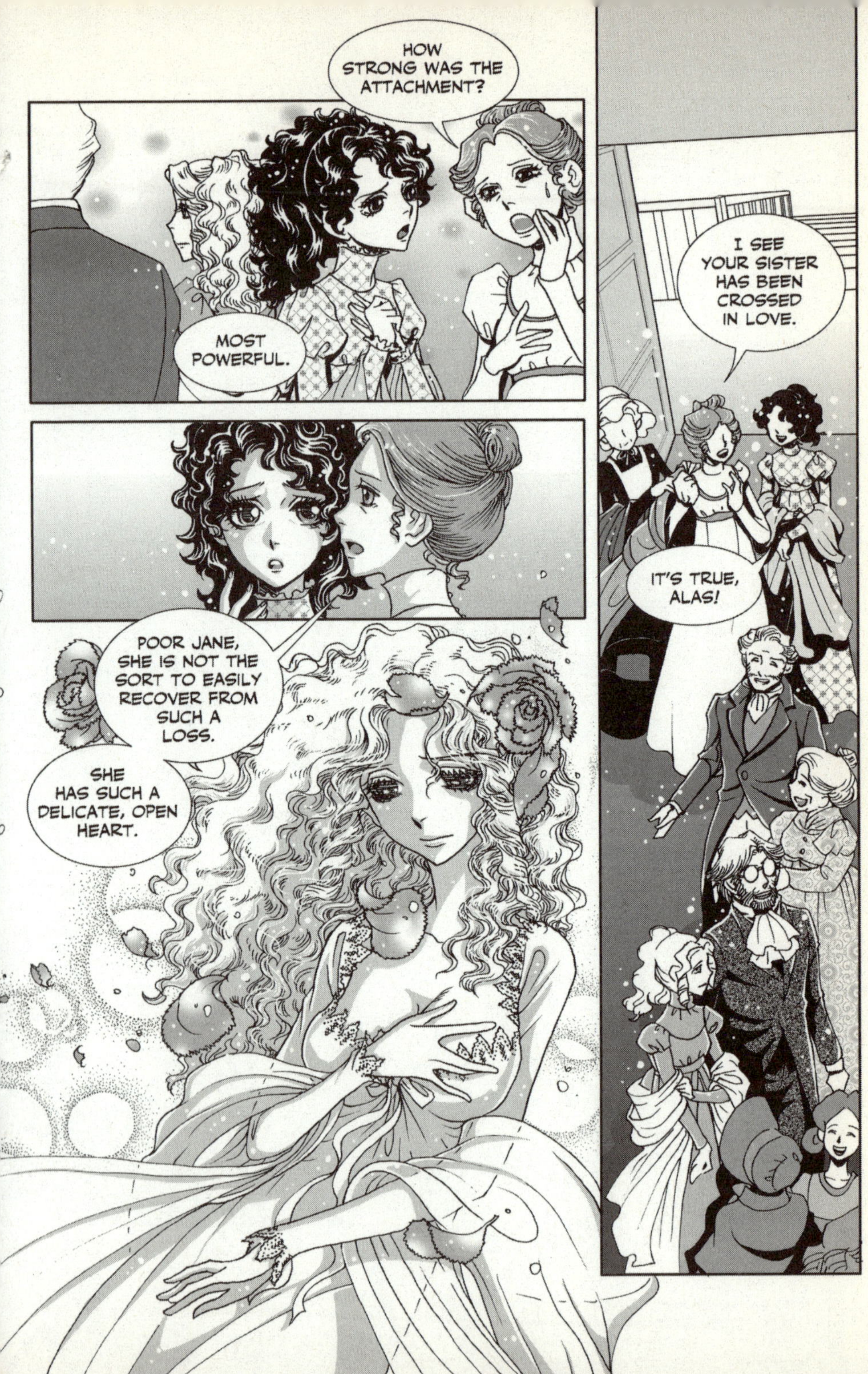
I SEE YOUR SISTER HAS BEEN CROSSED IN LOVE.
IT'S TRUE, ALAS!
HOW STRONG WAS THE ATTACHMENT?
MOST POWERFUL.
POOR JANE, SHE IS NOT THE SORT TO EASILY RECOVER FROM SUCH A LOSS.
SHE HAS SUCH A DELICATE, OPEN HEART.

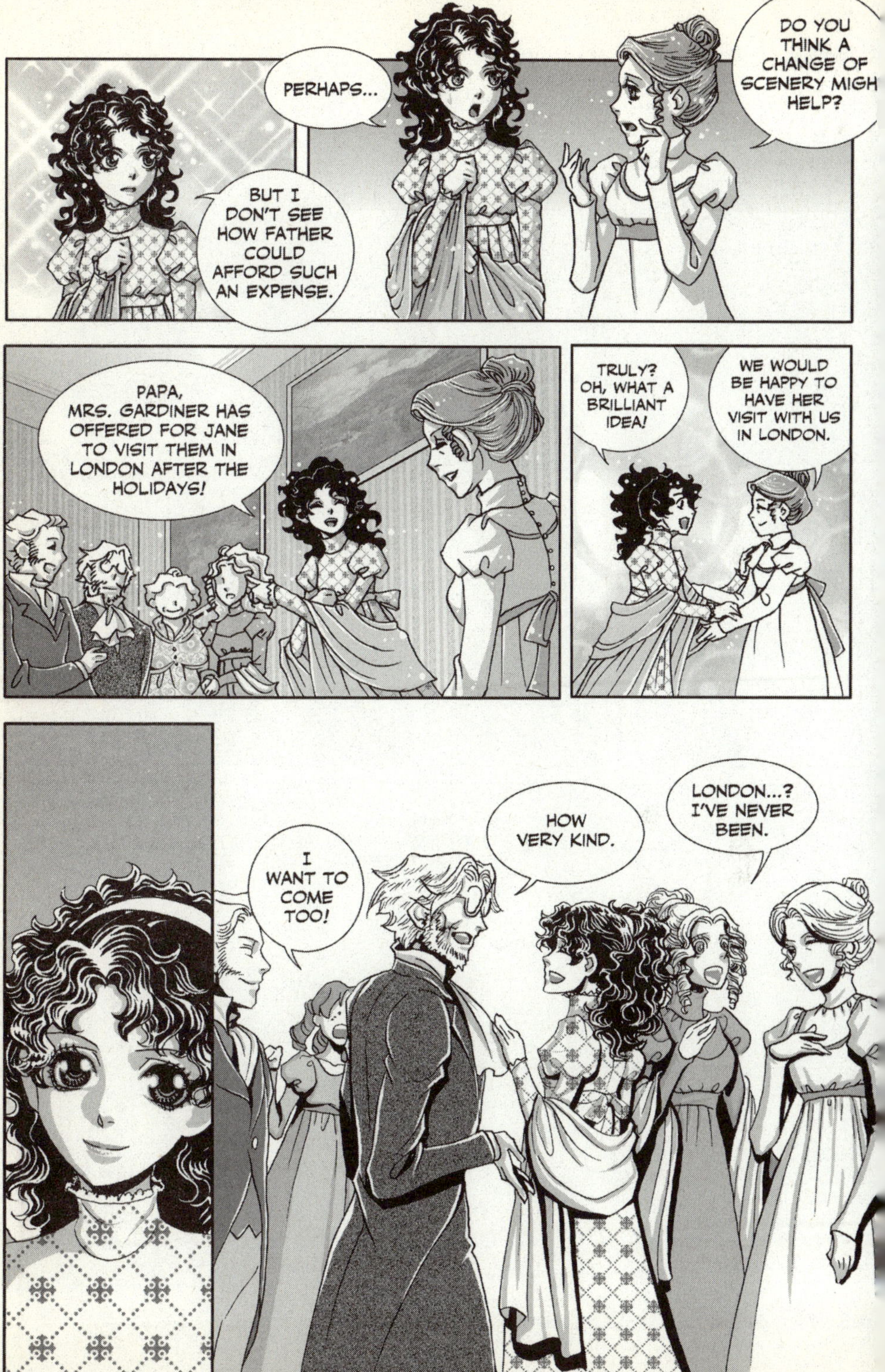

DO YOU THINK A CHANGE OF SCENERY MIGH HELP?
PERHAPS...
BUT I DON'T SEE HOW FATHER COULD AFFORD SUCH AN EXPENSE.
WE WOULD BE HAPPY TO HAVE HER VISIT WITH US IN LONDON.
TRULY? OH, WHAT A BRILLIANT IDEA!
PAPA, MRS. GARDINER HAS OFFERED FOR JANE TO VISIT THEM IN LONDON AFTER THE HOLIDAYS!
LONDON...? I'VE NEVER BEEN.
HOW VERY KIND.
I WANT TO COME TOO!

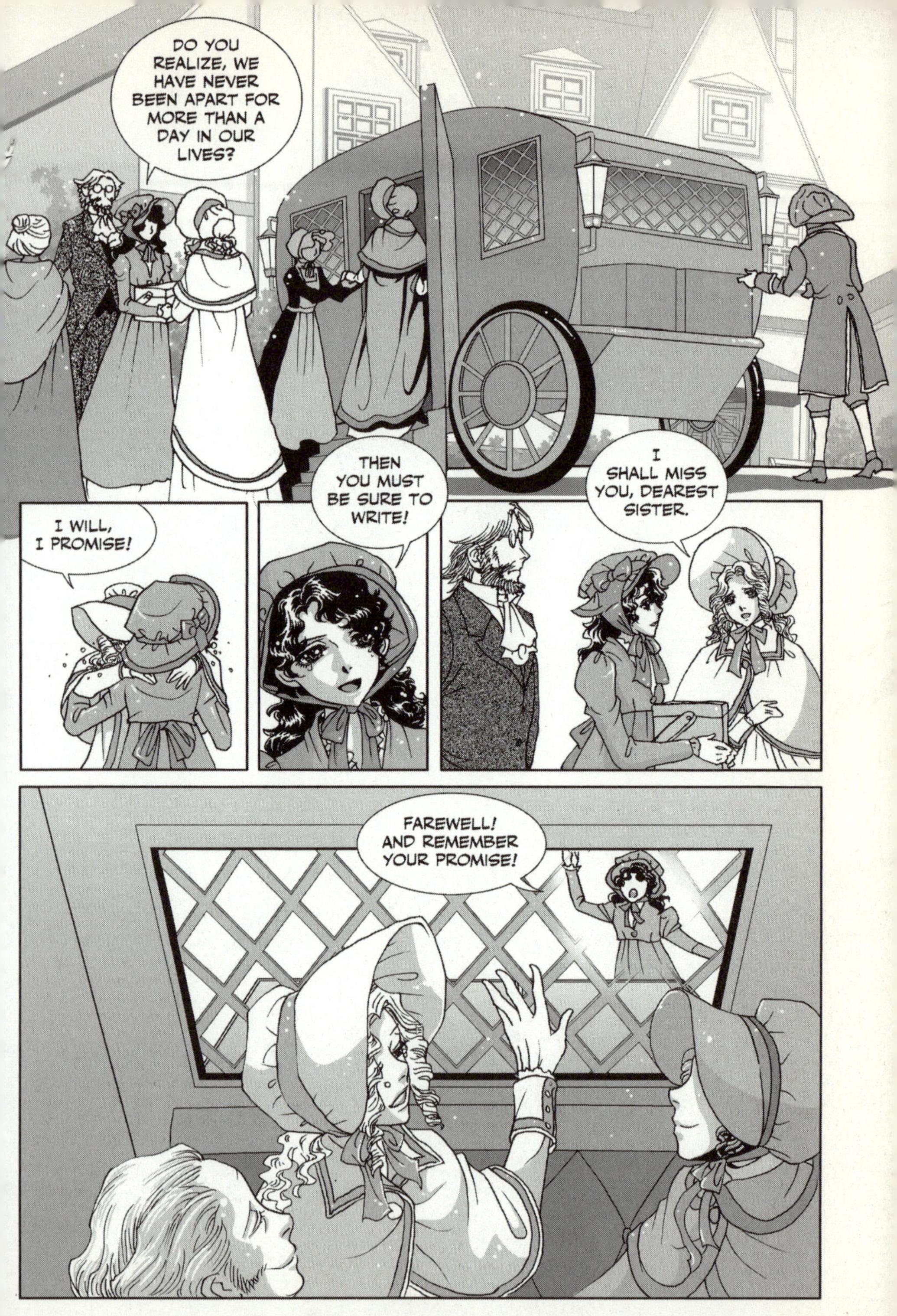
DO YOU REALIZE, WE HAVE NEVER BEEN APART FOR MORE THAN A DAY IN OUR LIVES?
I SHALL MISS YOU, DEAREST SISTER.
THEN YOU MUST BE SURE TO WRITE!
I WILL, I PROMISE!
FAREWELL! AND REMEMBER YOUR PROMISE!

London, January

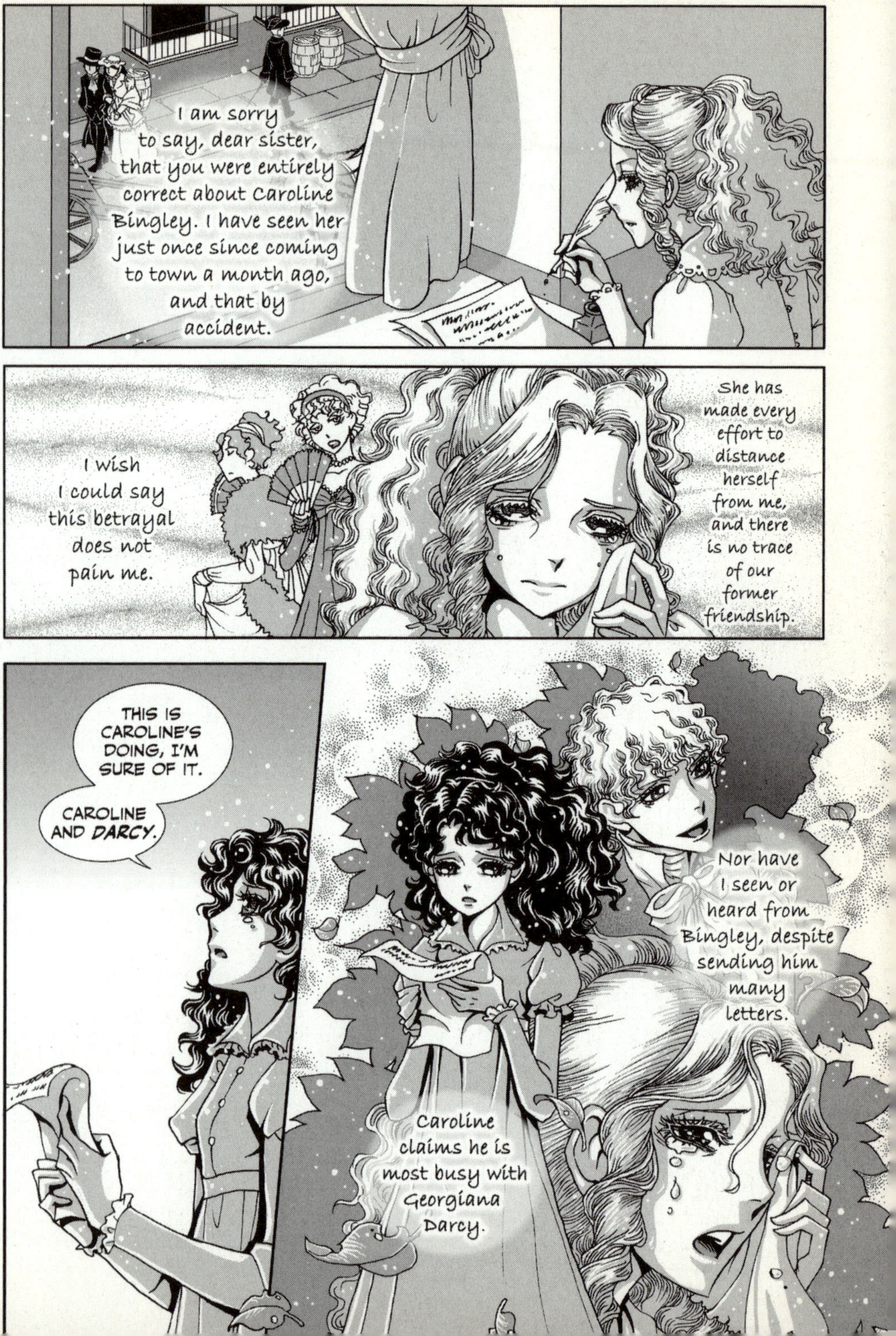
I am sorry to say, dear sister, that you were entirely correct about Caroline Bingley. I have seen her just once since coming to town a month ago, and that by accident.
She has made every effort to distance herself from me, and there is no trace of our former friendship.
I wish I could say this betrayal does not pain me.
Nor have I seen or heard from Bingley, despite sending him many letters.
Caroline claims he is most busy with Georgiana Darcy.
THIS IS CAROLINE'S DOING, I'M SURE OF IT.
CAROLINE AND *DARCY*.

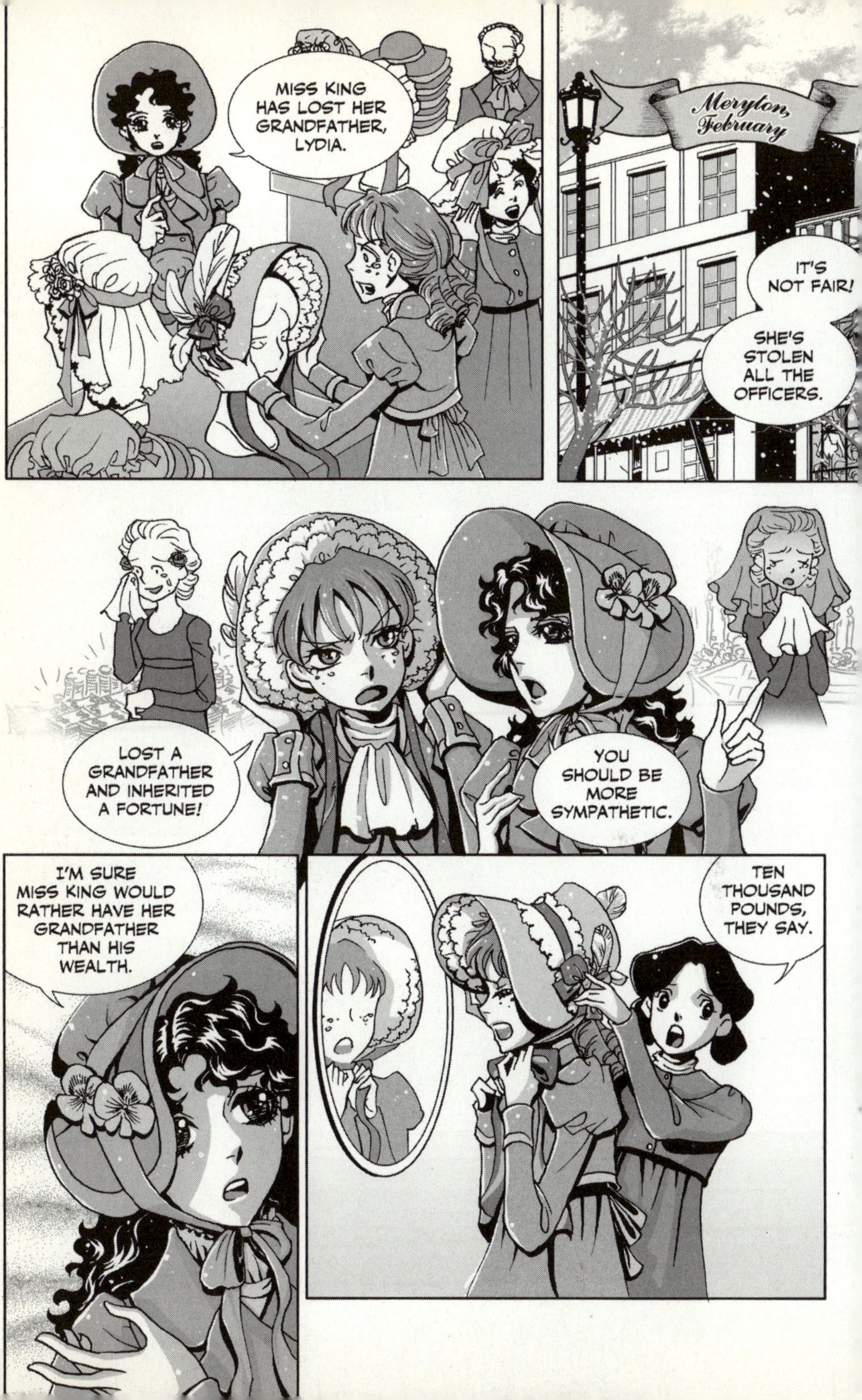
Meryton, February
IT'S NOT FAIR!
SHE'S STOLEN ALL THE OFFICERS.
MISS KING HAS LOST HER GRANDFATHER, LYDIA.
YOU SHOULD BE MORE SYMPATHETIC.
LOST A GRANDFATHER AND INHERITED A FORTUNE!
TEN THOUSAND POUNDS, THEY SAY.
I'M SURE MISS KING WOULD RATHER HAVE HER GRANDFATHER THAN HIS WEALTH.

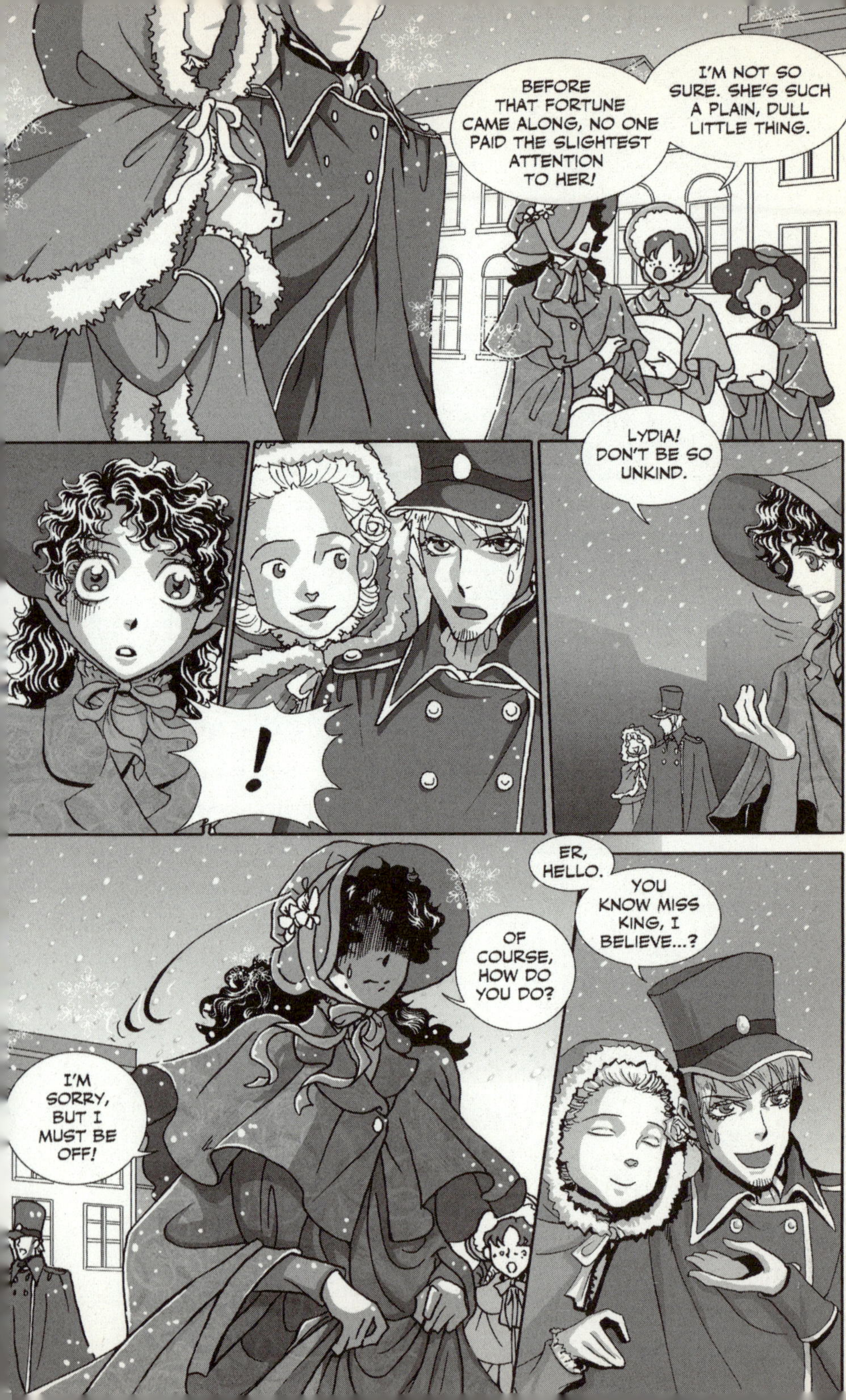
I'M NOT SO SURE. SHE'S SUCH A PLAIN, DULL LITTLE THING.
BEFORE THAT FORTUNE CAME ALONG, NO ONE PAID THE SLIGHTEST ATTENTION TO HER!
LYDIA! DON'T BE SO UNKIND.
!
ER, HELLO.
YOU KNOW MISS KING, I BELIEVE...?
OF COURSE, HOW DO YOU DO?
I'M SORRY, BUT I MUST BE OFF!

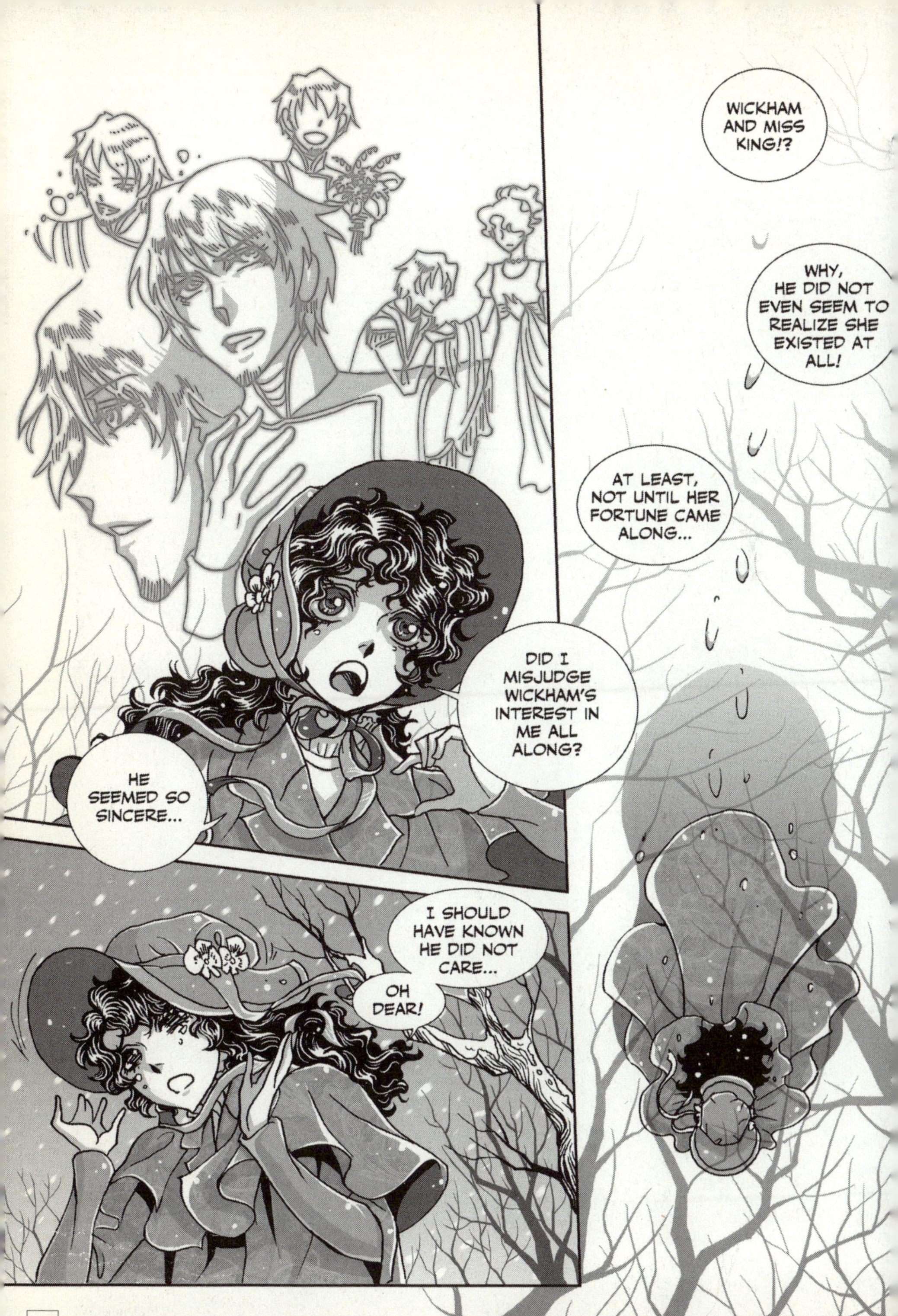
WICKHAM AND MISS KING!?
WHY, HE DID NOT EVEN SEEM TO REALIZE SHE EXISTED AT ALL!
AT LEAST, NOT UNTIL HER FORTUNE CAME ALONG...
DID I MISJUDGE WICKHAM'S INTEREST IN ME ALL ALONG?
HE SEEMED SO SINCERE...
I SHOULD HAVE KNOWN HE DID NOT CARE...
OH DEAR!

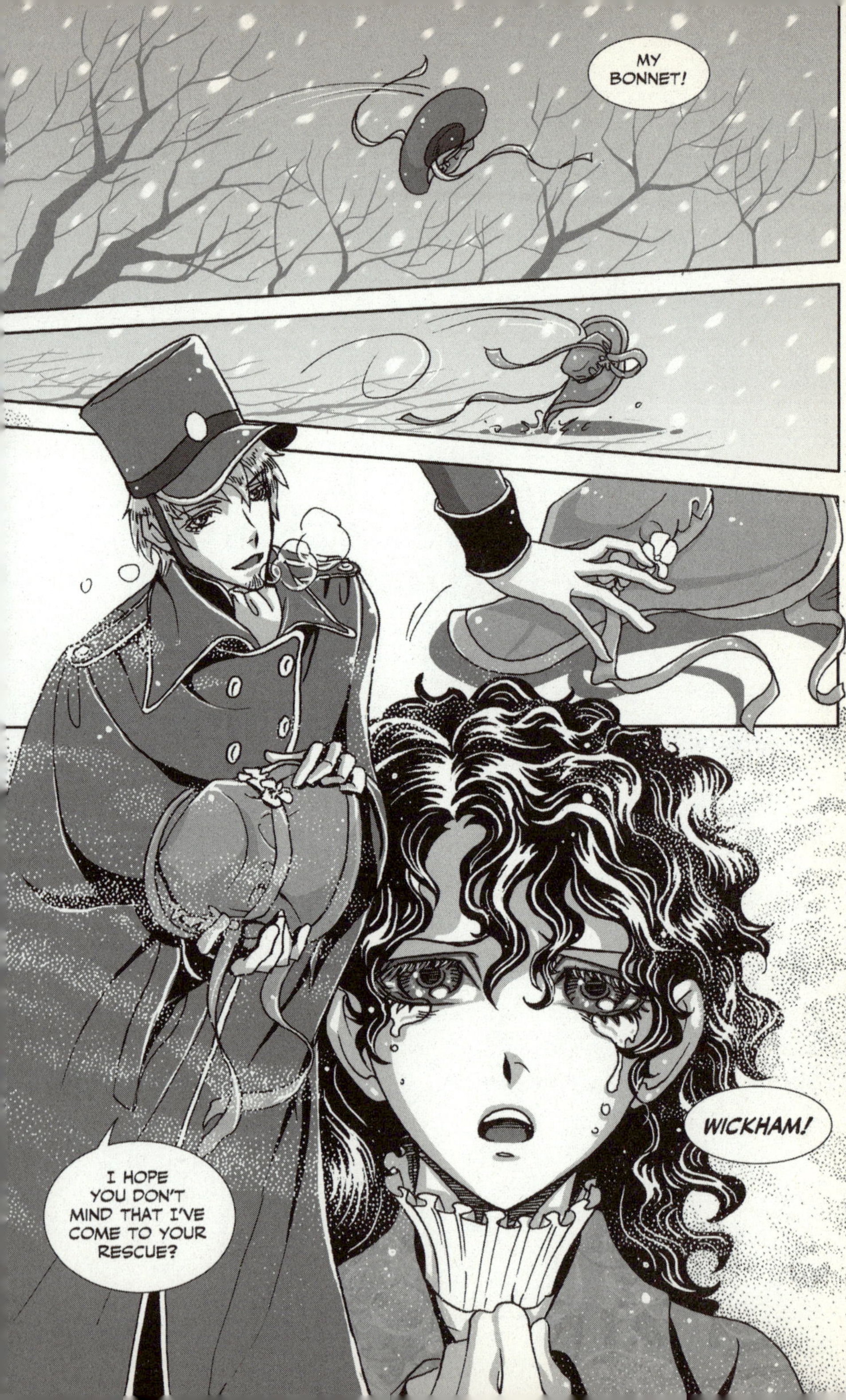
MY BONNET!
WICKHAM!
I HOPE YOU DON'T MIND THAT I'VE COME TO YOUR RESCUE?

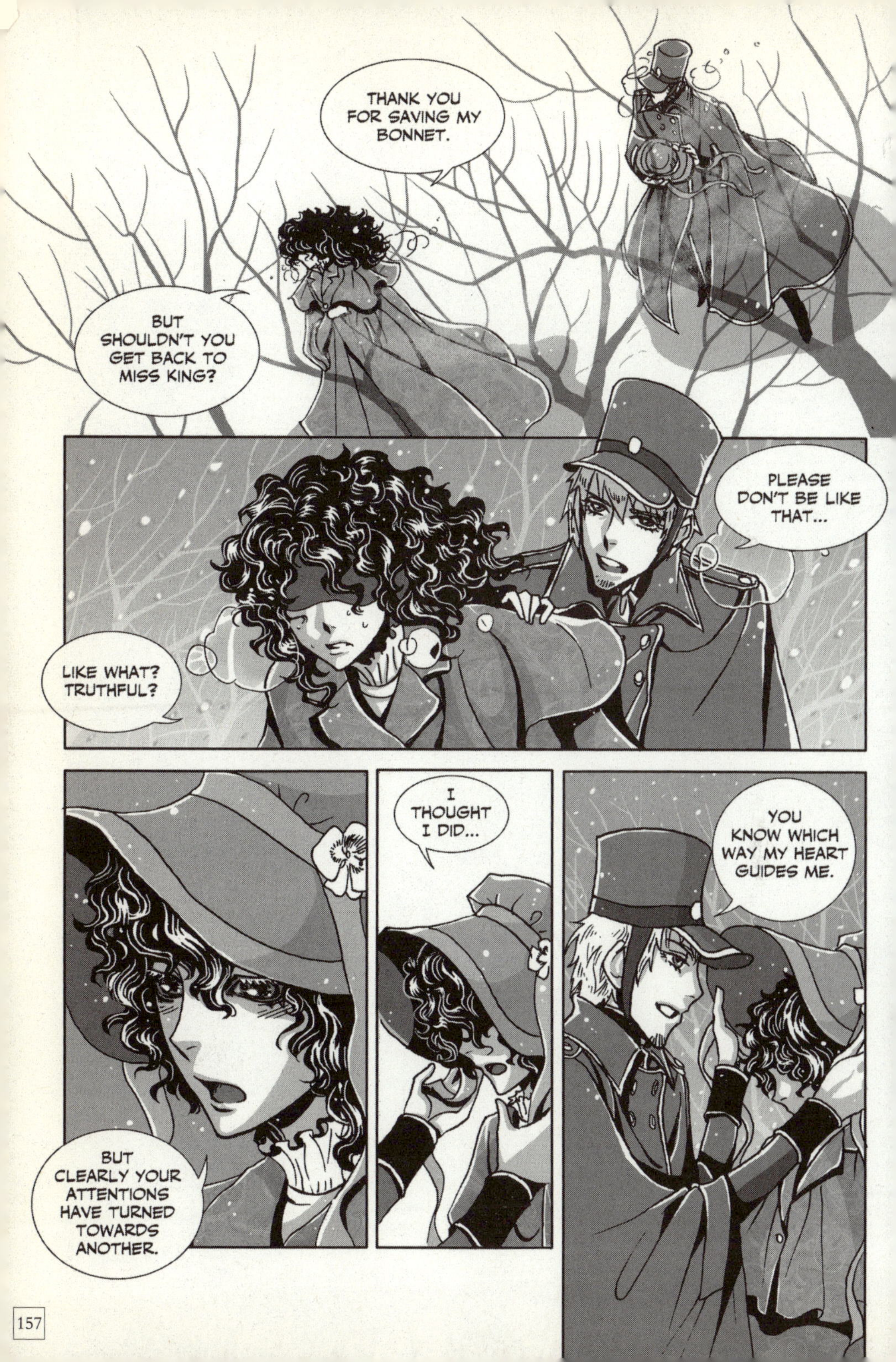
THANK YOU FOR SAVING MY BONNET.
BUT SHOULDN'T YOU GET BACK TO MISS KING?
PLEASE DON'T BE LIKE THAT...
LIKE WHAT? TRUTHFUL?
YOU KNOW WHICH WAY MY HEART GUIDES ME.
I THOUGHT I DID...
BUT CLEARLY YOUR ATTENTIONS HAVE TURNED TOWARDS ANOTHER.

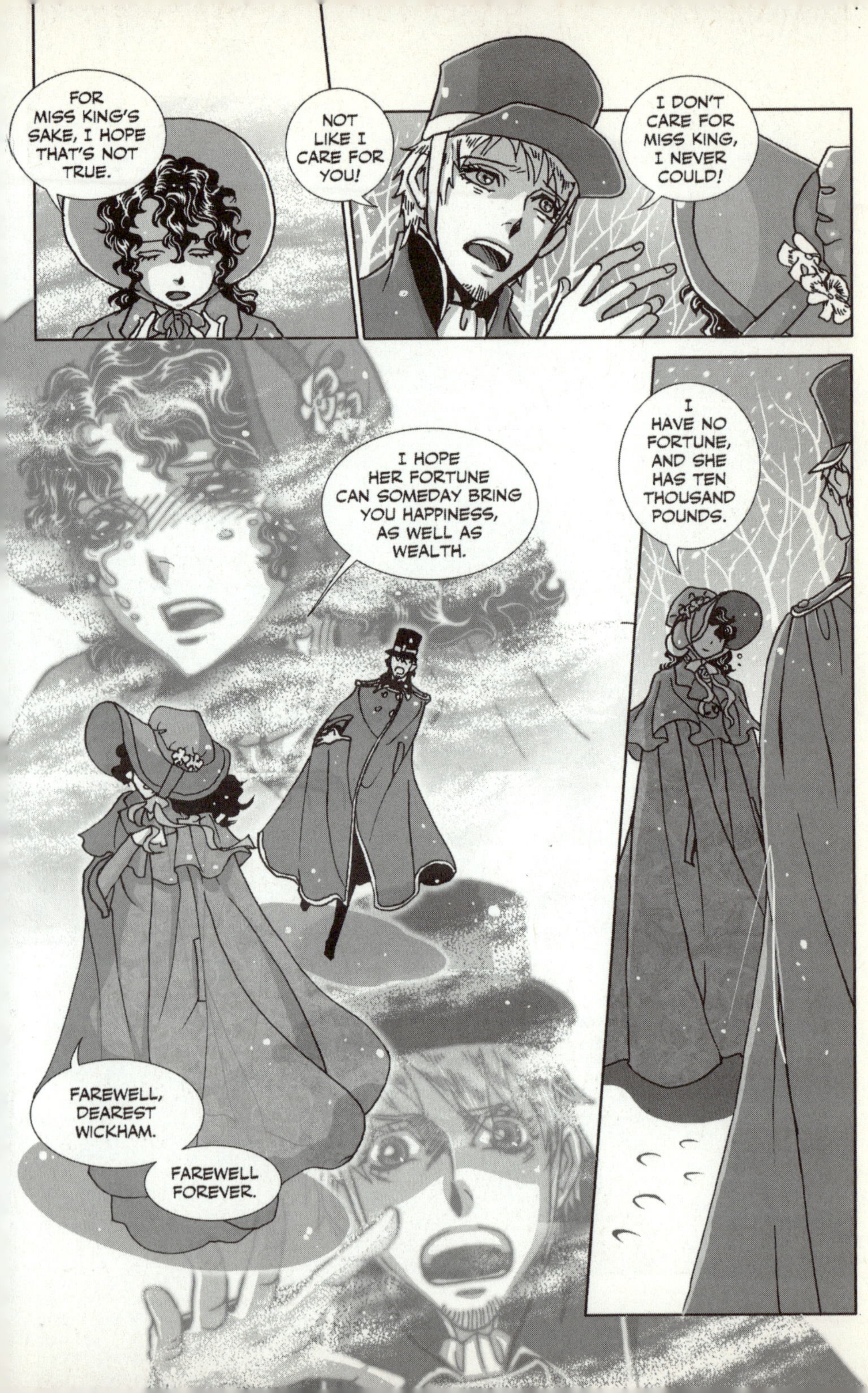
I DON'T CARE FOR MISS KING, I NEVER COULD!
NOT LIKE I CARE FOR YOU!
FOR MISS KING'S SAKE, I HOPE THAT'S NOT TRUE.
I HAVE NO FORTUNE, AND SHE HAS TEN THOUSAND POUNDS.
I HOPE HER FORTUNE CAN SOMEDAY BRING YOU HAPPINESS, AS WELL AS WEALTH.
FAREWELL, DEAREST WICKHAM.
FAREWELL FOREVER.

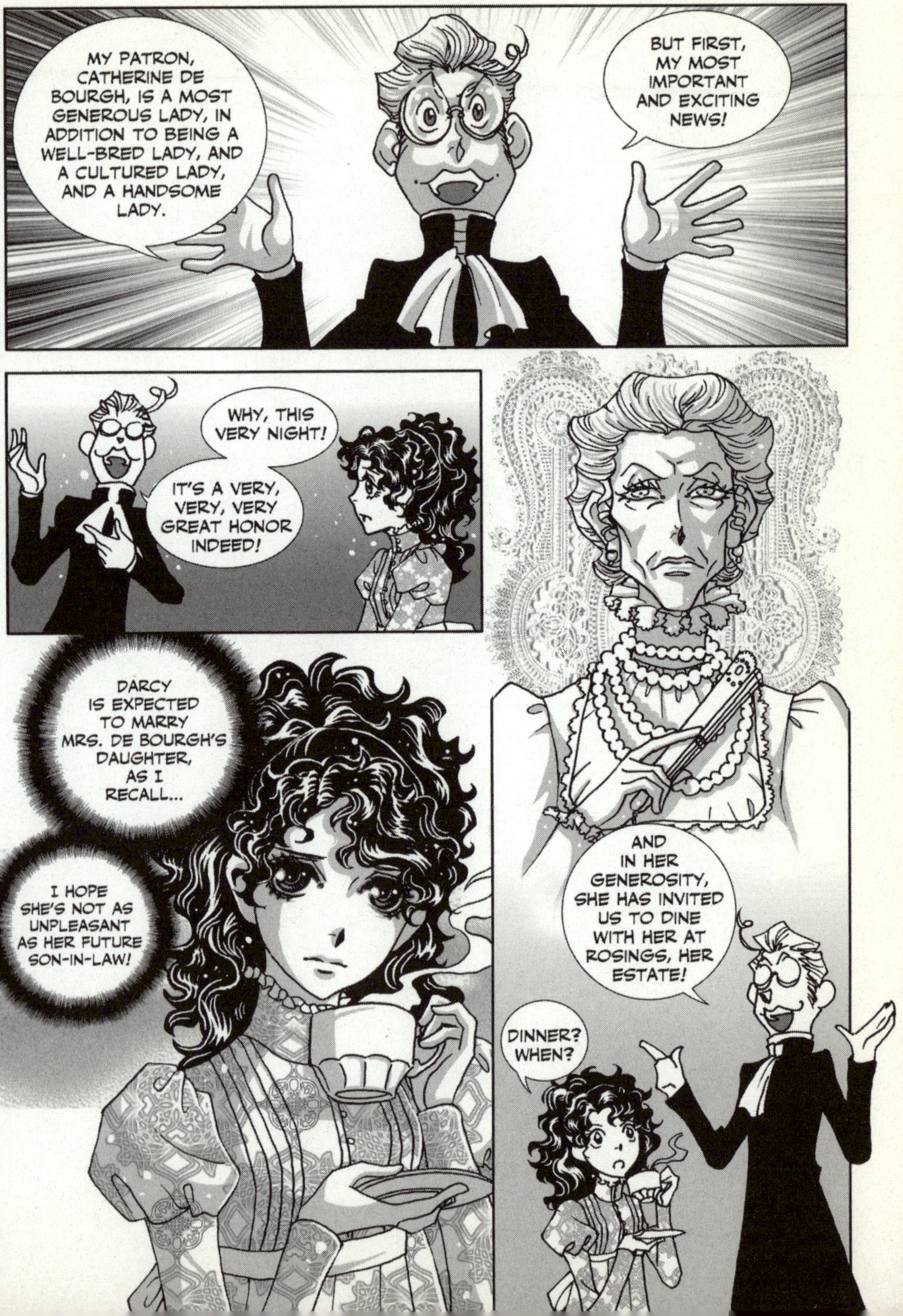
BUT FIRST, MY MOST IMPORTANT AND EXCITING NEWS!
MY PATRON, CATHERINE DE BOURGH, IS A MOST GENEROUS LADY, IN ADDITION TO BEING A WELL-BRED LADY, AND A CULTURED LADY, AND A HANDSOME LADY.
AND IN HER GENEROSITY, SHE HAS INVITED US TO DINE WITH HER AT ROSINGS, HER ESTATE!
DINNER? WHEN?
WHY, THIS VERY NIGHT!
IT'S A VERY, VERY, VERY GREAT HONOR INDEED!
DARCY IS EXPECTED TO MARRY MRS. DE BOURGH'S DAUGHTER, AS I RECALL...
I HOPE SHE'S NOT AS UNPLEASANT AS HER FUTURE SON-IN-LAW!

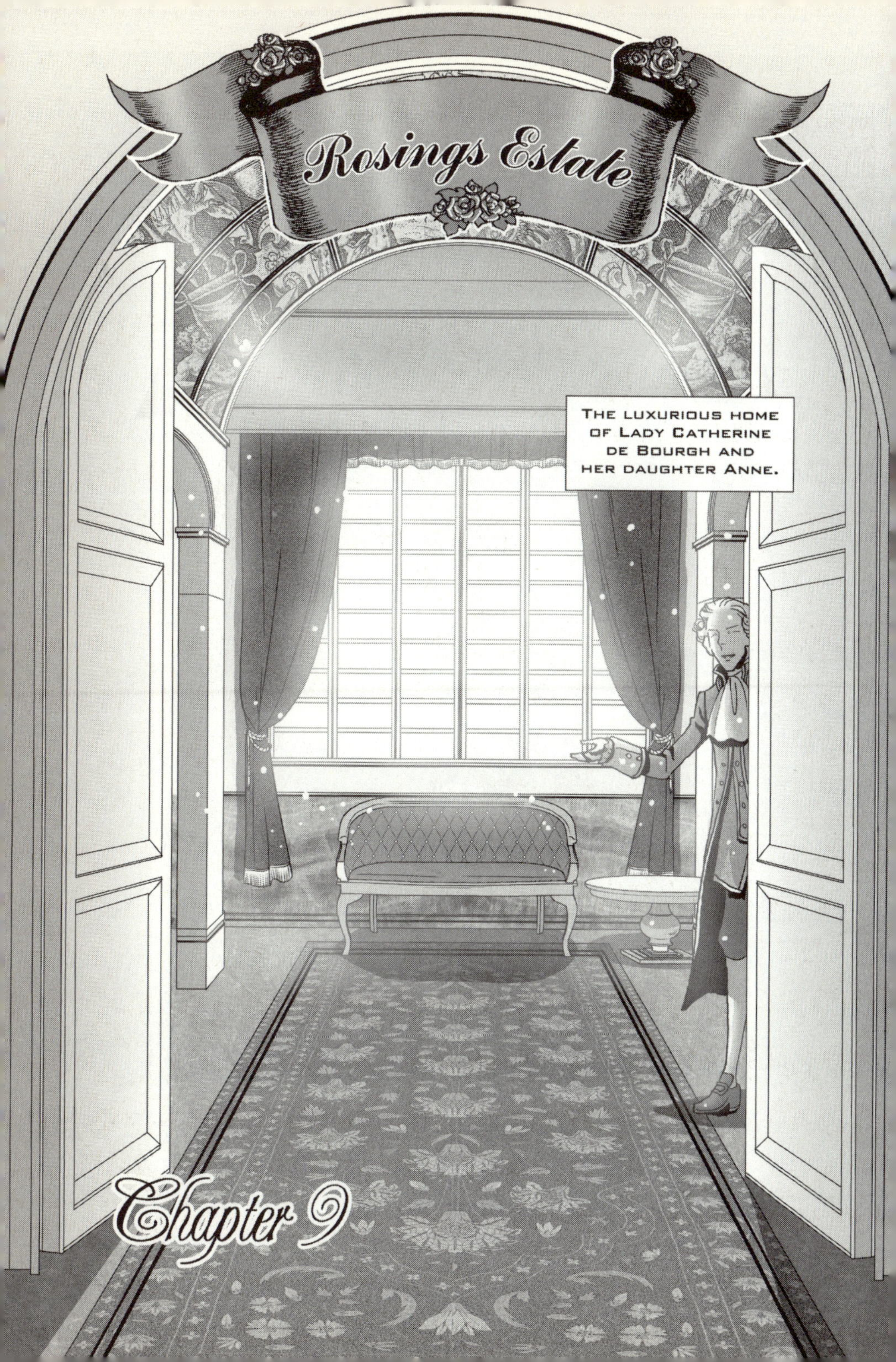
Rosings Estate
THE LUXURIOUS HOME OF LADY CATHERINE DE BOURGH AND HER DAUGHTER ANNE.
Chapter 9

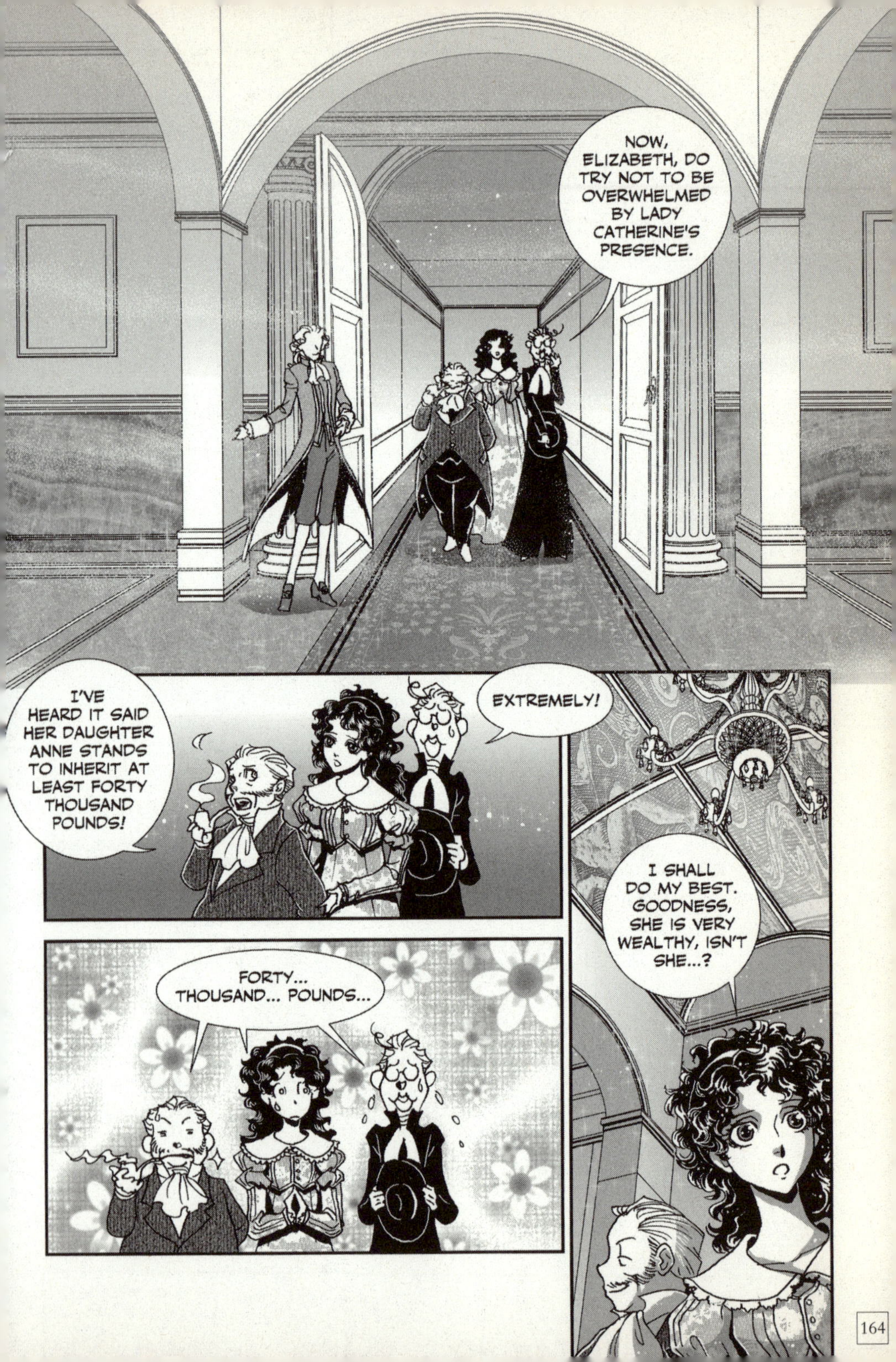
NOW, ELIZABETH, DO TRY NOT TO BE OVERWHELMED BY LADY CATHERINE'S PRESENCE.
I SHALL DO MY BEST. GOODNESS, SHE IS VERY WEALTHY, ISN'T SHE...?
EXTREMELY!
I'VE HEARD IT SAID HER DAUGHTER ANNE STANDS TO INHERIT AT LEAST FORTY THOUSAND POUNDS!
FORTY... THOUSAND... POUNDS...

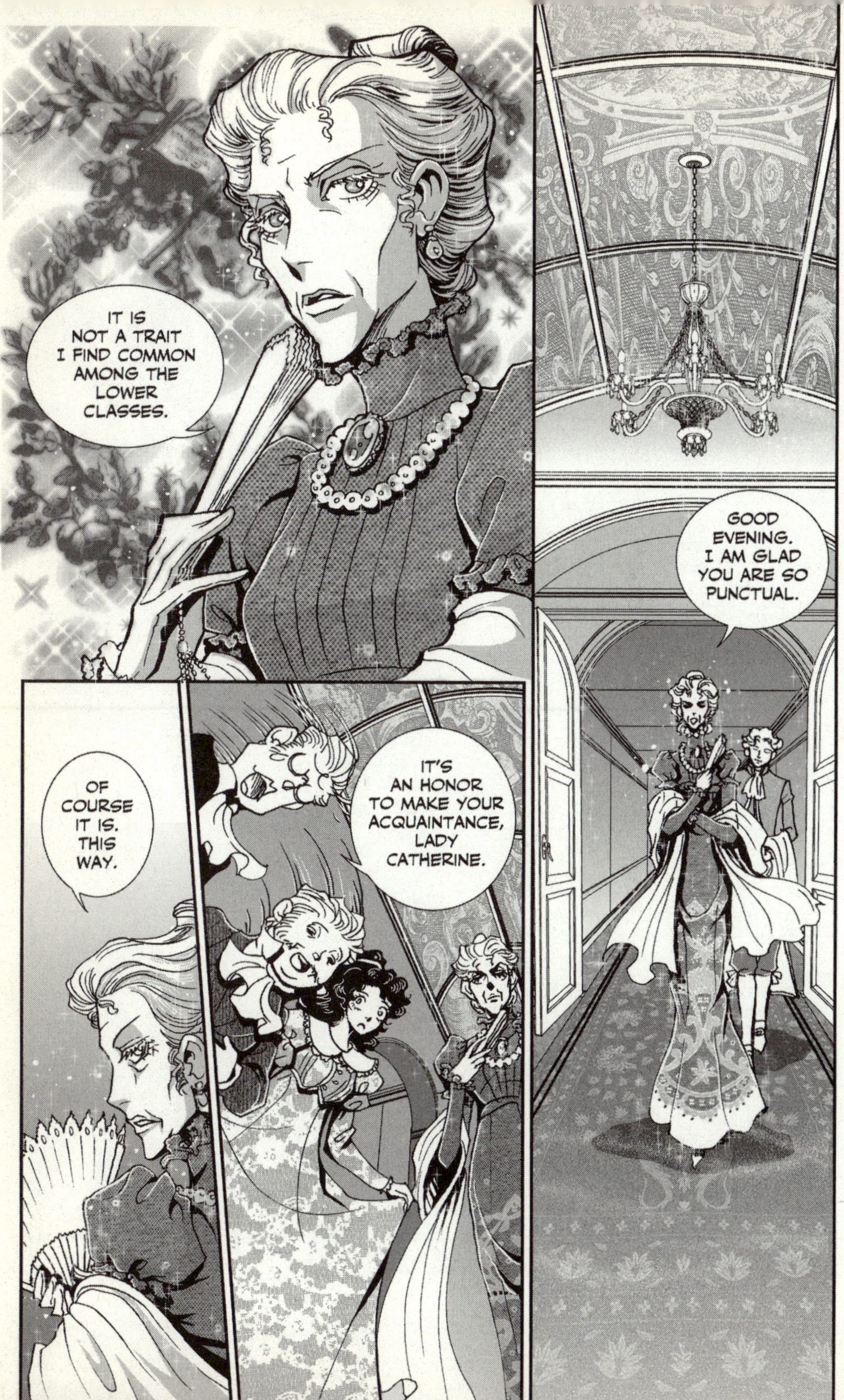
GOOD EVENING. I AM GLAD YOU ARE SO PUNCTUAL.
IT IS NOT A TRAIT I FIND COMMON AMONG THE LOWER CLASSES.
IT'S AN HONOR TO MAKE YOUR ACQUAINTANCE, LADY CATHERINE.
OF COURSE IT IS. THIS WAY.

166

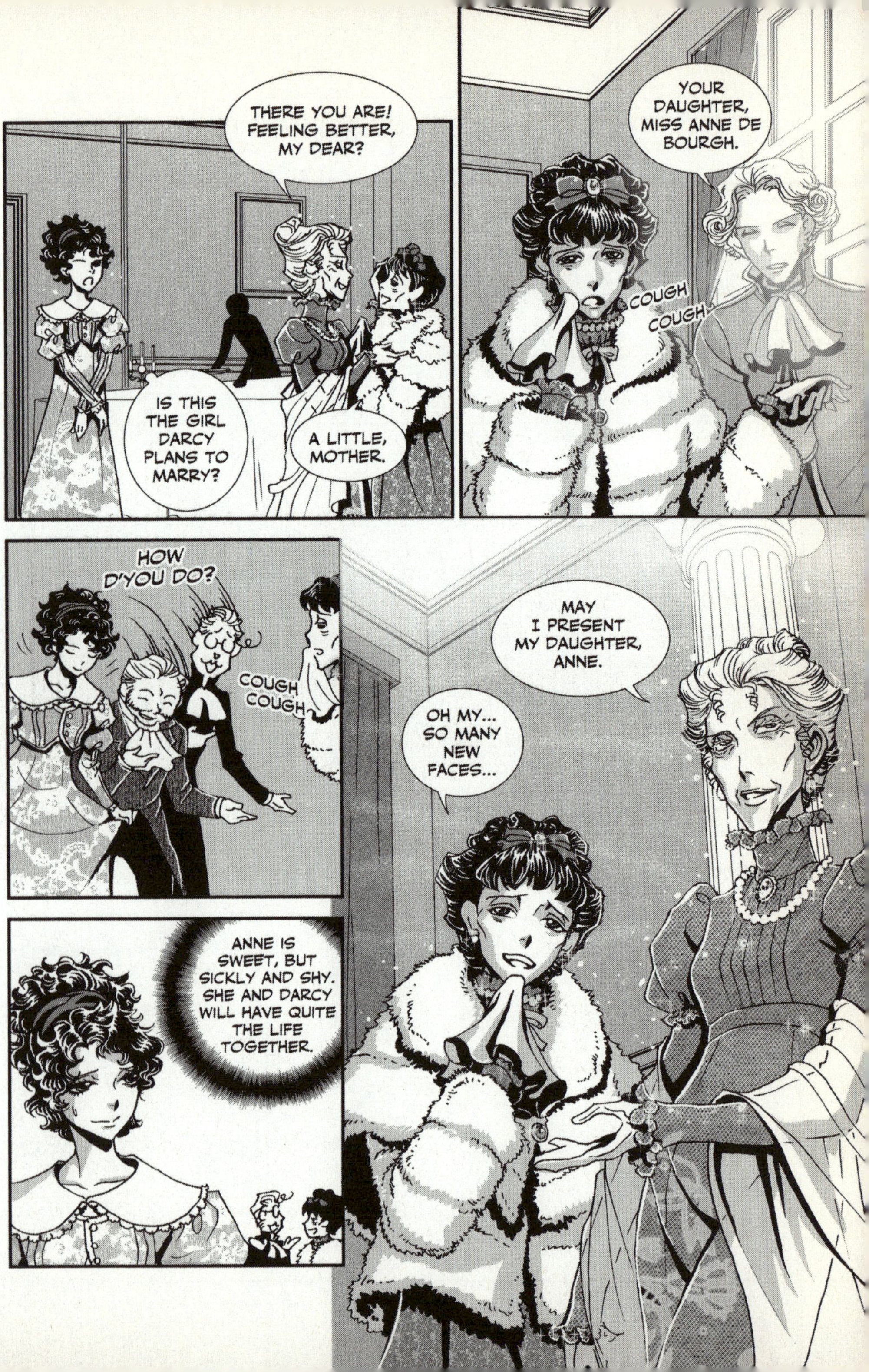
YOUR DAUGHTER, MISS ANNE DE BOURGH.
COUGH
COUGH
THERE YOU ARE! FEELING BETTER, MY DEAR?
A LITTLE, MOTHER.
IS THIS THE GIRL DARCY PLANS TO MARRY?
MAY I PRESENT MY DAUGHTER, ANNE.
OH MY... SO MANY NEW FACES...
HOW D'YOU DO?
COUGH COUGH
ANNE IS SWEET, BUT SICKLY AND SHY. SHE AND DARCY WILL HAVE QUITE THE LIFE TOGETHER.

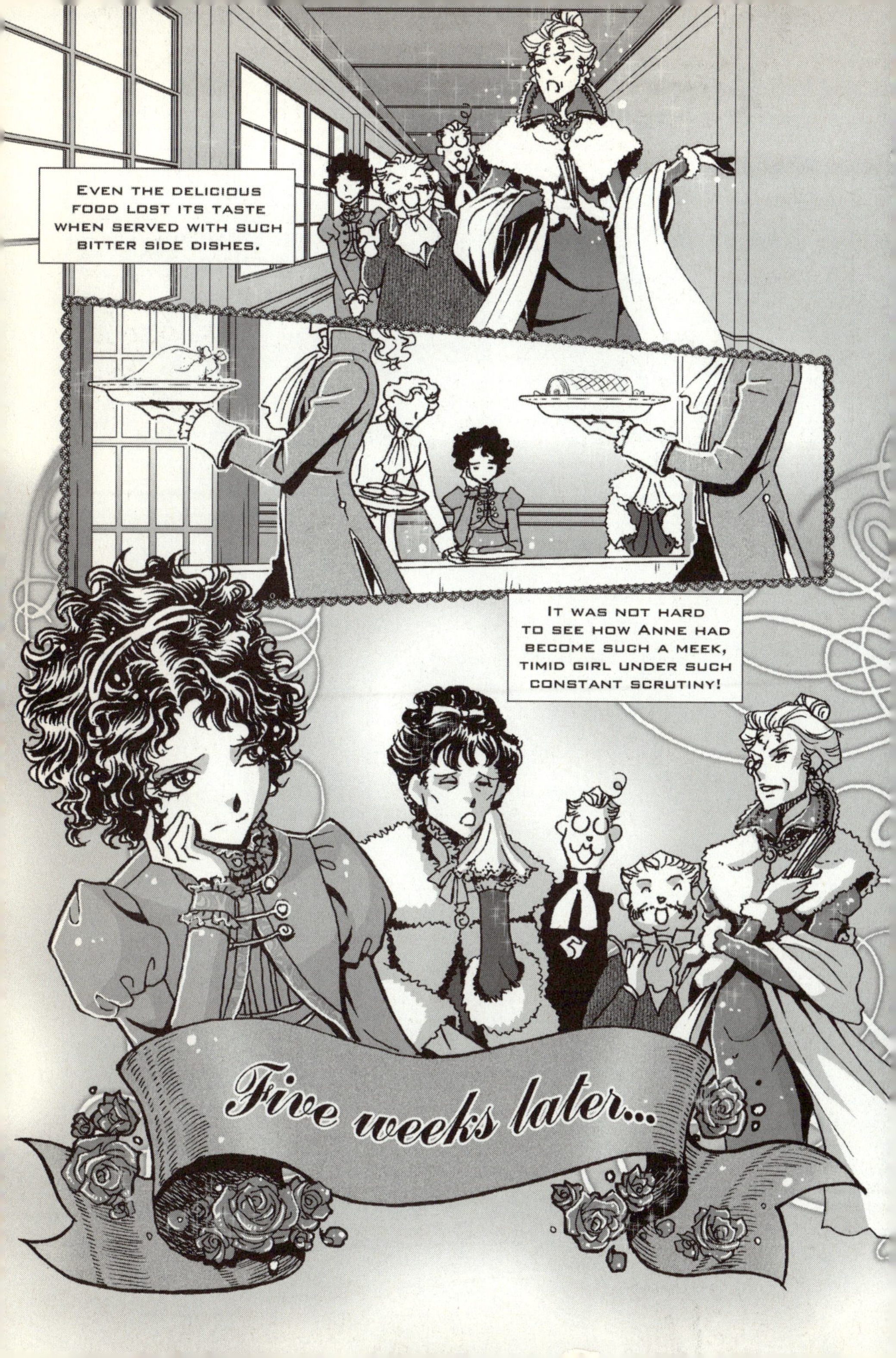
Even the delicious food lost its taste when served with such bitter side dishes.
It was not hard to see how Anne had become such a meek, timid girl under such constant scrutiny!
Five weeks later...

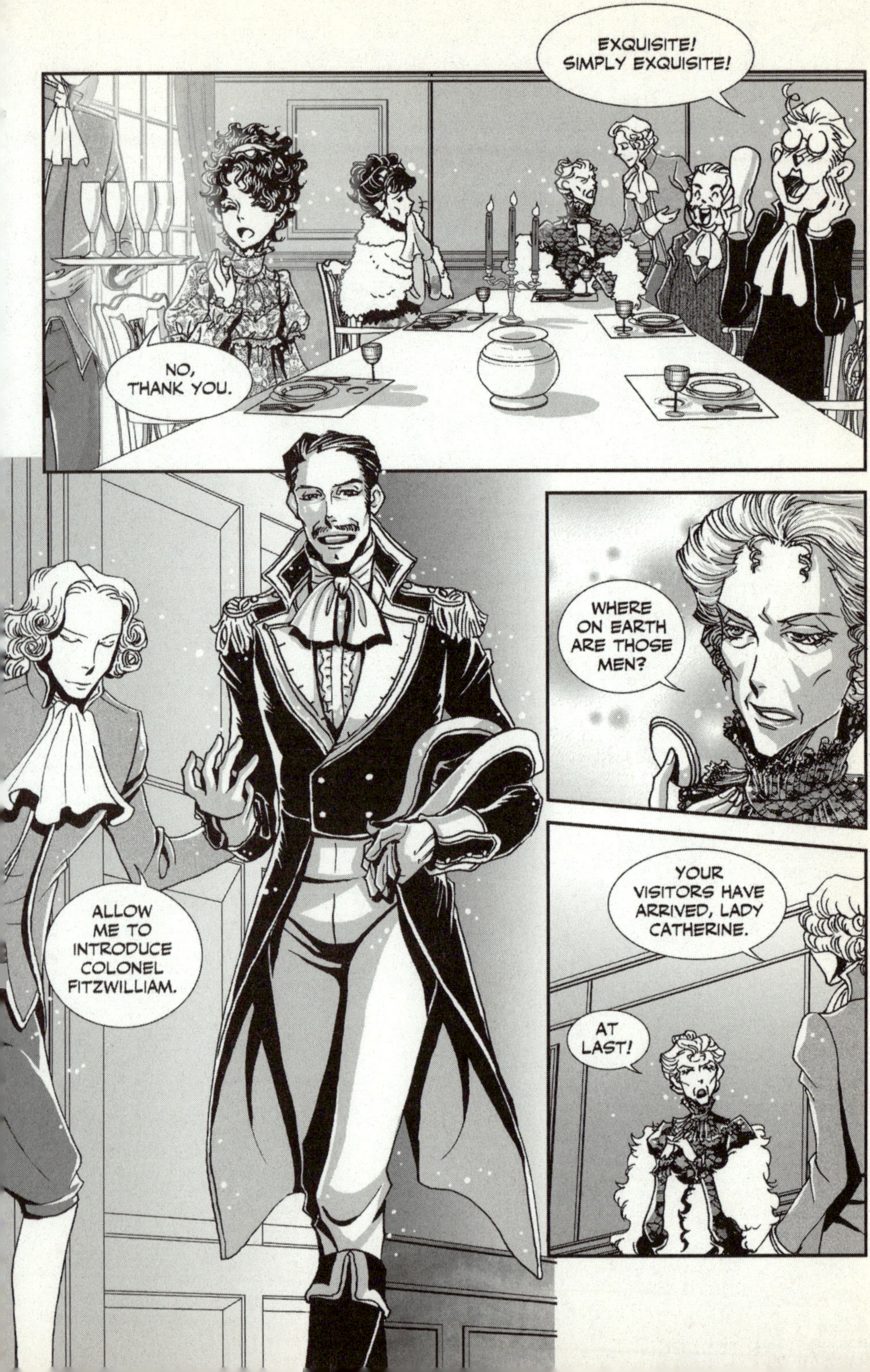
EXQUISITE! SIMPLY EXQUISITE!
NO, THANK YOU.
WHERE ON EARTH ARE THOSE MEN?
YOUR VISITORS HAVE ARRIVED, LADY CATHERINE.
AT LAST!
ALLOW ME TO INTRODUCE COLONEL FITZWILLIAM.

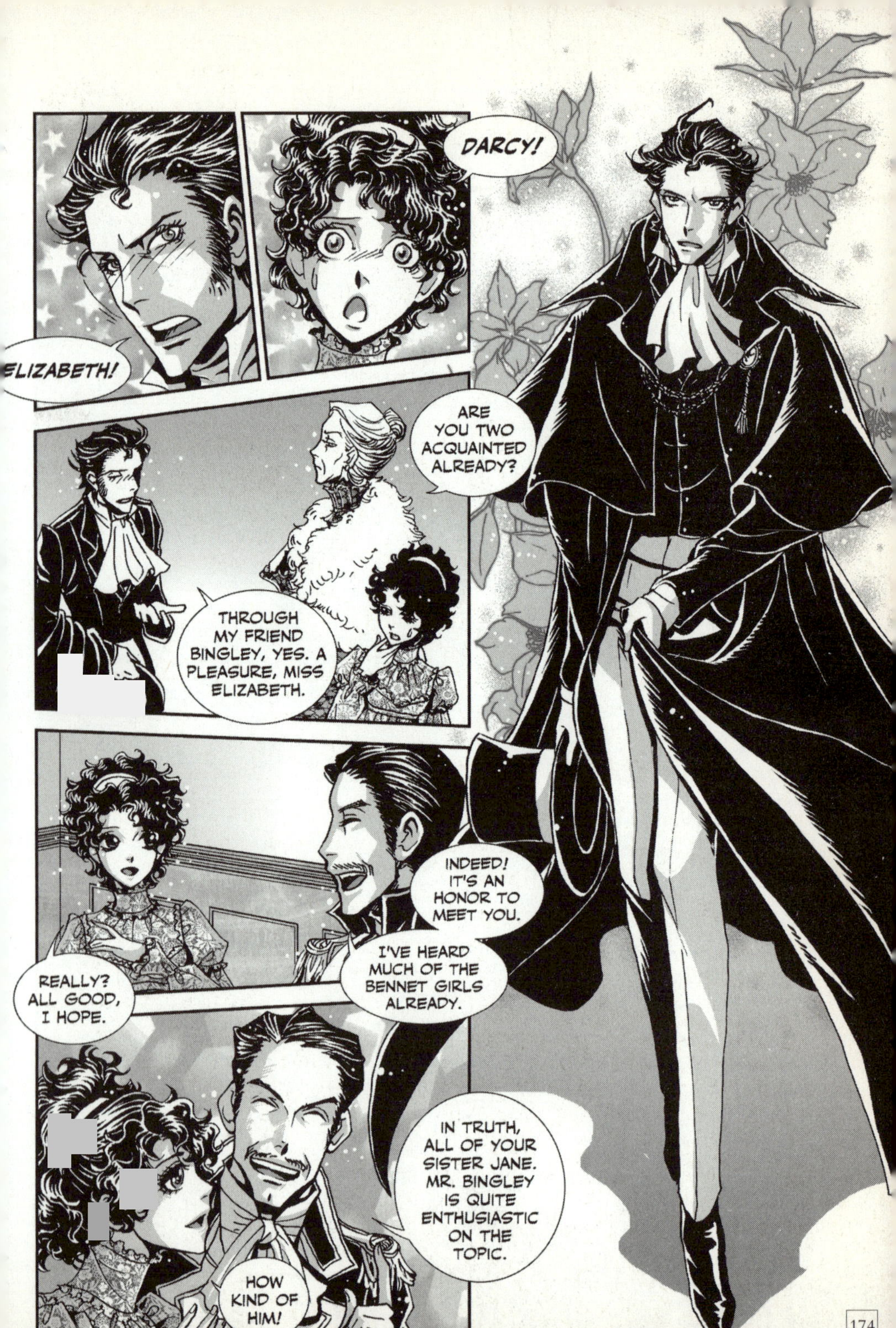
DARCY!
ELIZABETH!
ARE YOU TWO ACQUAINTED ALREADY?
THROUGH MY FRIEND BINGLEY, YES. A PLEASURE, MISS ELIZABETH.
INDEED! IT'S AN HONOR TO MEET YOU.
I'VE HEARD MUCH OF THE BENNET GIRLS ALREADY.
REALLY? ALL GOOD, I HOPE.
IN TRUTH, ALL OF YOUR SISTER JANE. MR. BINGLEY IS QUITE ENTHUSIASTIC ON THE TOPIC.
HOW KIND OF HIM!

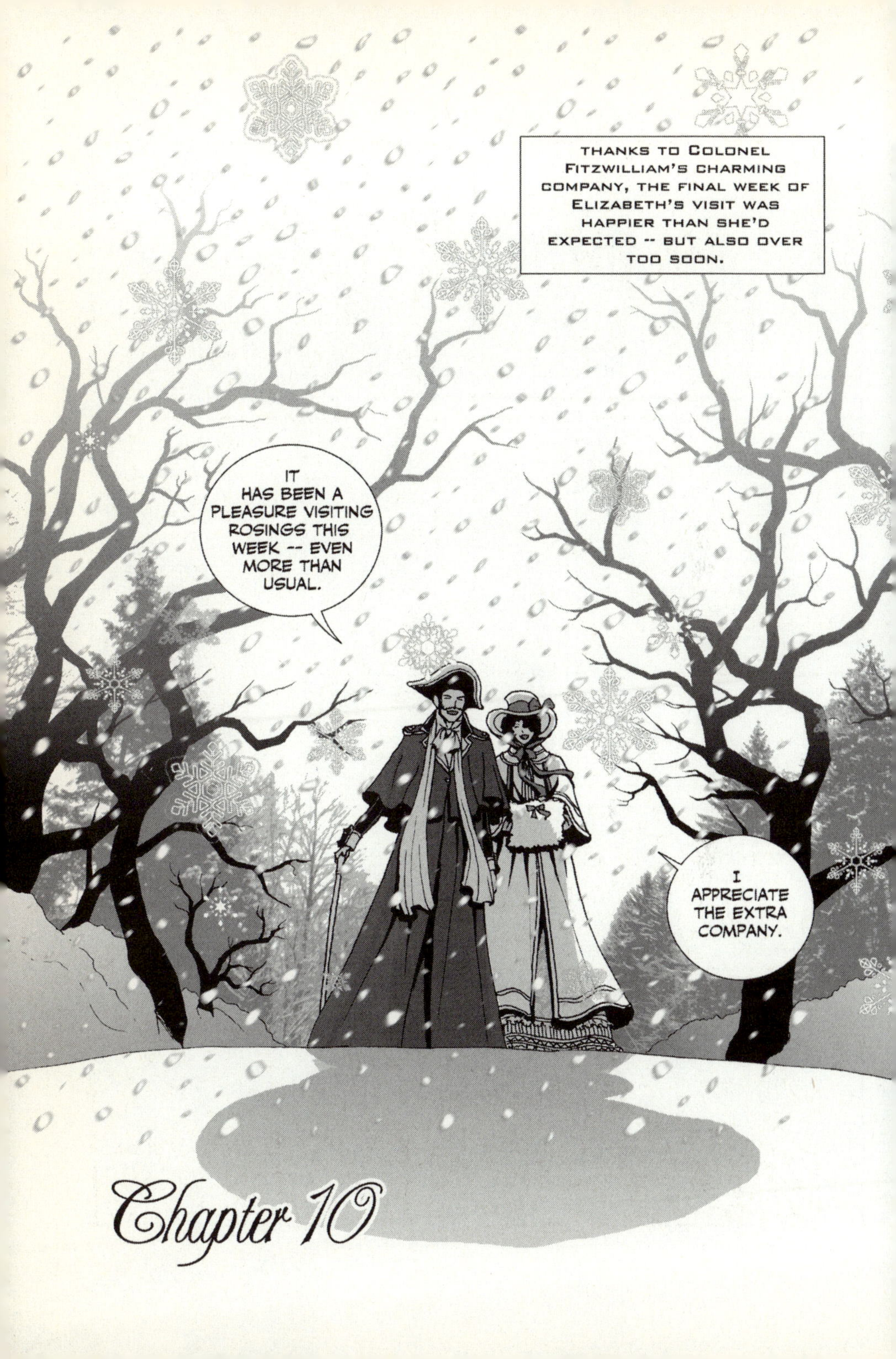
THANKS TO COLONEL FITZWILLIAM'S CHARMING COMPANY, THE FINAL WEEK OF ELIZABETH'S VISIT WAS HAPPIER THAN SHE'D EXPECTED -- BUT ALSO OVER TOO SOON.
IT HAS BEEN A PLEASURE VISITING ROSINGS THIS WEEK -- EVEN MORE THAN USUAL.
I APPRECIATE THE EXTRA COMPANY.
Chapter 10

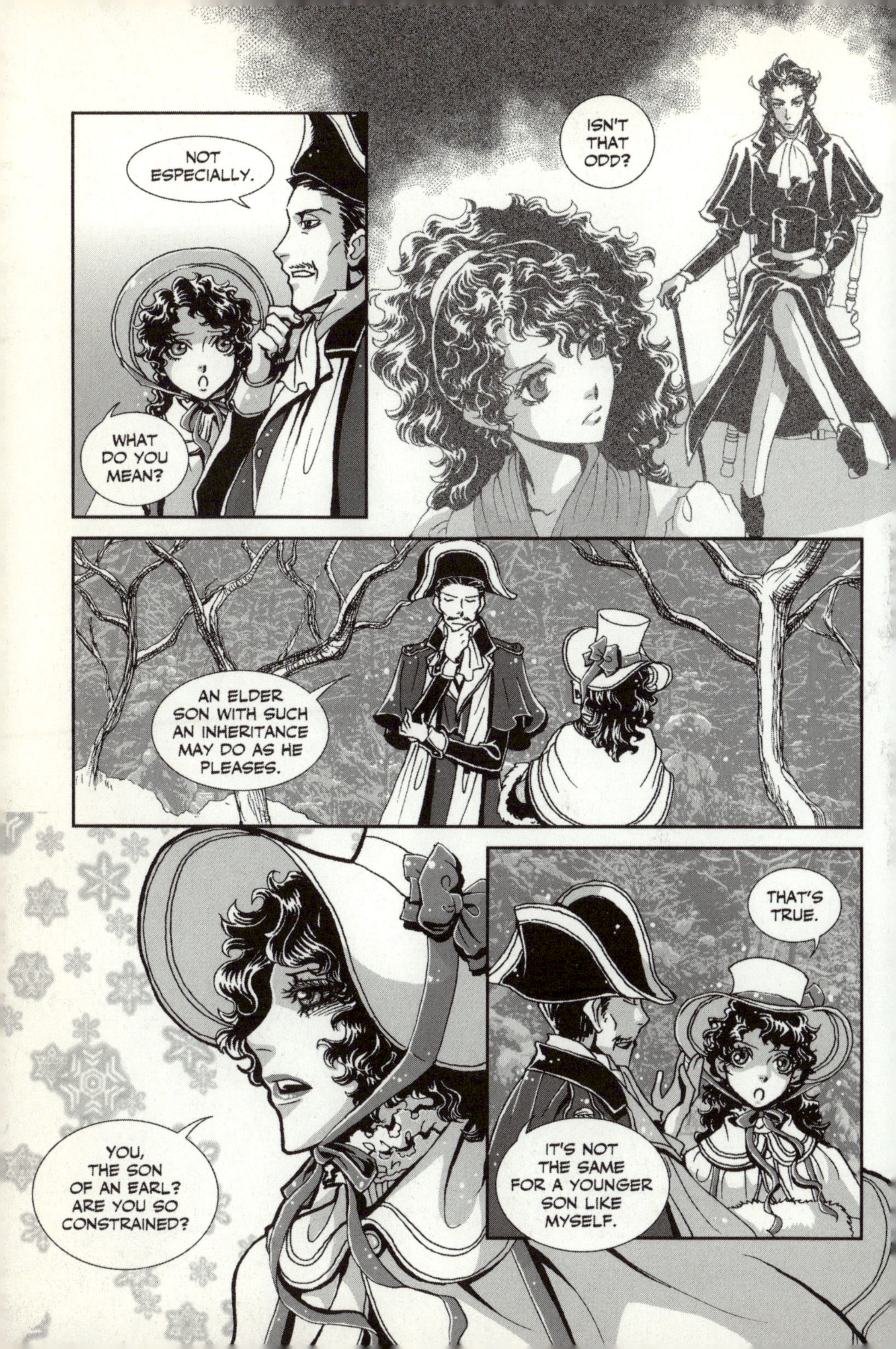
ISN'T THAT ODD?
NOT ESPECIALLY.
WHAT DO YOU MEAN?
AN ELDER SON WITH SUCH AN INHERITANCE MAY DO AS HE PLEASES.
THAT'S TRUE.
IT'S NOT THE SAME FOR A YOUNGER SON LIKE MYSELF.
YOU, THE SON OF AN EARL? ARE YOU SO CONSTRAINED?

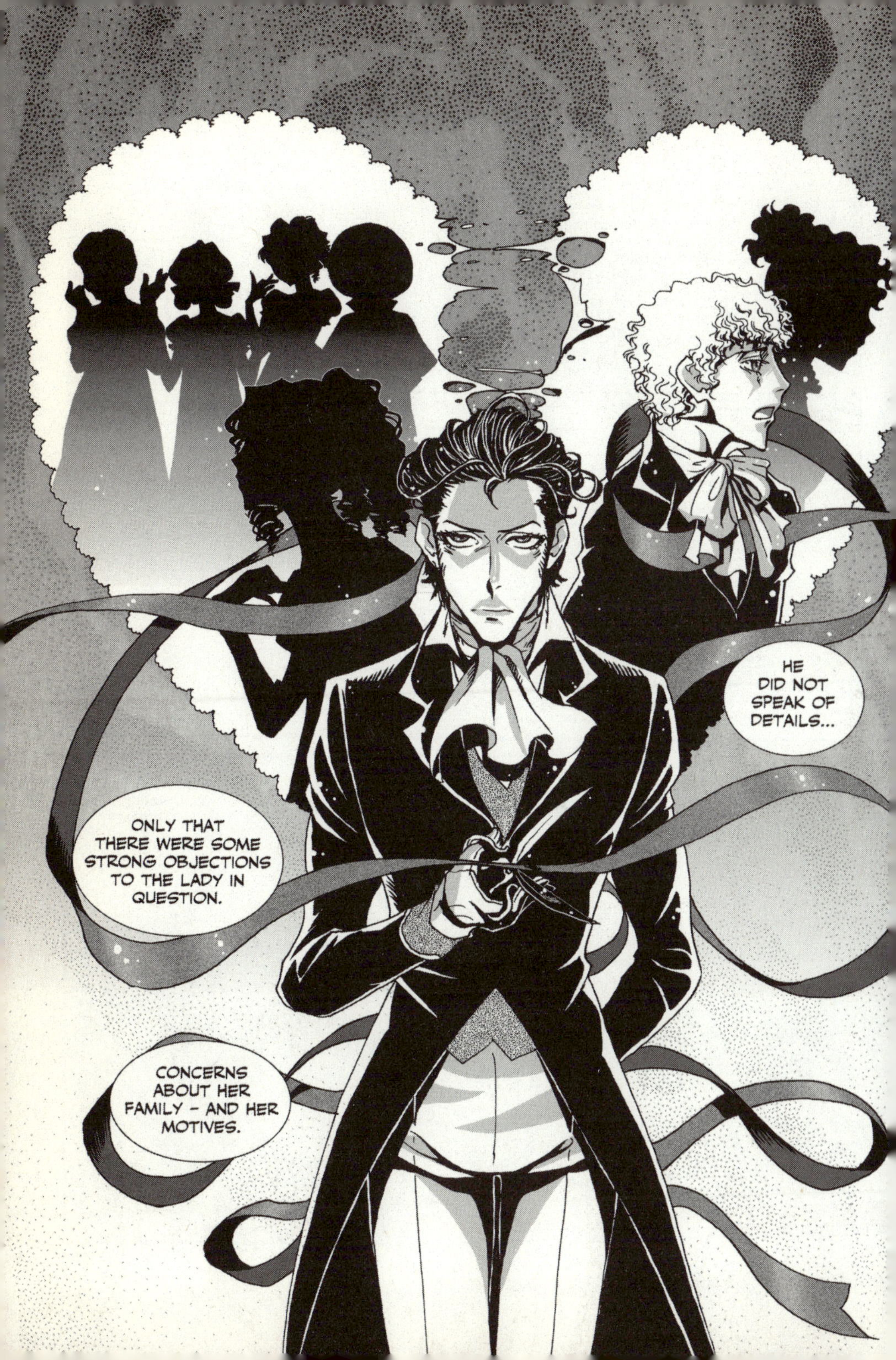
HE DID NOT SPEAK OF DETAILS...
ONLY THAT THERE WERE SOME STRONG OBJECTIONS TO THE LADY IN QUESTION.
CONCERNS ABOUT HER FAMILY - AND HER MOTIVES.

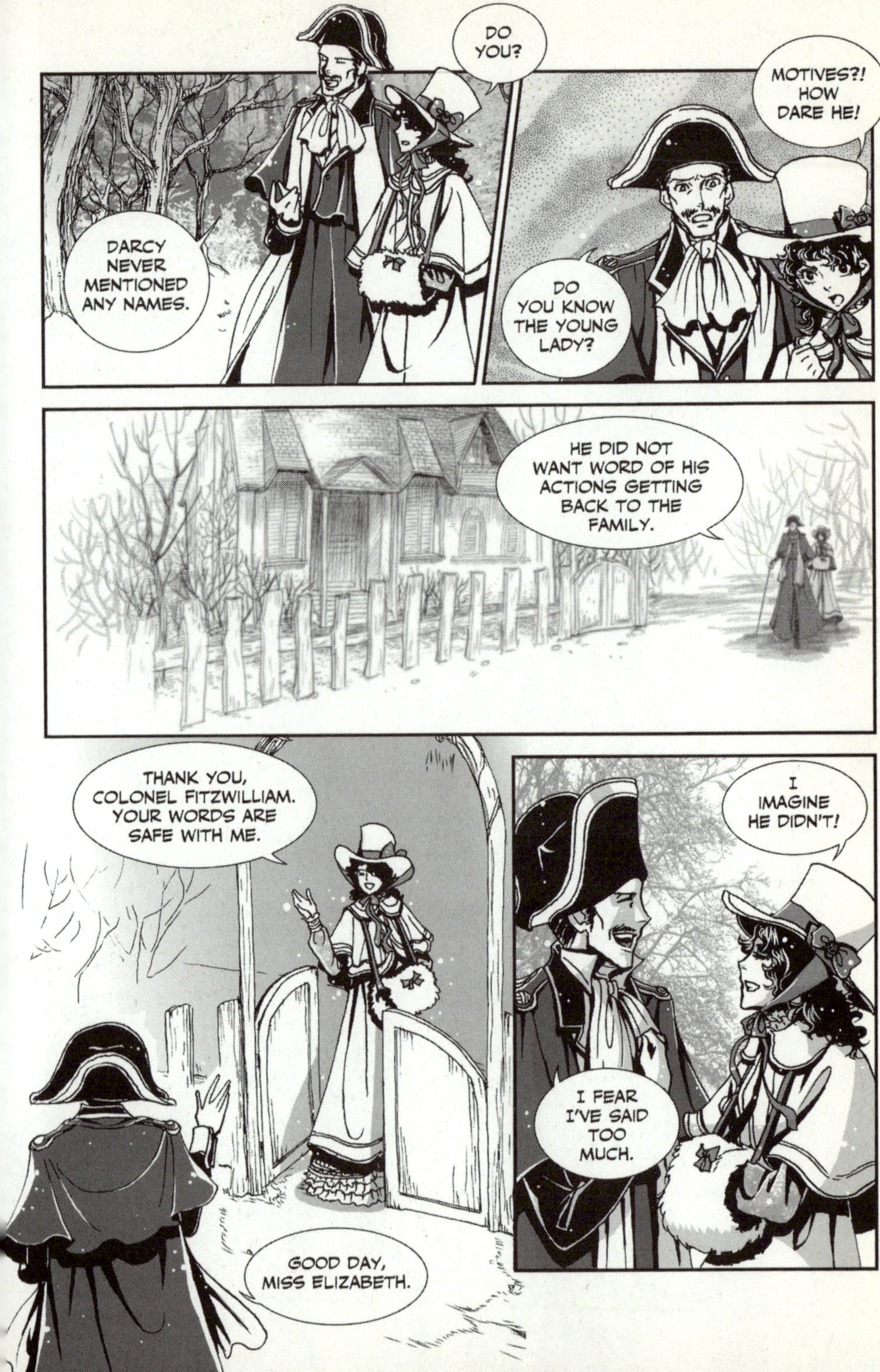

MOTIVES?! HOW DARE HE!
DO YOU KNOW THE YOUNG LADY?
DO YOU?
DARCY NEVER MENTIONED ANY NAMES.
HE DID NOT WANT WORD OF HIS ACTIONS GETTING BACK TO THE FAMILY.
I IMAGINE HE DIDN'T!
I FEAR I'VE SAID TOO MUCH.
THANK YOU, COLONEL FITZWILLIAM. YOUR WORDS ARE SAFE WITH ME.
GOOD DAY, MISS ELIZABETH.

THEY'VE GONE TO VISIT LADY CATHERINE AGAIN.

CHARLOTTE? MR. COLLINS?

HE IS THE CAUSE OF ALL JANE HAS SUFFERED!

HE HAS RUINED EVERY HOPE OF HAPPINESS FOR THE MOST AFFECTIONATE, GENEROUS HEART IN THE WORLD!

THERE CAN BE NO DOUBT. DARCY IS RESPONSIBLE FOR TEARING JANE AND BINGLEY APART!

I'M COMING!

KNOCK! KNOCK!

WHO CAN THAT BE?

THAT CRUEL, PROUD MAN! I SHALL NEVER BE ABLE TO FORGIVE HIM.

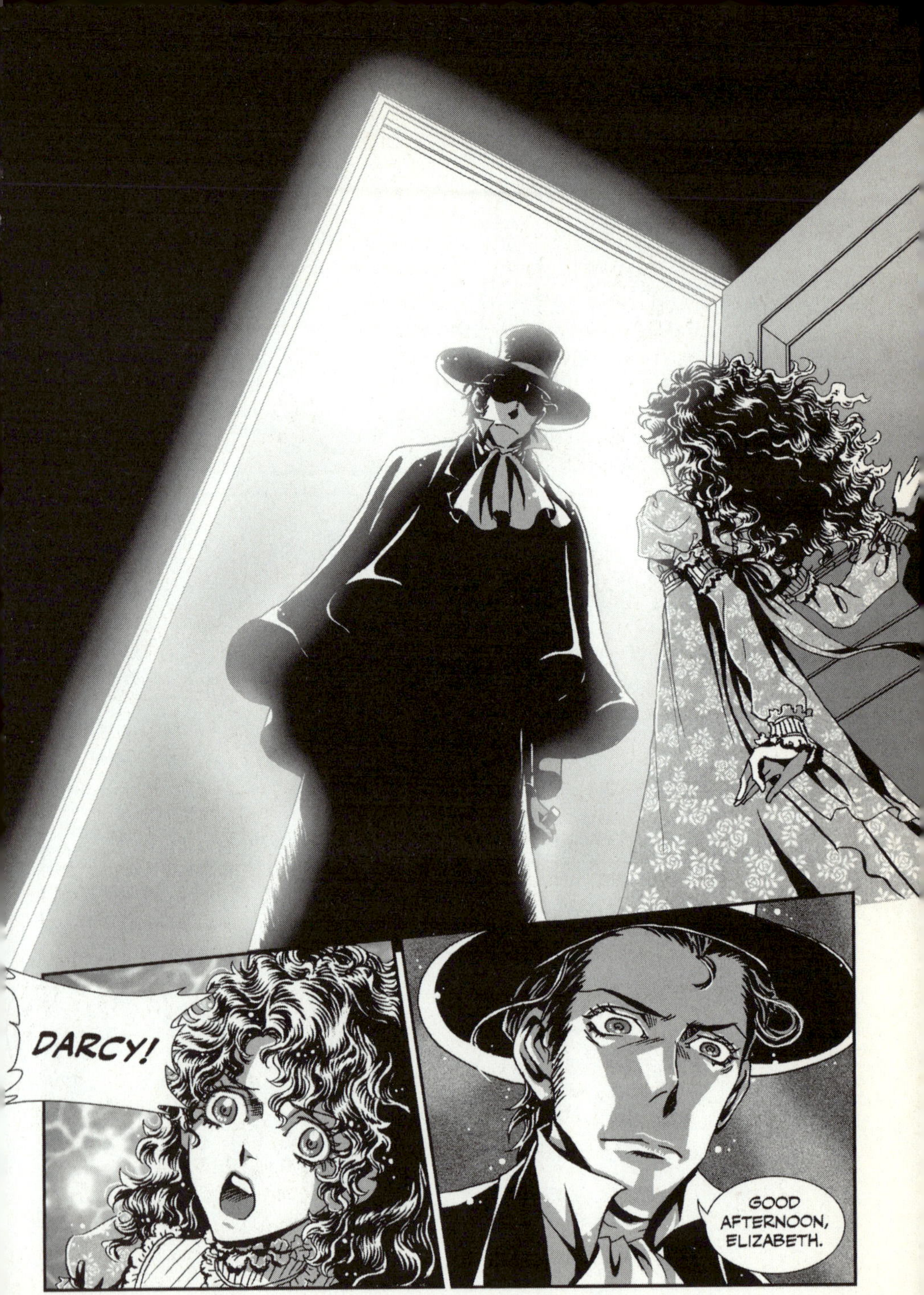
GOOD AFTERNOON, ELIZABETH.
DARCY!

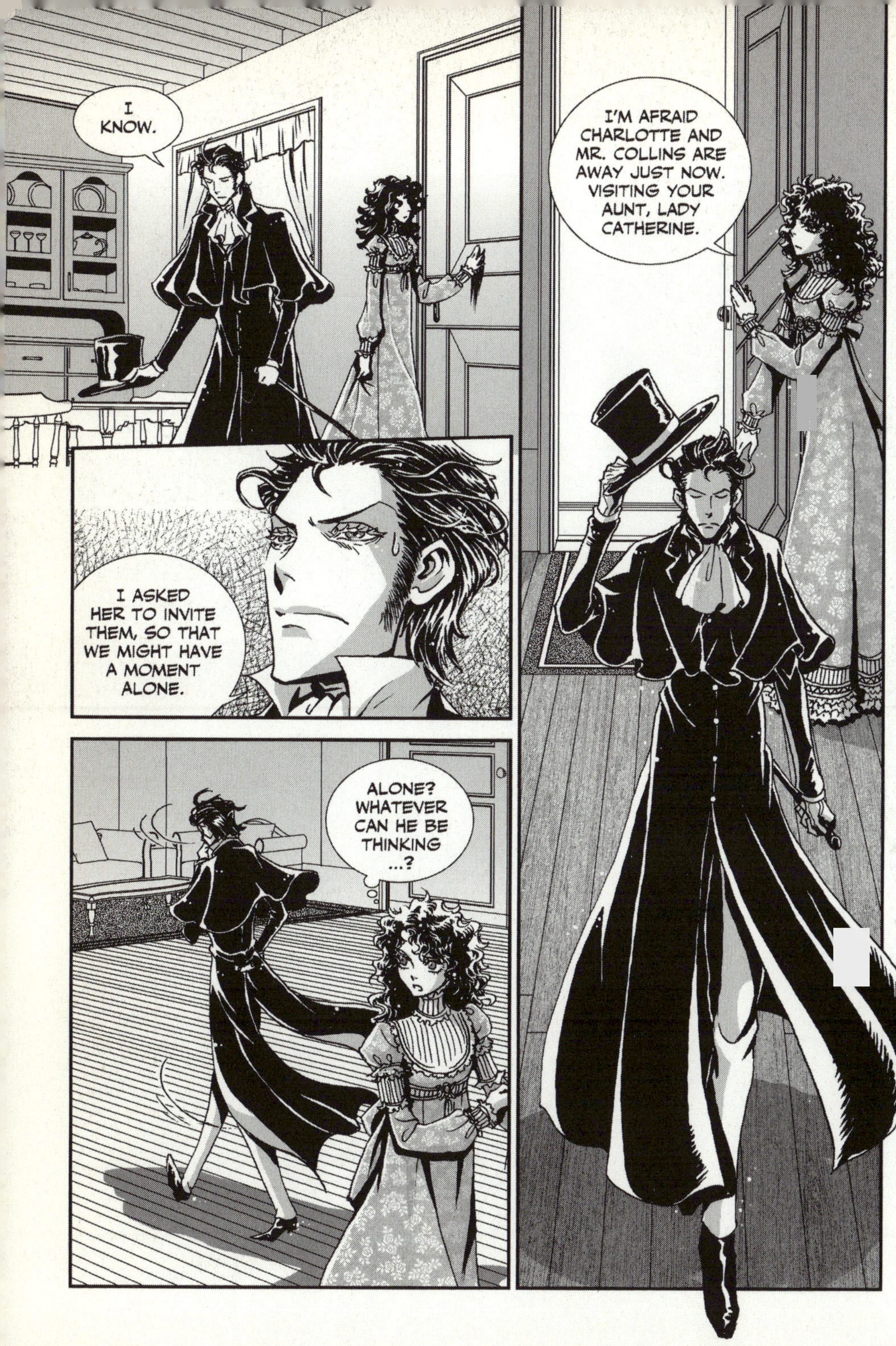
I'M AFRAID CHARLOTTE AND MR. COLLINS ARE AWAY JUST NOW. VISITING YOUR AUNT, LADY CATHERINE.
I KNOW.
I ASKED HER TO INVITE THEM, SO THAT WE MIGHT HAVE A MOMENT ALONE.
ALONE? WHATEVER CAN HE BE THINKING ...?

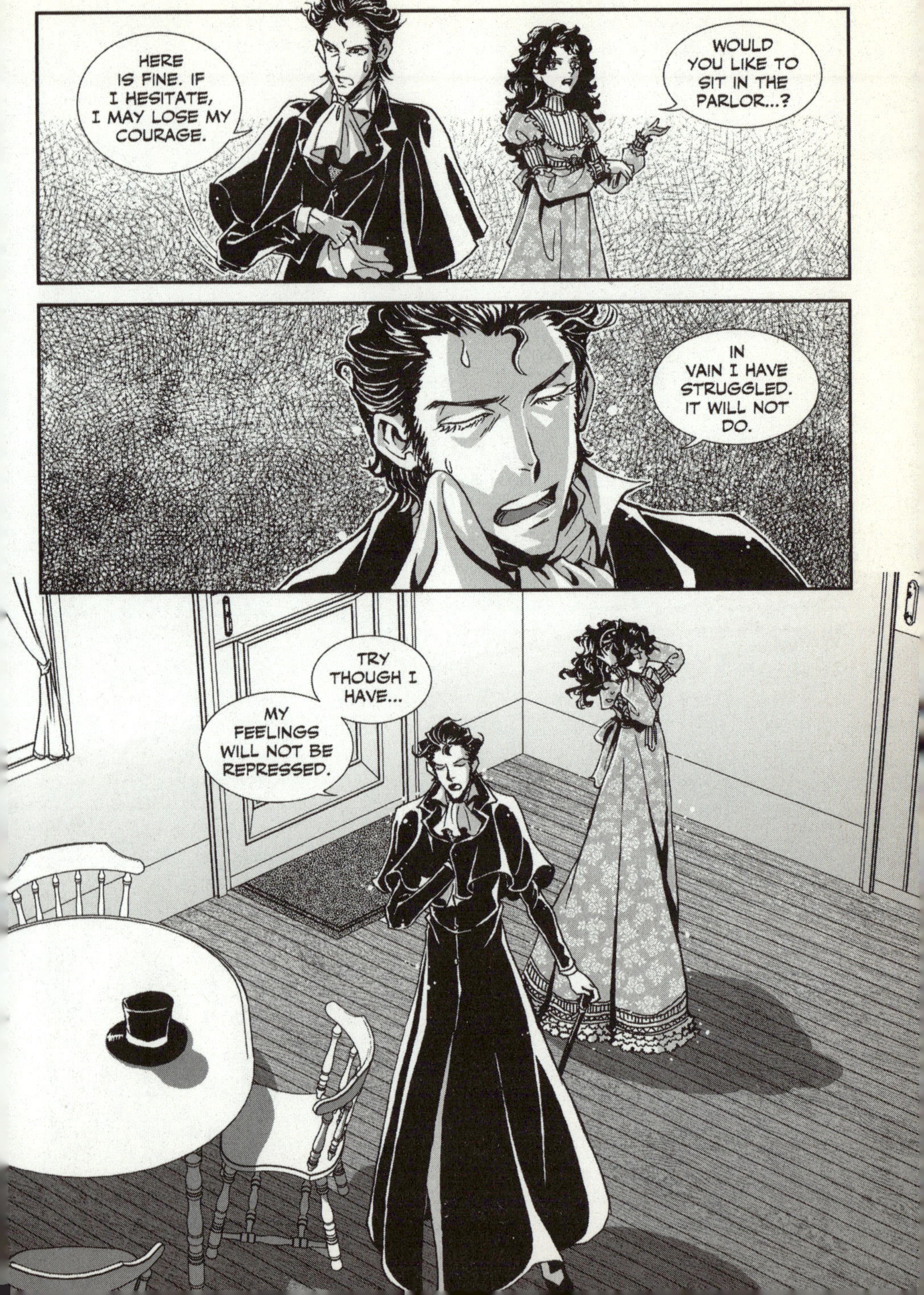
WOULD YOU LIKE TO SIT IN THE PARLOR...?
HERE IS FINE. IF I HESITATE, I MAY LOSE MY COURAGE.
IN VAIN I HAVE STRUGGLED. IT WILL NOT DO.
TRY THOUGH I HAVE...
MY FEELINGS WILL NOT BE REPRESSED.

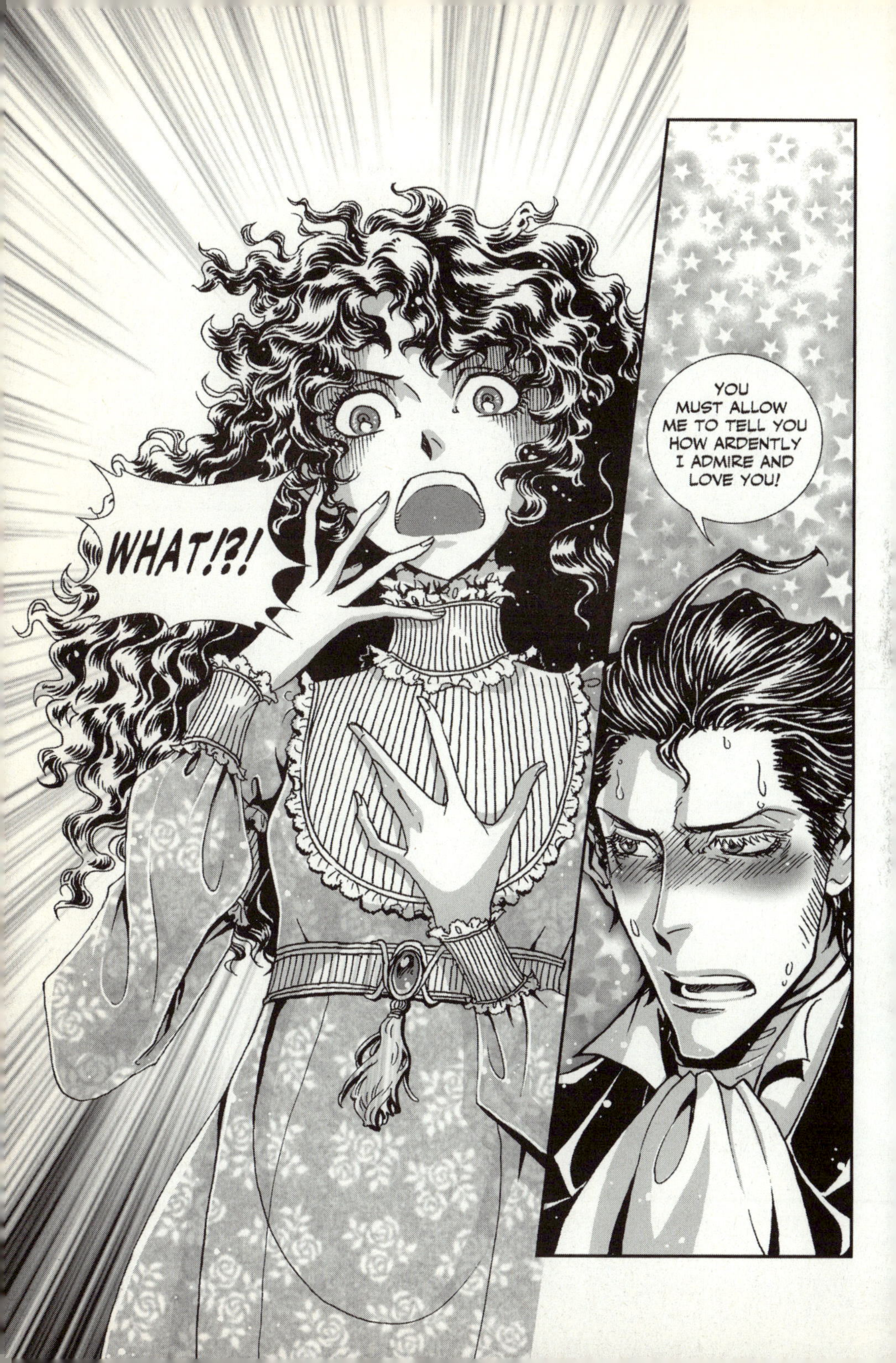
YOU MUST ALLOW ME TO TELL YOU HOW ARDENTLY I ADMIRE AND LOVE YOU!
WHAT!?!

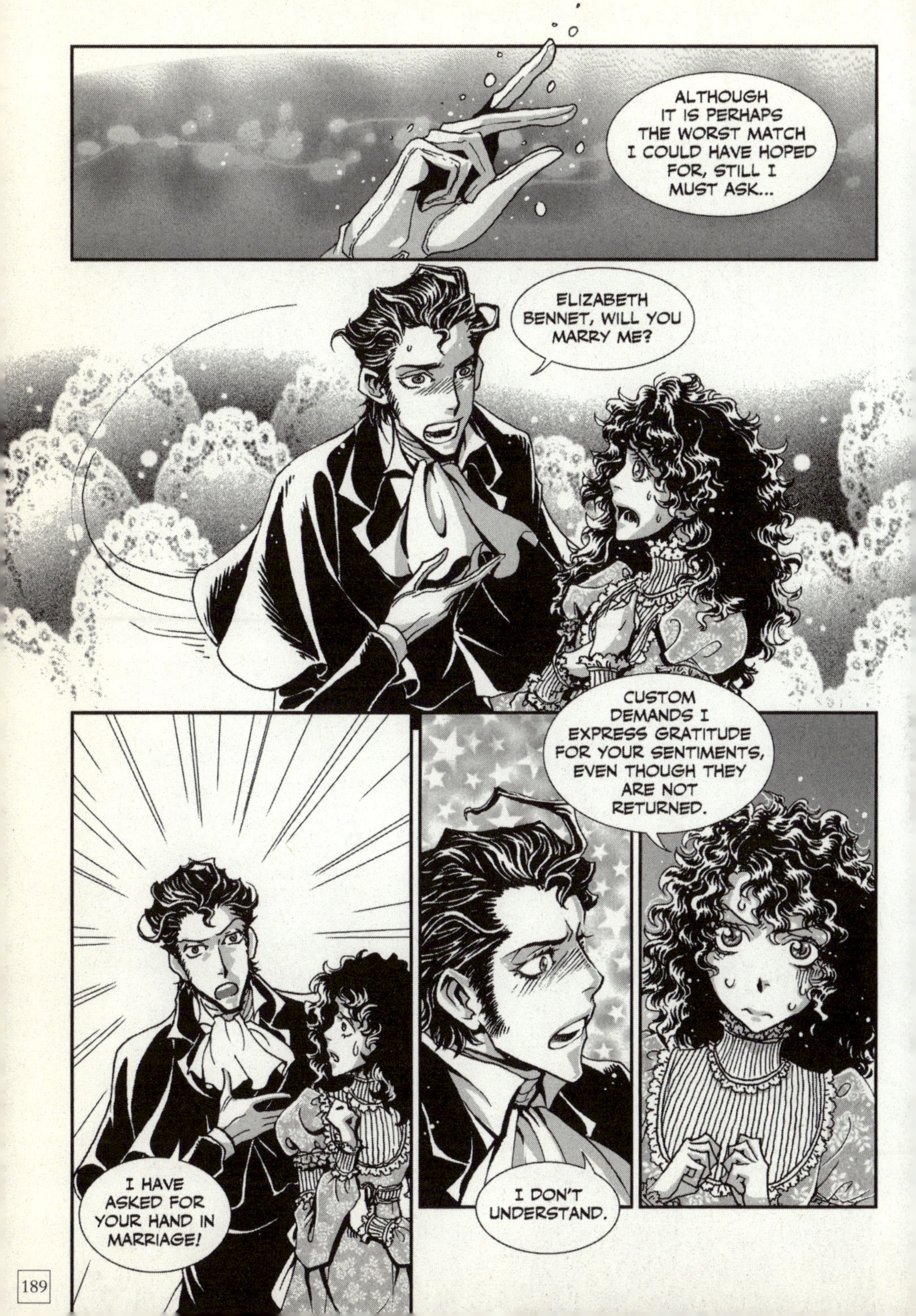
ALTHOUGH IT IS PERHAPS THE WORST MATCH I COULD HAVE HOPED FOR, STILL I MUST ASK...
ELIZABETH BENNET, WILL YOU MARRY ME?
CUSTOM DEMANDS I EXPRESS GRATITUDE FOR YOUR SENTIMENTS, EVEN THOUGH THEY ARE NOT RETURNED.
I DON'T UNDERSTAND.
I HAVE ASKED FOR YOUR HAND IN MARRIAGE!

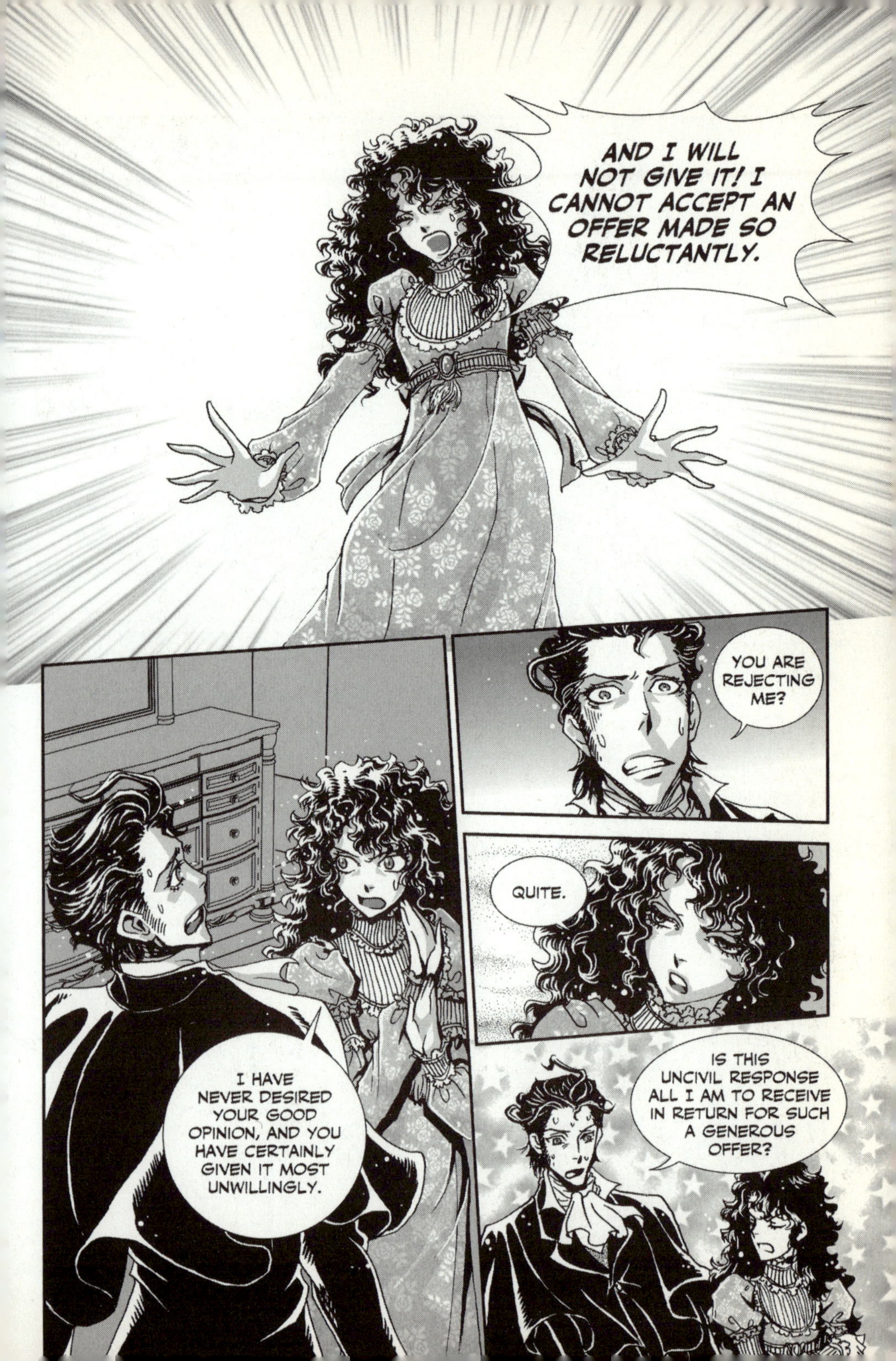
AND I WILL NOT GIVE IT! I CANNOT ACCEPT AN OFFER MADE SO RELUCTANTLY.
YOU ARE REJECTING ME?
QUITE.
IS THIS UNCIVIL RESPONSE ALL I AM TO RECEIVE IN RETURN FOR SUCH A GENEROUS OFFER?
I HAVE NEVER DESIRED YOUR GOOD OPINION, AND YOU HAVE CERTAINLY GIVEN IT MOST UNWILLINGLY.

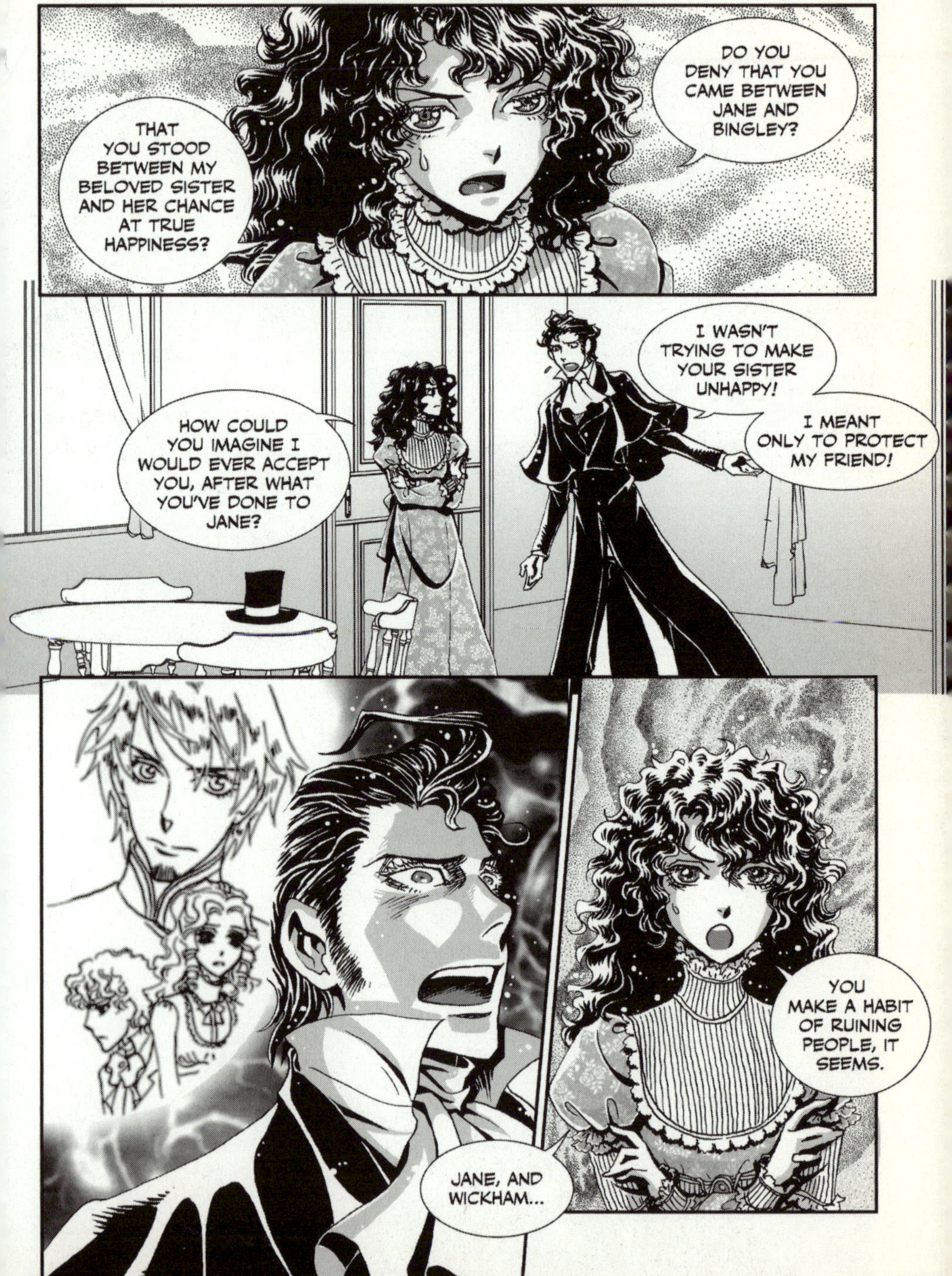
DO YOU DENY THAT YOU CAME BETWEEN JANE AND BINGLEY?
THAT YOU STOOD BETWEEN MY BELOVED SISTER AND HER CHANCE AT TRUE HAPPINESS?
I WASN'T TRYING TO MAKE YOUR SISTER UNHAPPY!
I MEANT ONLY TO PROTECT MY FRIEND!
HOW COULD YOU IMAGINE I WOULD EVER ACCEPT YOU, AFTER WHAT YOU'VE DONE TO JANE?
YOU MAKE A HABIT OF RUINING PEOPLE, IT SEEMS.
JANE, AND WICKHAM...

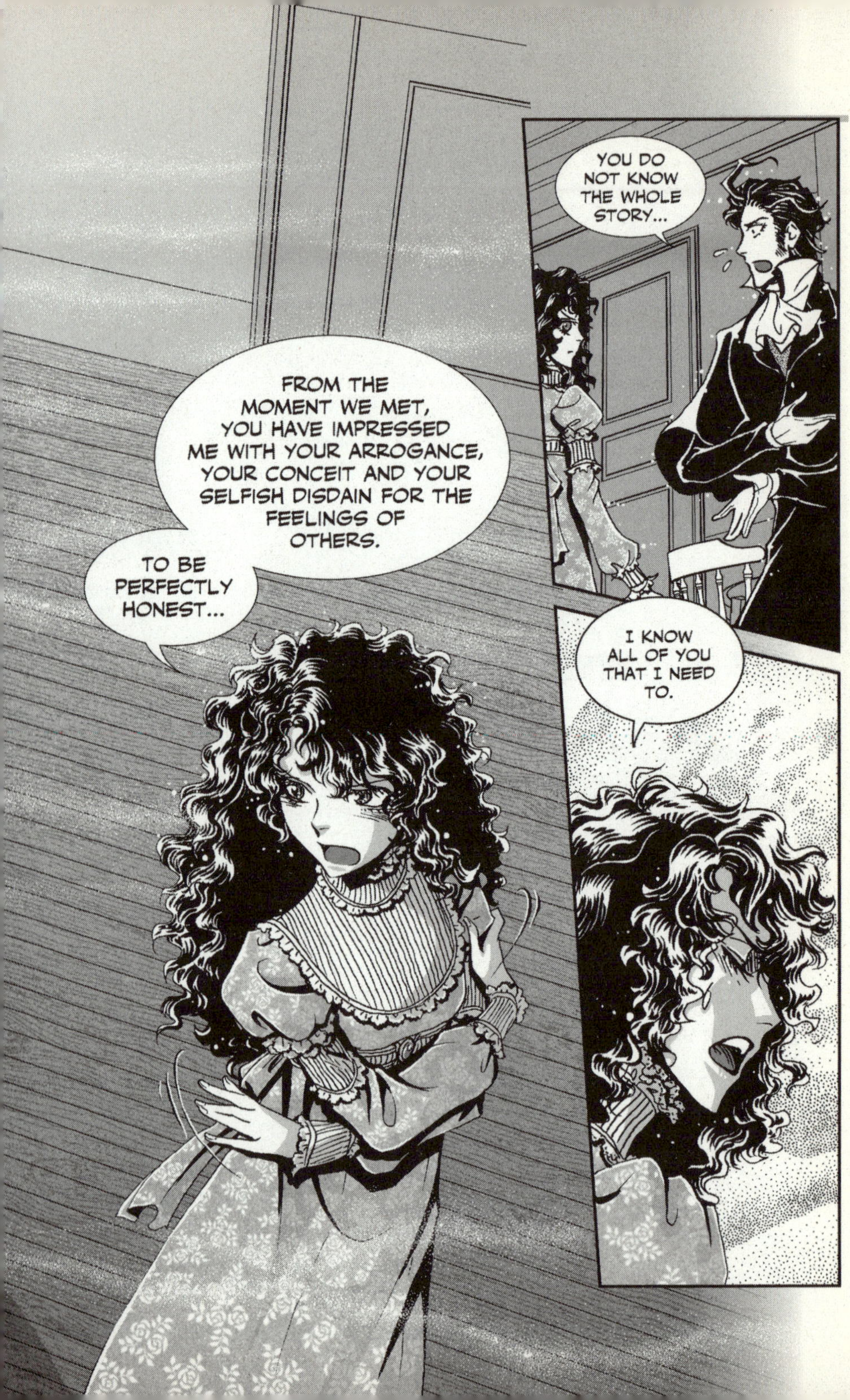
YOU DO NOT KNOW THE WHOLE STORY...
I KNOW ALL OF YOU THAT I NEED TO.
FROM THE MOMENT WE MET, YOU HAVE IMPRESSED ME WITH YOUR ARROGANCE, YOUR CONCEIT AND YOUR SELFISH DISDAIN FOR THE FEELINGS OF OTHERS.
TO BE PERFECTLY HONEST...

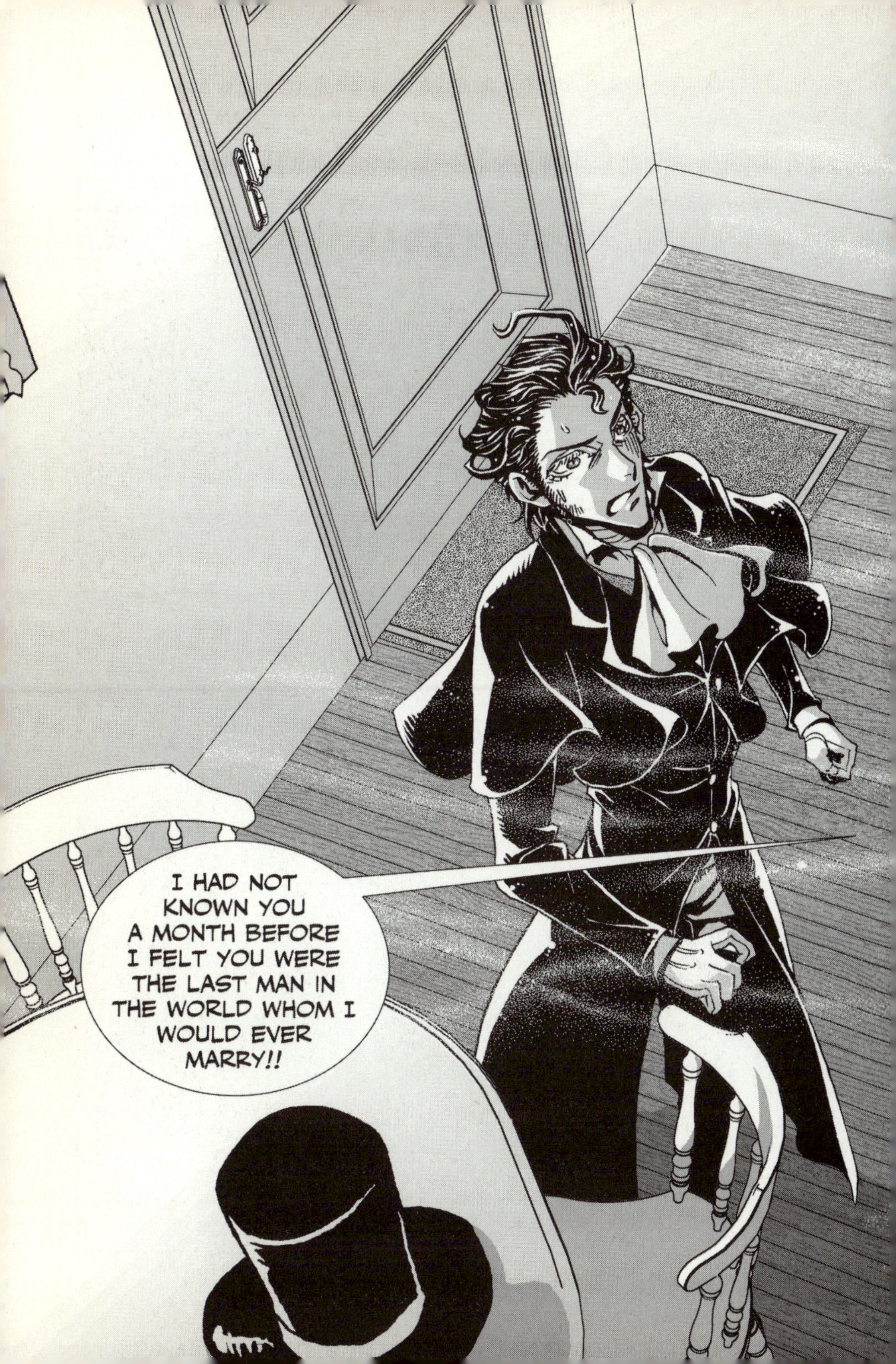
I HAD NOT KNOWN YOU A MONTH BEFORE I FELT YOU WERE THE LAST MAN IN THE WORLD WHOM I WOULD EVER MARRY!!

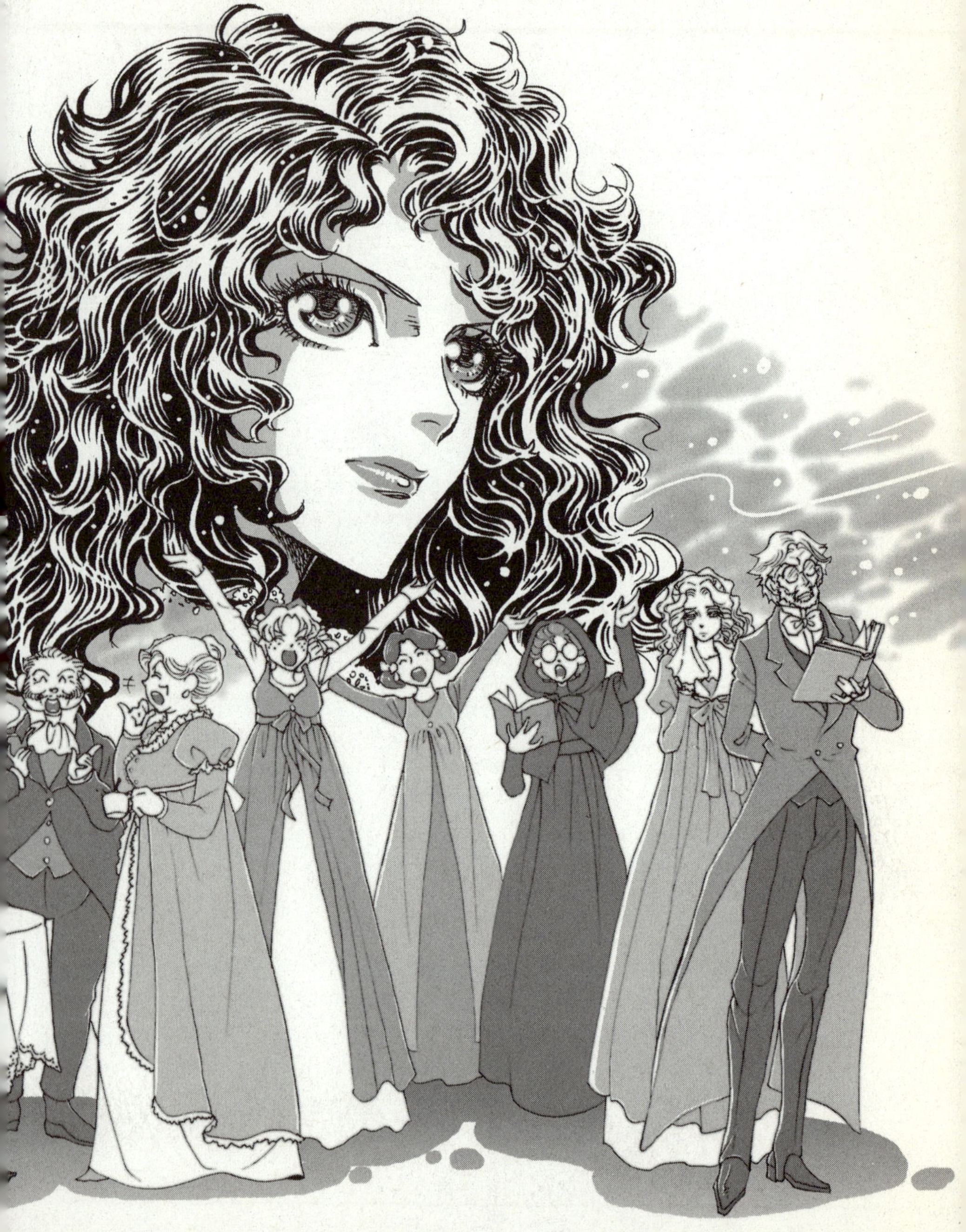

Chapter 11

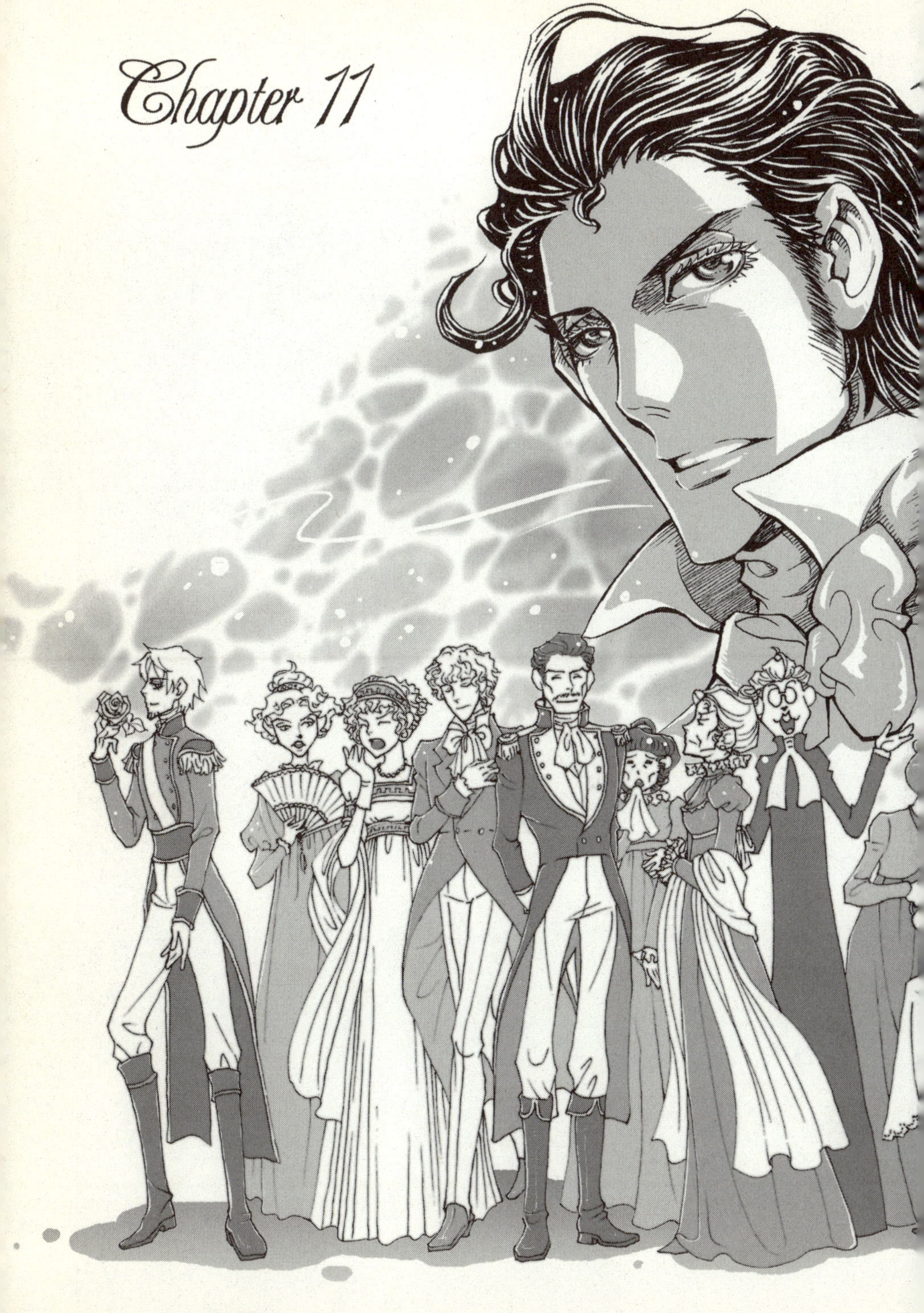

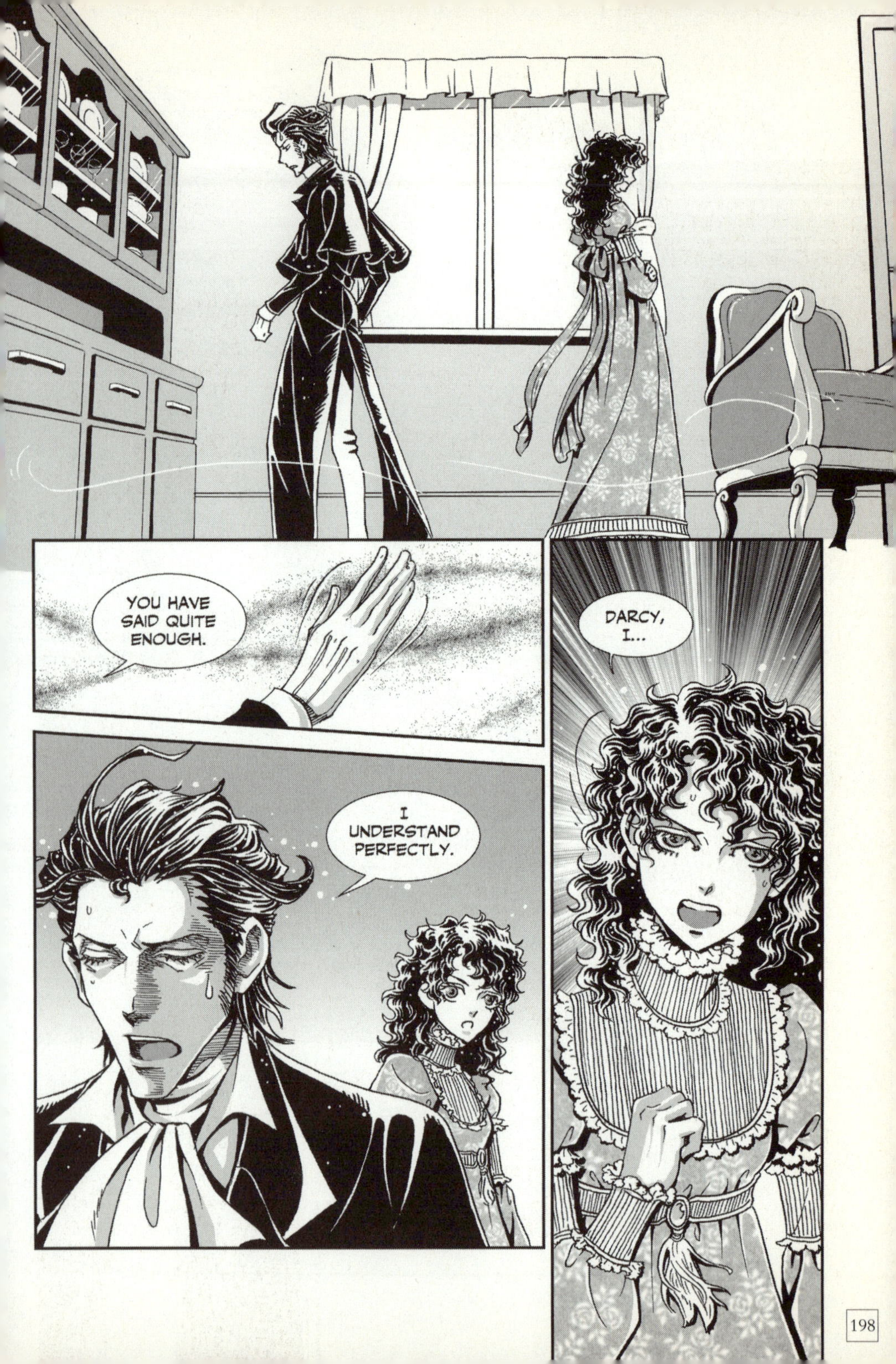
DARCY, I...
YOU HAVE SAID QUITE ENOUGH.
I UNDERSTAND PERFECTLY.

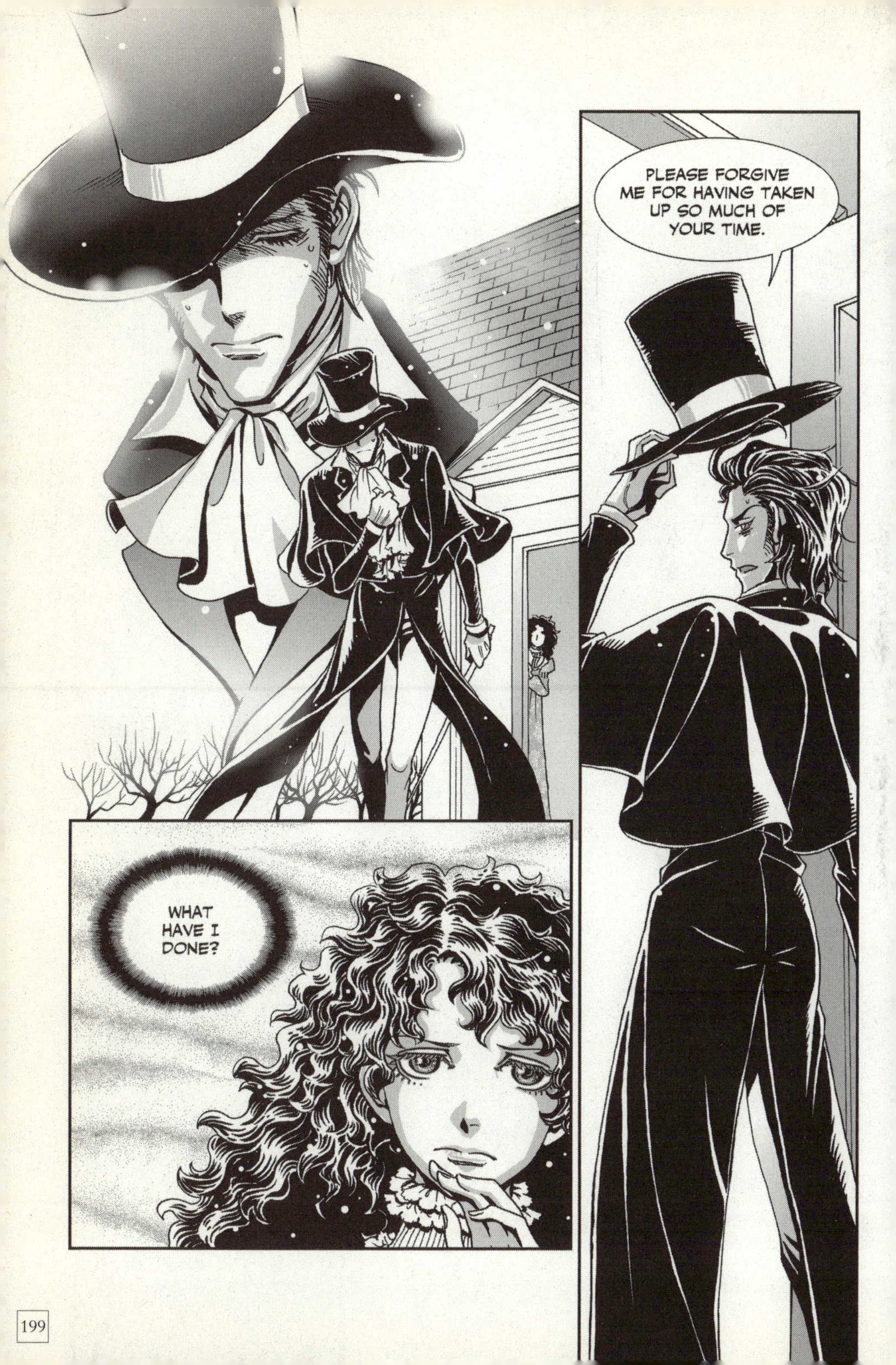
PLEASE FORGIVE ME FOR HAVING TAKEN UP SO MUCH OF YOUR TIME.
WHAT HAVE I DONE?

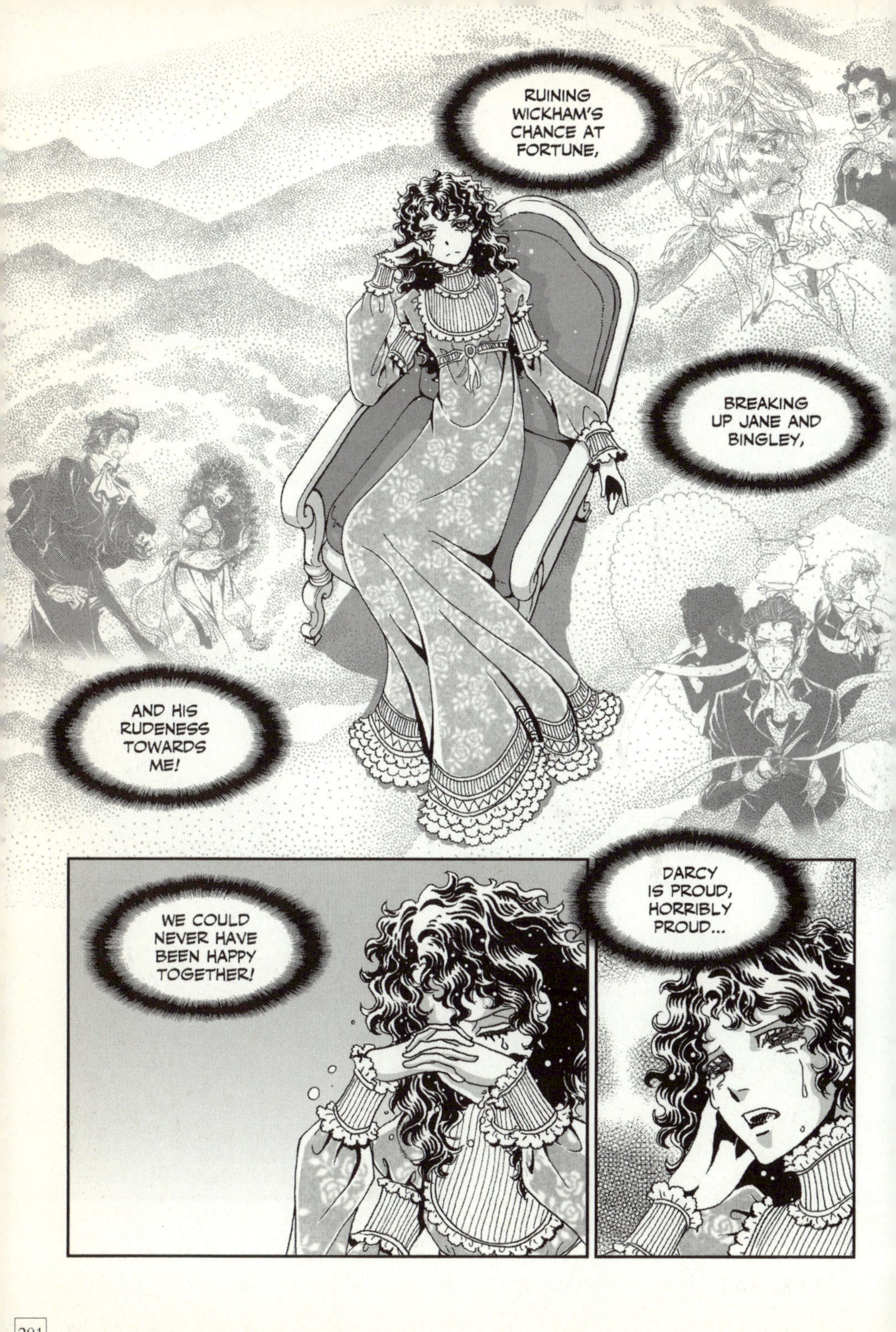
RUINING WICKHAM'S CHANCE AT FORTUNE,
BREAKING UP JANE AND BINGLEY,
AND HIS RUDENESS TOWARDS ME!
DARCY IS PROUD, HORRIBLY PROUD...
WE COULD NEVER HAVE BEEN HAPPY TOGETHER!

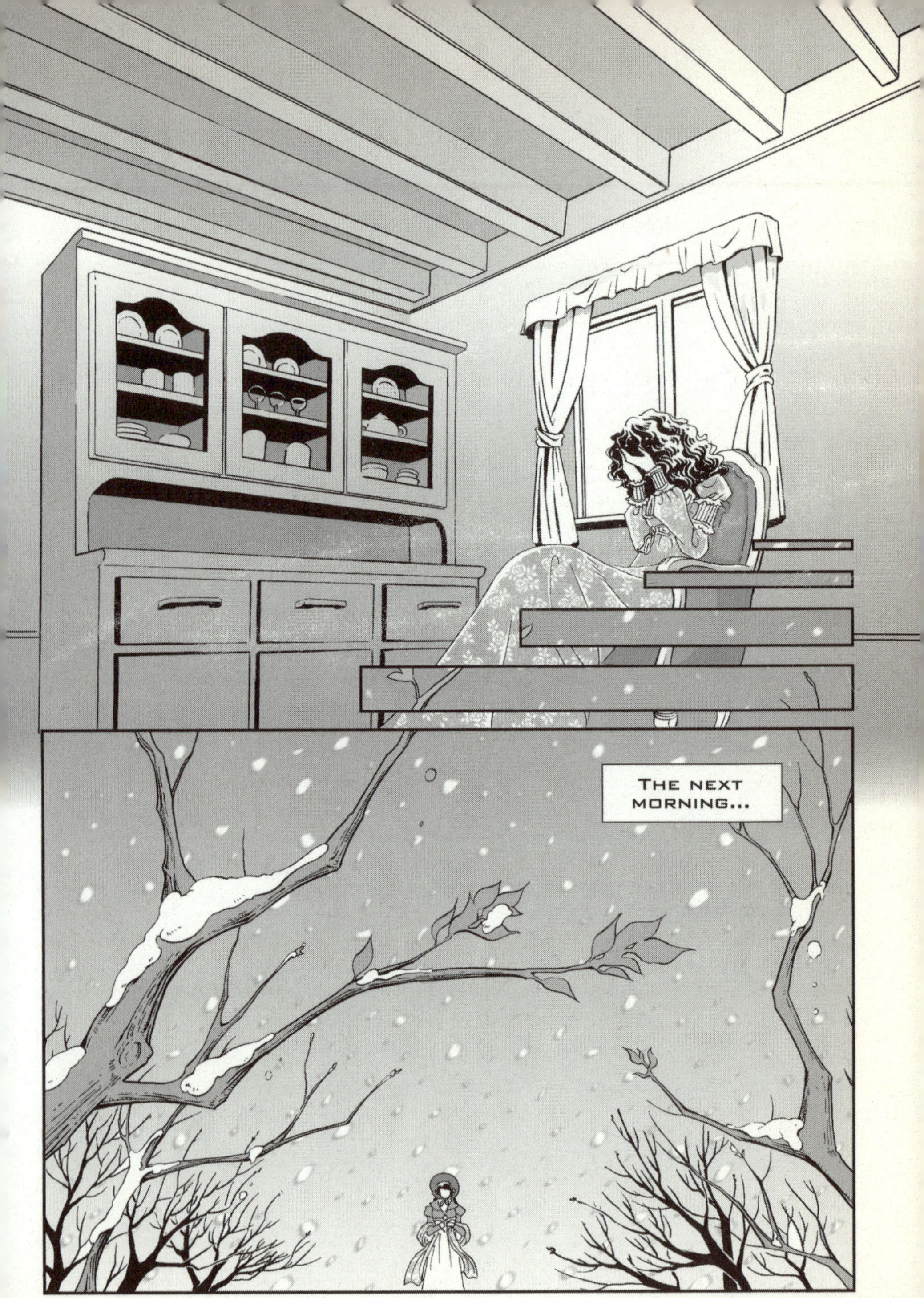
THE NEXT MORNING...

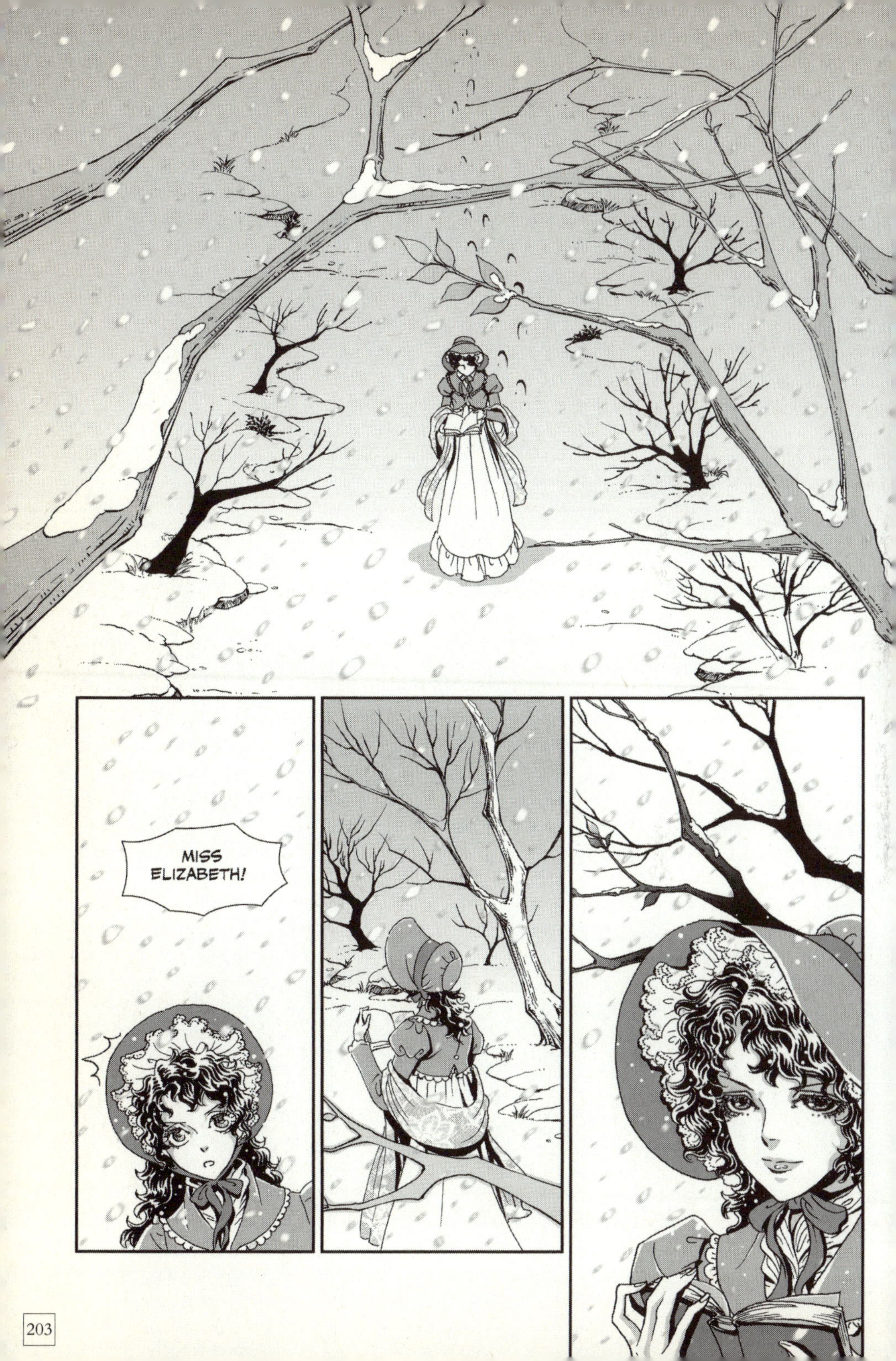
MISS ELIZABETH!

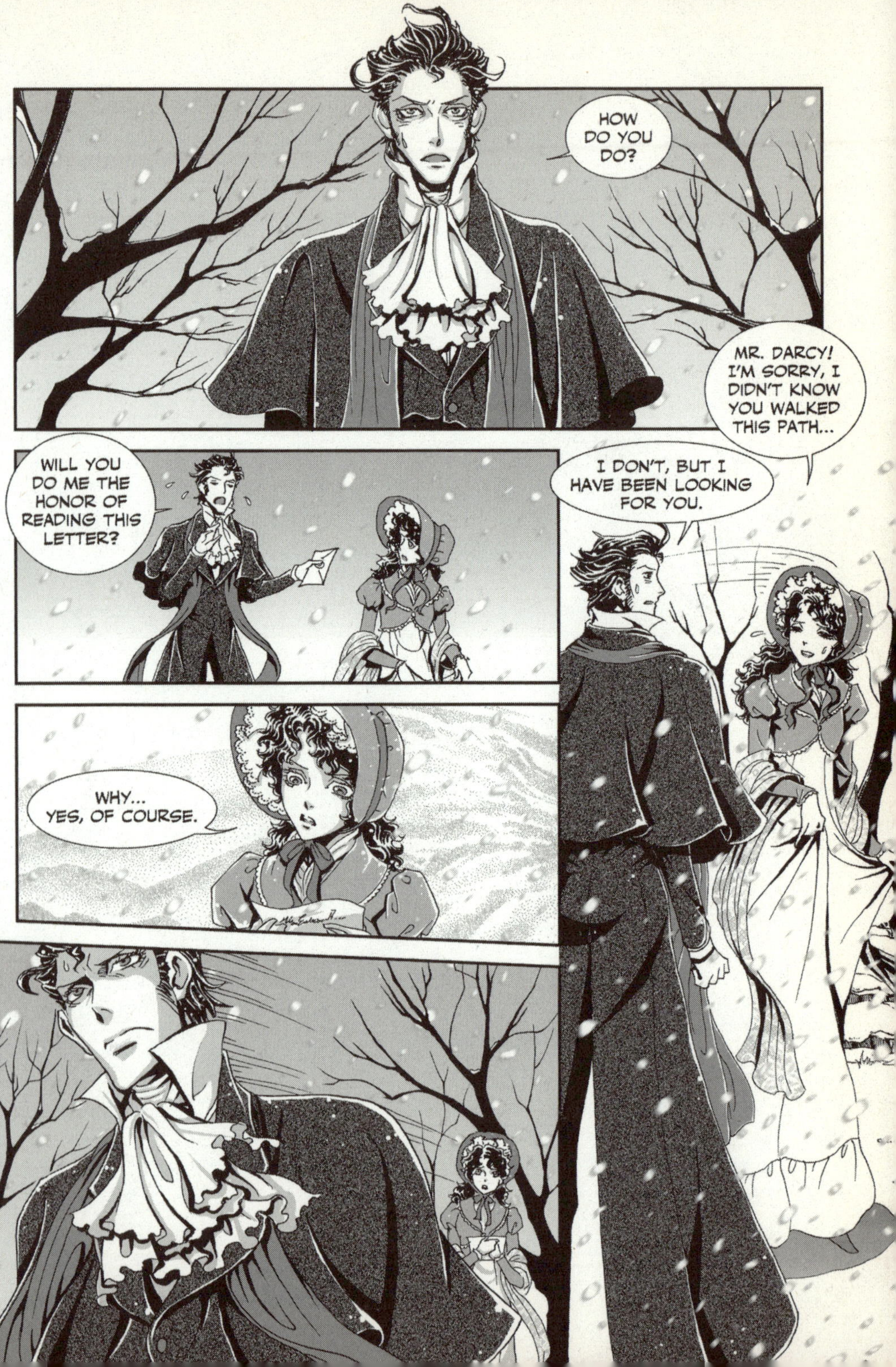
HOW DO YOU DO?
MR. DARCY! I'M SORRY, I DIDN'T KNOW YOU WALKED THIS PATH...
I DON'T, BUT I HAVE BEEN LOOKING FOR YOU.
WILL YOU DO ME THE HONOR OF READING THIS LETTER?
WHY... YES, OF COURSE.

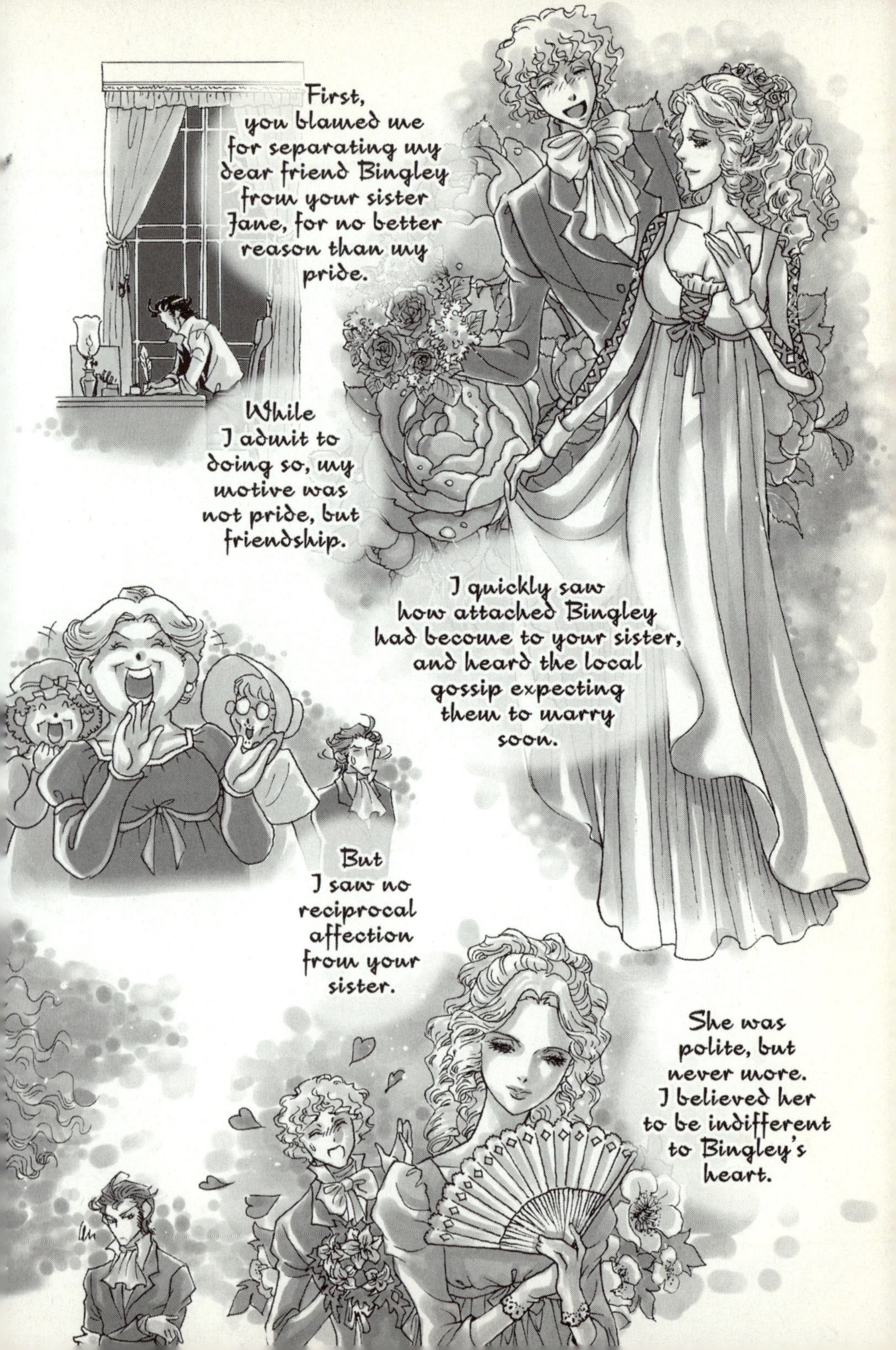
First, you blamed me for separating my dear friend Bingley from your sister Jane, for no better reason than my pride.
While I admit to doing so, my motive was not pride, but friendship.
I quickly saw how attached Bingley had become to your sister, and heard the local gossip expecting them to marry soon.
But I saw no reciprocal affection from your sister.
She was polite, but never more. I believed her to be indifferent to Bingley's heart.

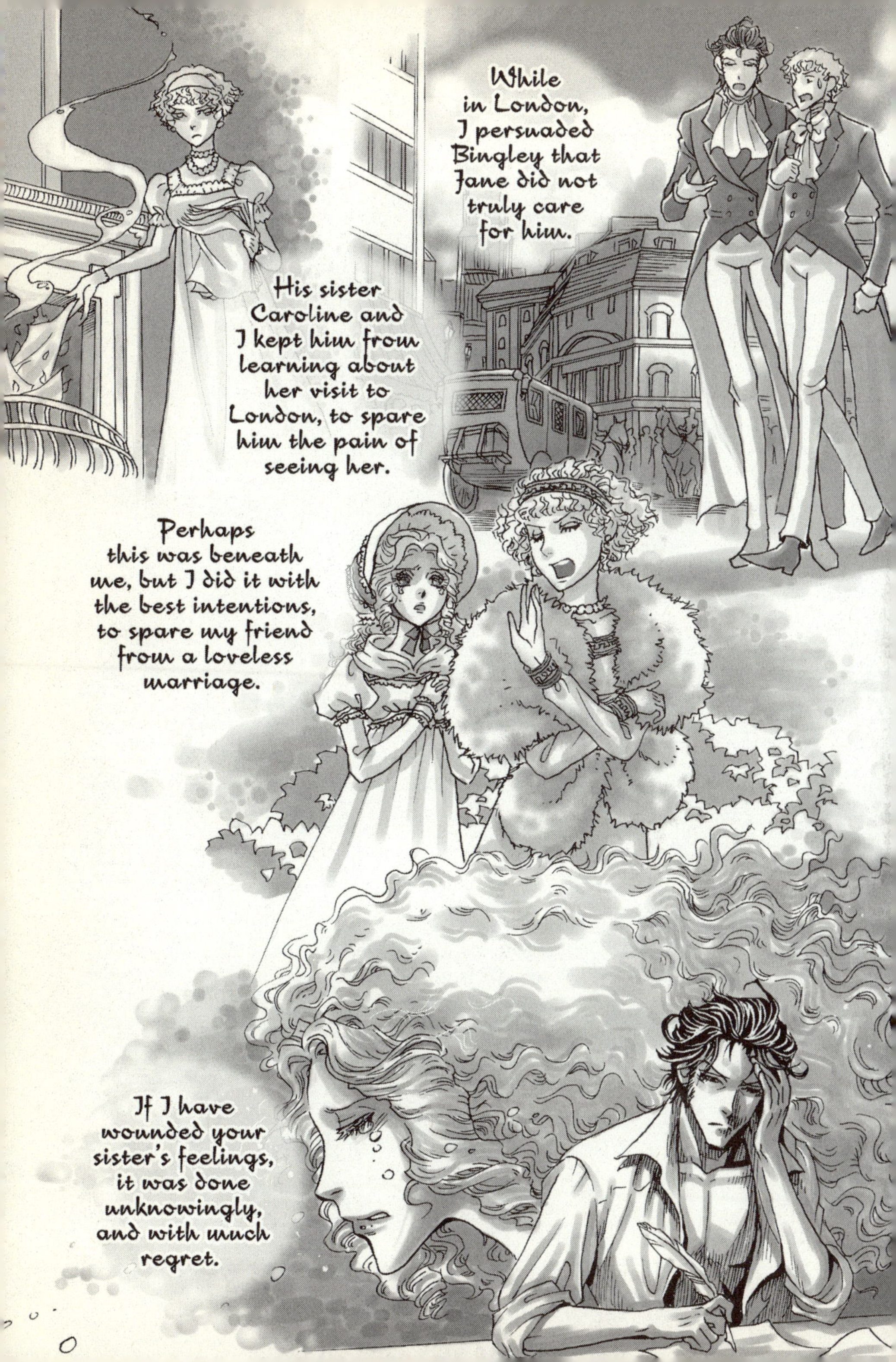
While in London, I persuaded Bingley that Jane did not truly care for him.
His sister Caroline and I kept him from learning about her visit to London, to spare him the pain of seeing her.
Perhaps this was beneath me, but I did it with the best intentions, to spare my friend from a loveless marriage.
If I have wounded your sister's feelings, it was done unknowingly, and with much regret.

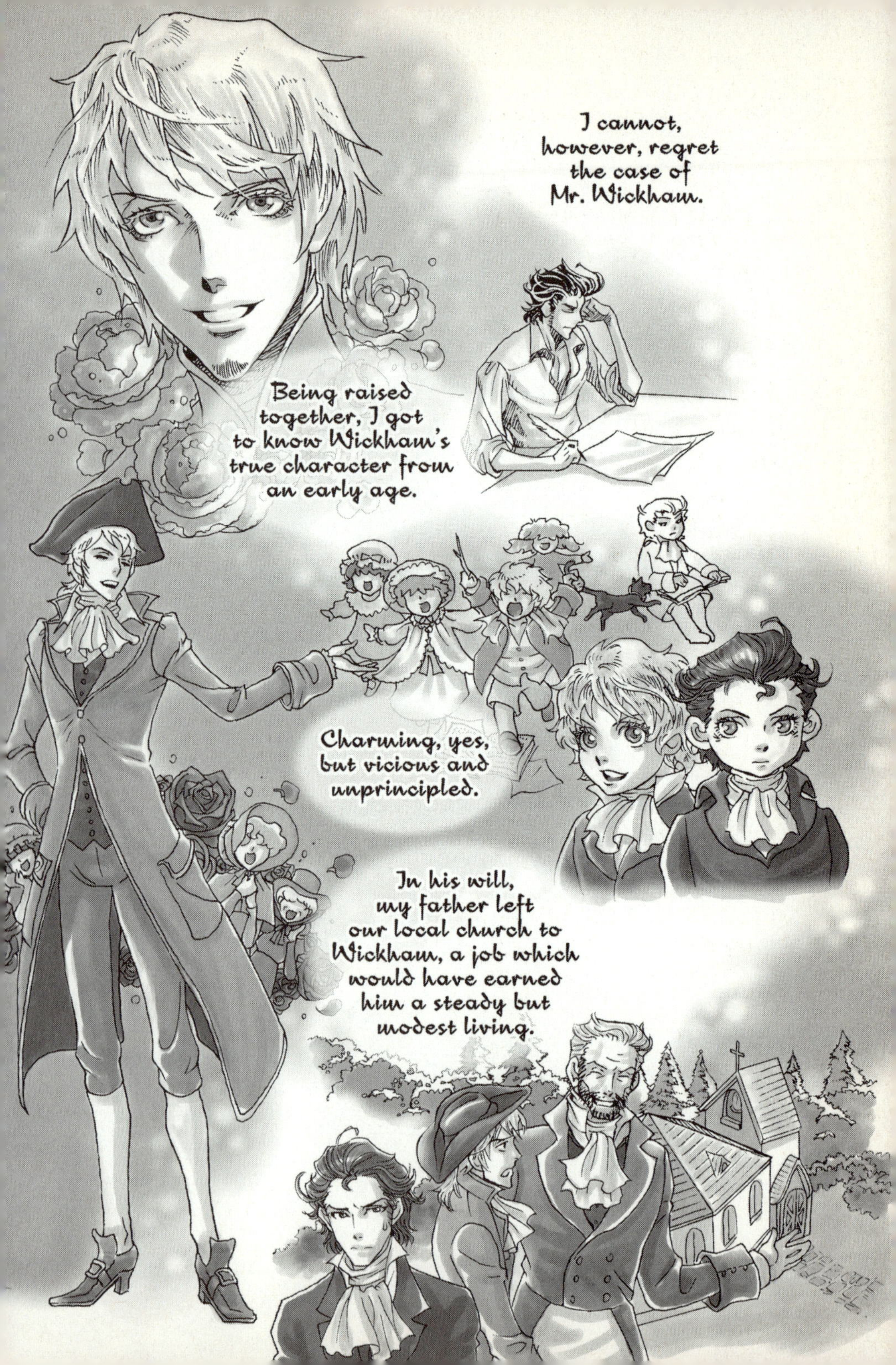
I cannot, however, regret the case of Mr. Wickham.
Being raised together, I got to know Wickham's true character from an early age.
Charming, yes, but vicious and unprincipled.
In his will, my father left our local church to Wickham, a job which would have earned him a steady but modest living.

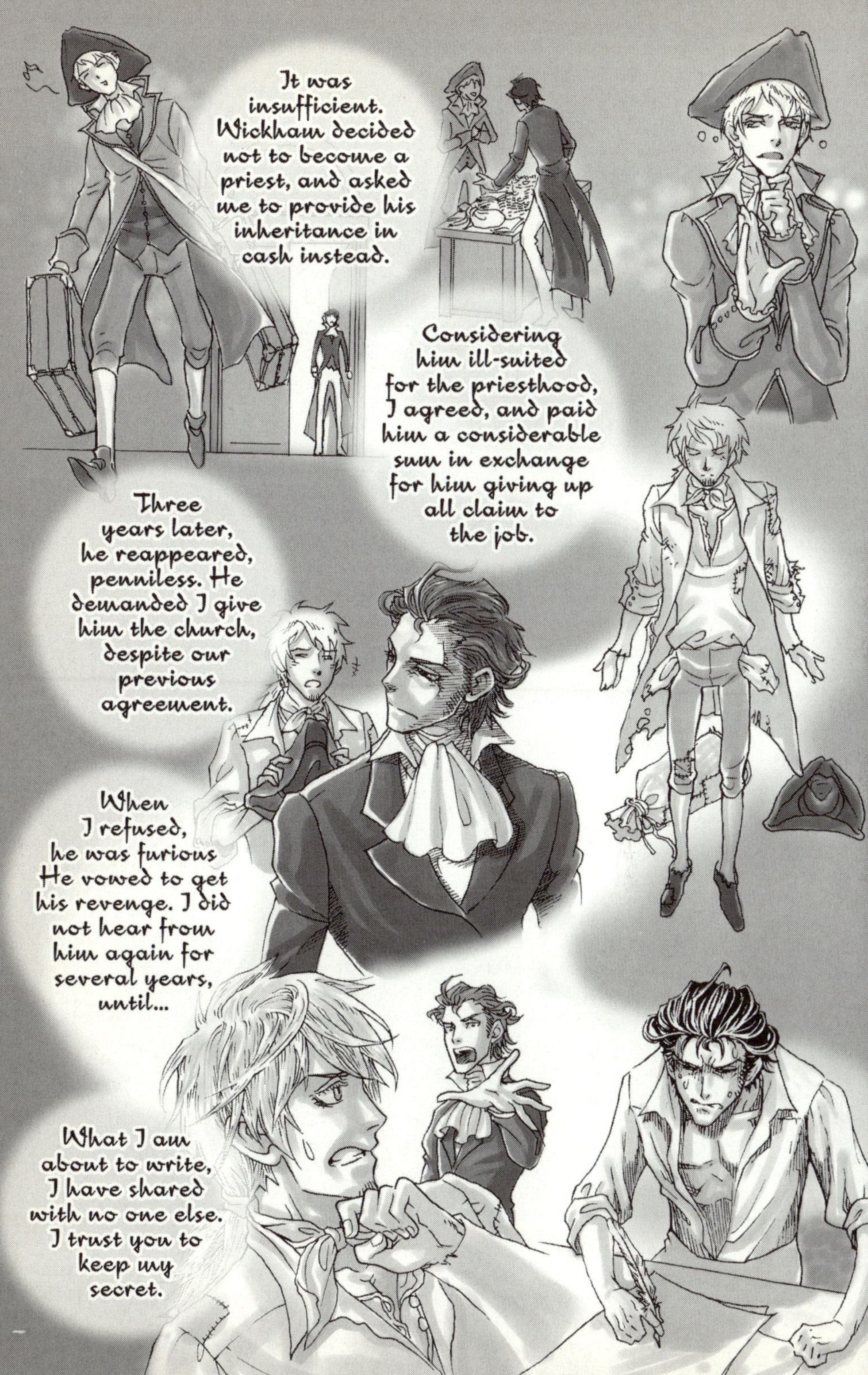
It was insufficient. Wickham decided not to become a priest, and asked me to provide his inheritance in cash instead.
Considering him ill-suited for the priesthood, I agreed, and paid him a considerable sum in exchange for him giving up all claim to the job.
Three years later, he reappeared, penniless. He demanded I give him the church, despite our previous agreement.
When I refused, he was furious He vowed to get his revenge. I did not hear from him again for several years, until...
What I am about to write, I have shared with no one else. I trust you to keep my secret.

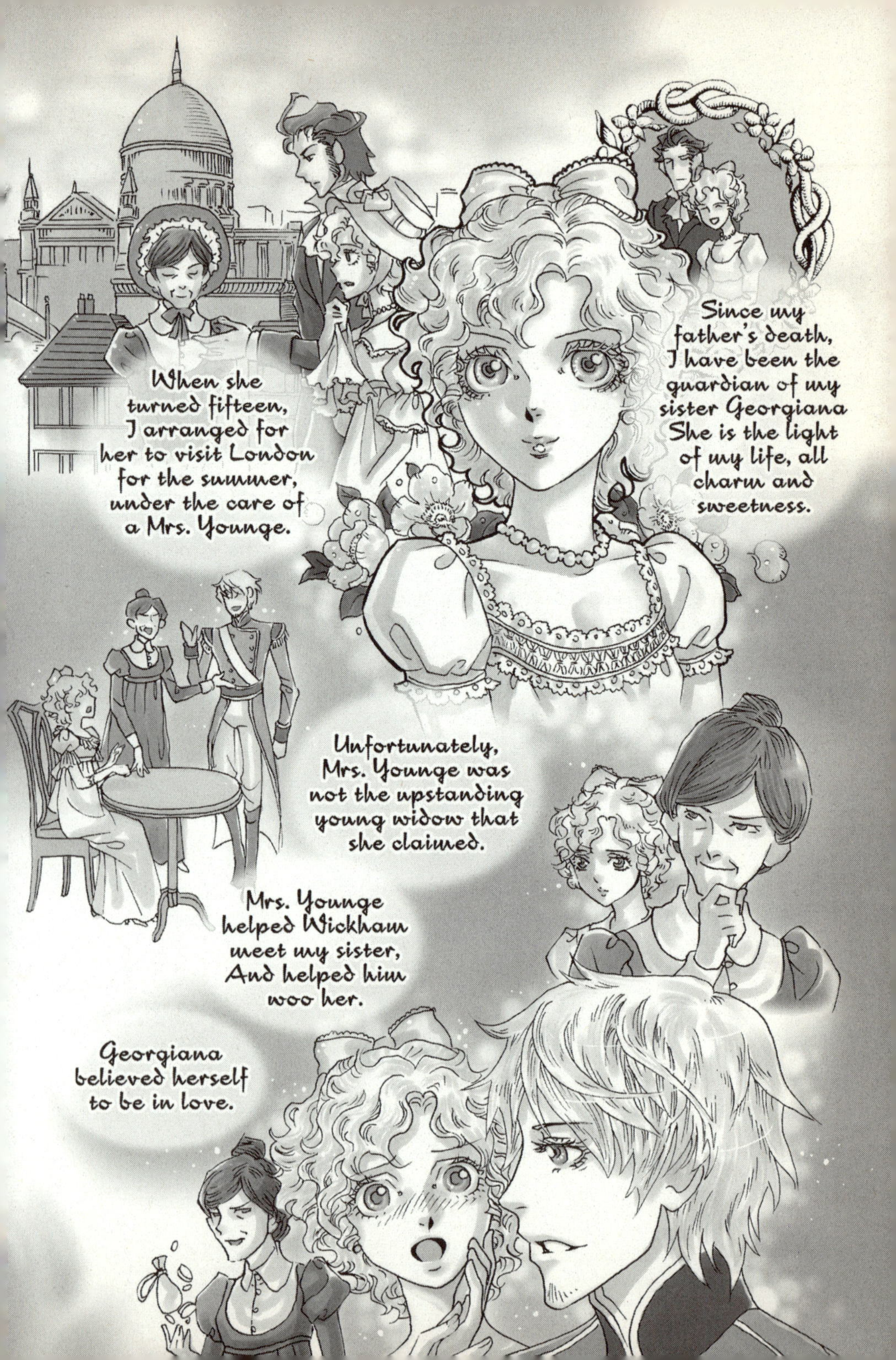
Since my father's death, I have been the guardian of my sister Georgiana She is the light of my life, all charm and sweetness.
When she turned fifteen, I arranged for her to visit London for the summer, under the care of a Mrs. Younge.
Unfortunately, Mrs. Younge was not the upstanding young widow that she claimed.
Mrs. Younge helped Wickham meet my sister, And helped him woo her.
Georgiana believed herself to be in love.

Swept up in romance, she agreed to elope.
Only a last-minute letter saved her from a terrible fate.
You may imagine what I felt and how I acted.
Wickham was after my sister's fortune, but it would have been revenge upon me as well.
If you cannot bring yourself to take this as truth, Colonel Fitzwilliam can verify it all.

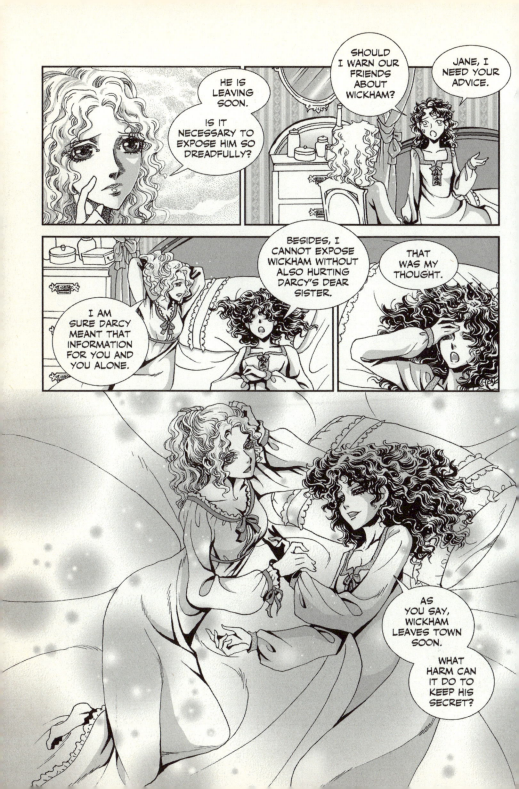

~AWKWARD

FINALLY, MY FAVORITE COURSE. DESSERT!

ISN'T IT MARVELOUS?

MRS. FORSTER'S ASKED ME TO JOIN HER IN BRIGHTON!

Chapter 13

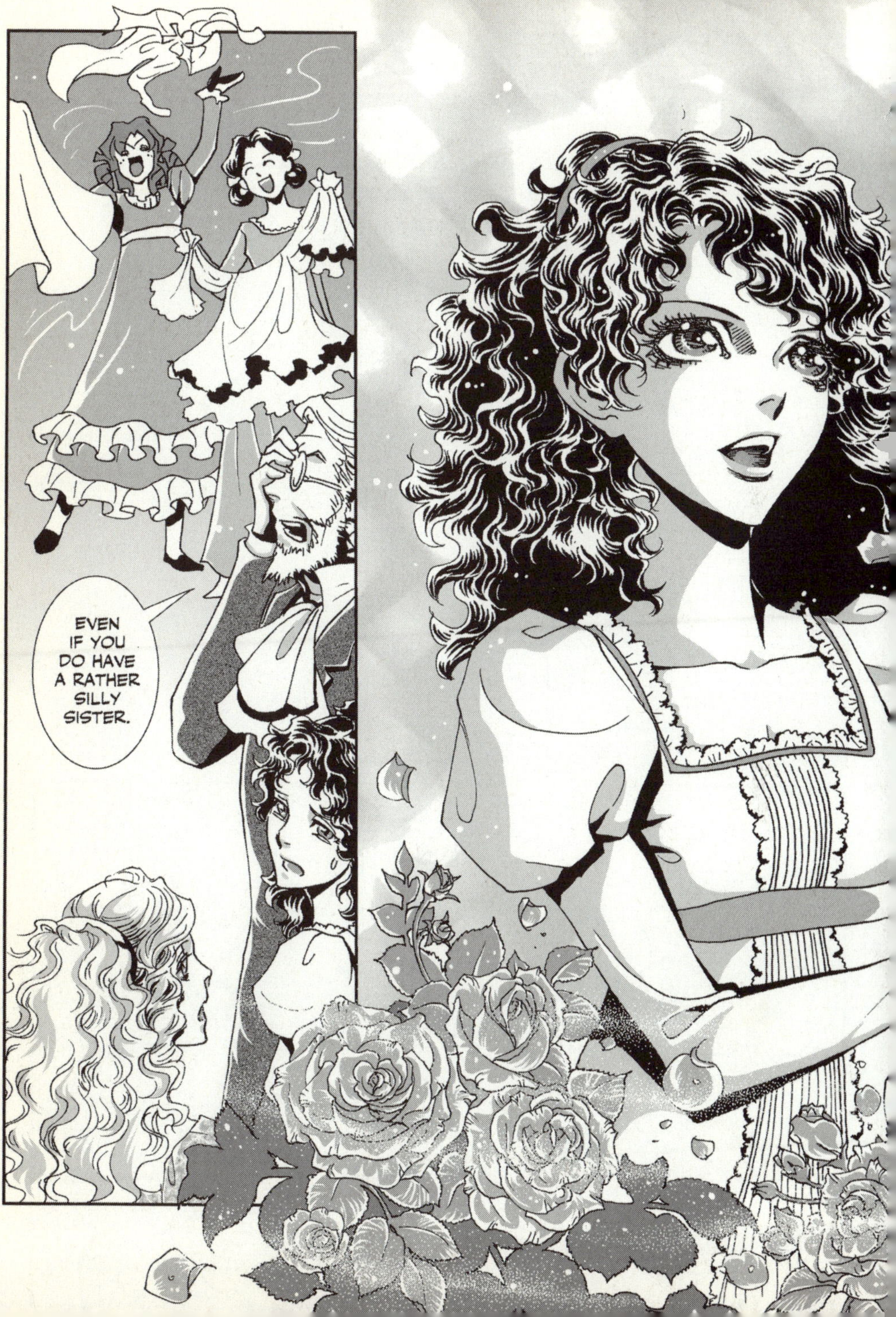
EVEN IF YOU DO HAVE A RATHER SILLY SISTER.

JANE! THERE'S A LETTER FROM LYDIA!

AND THIS ONE TAKES UP ALMOST HALF THE PAGE!

THEN COME WITH US, AND SPARE ME THE EFFORT OF WRITING!

I SUPPOSE SHE IS TOO BUSY SEEING THE SIGHTS TO WRITE LETTERS. YOU'LL BE THE SAME ON YOUR TRIP.

WHAT, ANOTHER ONE? THAT'S TWICE IN TWO MONTHS!

241

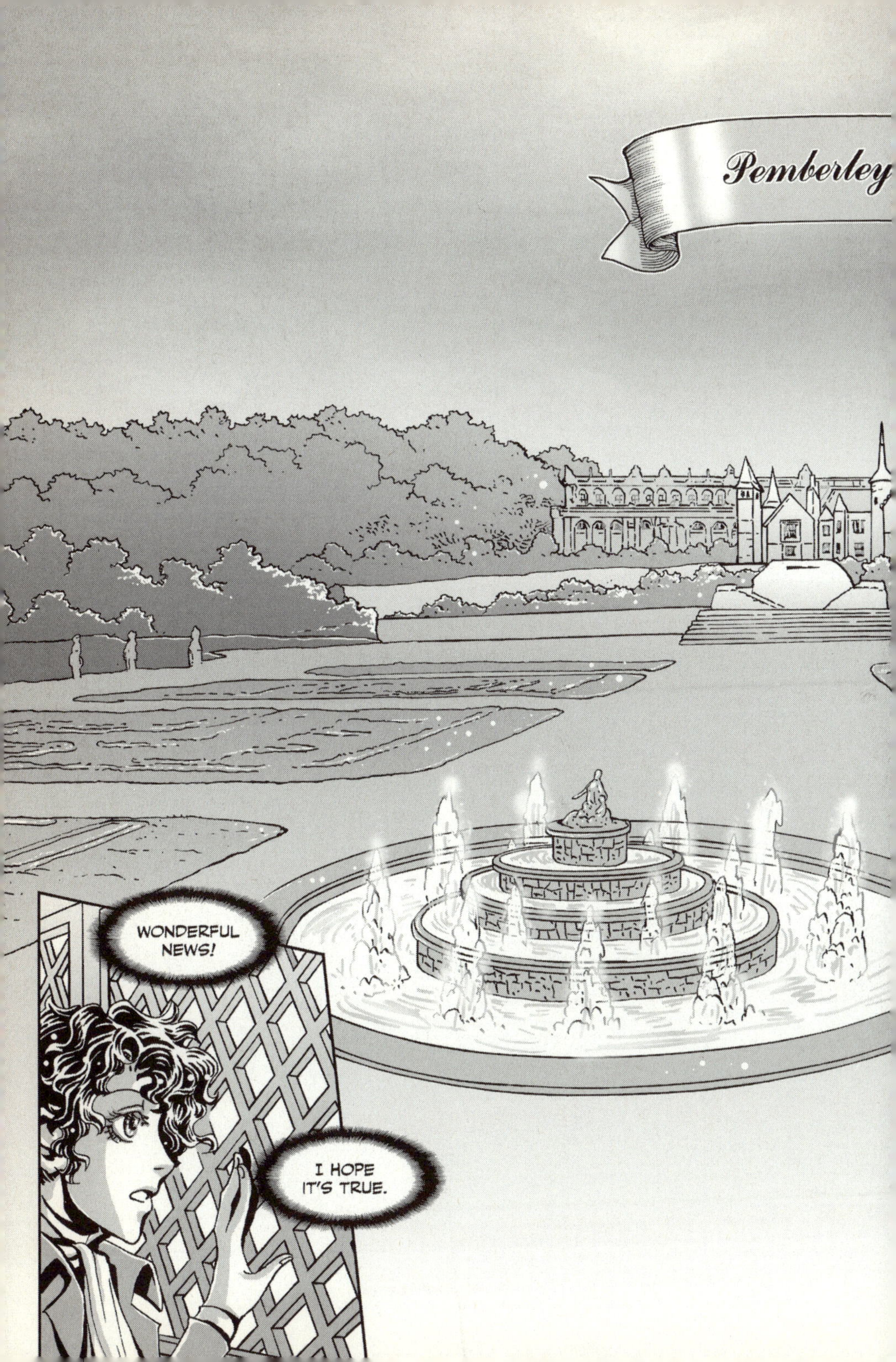
Pemberley
WONDERFUL NEWS!
I HOPE IT'S TRUE.

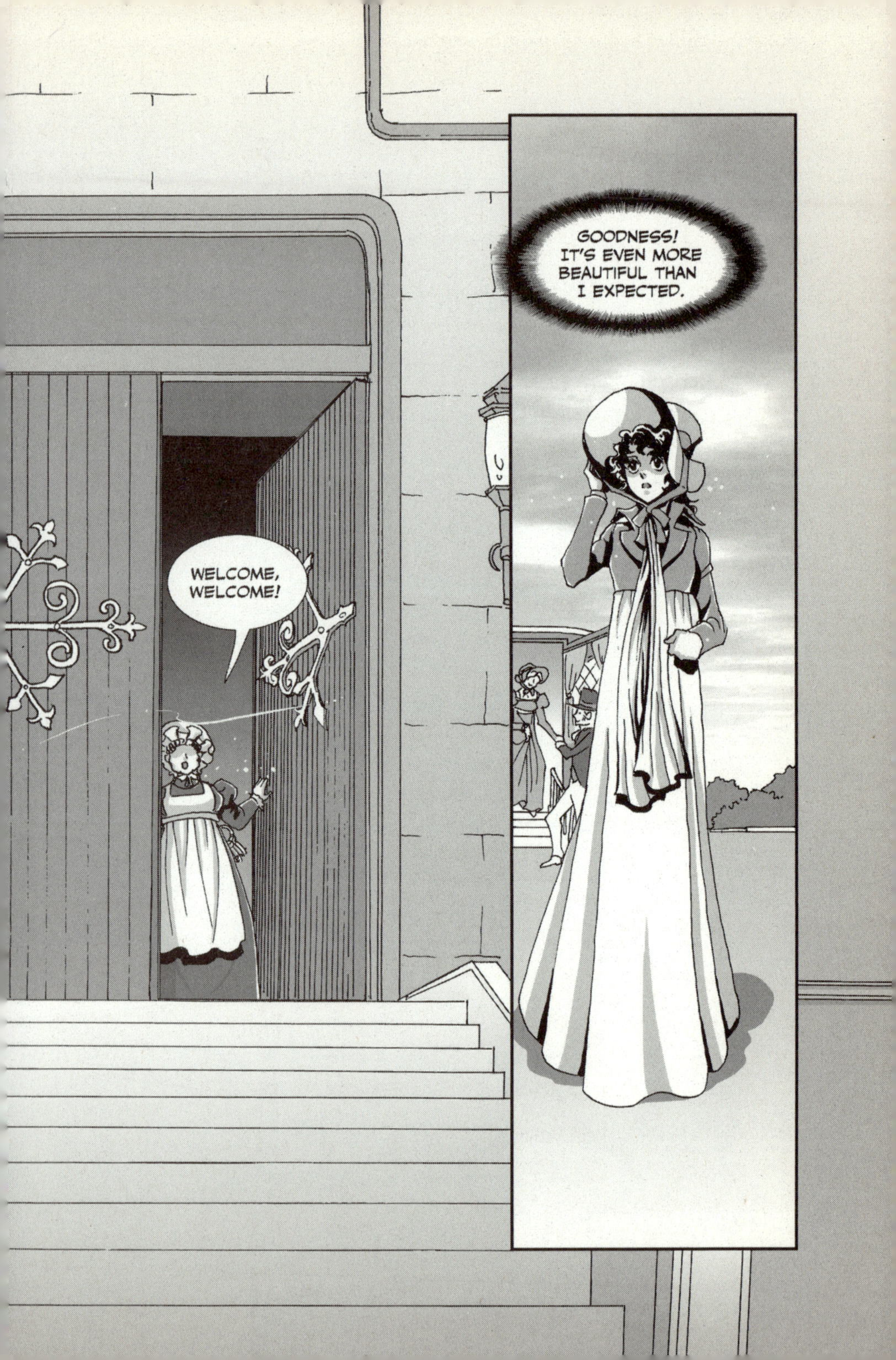
GOODNESS! IT'S EVEN MORE BEAUTIFUL THAN I EXPECTED.
WELCOME, WELCOME!

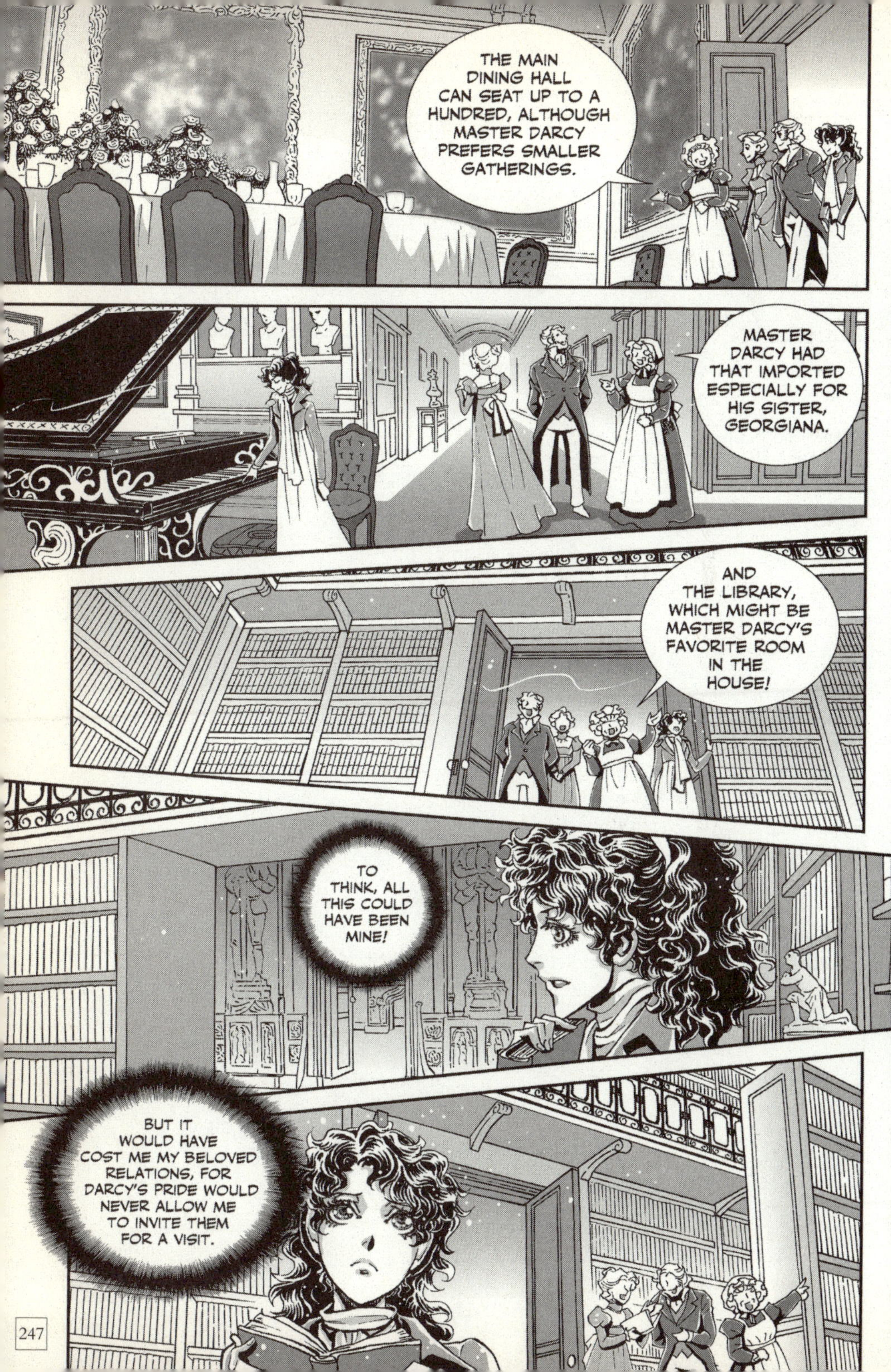
THE MAIN DINING HALL CAN SEAT UP TO A HUNDRED, ALTHOUGH MASTER DARCY PREFERS SMALLER GATHERINGS.
MASTER DARCY HAD THAT IMPORTED ESPECIALLY FOR HIS SISTER, GEORGIANA.
AND THE LIBRARY, WHICH MIGHT BE MASTER DARCY'S FAVORITE ROOM IN THE HOUSE!
TO THINK, ALL THIS COULD HAVE BEEN MINE!
BUT IT WOULD HAVE COST ME MY BELOVED RELATIONS, FOR DARCY'S PRIDE WOULD NEVER ALLOW ME TO INVITE THEM FOR A VISIT.

248

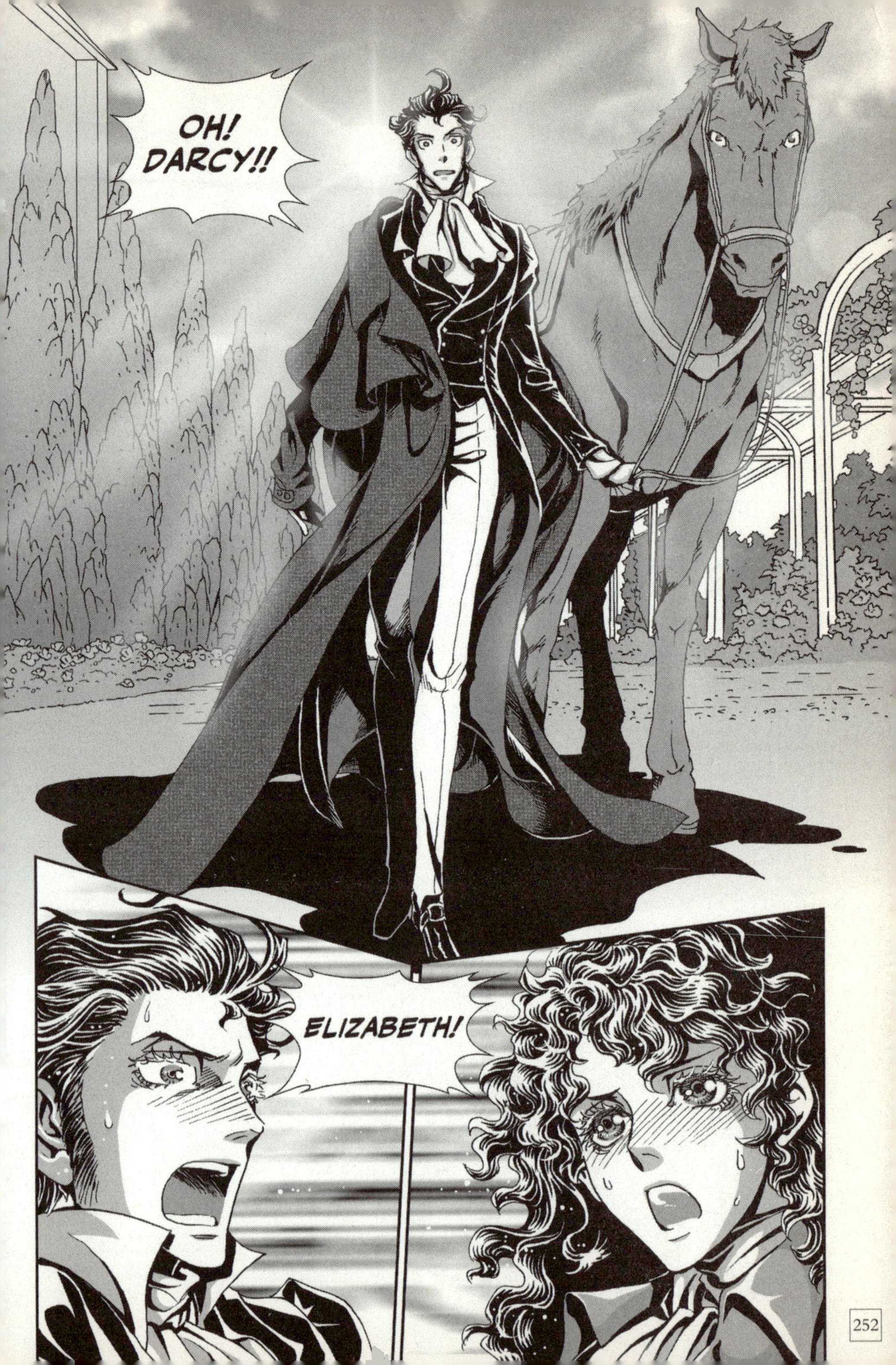
OH! DARCY!!
ELIZABETH!

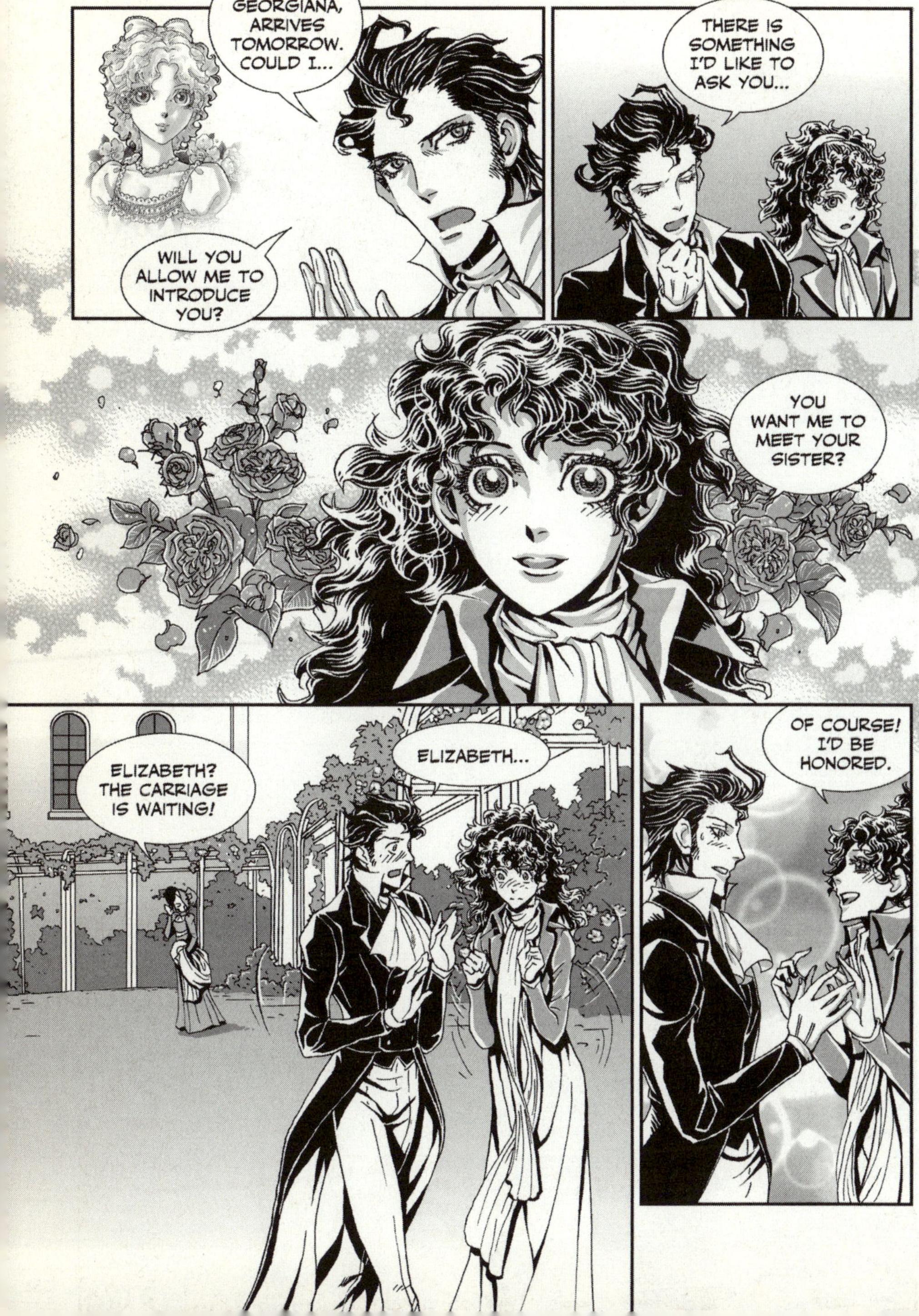
THERE IS SOMETHING I'D LIKE TO ASK YOU...
MY SISTER, GEORGIANA, ARRIVES TOMORROW. COULD I...
WILL YOU ALLOW ME TO INTRODUCE YOU?
YOU WANT ME TO MEET YOUR SISTER?
OF COURSE! I'D BE HONORED.
ELIZABETH...
ELIZABETH? THE CARRIAGE IS WAITING!

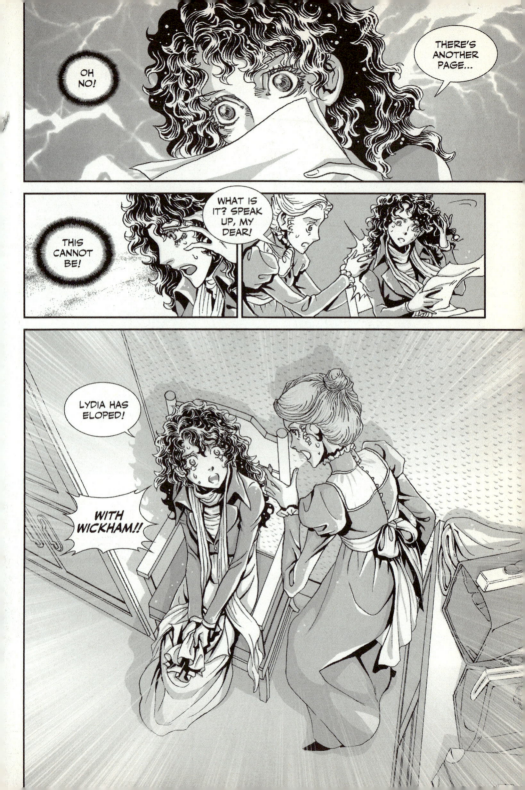

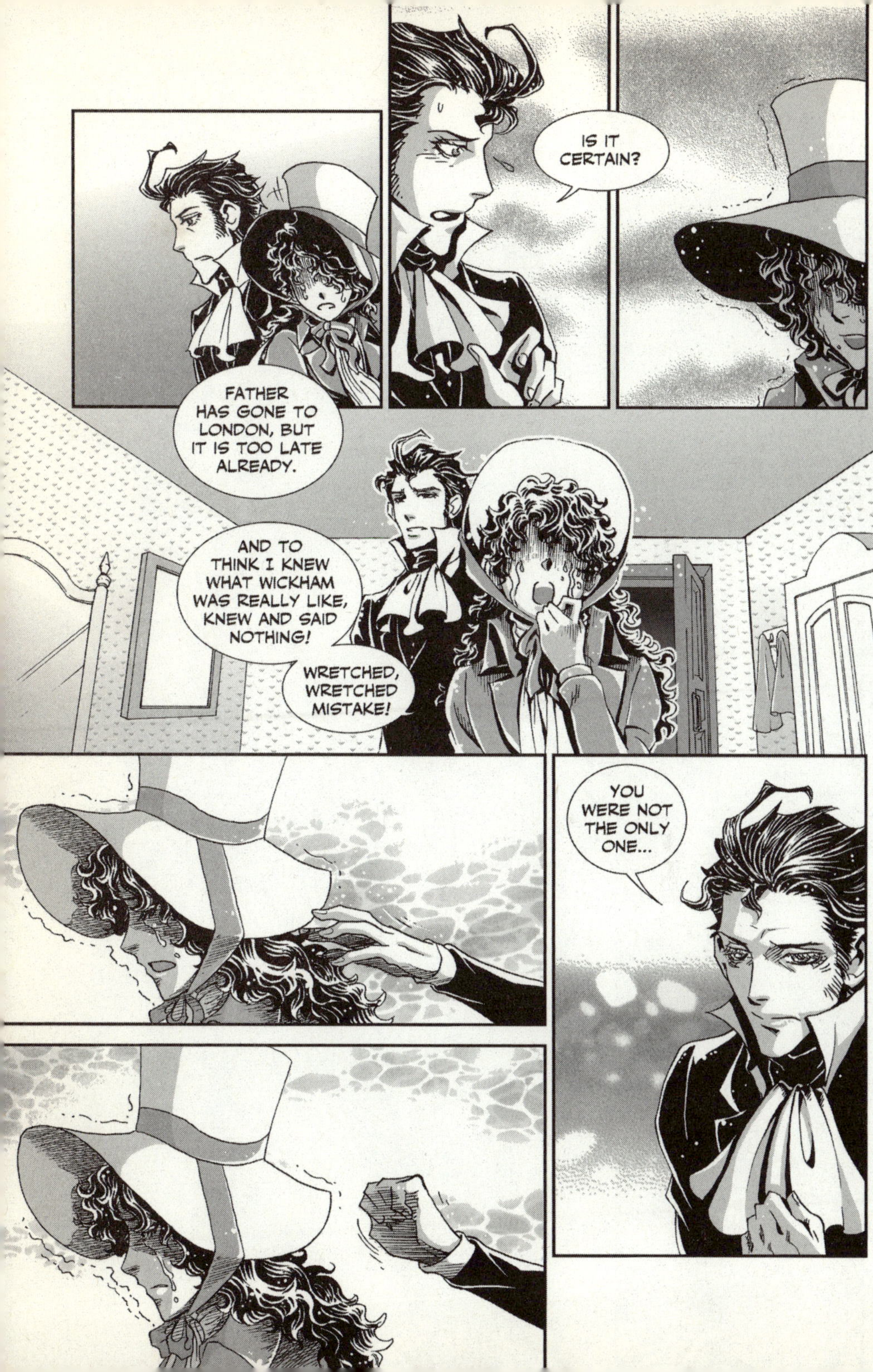
IS IT CERTAIN?
FATHER HAS GONE TO LONDON, BUT IT IS TOO LATE ALREADY.
AND TO THINK I KNEW WHAT WICKHAM WAS REALLY LIKE, KNEW AND SAID NOTHING!
WRETCHED, WRETCHED MISTAKE!
YOU WERE NOT THE ONLY ONE...

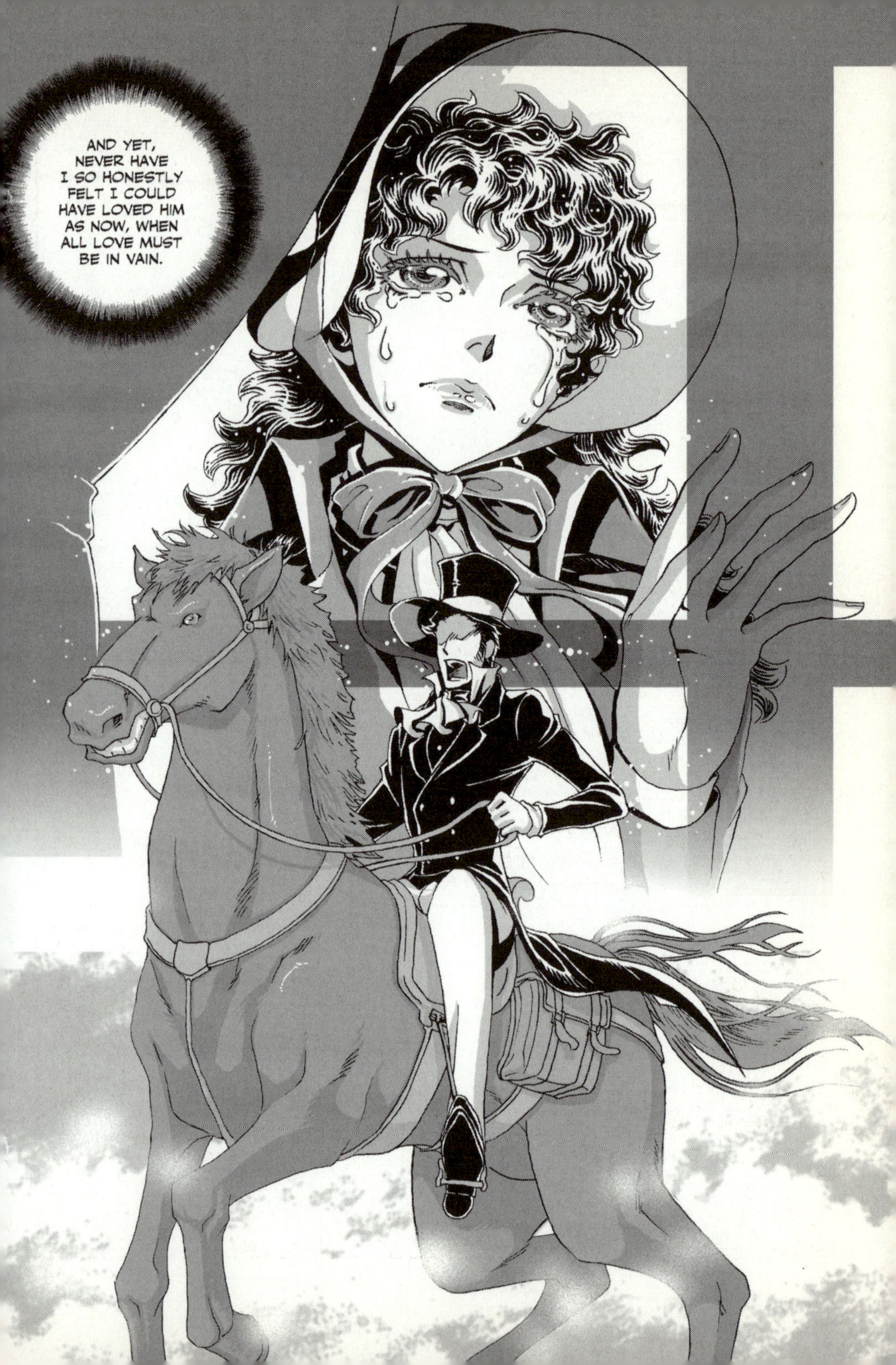
AND YET, NEVER HAVE I SO HONESTLY FELT I COULD HAVE LOVED HIM AS NOW, WHEN ALL LOVE MUST BE IN VAIN.

You will laugh when you know where I have gone...

although you must know with whom, for there is only one man in all the world whom I love.

to London

what a good joke it will be!

I shall write again when I can sign my name as Lydia Wickham.

A week goes by, and worries grow...

PLEASE TELL ME THAT'S A LETTER FROM LONDON!

HE OFFERS CONDOLENCES...

AND A HEARTY LECTURE ABOUT INDULGENT PARENTING, OF COURSE.

MR. COLLINS, ALAS!

THERE'S NOT A TRADESMAN IN TOWN WHO DOESN'T HAVE A TALE OF WICKHAM'S DEBTS – AND HIS WICKED WAYS TOWARDS THEIR DAUGHTERS!

IS THERE NO ONE WHO HAS NOT HEARD? MERYTON IS ABUZZ WITH STORIES, EACH ONE WORSE THAN THE LAST!

IS THAT ANOTHER LETTER?

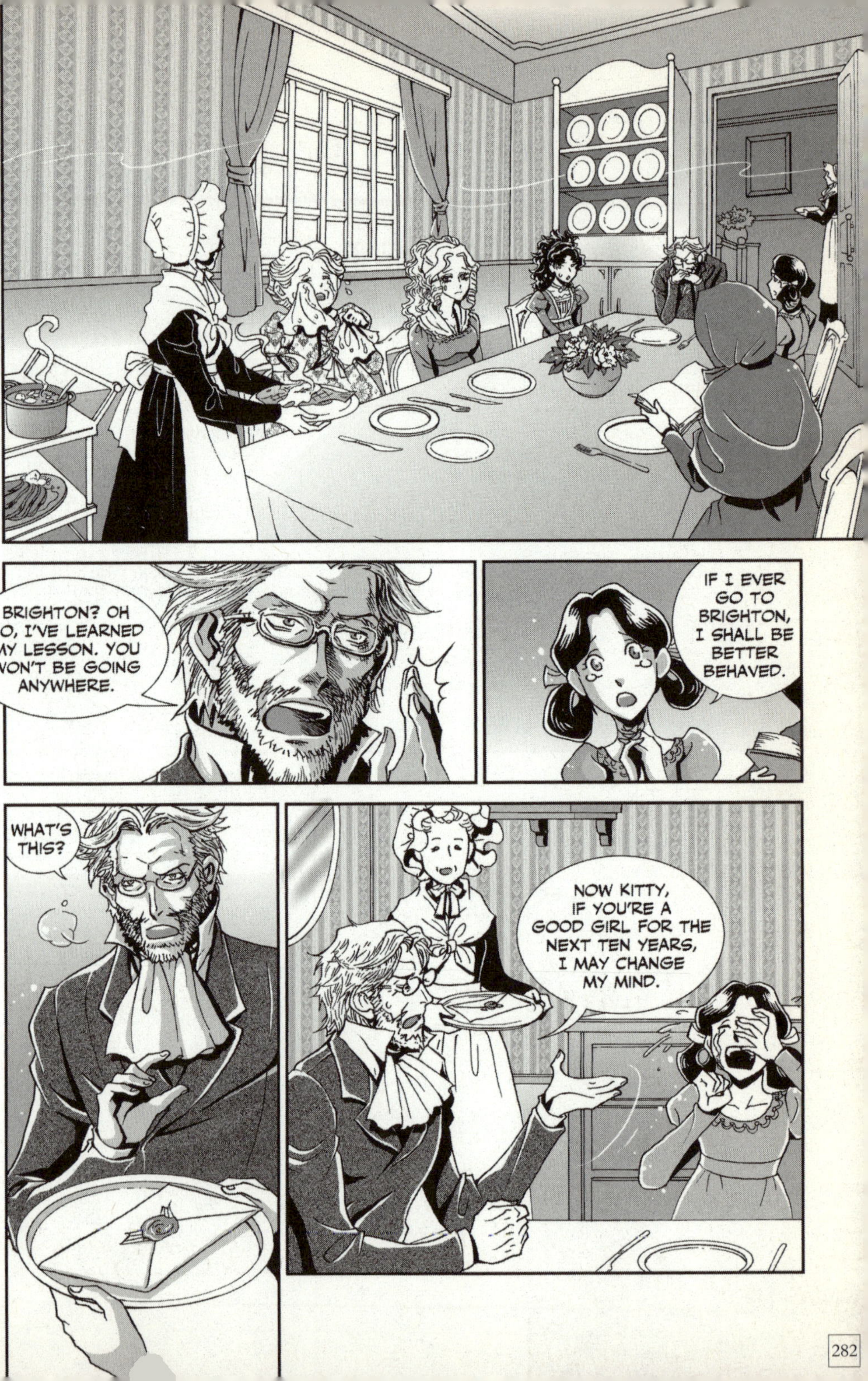
IF I EVER GO TO BRIGHTON, I SHALL BE BETTER BEHAVED.
BRIGHTON? OH NO, I'VE LEARNED MY LESSON. YOU WON'T BE GOING ANYWHERE.
NOW KITTY, IF YOU'RE A GOOD GIRL FOR THE NEXT TEN YEARS, I MAY CHANGE MY MIND.
WHAT'S THIS?

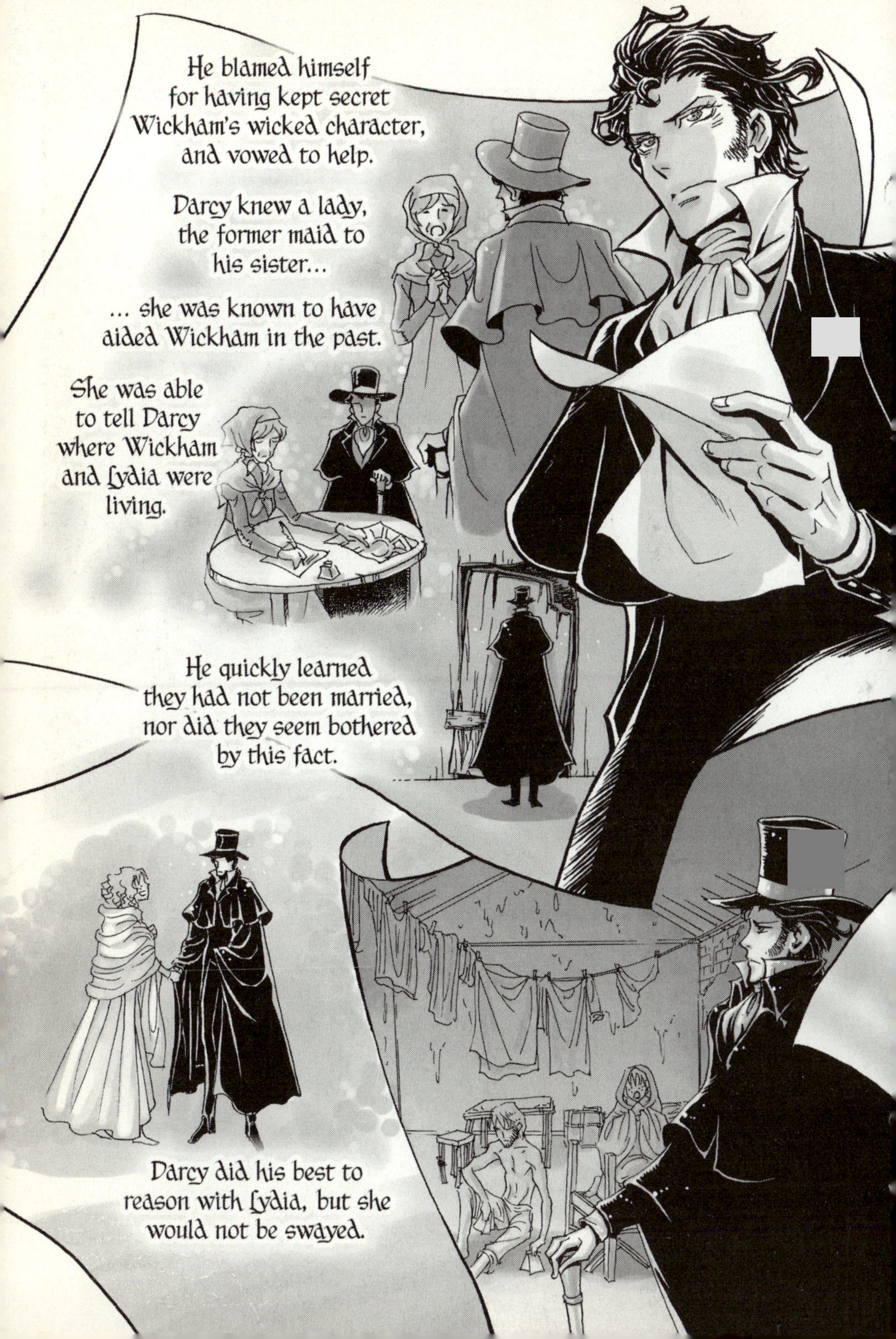
He blamed himself for having kept secret Wickham's wicked character, and vowed to help.
Darcy knew a lady, the former maid to his sister...
... she was known to have aided Wickham in the past.
She was able to tell Darcy where Wickham and Lydia were living.
He quickly learned they had not been married, nor did they seem bothered by this fact.
Darcy did his best to reason with Lydia, but she would not be swayed.

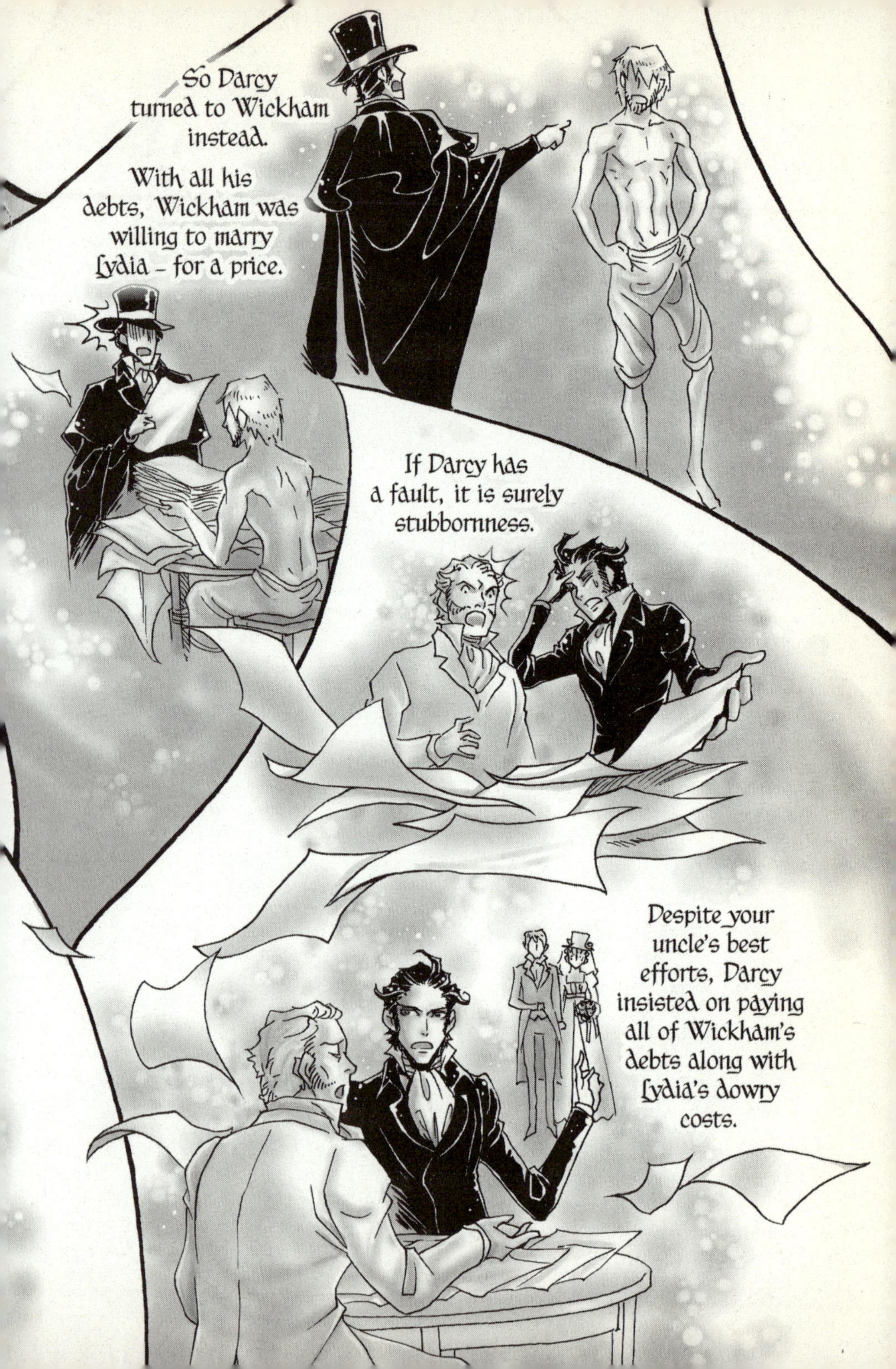
So Darcy turned to Wickham instead.
With all his debts, Wickham was willing to marry Lydia – for a price.
If Darcy has a fault, it is surely stubbornness.
Despite your uncle's best efforts, Darcy insisted on paying all of Wickham's debts along with Lydia's dowry costs.

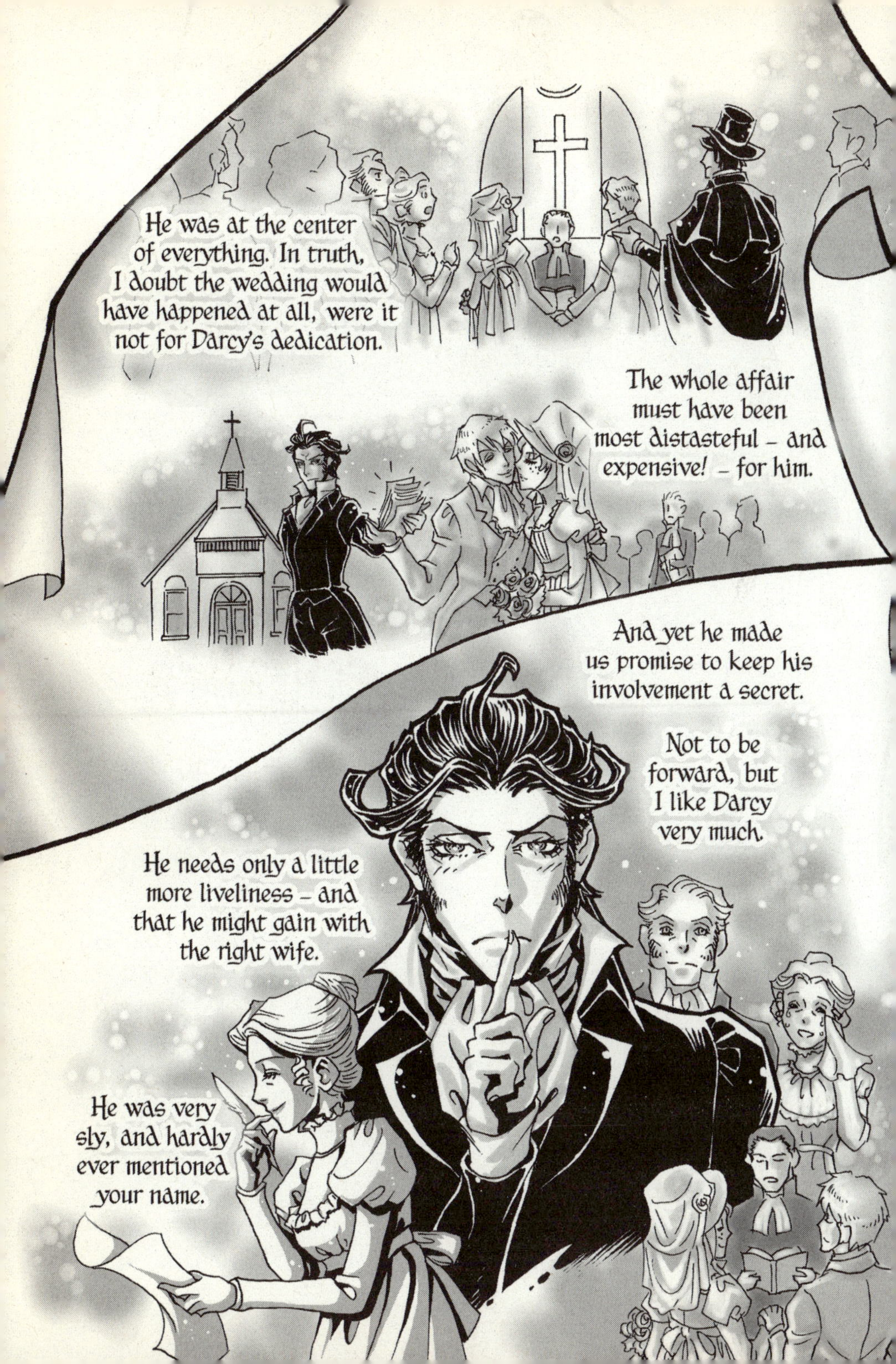
He was at the center of everything. In truth, I doubt the wedding would have happened at all, were it not for Darcy's dedication.
The whole affair must have been most distasteful – and expensive! – for him.
And yet he made us promise to keep his involvement a secret.
Not to be forward, but I like Darcy very much.
He needs only a little more liveliness – and that he might gain with the right wife.
He was very sly, and hardly ever mentioned your name.

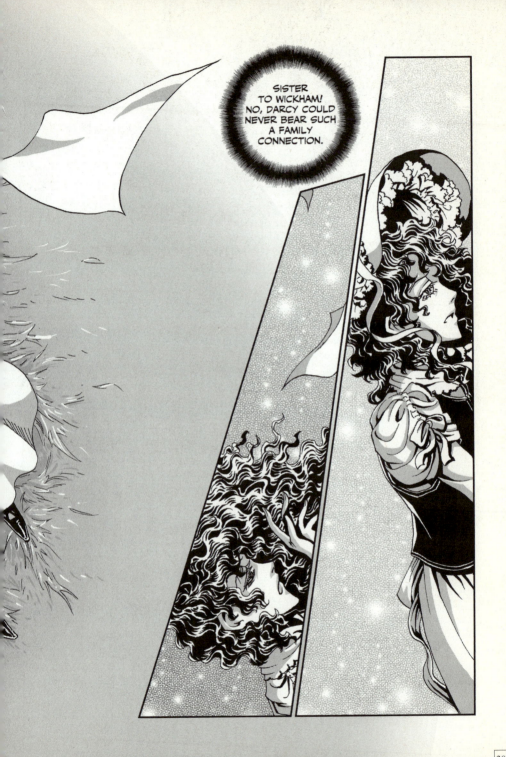

Chapter 17

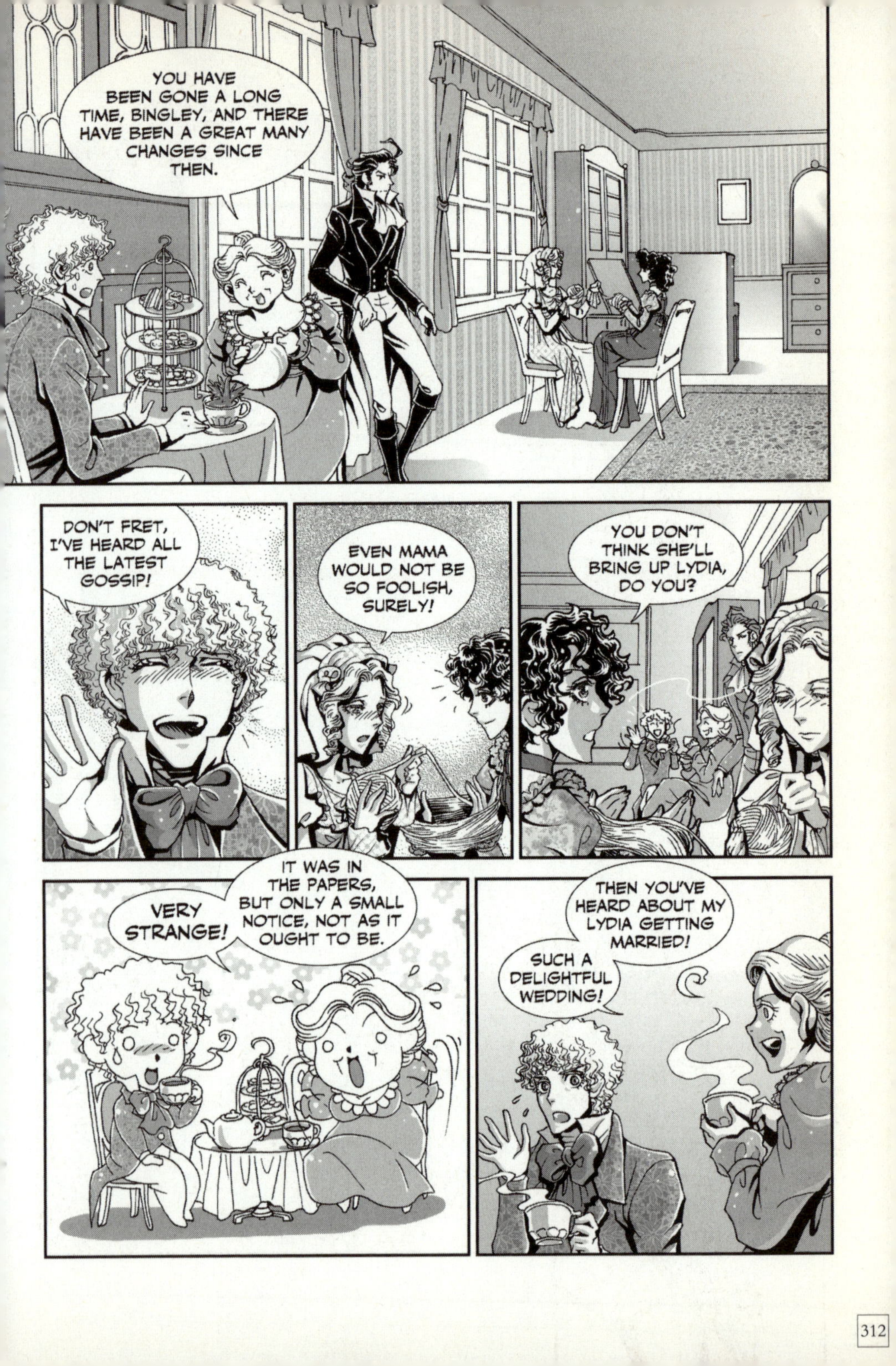
YOU HAVE BEEN GONE A LONG TIME, BINGLEY, AND THERE HAVE BEEN A GREAT MANY CHANGES SINCE THEN.
YOU DON'T THINK SHE'LL BRING UP LYDIA, DO YOU?
EVEN MAMA WOULD NOT BE SO FOOLISH, SURELY!
DON'T FRET, I'VE HEARD ALL THE LATEST GOSSIP!
THEN YOU'VE HEARD ABOUT MY LYDIA GETTING MARRIED!
SUCH A DELIGHTFUL WEDDING!
IT WAS IN THE PAPERS, BUT ONLY A SMALL NOTICE, NOT AS IT OUGHT TO BE.
VERY STRANGE!

WASN'T THAT KIND OF ME, TO SPARE YOU FROM DARCY'S COMPANY?

SUCH A DISAGREEABLE MAN!

YES, MAMA. VERY KIND.

YOU WILL SEE. HE COMES FOR TEA TOMORROW.

HOW LONG WILL YOU KEEP UP THIS CHARADE?

YOU SEE? WE ARE NOTHING BUT FRIENDS NOW.

THE NEXT DAY...

GIRLS! I NEED YOUR HELP!

JUST A FEW MORE STITCHES.

OH, THAT'S NOT OBVIOUS AT ALL.

COME, ELIZABETH!

NOT YOU, JANE, BUT THE REST OF YOU.

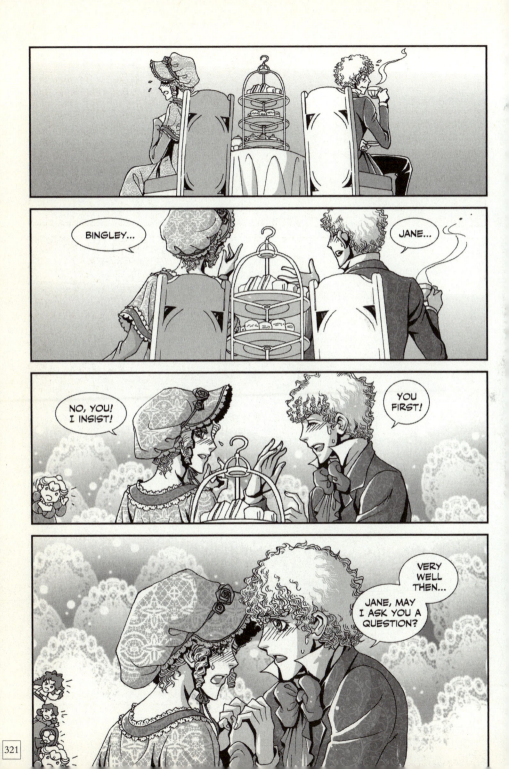

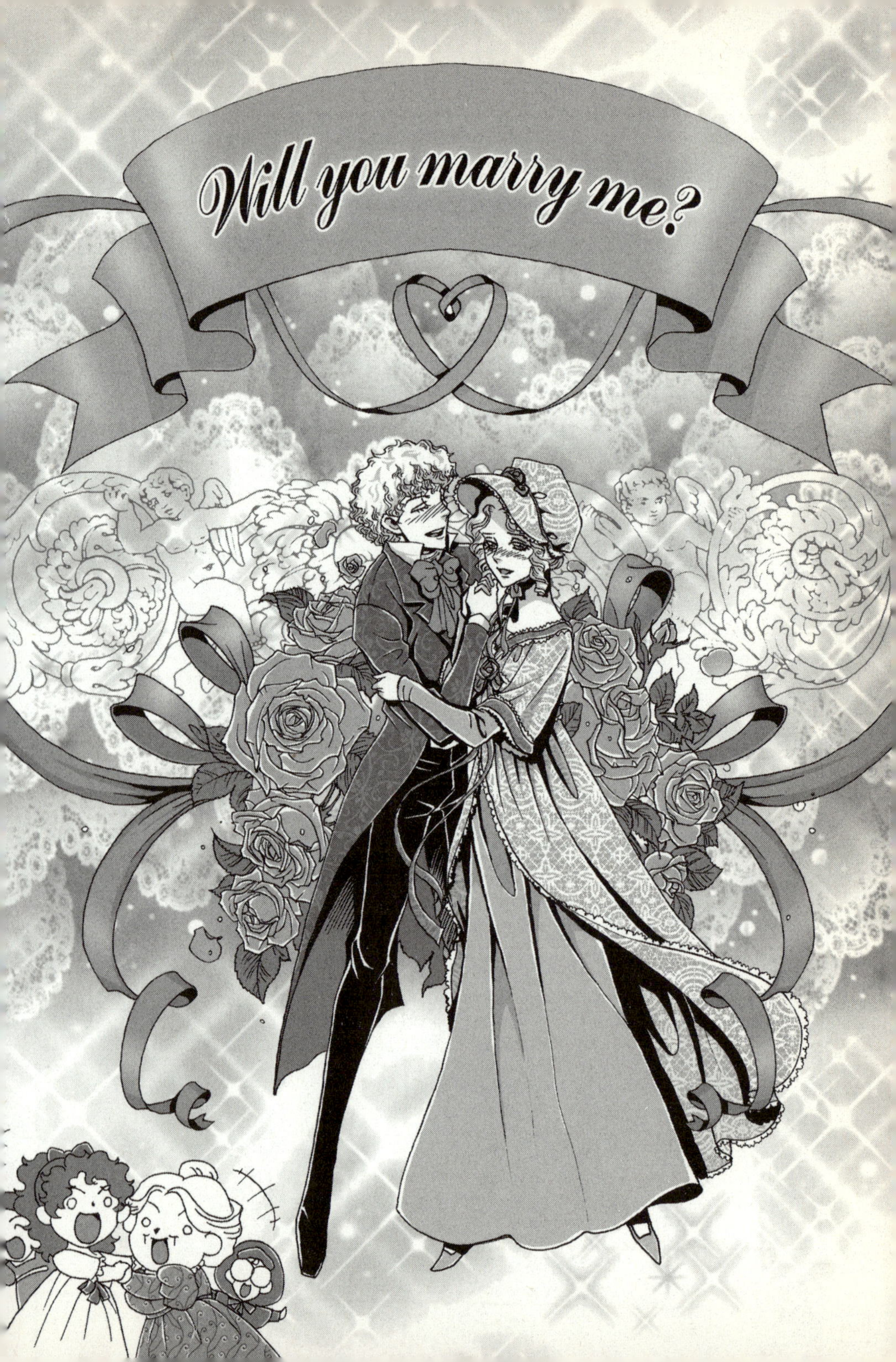
Will you marry me?

PREPARATIONS FOR JANE'S WEDDING BEGAN AT ONCE. WITHIN A WEEK, THE BENNET ESTATE WAS BUSTLING WITH MATRIMONIAL ACTIVITY -- AND UNEXPECTED VISITORS!

THERE'S A CARRIAGE COME! THE MOST EXPENSIVE ONE I'VE EVER SEEN!

AND ME IN MY SHABBIEST GOWN! OH, I WONDER WHO IT COULD BE?

YOU MET HER WHEN YOU VISITED MR. COLLINS, DIDN'T YOU?

YES, BUT I DON'T THINK I MADE A VERY GOOD IMPRESSION.

WHY, IT'S LADY CATHERINE! WHAT COULD SHE BE DOING HERE?

Chapter 18

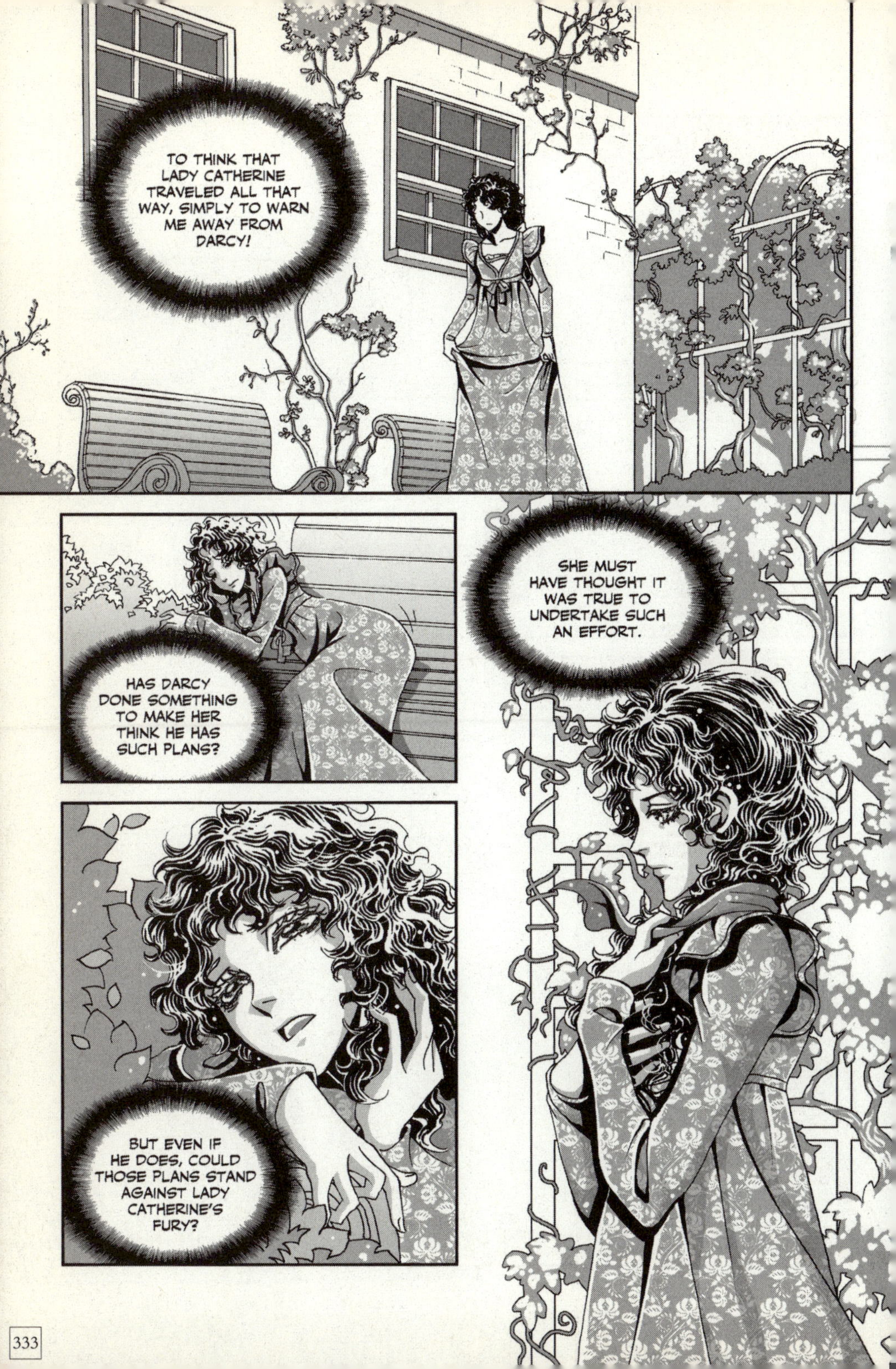
TO THINK THAT LADY CATHERINE TRAVELED ALL THAT WAY, SIMPLY TO WARN ME AWAY FROM DARCY!
SHE MUST HAVE THOUGHT IT WAS TRUE TO UNDERTAKE SUCH AN EFFORT.
HAS DARCY DONE SOMETHING TO MAKE HER THINK HE HAS SUCH PLANS?
BUT EVEN IF HE DOES, COULD THOSE PLANS STAND AGAINST LADY CATHERINE'S FURY?

DARCY IS AN INDEPENDENT MAN, BUT HE VALUES FAMILY AND CONNECTIONS.

OR PERHAPS, AS MY FATHER THINKS, HE NO LONGER LOOKS AT ME THAT WAY?

OH! THE SITUATION IS TOO IMPOSSIBLE!

PERHAPS LADY CATHERINE'S OBJECTIONS WILL BE ENOUGH TO SWAY HIM?

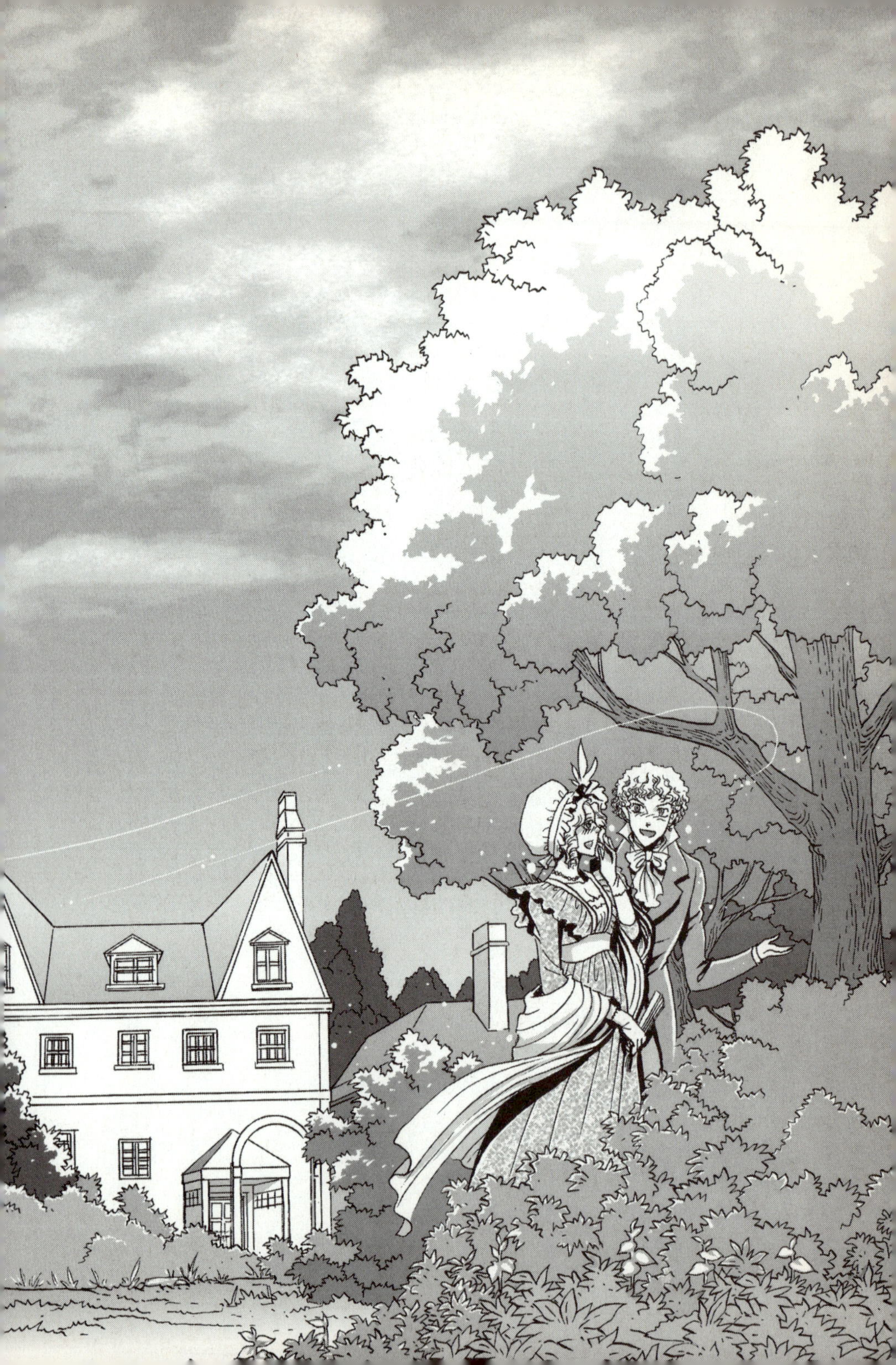

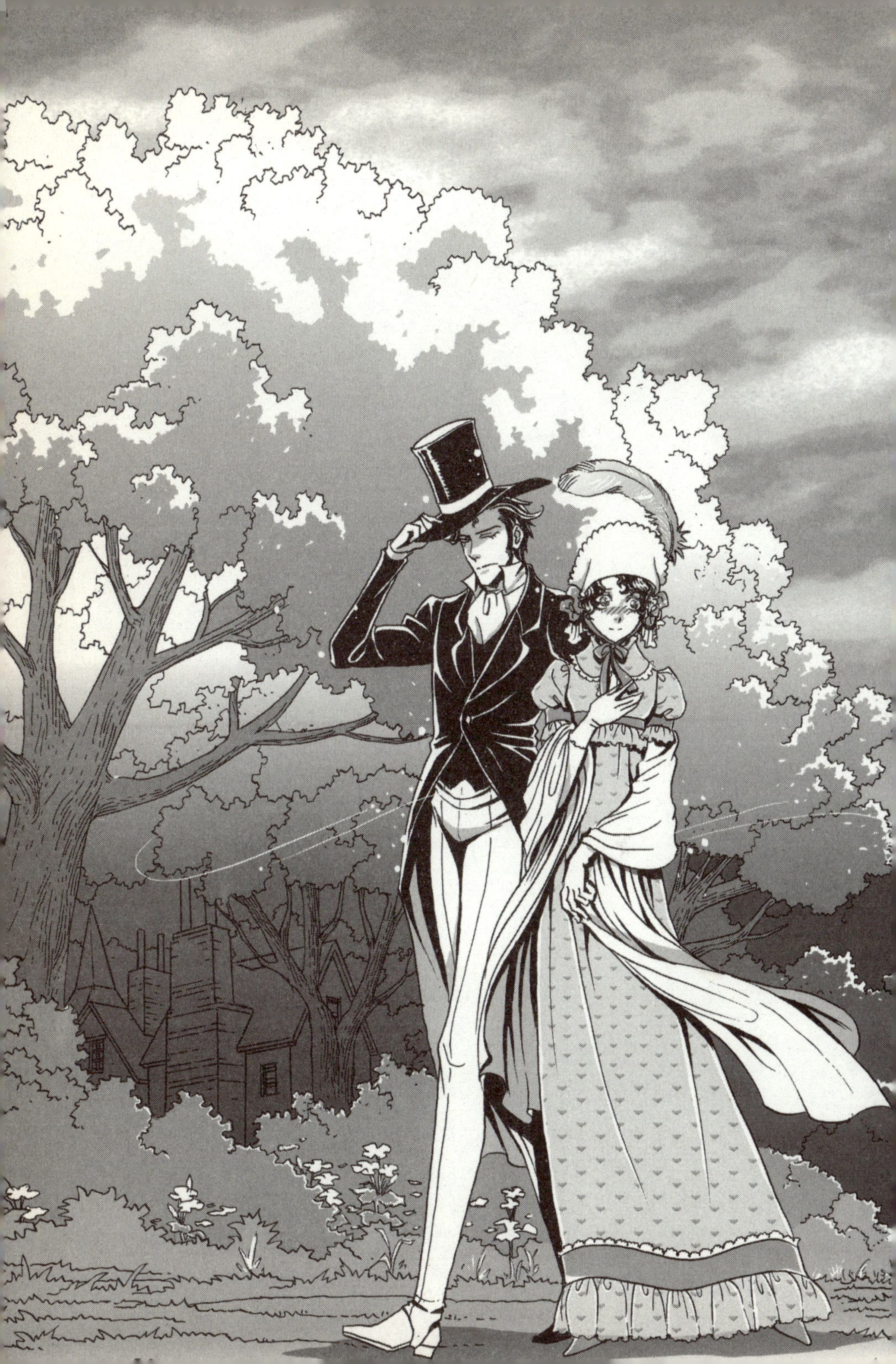

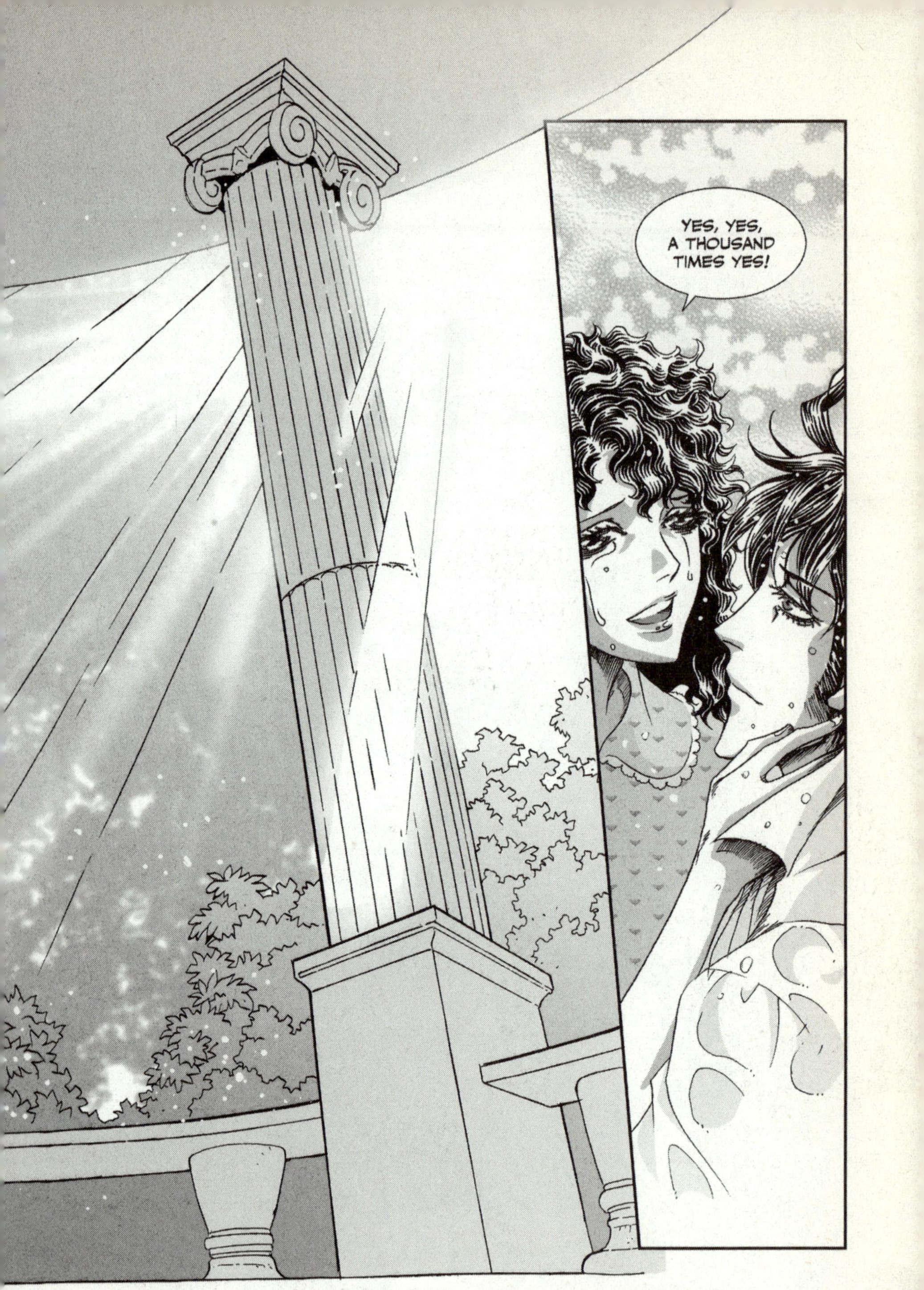
YES, YES, A THOUSAND TIMES YES!

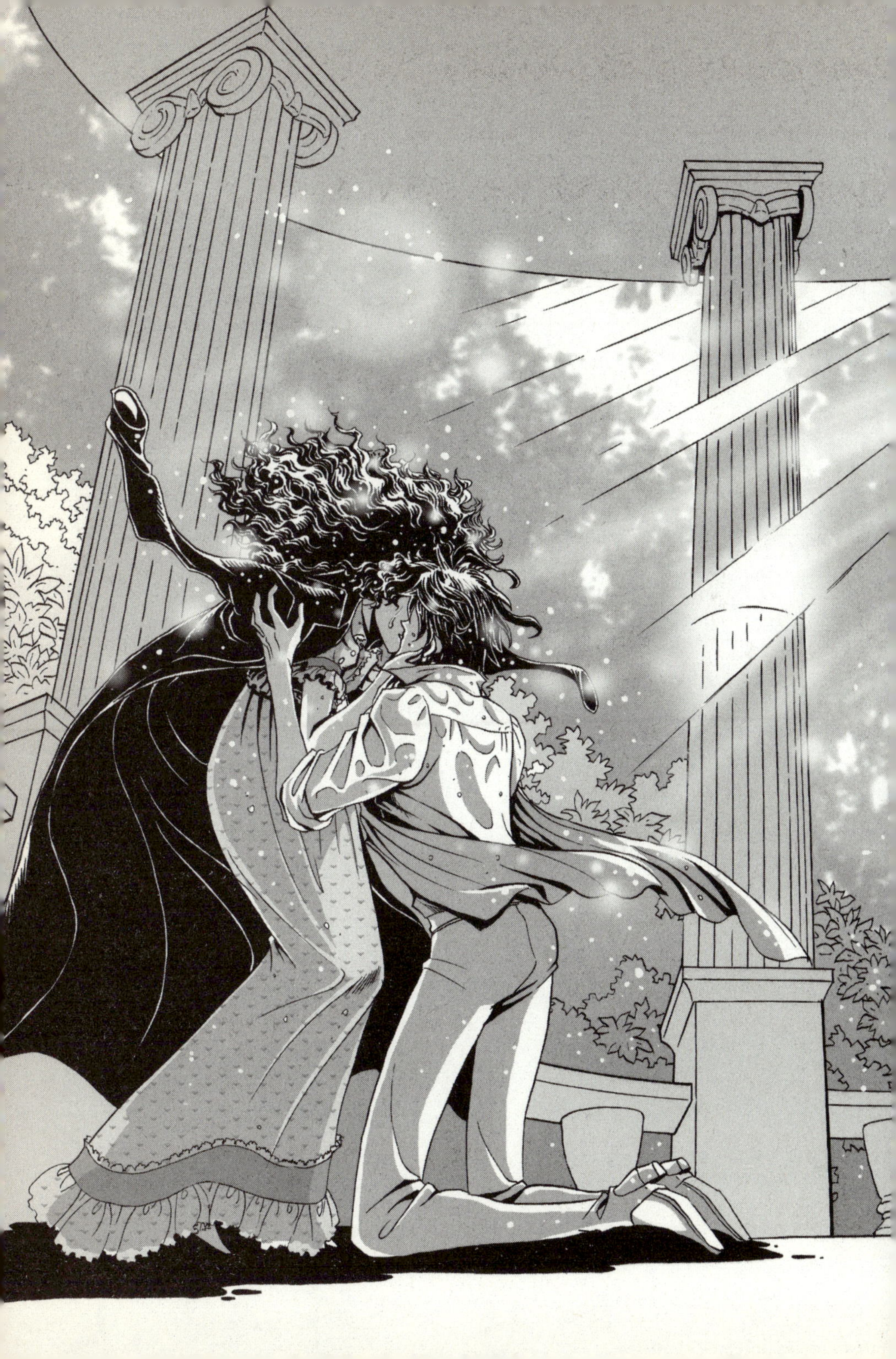

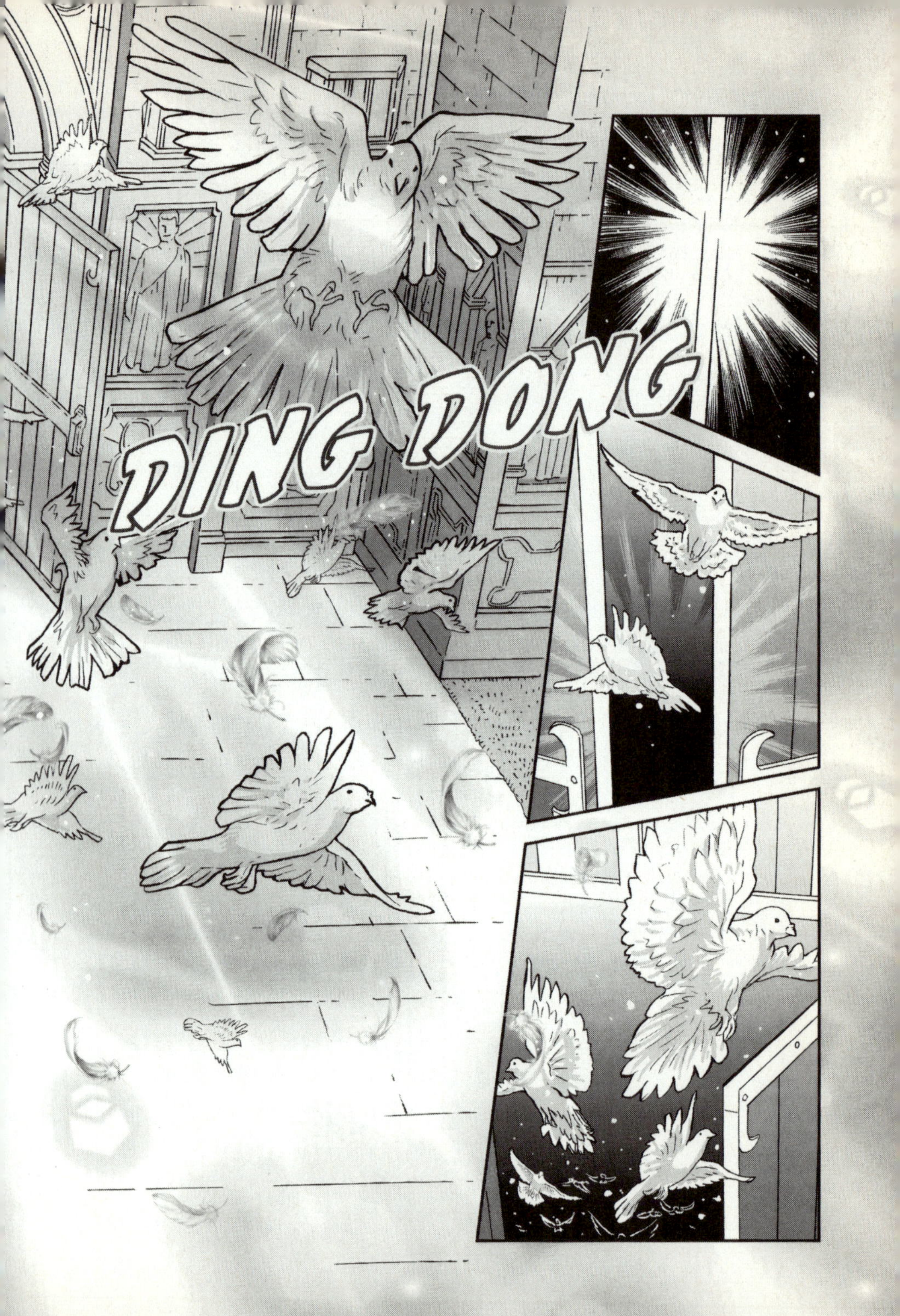
DING DONG

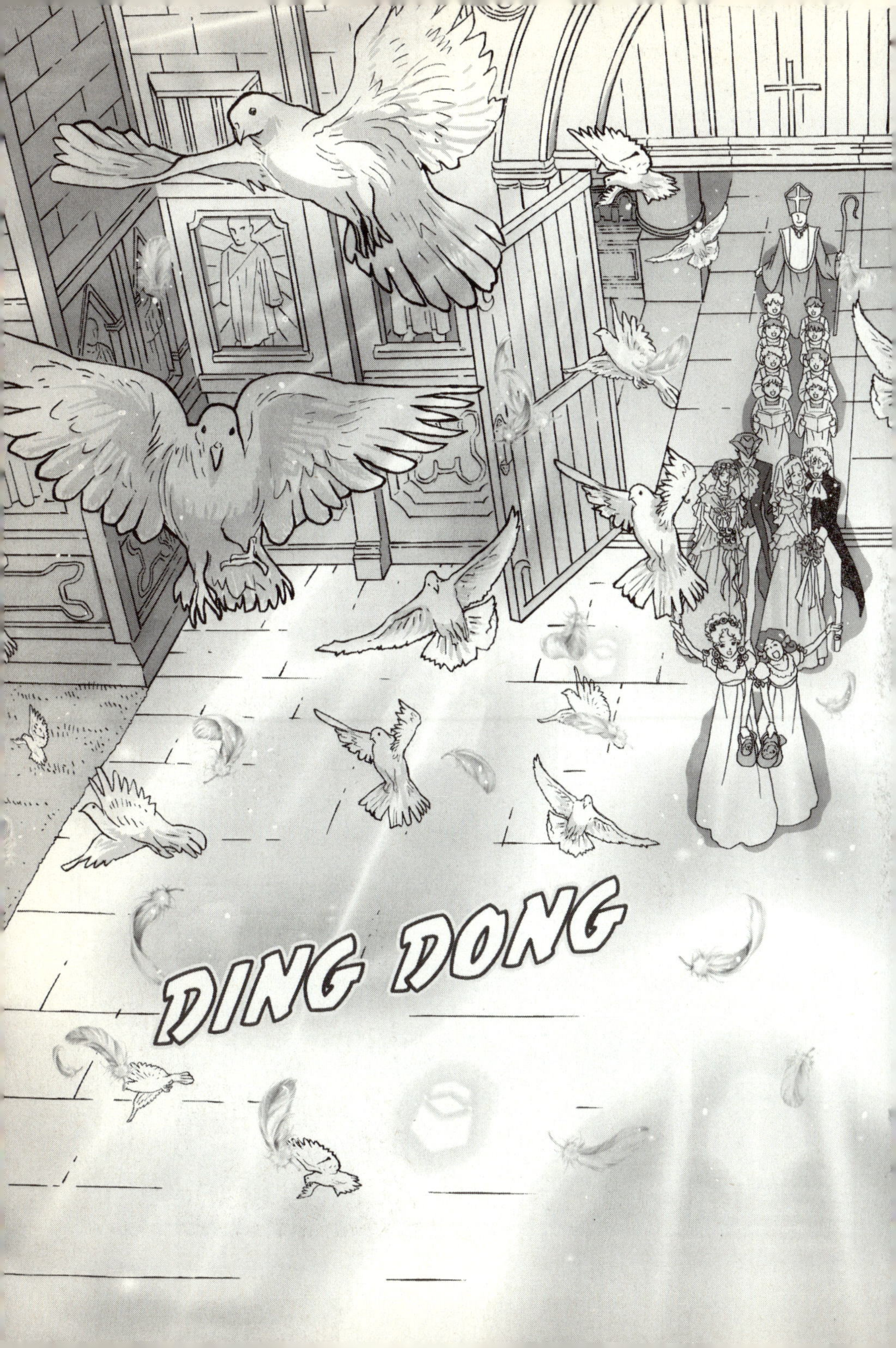
DING DONG

AND SO,
DESPITE HIS PRIDE
AND HER PREJUDICE,
ELIZABETH AND DARCY
FOUND THEIR PERFECT
MATCH IN ONE ANOTHER.

I WISH I COULD SAY, FOR THE SAKE OF HER FAMILY, THAT THE MARRIAGE OF HER CHILDREN TRANSFORMED MRS. BENNET INTO A SENSIBLE, WELL-INFORMED WOMAN FOR THE REST OF HER LIFE.

ALAS, THIS WAS NOT THE CASE.

KITTY AND MARY OFTEN VISITED THEIR OLDER SISTERS, TAKING ADVANTAGE OF THE EDUCATION AND ELEGANT SOCIETY TO BECOME LESS IRRITABLE, LESS IGNORANT AND LESS INSIPID.

ALTHOUGH PERHAPS MR. BENNET WAS HAPPY WITH HER JUST AS THINGS WERE.

GEORGIANA HAD THE HIGHEST OPINION IN THE WORLD OF ELIZABETH, AND THEY GREW TO LOVE ONE ANOTHER AS TRUE SISTERS.

LADY CATHERINE REMAINED HIGHLY INDIGNANT ABOUT THE MARRIAGE OF HER NEPHEW.

LYDIA AND WICKHAM WERE ALWAYS MOVING ABOUT FROM PLACE TO PLACE IN QUEST OF A CHEAP SITUATION, WHILE SPENDING MORE THAN THEY OUGHT. LYDIA WROTE TO ELIZABETH FROM TIME TO TIME, NEVER GIVING UP HOPE THAT DARCY MIGHT BE PERSUADED TO HELP ADVANCE WICKHAM'S CAREER.

As a life-long Jane Austen fan, I was both thrilled and terrified at the prospect of adapting her best-known work to a graphic novel format. Hiding within the apparent simplicity of Austen's plots is a complex understanding of human nature, one that I think still applies in so many ways – even to the high school dating scene! Imagine snubbing the plain girl who turns into a hottie over the summer holidays, and realizing how hard it will be to make up for your mistake... or keeping a nasty secret about your ex, only to be torn when your best friend starts dating him.

Clothing styles – and women's rights – have changed a lot in the last two centuries, but the challenges of human relationships remain as constant as Darcy's affection for Elizabeth. I hope this new adaptation, with its beautiful artwork and accessible design, will help both new and repeat readers discover the wonders of Austen's writing for themselves.

I'd like to express my gratitude to Po Tse and his studio assistants for bringing their remarkable art talents to this book. Many times, when I was unsure if the scene I'd written would capture the full emotions of the characters, I was reassured by knowing that Po's visuals would make up for any lack in my script! Thanks as well to Janice Leung, who helped both with organizing this project and providing translation help when needed. Above all, many thanks to Erik Ko and Andy Hung for helping to inspire and guide this book from initial idea to final creation, and for trusting me with the opportunity to work on such a wonderful and fulfilling adaptation.

I hope you enjoy this book as much as we enjoyed creating it!

Stacy King

Afterwords from PO

Hello to my dear Janeite (Fans of Jane Austen). Glad to share my thoughts with my fellow Janeite on this section. The charming relationship between Lizzy and Mr. Darcy captivated us. From their quarrel at first sight, to how their relationship eventually developed made it very enjoyable for all of us. Who can forget Miss Austen, for she was the one who created the first "Tsundere(ツンデレ)" character on Mr. Darcy, god bless her! I had a lot of fun making this manga. I especially enjoy Mr. Darcy's character. How to express his true feelings from under his emotionless face posed an enjoyable challenge for me. How did I do on that?

I would like to thank Mr.Erik Ko and Mr.Andy Hung, for giving me the opportunity to join this project, thanks for enduring all the delays from time to time, and for helping me with making it possible for Janeite to enjoy this exquisite manga! I give my gratitude to Stacey King for the perfect adaptation of the script, great job on the script of Lizzy & Mr. Darcy --- Thanks to Mr. Tai for the great arrangment. Kuma san, CL, Ahshu & Vincent Lau (also the other helpers), thanks for creating the background and manga effects. Last but not least, to my dear Jessica, thanks for everything!! Thank you to everyone involved --- see you all next time (And please visit my online pages too)!!

My Blog : http://lemonpo.blogspot.hk/
My devaintArt gallery : http://lemonpo.deviantart.com/

◆ ! WHOOPS ◆ !

This is the back of the book!

UDON's Manga Classics books follow the Japanese comic (aka Manga!) reading order. Traditional manga is read in a "reversed" format starting on the right and heading towards the left. The story begins where English readers expect to find the last page because the spine of the book is on the opposite side. Flip to the other end of the book and start reading your Manga Classics!

Pride and Prejudice
— JANE AUSTEN —

Art by: Po Tse
Story Adaptation by: Stacy King

Lettering: Morpheus Studios
Lettering Assist: Shane Law

UDON STAFF:

UDON Chief: Erik Ko
Managing Editor: Matt Moylan
Director of Marketing: Christopher Butcher
Marketing Manager: Stacy King
Associate Editor: Ash Paulsen
Production Manager: Janice Leung
Copy Editing Assistant: Michelle Lee
Japanese Liaisons: Steven Cummings

MORPHEUS STAFF:

Morpheus Chief: Andy Hung
Production Manager: Tai
Art Assistants: Kuma, Oldman,
Roy, Ben Tsui,
Ashton Nokman Poon,
Touyu, DORA,
Jessica, VIP 96neko,
Stoon, Mingsin Song

Manga Classics: Pride and Prejudice. Published by UDON Entertainment Inc. 118 Tower Hill Road, C1, PO Box 20008, Richmond Hill, Ontario, L4K 0K0, Canada. Any similarities to persons living or dead are purely coincidental. No portion of this publication may be used or reproduced by any means (digital or print) without written permission from UDON Entertainment Inc. and Morpheus Publishing Limited except for review purposes. All artwork © UDON Entertainment Inc. and Morpheus Publishing Limited. **Printed in Canada**

First Printing August 2014.
Hard Cover Edition ISBN # 978-1-927925-17-1   Soft Cover Edition ISBN # 978-1-927925-18-8

www.mangaclassics.com

An UDON Entertainment Production, in association with Morpheus Publishing Limited.
www.udonentertainment.com   www.morpheuspublishing.com

UDON

morpheus